"I Will Wear No Chain!"

"I WILL WEAR NO CHAIN!"

A Social History of
African American Males

Christopher B. Booker

PRAEGER

Westport, Connecticut
London

Dedicated to Douglas G. "Damu" Booker, 1953–1997

Library of Congress Cataloging-in-Publication Data

Booker, Christopher B. (Christopher Brian), 1949–
 "I will wear no chain!" : a social history of African American males / Christopher B. Booker.
  p. cm.
 Includes bibliographical references and index.
 ISBN 0–275–95637–7 (alk. paper)
 1. Afro-American men—History. 2. Afro-American men—Social conditions. 3.
Masculinity—United States—History. 4. Sex role—United States—History. I. Title.
E185.86.B635 2000
 305.38′896073′09—dc21   99–086221

British Library Cataloguing in Publication Data is available.

Library of Congress Catalog Card Number: 99–086221
ISBN: 0–275–95637–7

First published in 2000

Praeger Publishers, 88 Post Road West, Westport, CT 06881
An imprint of Greenwood Publishing Group, Inc.
www.praeger.com

Printed in the United States of America

The paper used in this book complies with the
Permanent Paper Standard issued by the National
Information Standards Organization (Z39.48–1984).

10 9 8 7 6 5 4 3

Copyright Acknowledgment

The author and publisher wish to acknowledge University of California Press (Berkeley) for permission to use extracts from *Marcus Garvey: Life and Lessons*, edited by Robert A. Hill and Barbara
Bair (1987).

Contents

Introduction

> Though we ordinarily speak of the Negro problem as though it were
> one unchanged question, students must recognize the obvious facts that
> this problem, like others, has a long historical development, has changed
> with the growth and evolution of the nation; moreover, that it is not one
> problem, but rather a plexus of social problems, some new, some old,
> some simple, some complex; and these problems have their one bond
> of unity in the act that they group themselves about those Africans whom
> two centuries of slavetrading brought into the land.
>
> —W.E.B. Du Bois, 1898[1]

This book is intended to acquaint readers with the broad outline of the centuries-old history of the African American male and, in doing so, help foster insight into his present dilemma. Hopefully, systematically studying the persisting problems confronting African American males across the generations will illuminate and help resolve the current problems that confront them by identifying persisting barriers to their collective development and by shedding light on the process of social change. The challenge for contemporary black males is to surmount the legacy of slavery and Jim Crow while confronting new forms of inequities evolving within the context of an increasingly globalized economy and polity. The reality of the massive criminalization of the black male population created by the lack of legitimate career opportunities for millions combined with the proliferation of a materialism embodied in the quest for status-granting consumer goods accounts for much of the current dilemma. Overcoming the lack of wealth, educational background, and social status represents a daunting challenge for millions of African American boys and men as it is for African American women and girls. The contemporary male role, however, leads males into a form of risk-taking behavior within a culture of risk. While earning millions of dollars in illegal income, primarily through the sale of drugs, millions of black men have become enmeshed within the criminal justice system. As this sector of the African

American economy perpetuates itself through the generations, the accompanying culture, with its attendant worldview and values, spreads and, to varying degrees, insinuates itself throughout society, deepening the social and economic crisis of the national black community. Clearly, this all-sided crisis for African American males is inseparable from that facing black females; yet, distinguishing their specificities is a critical step in the formulation of feasible strategies of social change.

Tracing the positioning of a diverse population of African American males within the evolving economic system from the early days of European settlement in the United States to the present illustrates the myriad forces impeding or propelling racial progress. While a dearth of economic opportunities for black men has been a continual, never-ending dynamic connecting every moment of African American history, the character of those limitations and the ability of individuals to successfully overcome them have varied in many ways. All too often throughout American history, the assumption that African American males have failed to take full advantage of the opportunities presented them has been made into an implicit or explicit explanation for their contemporary socioeconomic problems. Beneath this lay an underlying assumption that other people similarly situated, but more ambitious and capable, were better able to pull themselves (and their families) out of poverty.

Interwoven with the economic relationships of African American males historically is a distinct set of social experiences. The male's economic role during slavery was inextricably linked to a limited range of social roles that were able to support, coexist with, or survive the degradation. The antebellum male role and cultural heritage surrounding familial roles, the importance of male friends and peers, and the resistance to social restrictions exerted a powerful formative influence on black male culture. Controversies during the post–World War II era illustrate the continuing significance of the question of the character of the African American male's role in family life. The question of the criminality of the black male and the charge that it is at the core of his nature, seemingly given more credence by the economic circumstances of the post–industrial urban areas, are illustrative of the persistence of the battle of black males for basic respect as human beings.

By tracing the perception and reality of the black male image as a "criminal" through the slave, Reconstruction, Jim Crow, and modern eras, both the continuity and evolution of change can be discerned. Historically, this image has served to reinforce the status quo and legitimate the social order and the lowly status of black males within it. Commercialized early in American history, this image has recently taken on a life of its own, being driven, at least partially, by the engines of profit. Politically and ideologically, the image of the black male has been the site of fierce combat. Throughout American history politicians have repeatedly attempted to mobilize white voters by means of frightening them with the specter of upward black male social mobility, especially that which implies closer social interaction between whites and the pariah group. From Senator Stephen A. Douglas, through President Theodore Roosevelt, to President George Bush and his trope "Willie Horton," the use of the symbolism of the black male as the society's greatest internal threat or enemy has proved useful to political ambition.[2]

Previous research has shown that while many elements within the values, attitudes, and behaviors of white and black males are shared, their total configuration differs in terms of quantity, quality, and their relationship to each other.[3] Of singular importance in this regard is the evolving male role as African American males themselves perceived it, in contrast to the perception of the larger white society. Those scholars who pinpoint the black male dilemma as deriving basically from the gap existing between the ideal male gender role for the overall American society and the actual ability of black males to realize it miss the mark. Throughout American history, most white Americans have not expected black men to be able to fulfill the ideal male gender role. Indeed, it was often made abundantly clear that severe repercussions would follow if they made serious and steadfast efforts to live up to the white standards of masculinity. During the antebellum and Jim Crow periods in particular, violence threatened black men bent on obtaining financial, social, cultural, or political power. Since these barriers to advancement were well known within African American communities, the emergence of standards by which to evaluate black masculinity were altered accordingly. These standards of acceptable masculine behavior and achievement, were adapted, to a considerable extent, to the reality of the unjust conditions that these males confronted.

A dialectic exists between the development of white males historically and the underdevelopment of African American males. The long decades of racial oppression served to transfer resources from blacks to whites. For the black male the abbreviated and aborted careers and the lack of property accumulation have meant that successive generations have been burdened by a mounting racial disparity in wealth and resources. While trade union exclusion, the lack of education, the prohibition on black labor and commerce, and the lack of spatial mobility were important factors in the sub-par black male economic status, the repeated ousting of black males from trades where they had dominated for decades had perhaps the most permanent deleterious impact. The black stableman who was pushed out of his position during the 1840s by an Irish immigrant was unable to pass along the wealth he might have accumulated to his children.[4] The loss of such a skilled position has lasting consequences on family stability, business formation, and the storehouse of inspiration needed to fuel the aspirations of the next generation.

Black masculinity in America has always been influenced by the prevalent forms of masculinity of white America. Since the mid-nineteenth century when the characteristic masculinity of the "self-made man" displaced the earlier types according to Michael Kimmel, the "genteel patriarch" and the "heroic artisan" black males have felt the impact of these mainstream values, standards, and behaviors. This "self-made man," epitomized by the rise of President Andrew Jackson to popularity, involved, to a considerable extent, the buying, selling, and working of African Americans as the quickest route to wealth.[5]

By the end of the nineteenth century white manhood in America faced several converging problems: the entry of African Americans, immigrant males and women into an unstable and increasingly competitive labor market; the end of the frontier in the American West; and the rise of white-collar work.[6] By the turn of the century American men were increasingly insecure about their manhood as brawling, hard drinking, and other manifestations of this became more visible. Changing manhood was evident in the rise in mass participation in athletic activities and the emergence of organized and professional sports.[7] National concern over the state of American men had risen markedly by the eve of World War I as a "fatherhood movement," a new, muscular version of Christianity, and emergent social institutions such as the Young Men's Christian Association (YMCA) attempted to compensate for changes wrought by urbanization, industrialization, and perceived feminization. One expert argued that boys should have at least one fight daily to hone their budding manhood—such was the fear of men's becoming feminized.[8] By the late twentieth century American manhood continued to be in flux, battered by new conceptions of masculinity, corporate anonymity, and hypermasculine tendencies.[9]

In striking contrast to the rhythms and themes of white American masculinity, black masculinity, from the Nat Turner slave revolt in 1831, to the memorable determination displayed by a gagged and bound Black Panther leader, Bobby Seale over a century later, has often taken the form of defiance and resistance against deeply felt injustices. While not the only form of black manhood, this type of black masculine practice has exerted a significant influence during every phase of African American history. The acquiescent form of masculinity, an aberrant deviation from the main thrust of African American history, took its most outstanding form under the accommodationist leadership of Booker T. Washington, who counseled black males to be meek and subservient. The early decades of the twentieth century witnessed the flowering of middle-class, black expressions of masculinity represented by Monroe Trotter, W.E.B. Du Bois., and the National Association for the Advancement of Colored People. In marked contrast, the black nationalist expressions of black masculinity embodied in the Universal Negro Improvement Association, the Nation of Islam, and the Black Panther Party all used the symbolism and language of an assertive black masculinity as an effective mobilizing instrument.

Today, as in the past, among African Americans the ability to earn a decent living is perhaps the most important component of manhood. This is seen as critical to the fulfillment of a man's responsibilities to his family and loved ones. As a value, its influence impacts other personality characteristics critical to the achievement of manhood, such as independence. These manhood values, while seemingly neutral, acquire a special significance within the context of today's rampant materialism, family fragmentation, and increasingly globalized economy. Within an environment of scarcity and competition, a world where the family has shattered into small pieces of what once was a more cohesive unit, these manhood values become the key factors in an explosion of both rational and irrational violence.

An important route to the achievement of African American manhood in contemporary America involves the command over scarce material resources. Money and sought-after consumer goods play a prominent role in the lyrics of many of today's rap songs, including the notable example of the late Biggie Smalls. The feverish thirst for money, consumer goods, and social status is at the heart of the upsurge in black male homicides since the early 1980s, as fully 43.3 percent of black males under the age of 18 are impoverished compared to only 12.2 percent of comparable white males.[10]

Many statistics on the contemporary condition of African American males are grim indeed, but historically, each generation has faced severe threats to its status and managed to register sufficient progress for the next generation to build on. For the black male, wisdom comes from the realization that sheer force or power and sheer ability or intelligence are not enough. Adroitness, flexibility, malleability, slickness, drive, patience, forbearance, and humility are also necessary to achieve the desired personal goals. Even for the most prominent male figures in black history, their efforts to provide for their family and loved ones have met with some frustration. Frederick Douglass, indisputably one of the truly great men of the nineteenth century, not only was denied any consideration for the highest offices of the land but had to confine his bureaucratic ambitions to the "Negro" posts of recorder of deeds in the District of Columbia and ambassador to Haiti. For thousands of others, the attractiveness of positions such as post office letter carrier and Pullman porter testified less to their lack of ambition than to the dearth of positions of high status available to African Americans.[11]

Chapter 1 of this study provides the necessary context for the consideration of the ranges of black masculinities developed during the slave era. Chapter 2 discusses the microsocial aspects of African American male slave life, using examples that traverse the range of individual experiences. Chapter 3 traces the development of masculinity among unenslaved blacks during the antebellum era.

Chapter 4 discusses the significance of the unique role that African American males played during the Civil War. Chapter 5 outlines the developments following the war and the struggle for black families to forge an independent and prosperous life and to participate equally in southern life. Chapter 6 focuses primarily on the philosophy and actions of Booker T. Washington with respect to black masculinity. The demise of the philosophy of accommodationism is described in the context of the Brownsville affair, the politics of Theodore Roosevelt, and the opposition to Washington led by William Monroe Trotter and W.E.B. Du Bois. Chapter 7 looks at the problem of lynching and the efforts to banish it from American life. Marcus Garvey's influence on black masculinity is traced in Chapter 8 in the context of the new, urbanized existence for black male America.

Chapter 9 looks at the black masculinity of the post–World War Two era, focusing on the role of the Civil Rights movement, the Black Power movement, and the summer riots as important forces in its development. Chapter 10 discusses the most important events and developments of the 1980s and 1990s with respect to their impact upon black male America. The Million Man March, black male criminalization, and patriarchalism in the black community are explored to conclude the study.

Black masculinity continues to evolve, today impacted by new forces in a rapidly changing global environment. It is influenced by multiple sources, including music, the workplace, the streets, the playing field, the household, and other sources. African Americans have always been a diverse people, individual variations influenced by ethnicity, class, language, status, occupation, outlook, religion, color, sexual orientation, and region, and with twenty-first century they continue to become more diverse. While this study focuses on the African American population with deep roots in the United States, African Americans are increasingly an ethnically diverse population with a healthy influx of immigrants primarily from Africa, Latin America, and the Caribbean. The options for African American males have gradually expanded so that by the end of the twentieth century, with new technological conditions and a more globalized economic context, there were broader horizons for millions of black males. Yet millions are unable to take advantage of these opportunities due to the legacies of slavery, poverty, joblessness, and lack of education. The following chapters hopefully explain how this paradoxical contemporary situation came into being and thereby contribute to a strategy to finally resolve these age-old problems.

NOTES

1. W.E.B. Du Bois, "The Study of the Negro Problem," *Annals of the American Academy of Political and Social Science* 11 (January 1898): 1–23.

2. See David R. Roediger, *The Wages of Whiteness: Race and the Making of the American Working Class* (London: Verso, 1991), 142; Michael Goldfield, *The Color of Politics: Race and the Mainsprings of American Politics* (New York: The New Press, 1997), 8.

3. Valuable sources include Jewell Taylor Gibbs *Young, Black, and Male in America: An Endangered Species* (Dover, MA: Auburn House, 1988); Michael Kimmel, *Manhood in America: A Cultural History* (New York: The Free Press, 1996); Susan Jeffords, *The Remasculinization of America: Gender and the Vietnam War* (Bloomington: University of Indiana Press, 1989; David D. Gilmore, *Manhood in the Making: Cultural Concepts of Masculinity* (New Haven, CT: Yale University Press, 1990). Kenneth Clatterbaugh, *Contemporary Perspectives on Masculinity* (Boulder, CO: Westview Press, 1990); Lawrence E. Gary, Christopher B. Booker, and Abeba Fekade, *African American Males: An Analysis of Contemporary Values, Attitudes and Perceptions of Manhood* (Washington, DC: Howard University School of Social Work, 1993); Noel A. Cazenave, "Black Men in America: The Quest for Manhood," in Harriette P. McAdoo (ed.), *Black Families* (Beverly Hills, CA: Sage, 1981), 176–186; Richard Majors and Janet Billson, *Coolpose: The Dilemmas of Black Manhood in America* (New York: Lexington Books, 1992); Robert Staples, *Black Masculinity: The Black Males' Role in American Society* (San Francisco: Black Scholar Press, 1982); Mifflin W. Gibbs, *Shadow and Light: An Autobiography* (New York Arno Press and the New York Times, 1968);Gary Donaldson. *The History of African-Americans in the Military, Double V* (Malabar, FL: Krieger, 1991); Joe I. Dubbert, *A Man's Place: Masculinity in Transition* (Englewood Cliffs, NJ: Prentice-Hall, 1979).

4. Phillip S. Foner, *Organized Labor and the Black Worker, 1619–1981* (New York: International Publishers, 1981), 6.

5. James Oakes, *The Ruling Race: A History of American Slaveholders* (New York: Alfred A. Knopf, 1982), 73.

6. Michael Kimmel,*Manhood in America*, 78. See also, Peter G. Filene,*Him/Her/Self: Sex Roles in Modern America* (Baltimore: Johns Hopkins University Press, 1974), 73–78.

7. Kimmel *Manhood in America*,138.

8. Ibid., 160–61.

9. Ibid., 245–52.

10. U.S. Bureau of the Census, "Table 15. Selected Characteristics of the Population below the Poverty Level in 1994, by Region and Race," (Washington, DC, May1996).

11. William S. McFeely, *Frederick Douglass* (New York: W. W. Norton, 1991).

Chapter 1

Slavery and the Development of Black Masculinity, 1619–1860

> Years ago, while a toiling slave in Tennessee, I resolved, that with the help of God, and the energies he had given me, I would cast off the chain and be a slave no longer. "Liberty or Death!" never came from a more earnest breast than when I uttered it there before my God! I will be no man's slave, be he called friend or foe—be he in a church or out. God helping me, I will be a MAN—I will wear no chain!
>
> —Jermain Wesley Loguen, March 1855[1]

By the American Revolution of 1776, slavery had existed over a century and a half in the British colonies. During this period of upheaval, the currents of liberty ran more freely than ever among the American settlers. With the change in the world economy and the declining slave economics of the Chesapeake and Tidewater regions, a growing distaste for slavery in the North, and a favorable ideological climate, prospects for mass black liberty looked rosy indeed. Only six years earlier in March, Crispus Attucks, a black fugitive slave, had sacrificed his life for the cause of the young American nation, and private manumissions seemed to be increasingly in vogue. For the Africans in America, whose population had increased from approximately 250,000 in 1750, to 750,000 in 1790, this was the first realistic prospect for mass freedom.[2]

This chapter lays the basis for a more detailed discussion of conditions confronting African American males and their response to them during the era of slavery. The macrolevel social, economic, political, and ideological factors impacting upon Africans in early America are discussed with a special emphasis on the male role and the contemporary gender-role distinctions. The second half of the chapter focuses on the antebellum development of the black male image in America.

African American history begins with countless crimes of violence. The seizure of thousands upon thousands of human beings on Africa's west coast—Bambara, Fulani, Fanti, Ga, Ibo, Yoruba, Coromantees, and others—was accompanied by other grave crimes that set in motion a process that led to the creation of a new people—African-Americans—whose history was to revolve around the dialectic of freedom and slavery. Those captured endured the Middle Passage and first tasted the lash of slavery and the excruciatingly difficult choices it presented them. Clearly, the voyage to America and adaptation to the new slave setting served as a rigorous screening process by which the individual's ability to endure a regimen of physical, psychological, and social terror was put to a severe test. Those too sensitive to pain, physical or emotional, too impatient for revenge, or too physically frail would succumb to one of the many hazards of being black and enslaved.[3]

Olaudah Equaino typified the state of shock the captives shared. Registering his shock over the strange appearance of the whites, he learned that the captives "were to be carried to these white people's country to work for them." The thought of merely being reduced to constant work, at this point, didn't bother him, he recalled later. Other Africans, however, leaped from the sides of the vessels to their deaths whenever the opportunity presented itself. Almost as feared as the crew's whips and assorted torture devices were the stench and horror below decks.[4] "The shrieks of the women with the groans of the dying rendered the whole scene of horror almost inconceivable." J. Taylor Wood participated in the capture of a slave ship, after the international slave trade had been banned:

From the time we first got on board we had heard moans, cries, and rumblings coming from below, and as soon as the captain and crew were removed, the hatches had been taken off, when there arose a hot blast as from a charnel house, sickening and overpowering. In the hold were three or four hundred human beings, gasping, struggling for breath, dying; their bodies, limbs, faces, all expressing terrible suffering.[5]

While both males and females shared a determination to break free of their captors by whatever means they could avail themselves of, prior socialization in Africa would make it probable that the black male felt the psychological humiliation of military defeat more acutely. Already, on the slave ship, the white male captors had taken the military capacity of the African males into account as they tended to shackle them below decks while leaving females unshackled above deck Clearly, the first generations captured and enslaved had a different outlook from that of subsequent generations raised under slavery; armed revolt was never completely stamped out among African American slaves, although the opportunities for large-scale revolt were not as favorable as in areas featuring black slave majorities such as Bahia, Haiti, or Jamaica.[6]

Each colony featured unique politicomilitary conditions that evolved over time, some creating more favorable conditions for successful uprisings or the establishment of maroon colonies than others. In Louisiana, for example, strong maroon colonies developed in the cypress swamps, *la cipiere*, the waterways facilitating their movements. The Bambara settlements exerted a powerful lever in favor of justice to the blacks enslaved nearby on plantations. With the growth of a cypress industry in the middle of the eighteenth century, the maroon settlements likewise experienced growth, and, with arms, their defenses improved. The emergence of permanent maroon communities encouraged the growth of their agricultural production and other enterprises, while the raids on nearby plantations continued.[7]

The Bambara experience in Louisiana is but one example of the manner in which African American males and females took full advantage of geographic and demographic circumstances that made some kind of military response advantageous. Nevertheless, despite many variations and exceptions, Africans, upon arrival to America, were generally a conquered and traumatized people who had to first forge a new culture uniting various African ethnic and subethnic groups before they could begin to effectively reshape their environment according to their own designs. When armed resistance proved futile in terms of defeating the enemy and gaining liberty, the captured Africans were forced to come to terms with their new situation, however bleak it may have been. The end of collective armed resistance, however, did not mean that resistance ended. The economic sphere became the focus of the resistance of Africans on a daily basis; work, in all of its myriad forms, was the site of continual battles between slave and master.[8]

The character of work and the occupational structure of American slavery were determined, in large part, by the stress slave owners placed on the acquisition of profits and financial growth, as opposed to a focus on the paternalistic obligations of the master class toward those they claimed ownership over. Historian Eugene Genovese maintains that a "substantial number" of slaveholders were attracted not by the prospect of upward social mobility but rather by "a way of life reminiscent of self sufficient peasantries." While slave owners worked at a relatively leisurely pace, out of sync with the ideal bourgeois work ethic, they "operated in a capitalist world market" and "had to pay attention to profit-and-loss statements." Genovese concludes, therefore, that they adhered to the "Puritan work ethic," "but only so far as their slaves were concerned. Slaves ought to be steady, regular, continent, disciplined clock-punchers."[9] Yet, such enforcement of the suggested pace of work by means of a whip and other instruments clashes with the "paternalist" imagery promoted by the slaveholders during the mid-nineteenth century.[10]

James Oakes points to the fact that the bulk of the slaveholders were lured to the business by the promotional literature promising large profits in a brief amount of time. Many early European settlers to North Carolina were attracted by the claims that within only a few short years following the termination of their indentures, they would be able to acquire cheaply a large amount of land and slaves to work it.[11] In contrast to Genovese, Oakes stresses that cruelty, rather than an aberration of the system, was inherent to it and followed from its overriding goal of "material advancement."[12] Far from basing their actions on a sense of obligation infused with emotion, slaveholders resisted attempts to humanize Africans and battled to view the people as commodities for profit. In the final analysis, they were capital assets and a supply of labor. The slaveholders' ceaseless quest for expansion and wealth, embodied in a popular American ideology of upward social mobility, involved frequent migration, the sale of whole families and individuals, a whip-enforced, brutal pace of labor, and material deprivation. Often slave ownership, particularly for the larger slaveholders, was facilitated by a lucrative career as an attorney, artisan, or physician. For others it was the sole means of their quest for wealth. Hence, slave ownership became widely distributed in antebellum society—by the eve of the Civil War some 400,000 people held slaves. For many of the most ambitious southern whites, the prospect of enslaving blacks offered them the hope that they would be among the prosperous few by midlife. Slave ownership became a badge of success.[13] No wonder that some 20,000 artisans (including blacksmiths, carpenters, and mechanics), 21,000 businessmen and civil servants, and 27,000 doctors, attorneys, and other professionals owned slaves in 1850.[14]

BLACK MALE LABOR AND THE FOUNDATIONS OF THE EARLY AMERICAN ECONOMY

Much of the foundation for subsequent American prosperity was laid by the initial arduous labor of slaves involved in clearing the native forests for agricultural production. In the northern colonies, European settlers took advantage of the excellent natural harbors, temperate climate, abundant timber, and bountiful seas. The only element making for prosperous economic development that was lacking was human labor. The glut of available land for freeholding retarded the ability of the early colonial economy to maintain the minimum number of laborers needed to develop the settlements. The rejection of wage labor among white colonists was so universal that almost every colony resorted to some form of compulsory labor to resolve this acute shortage of workers. For whites, coerced labor took the form of indentured servitude, while for blacks, slavery was instituted.[15]

In New York, then known as New Amsterdam, the first 11 Africans arrived in 1626 and were immediately put to work on building the first roads, clearing bush, cutting trees, and constructing buildings.[16] By 1626 the Dutch West India Company began importing Africans as slaves to clear forests, build roads, and raise crops. Their early accomplishments led an increasing number of whites to gradually turn from fur trading to farming.[17]

While chattel slavery in New England began in 1637 with the swap of captured Pequot Indian males for black slaves from the Caribbean, it soon became widespread throughout the region.[18] With the incentive to trade in slaves, New England settlers soon developed a thriving slave trade industry whose profits fueled the growth of shipbuilding, liquor, and agriculture enterprises.[19] By the 1700s enslaved blacks worked in every phase of the colonial economy. In Philadelphia, New York, and Boston, slaves worked in almost every craft, occupying positions as assistants and apprentices to established white craftsmen. In these capacities they worked as bakers, coopers, tanners, weavers, blacksmiths, millers, goldsmiths, and cabinetmakers, seriously competing with whites, whose business suffered from the competition.[20] Industry in the colonial North was also heavily dependent on slave labor, as were the maritime industries. This dependence on black labor in the North, however, was not without its cost in terms of white anxieties. Any opportunity to exercise a modicum of liberty was taken advantage of by the slaves. Complete control was impossible, as simple tasks such as carrying water or caring for horses could be used to find moments to gather in the streets to socialize or take care of personal business. By the early 1700s laws prohibiting gatherings by slaves and mandating stringent curfews were common in the northern colonies.[21]

In South Carolina the successful production of rice with slave labor required that large tracts of land be cleared of trees. The need for massive tracts of cleared land can be seen from the fact that roughly 500 acres was considered sufficient for as few as ten African slaves to work. Trees alone proved to be enough to fuel a very profitable industry, while the need to produce timber for convenient export created an acute demand for sawyers. For an entire generation or more, black men working in pairs spent their lives clearing forests and sawing timber.[22]

African males in early colonial America also engaged in other subsidiary trades. For example, almost from the beginning of European settlement, blacks came to dominate the cooper's trade in South Carolina.[23] The production of timber-related products, including turpentine, pitch, and tar became an important industry that occupied the labor of enslaved Africans in the state. This was dangerous and painstaking work, requiring a tall man to chop channels in a pine tree in order that the liquid would drain onto boards below and constructing kilns to produce the tar. The kilns then had to be watched constantly for several days and night, a task necessitating considerable skill in maintaining the proper temperature—a mistake could lead to a fatal explosion.

As slavery consolidated itself in the colonies, there was a progressive differentiation of the black occupational structure within the bowels of the institution. The increasing number of economic roles played by enslaved Africans included careers as barbers, cooks, waiters, butchers, gardeners, shoemakers, carpenters, tanners, bricklayers, and plasterers. In New York City, which had the highest proportion of skilled slaves during the colonial era, black males worked as coopers, tailors, goldsmiths, glaziers, and blacksmiths and in numerous other trades.[24] The competition of these slave occupations with those of free, white workingmen led to restrictive legislation being passed in some areas. In Charleston, too, slaves were involved in dozens of skilled occupations, working as bakers, tailors, plasterers, and coopers and in other trades. Mills and other manufacturing enterprises in the city depended heavily on black slave labor. By the eve of the Civil War, for example, the West Point Rice Mills, the largest in the state, relied on the 160 slaves it owned. The human property included men skilled at carpentry, bricklaying, blacksmithing, and other trades.[25] The city's waterfront, as in the northern cities, also drew heavily on the labor power of slaves who worked there as stevedores and wharf hands. In Charleston and in other antebellum urban areas, the rigidity of the slave system was relieved somewhat by the provision of the option of "hiring out" slaves.[26] In Charleston the spread of the practice of using slaves for an ever-widening number of jobs led to periodic protests by the city's white working population. In 1826, for example, the Charleston City Council deplored the increasing number of slaves working as clerks and salesmen. The problem was the spread of slave labor to jobs "which require the exercise of greater intelligence & improvement," a situation that threatened to disrupt the fabric of society.[27] By this date the significance of the types of work slaves performed was clear, since only years before, Charleston whites had narrowly avoided the necessity to quash a massive slave rebellion. In its aftermath it was clear that these types of black slaves, enjoying mobility, somewhat challenging work, an elevated social status, and a greater sense of liberty, represented a distinct threat to the stability of the slave system. The literacy, sense of organization, and familiarity with the urban scene gave rebel leader and former seaman Denmark Vesey, harness maker Monday Gell, and other rebel leaders the confidence to launch their audacious, yet ultimately ill-fated, attempt at insurrection.

Imported African culture played a more important role in some areas than in others. In contrast to the European settlers, for example, the Africans imported into South Carolina were accustomed to the open grazing of cattle, as was common along the Gambia River. Their skills in husbandry, horsemanship, and herding were brought with them from Africa.[28] In a similar manner, many Africans were quite adept at rice cultivation, processing, and utilization, and passed on their knowledge to Europeans.[29] In rural areas across the plantation South, where the vast majority of slaves were held, plowing, planting, weeding, hoeing, picking, and other activity generally occupied the black male slave from sunup to past sundown. On Nicolas Massenburg's North Carolina plantation males cut timber, raked manure, dug ditches, and thrashed oats, among other tasks. While they performed the bulk of the plowing, women were involved in this work activity also. This was not true, however, of the ditch-digging, road work, and timber-cutting tasks.[30]

The slave occupational structure was characterized by hierarchy, associated with status, privilege, and material status, consisting of the house slaves, slave drivers and overseers, slave craftsmen, and other especially skilled individuals.[31] Slave artisans could derive some amount of satisfaction from their crafts and from the material rewards and prestige their accomplishments generated. This "elite" often could take advantage of being "hired out" to work, which allowed for more independence and income than other slaves had.[32]

While the nature and variety of tasks varied with the region, the crops produced, and the historical era, during colder months slaves generally performed tasks such as fixing fences, baling hay, and repairing roads.[33] In cotton areas, January and February meant ginning, moting, and sorting as well as digging ditches. The months of March and April meant preparing the cotton ground by bedding, planting, and more digging of ditches and fencing and hoeing. Hoeing dominated the summer months of May through August, and by the fall moting and ginning were again required.[34]

The variety of slave occupations and personal situations within agricultural areas, as well as in urban areas, is striking. Sella Martin was a house servant and boatman in North Carolina while a slave; Parke Johnson was a carpenter, farmhand, and shoemaker in Virginia; Reuben Madison was a "hired-out" rag merchant[35] ; and J. W. Lindsay was born free but was enslaved and made a blacksmith.[36] Slavery did not preclude involvement with heavy industry, as the success of ironmaster William Weaver's forges illustrates. The character of the slave labor of Weaver's forge is an example of the diversity within the antebellum South and the ability of the "peculiar" institution to adapt to a variety of social and economic exigencies.[37]

The gender-role flexibility characteristic of African American life was developed during the slave era as black women performed what would traditionally be considered male roles. Black men's work conformed to stereotypical, traditional gender role in its heavily physical quality and minimal demands on mental processes.[38] While enslaved females often spent their childhoods in the "big house," according to Elizabeth Fox-Genovese, they "matured into a distinct female sphere shaped by the assumptions of both slaveholders and slaves about gender relations (the proper relations between women and men) and gender roles (the proper occupations of women)."[39] On many plantations, women were forced to wield heavy "slave-time hoes," implements constructed from pig iron made to thwart all slave attempts to break them "accidentally." The black female's physical, emotional, and spiritual resources were stretched to the utmost as she was forced to labor alongside her male counterpart in the fields, exploited for her ability to bear future slaves and, driven by her regard for her family and mate, forced to work in the slave quarters to humanize the home environment to the extent possible.

The microeconomic realities of slaveholding gave owners sufficient incentive to interfere in the most intimate of matters, the reproductive, romantic, and sexual lives of African Americans. Thomas Jefferson, for example, celebrating the black slave "breeding" woman, stated that, "it is not their labor, but their increase which is the first consideration with us." Jefferson frankly stated, "I consider a woman who brings a child every two years more profitable than the best man of the farm. What she produces is an addition to the capital, while his labors disappear in mere consumption."[40] Angela Davis commented that, in the view of the slaveholders, "slave women were not mothers at all: they were simply instruments guaranteeing the growth of the slave labor force. They were 'breeders'—animals, whose monetary value could be precisely calculated."[41] As in wartime, a greater approximation of gender equality became necessary and values leaning toward greater role flexibility and gender equality became a feature of the slave's domestic life.

The hierarchy among slaves heightened the extent of diversity among antebellum African Americans. According to one estimate, one-quarter of enslaved males were supervisors, artisans, skilled laborers, or semiskilled laborers, such as gardeners, coachmen, and teamsters.[42] Perhaps the most pivotal and "political" role on the plantation was performed by the black drivers. The "ideal" traits of a driver in the eyes of the slaveholders were loyalty, reliability, and accountability, combined with mental and physical energy.[43] From daybreak, when the driver would awaken the field slaves and rush them through "breakfast," to nightfall, when checks would be made to ensure that slaves were in their cabins, drivers played a key role.[44] Much of the black driver's power flowed from his job of administering punishment, allocating rations, and evaluating work performance. The enhanced social, political, and financial status of the driver often led to his assumption of a leadership role within the social life of the slave quarters. Politically, the stance of the drivers varied from a complete identification and commitment to the slave owner, to complete loyalty to the black slave community. Slaveholders were wary of the pull that the African American slave community had on drivers. An article in the *The Farmers' Register* in 1836 advised that "the more the driver is kept aloof from the negroes, the better," as the emergence of a sense of "equality" between field hand and drivers would result in the loss of all "control." [45]

THE PRO-SLAVERY ARGUMENT AND ITS IMPACT ON THE BLACK MALE IMAGE

Prior to the introduction of the institution of slavery in North America, the perception of Africans among Europeans, while hardly positive, was not linked with slavery.[46] Lifetime bondage as a laborer was endured by tens of thousands of Europeans indentured during the seventeenth century, and, often, during the middle and latter decades of that century, indentured Africans and Europeans ran away from their masters together.[47] The notion of enslaving Indians was shattered after the 1622 slaughter of some 400 English colonists by the Powhatan Confederacy.[48] After the English gained direct access to the burgeoning trade in human beings via the Treaty of Breda in 1667, and tobacco was discovered to be an excellent export for the world market, large colonial landowners began to push to make African servitude lifelong and hereditary. This proved politically and socially feasible by exempting Europeans from bondage, isolating Africans, and gradually elaborating an ideology and a rationale for black bondage.[49]

The image of the African held by Americans in the early nineteenth century was heavily influenced by the writings of Thomas Jefferson, despite his vested interest in slavery as a large slaveholder. The contrast between Jefferson's opinions of the innate capacities of Native American males and those of African males is striking. From his masculinist perspective and relying primarily on environmental and cultural explanations for what he perceived to be Native American anatomy, culture, and social life, the Founding Father denied that they were lacking in "ardor" in comparison to whites.[50] Jefferson, terming enslavement of Indians an "inhuman practice [that] once prevailed in this country," assembled a series of arguments intended to demonstrate the equality of Indians and Europeans. Africans, Indians, and Europeans were found to be equally brave; however, the Africans' capacity for courage was found to stem from "a want of forethought, which prevents their seeing a danger till it be present."[51]

Jefferson believed blacks to be an emotional people whose gender relationships lacked tenderness and involved almost pure lust in comparison to whites. He assured readers that the Africans' "griefs are transient" and that they were "less felt, and sooner forgotten."[52] Blacks, to Jefferson, were a people who felt but did not reflect. In his *Notes on Virginia*, Jefferson wrote unfavorably of black intellect, writing that "in memory they are equal to the white; in reason much inferior," doubting that a single black could be found capable of comprehending Euclid's research. Blacks also lacked talent and creativity in music and the arts, in Jefferson's opinion, as he found them at once "tasteless and anomalous," although he later conceded that blacks had some musical talents. Worse still, their very existence in America posed a threat to whites since, if miscegenation occurred, the beauty of the white race would be fouled and replaced by an unattractive and "immoveable veil of black."[53]

Historian U. B. Phillips described African American slave laborers as "notoriously primitive, uncouth, improvident and inconstant," a trait deemed to be characteristic of their race. Happy and ignorant, they were totally ruled by both their passions and their white masters.[54] This follows Thomas Jefferson, who, earlier profferring similar views, apparently felt that Africans could become excellent craftsmen, mechanics, skilled workers, or artisans. His confidence in the slave artisans he owned can be gleaned from an exchange of letters in 1825 after the home of Francis Wayles Eppes, his grandson, suffered serious damage from a fire. In dispatching master carpenter John Hemings to repair the damage he wrote Eppes: "I will spare [John Hemings] to you and his two aids and he can repair everything of wood as well or perhaps better than anybody there."[55] The African Americans with whom Jefferson was closest in terms of blood ties, property ties, and personal contact, some of whom, centuries later, were shown to be his children, were encouraged to learn practical trades. Nevertheless, Madison Hemings was put under the wing of John Hemings, his uncle, who was a carpenter and learned to read only by "inducing the white children to teach" him "the letters and something more."[56]

Jefferson biographer John Chester Miller concluded that Jefferson labored "under powerful psychological compulsion to believe that the blacks were innately inferior." Privately, he went further in his charge of black inferiority. In 1807 he told a British diplomat that blacks were "as far inferior to the rest of mankind as the mule is to the horse, and as made to carry burthens."[57] Yet, Jefferson and other slaveholders made use of black mental and physical powers to the extent they could, given the political, social, cultural, and economic constraints.

Benjamin Bannecker, a free black, challenged some of Jefferson's views on race. Offering his own achievements as evidence, Bannecker sought to demonstrate the heights Africans could attain intellectually, even while hampered by a pervasive racism. In 1791 Jefferson himself had approved Bannecker's appointment as an assistant to Andrew Ellicott, surveyor of the newly planned American capital.[58] Later that year, he wrote to Jefferson, then the U. S. secretary of state. Bannecker reminded Jefferson in the letter of the statesman's image as a man who harbored no rigid prejudices and was "measurably friendly, and well disposed toward us."[59] If this was true, he asserted, then Jefferson should be eager "to eradicate that train of absurd and false ideas and opinions" that disparaged the mental and emotional capacities of Africans. The Maryland-born Bannecker assured Jefferson that he was "of the African race" and "of the deepest dye" in order to discourage the idea that a preponderance of white forebears was responsible for whatever intellectual abilities Jefferson perceived him to have.

Bannecker's anger seems barely contained, as he asked Jefferson to "wean" himself "from those narrow prejudices which" he had "imbibed with respect to blacks" and to "put your soul in their souls' stead." At one point he accused Jefferson and his countrymen of acting in conflict with the "Father of Mankind" by enslaving blacks. He remarked on "how pitiable" it was to witness Americans committing "that most criminal act, which you professedly detested in others." Bannecker, who authored six almanacs in 28 editions during the mid-1790s, finally presented Jefferson with a gift of an almanac, recounting that it was produced under many "difficulties and disadvantages."[60] Jefferson thanked him, yet again voiced doubts that blacks were equal to whites despite his most fervent desire that they be so. Later, Jefferson conceded that Bannecker knew "spherical trigonometry enough to make almanacs," accusing him of secretly being aided by Andrew Ellicott, his younger white supervisor. Uncharitably, Jefferson concluded Bannecker intellectually to be "of very common stature indeed." He concluded that blacks were "inferior to whites in the endowments both of body and mind."[61] A year later, Jefferson confided to a diplomat that the letters he received from Bannecker were of a "very childish and trivial" nature, perhaps still remembering the implied insults to his humanistic convictions.[62] Long-term public policy with regard to the issue of Africans in America, according to Jefferson, should be based on the two-pronged danger that blacks posed to the American nation. First, the danger of a "staining" and polluting racial intermixture—fueled by a perception of a large population of promiscuous black males intoxicated with desire for interracial sex—was to be avoided at all costs. The second problem was that of having "the wolf by the ears" and not being able to either "hold him, nor safely let him go." With whites afraid to "let go," African Americans had to be "safely" held down.[63] This implied a long-term strategy based on fear that would be primarily aimed at black males, who, it was feared, would be in a vengeful mood if they ever gained a semblance of political or military power. These conclusions led Jefferson to favor continued slavery until a time in the future when black emigration from America could be arranged.[64]

As slavery came under increasing attack, particularly in the North and in Europe, pro-slavery forces felt a need to elaborate a defense for the institution. By the time of the inception of the slave trade, the association of blackness in English culture with sexuality and evil was quite strong.[65] The earliest formal defense of slavery, authored by John Saffin, argued that it was "no evil thing to bring" Africans "out of their own Heathenish Country, [to] where they may have the knowledge of the One True God, be Converted and Eternally Saved." Saffin's text also included a poem describing blacks as "Cowardly," "Cruel," "Prone to Revenge," and hateful. They were murderous, "Libidinous," "Deceitful," and "Rude."[66] With the material incentive of profit for colonial planters, merchants, slave traders, and others, coupled with the social incentives of higher status for white laborers, these notions were reinforced as increasing numbers of African captives were imported into the colonies.[67] Bertram Wyatt-Brown stresses that the pro-slavery defenders were aiming to influence a particular audience: the growing chorus of critics of the institution in both the North and Britain.[68]

Defenders of the institution argued that slavery was a school of civilization for pagan blacks, inculcating Christianity and morality in them.[69] If slavery was necessary to force blacks to perform useful, moral, and socially redeeming roles, its abolition would be tantamount to unleashing wild hordes of Africans to plague the nation with their crime, idleness, and violence. By indulging the additional notion that Africans were happy in America under slavery, they were able to reduce their guilt and anxieties about the institution.[70] During the mid-1830s, William and Mary College professor Thomas R. Dew praised slavery, declaring that a "merrier being does not exist on the face of the globe than the negro slave."[71]

Thomas R. R. Cobb, in a manner similar to Jefferson's, argued that the subhuman character of Africans is such that their "natural affections are not strong," and they are "cruel" to their children. It followed that the family breakup endemic to slavery did not entail much suffering by those so victimized. Other ideologists of slavery agreed that blacks lacked the human emotions necessary to bind the family together, as love was seen as alien to the African, being overshadowed by impulses of "lust and beastly cruelty."[72] Instead, one of the roles of the patriarchal slave owner, in the view of the defenders of the institution, was to provide blacks with a loving and caring plantation "family." Historian William W. Freehling found a connection between this patriarchal ideal and the incredible impact that the Nat Turner revolt had on slaveholders. The revolt served to shatter the illusions of harmony and tranquillity among the slaves and the close proximity of apparently would-be Nat Turners to thousands of plantations across the nation sent a shiver down the spines of slaveholders. The Turner revolt raised several troubling questions. How many other slaves, ostensibly happy and contented, had a hidden side to their personalities? To what extent were these smiling faces mere masks? How could slaveholding whites trust their cooks, servants, and others whom they depended upon for every task?[73]

A good part of the lure of such patriarchal imagery for slaveholders was that it dissociated their practices from those of foreign slave traders and that it drew on biblical sources. Describing slavery as a *condition* and not a *moral* evil was a key element in presenting it as a God-decreed state of being.[74] The image of the southern planter as a benevolent, Abraham-like figure guiding clueless black "children" to a better way of living, saving their souls, and making a modest profit in the process was preferable to the image increasingly put forth by the abolitionists and other critics of slavery.[75] Reverend Joseph Wilson, a North Carolina Presbyterian minister and the father of President Woodrow Wilson, felt that slavery was a "scheme of politics and morals" that under "divine management, contributed to refine, exalt, and enrich its superior race."[76] A staple element within this thought was the view that blacks must be compelled to work.

One southerner told English traveler Harriet Martineau with no trace of irony that "it takes two white men, to make a black man work."[77]

On 6 February 1837 South Carolina senator John C. Calhoun delivered his landmark "Slavery a Positive Good" speech before the U. S. Senate. Bemoaning the spread of an "incendiary spirit," Calhoun declared slavery "a positive good," since it "brought together" two quite distinct races. Describing slaveholder rule as "patriarchal," he held that the "kind attention paid" to the slaves by the slave masters compared favorably with the conditions faced by the "tenants of the poor houses in the more civilized portions of Europe."[78]

Within this ideological context the evolving image of the African American male took form. Tilden G. Edelstein's analysis of two centuries of Othello performances sheds light on how this image changed over the decades. First performed in Newport, Rhode Island, in 1765, the playbill indicated that the moral of the story was the foolishness of Desdemona's father for despising Othello, a Moor, an account of his blackness. Such prejudices against humanity, while frequent, it said, were nevertheless "wrong."[79] When Abigail Adams saw Othello two decades later in 1786, she expressed discomfort with "the sooty appearance of the Moor" and experienced a sense of "disgust and horror" every time she saw him touch "gentle Desdemona." These scenes forced her to ponder whether witchcraft or "love potion" could be the cause of Desdemona's love for "what she scarcely dared to look upon."[80]

The ever-increasing antiblack sentiment prevalent in early America made it imperative to recast Othello until the play's racial-sexual content was within the bounds of acceptability. For Americans, the high status of the Moor Othello clashed with the almost universally debased status they viewed as appropriate for African American males. By 1820 Edmund Kean used makeup dramatically lighter in color to play the role of Othello, inaugurating the "bronze age" of Othello.[81] This greatly pleased Samuel Taylor Coleridge, who was sure that Shakespeare was not "so utterly ignorant as to make a barbarous negro plead royal birth," adding that it was "monstrous" to think of a "beautiful Venetian girl falling in love with a veritable negro."[82] Following this, Othello underwent a further lightening, but this failed to satisfy John Quincy Adams, who reviewed the play:

The great moral lesson of Othello is that black and white blood cannot be intermingled without a gross outrage upon the law of Nature; and that, in such violations, Nature will vindicate her laws. Upon the stage her fondling of Othello is disgusting. Who, in real life, would have her for a sister, daughter or wife. The character takes from us so much of the sympathetic interest in her sufferings that when Othello smothers her in bed, the terror and the pity subside immediately to the sentiment that she had her just desserts.[83]

This image of the black male as a sexual predator has deep roots in the American psyche. One pro-slavery writer stressed that the aims of the Denmark Vesey rebels in 1822 were to slay the men and take the women as their concubines. The captured rebel Rolla allegedly said that "When we have done with the men we know what to do with the women."[84]

One analysis of the eighteenth and nineteenth century press in Pennsylvania revealed a consistent stream of negative images of blacks during this long period. The local papers around Lancaster, Pennsylvania, featured a disproportionate number of negative portrayals of black males. As the years passed, the old image of the loyal and faithful black domestic gave way to that of the black thief, drunk, or fool. Gradually, as the Civil War approached, the images of black males as violent and thieving became predominant. Cowardly and predatory attacks, especially upon women, were depicted as perpetrated almost at random by black males. In this manner, the fear of being personally assaulted on the streets or in one's household by black males was systematically promoted over the course of decades by these newspapers.[85]

Even when blacks were portrayed as mentally adroit, it was in the context of indicating that they were "tricky" and would take advantage of unsuspecting whites. Incompetence, deceitfulness, and untruthfulness were also prominent in commentaries on black males within these newspapers. Those positive characteristics promoted by the press were consistent with the paternalist imagery emanating from the South regarding the proper role for blacks in society. Musical ability, obsequiousness and deference, vigor and good health, and, most important, loyalty were all celebrated as ideal qualities. A slave's willingness to risk his life in order to save a slave master was perhaps the standard for gauging slave loyalty, for the ideal slave would identify with the slave master to such an extent that life itself was inconceivable without his guidance.[86]

THE BLACK MALE AS BOY: THE EMERGENCE OF SAMBO

Perhaps the most important historical personification of the black male to emerge during the slave era was the image of "Sambo," which became a ubiquitous figure in American culture. Stanley M. Elkins writes that southern lore typically portrays him as "docile but irresponsible, loyal but lazy, humble but chronically given to lying and stealing; his behavior was full of infantile silliness and his talk inflated with childish exaggeration. His relationship with his master was one of utter dependence and childlike attachment: it was indeed the childlike quality that was the very key to his being."[87]

In his extensive study of this fool figure, Joseph Boskin described how the ubiquitous Sambo became unmatched in his ability to reduce audiences to paroxysms of laughter. Boskin writes that Sambo was found in "journals, weeklies, newspapers, magazines, travel reports," all forms of literary production, and in many commodities of American popular culture. The image of Sambo was that of the black male as perpetual child existing to serve whites with a smiling face, perform hard labor, and act as a lightning rod for humor. Sambo was a key feature in the effort to forge a worldview that rendered the image of the black male harmless. Remaking the black male in humorous terms, as a buffoon, cemented his status as a perpetual child, deprived of manhood, not worthy of being taken seriously. What else could he do save follow orders?[88]

By the 1820s the minstrel show featuring white entertainers in blackface had emerged. These shows presented the black male in two forms: the "darky" and the "dandy," the former representing a rural figure, and the latter, an urban figure. In 1828 Thomas Rice was inspired by an older black man saddled with rheumatism to begin his Jim Crow performances in blackface.[89] Using a "darky" accent, Rice became an instant sensation on stages across the nation. White males in blackface had portrayed black males as buffoons prior to the American Revolution, but the new form of blackface took off in terms of popularity. As blackface swept the nation and became a fixture of American culture, the "Sambo" image became lodged deeply into the American psyche.[90]

The second half of the minstrel show, the *olio*, featured a monologue by a blackfaced actor that invariably included mangled words and terms. The humorous oratory could touch on a variety of controversial social, political, and cultural subjects. Garbled words and confused meanings allowed the audience to reach heights of frenzied humor at the expense of antebellum urban black males.[91] Caricatures of the African appearance, culture, language, music, and nonverbal behavior all were distorted in the effort to portray black males as foolish, imbecilic, incompetent, and generally inferior creatures.[92]

Targeting northern black males, beset by discrimination and exclusion in every area, minstrel shows focused on stereotypic, narcissistic "dandy darkies," who laughingly believed they were handsome with their outrageously deformed African physical characteristics. Having them perform skits in which they were learning new inventions, and discussing the issues of the day or their social lives, the minstrel acts were able to depict humorously the black males' incurable incompetence and hardheadedness. Minstrels shied away from the stock images of the black male as a sexual predator but were more likely to portray the black male as an overgrown child. "Old Darky" was about as positive as the minstrel images got, as his asexual and comforting ways were not intimidating to white audiences. The image of Old Darky was appealing since it played on the nostalgic images of mutual devotion and love on the plantation. One common scene, of the Master dying, depicted Old Darky's profound grief. With tears pouring from his eyes, what would dependent Old Darky do now?[93]

Eric Lott focuses his analysis of blackface on what he observes as a "cross-racial desire" characterized by both fascination and defensive derision of black male culture. It represented not so much "a sign of absolute white power and control" as it did their "panic, anxiety, terror, and pleasure" in their appropriation of a slice of black male culture. For the working-class white male of Jacksonian America, putting on blackface meant "to become black, to inherit the cool, virility, humility, abandon" that they perceived black males to enjoy. Lott maintains that this historical association of black male culture with masculinity, occurring largely unconsciously on the part of white males, has persisted throughout American history.[94]

Nevertheless, the blackface audiences suffered from a social, psychological, and cultural dissonance, being at once attracted to, and repulsed by, black males, a phenomenon occasionally giving rise to antiblack mobs.[95] Frederick Douglass was once moved to describe the performers of blackface as "the filthy scum of white society, who have stolen from us a complexion denied to them by nature, in which to make money, and pander to the corrupt taste of their white fellow citizens."[96] Against these images, articles and books produced by African Americans and other antislavery forces in the nation consisted, in large part, of narratives of slaves, a portion of whom depicted the black male in heroic terms. One commentator noted that the first major portrayal of a black male in American literature was the *Narrative of the Life of Frederick Douglass.*[97]

There is considerable evidence that even the most fervent adherents of the Sambo view of the black male as an overgrown, passive, and faithful child were unable to fully convince themselves of this. In her *Diary from Dixie*, South Carolinian Mary Chesnut wavered between an arrogant confidence that the scores of slaves surrounding her were absolutely faithful and a grim realization that she possibly lay vulnerable to their resentment and revenge. In 1861 Chesnut considered the possibilities that her and her husband's trusted body servant Lawrence would flee to the North after being entrusted with the care "of all Mr. Chesnut's things—watch, clothes, and two or three hundred gold pieces that lie in the tray of his trunk." The slave was instructed to bring these valuables to Mary Chesnut if her husband should meet with death or other misfortune. Chesnut speculated, however: "Maybe he will pack off to the Yankees and freedom with all that. Fiddlesticks! He is not going to leave me for anybody else. After all, what can he ever be, better than he is now—a gentleman's gentleman?"[98]

By 1864 Mary Chesnut's personal situation had greatly deteriorated, as she was a virtual refugee and had descended to the level of a pauper. Lawrence loyally presented her with the $600 her husband had entrusted him with. Chesnut told him, "Now I am pretty sure you do not mean to go to the Yankees, for with that pile of money in your hands you must have known there was your chance." Lawrence smiled but remained silent.[99]

Unfree black male labor played an essential role in laying the foundations for agricultural and industrial development in America. The character of this labor was of fundamental importance in shaping the subsequent social history of African Americans. As black males emerged from the traumas of capture, the rupture of family and community ties, the Middle Passage, and the seasoning process, they found themselves victimized by a pernicious and pervasive image that became iconic in American culture. While literally enchained, a fool figure called Sambo was foisted upon the black male. This all-sided structural, institutional, and individual racial slavery inevitably had damaging consequences for the black male's familial, romantic, friendship, and other social relationships. Their spirited resistance, however, generally would not allow a surrender to despair despite the grimness of the long decades of slavery. In every way, African American males, joined by their female counterparts, fought back to attempt to salvage meaning, purpose, and happiness in their lives. In this effort, they forged a body of concrete achievements and, in so doing, laid the basis for the future progress of the African American people.

NOTES

1. Jermain Wesley Loguen, Letter to Frederick Douglass. March 1855, in Peter Ripley et al. (eds.), *The Black Abolitionist Papers* (New York: Microfilm Corporation of America, 1981), 271.

2. Reynolds Farley, *Growth of the Black Population: A Study of Demographic Trends* (Chicago: Markham, 1970), 22.

3. Nathan Irvin Huggins, *Black Odyssey: The African American Ordeal in Slavery* (New York: Random House, 1977), 3.

4. Olaudah Equiano, "A Multitude of Black People.Chained Together," *The Interesting Narrative of the Life of Olaudah Equiano or Gustavus Vassa the African* (London, 1789).

5. J. Taylor Wood, "The Capture of a Slaver," *Atlantic Monthly* (1900): 451–63.

6. Herbert Aptheker, *American Negro Slave Revolts* (New York: International Publishers 1978), 3–4, See also Deborah Gray White, *Ar'n't I A Woman?: Female Slaves in the Plantation South* (New York: W. W. Norton, 1985), 63.

7. Gwendolyn Midlo Hall, *Africans in Colonial Louisiana: The Development of Afro-Creole Culture in the Eighteenth Century* (Baton Rouge: Louisiana State University Press, 1992), 159.

8. Raymond A. Bauer and Alice H. Bauer, "Day to Day Resistance to Slavery," *Journal of Negro History* 27, no. 4(October 1942): 388–419. See also Eugene Genovese, *From Rebellion to Freedom: Afro-American Slave Revolts in the Making of the Modern World* (Baton Rouge: Louisiana State University Press, 1979).

9. Eugene D. Genovese, *Roll, Jordan, Roll: The World the Slaves Made* (New York: Pantheon Books, 1974), 297.

10. James Oakes, *The Ruling Race: A History of American Slaveholders* (New York: Alfred A. Knopf, 1982), 7.

11. Ibid., 7.

12. Ibid., 25.

13. Ibid., 123.

14. Ibid., 59–61.

15. Edgar J. McManus, *Black Bondage in the North* (Syracuse, NY: Syracuse University Press, 1973), 2.

16. Roi Ottley and William J. Weatherby (eds.) *The Negro in New York: An Informal Social History* (New York: New York Public Library, 1967), 2–3.

17. McManus, *Black Bondage*, 3.

18. McManus, 6.

19. McManus, 10.

20. McManus, 42.

21. McManus, 82.

22. Peter H. Wood, *Black Majority: Negroes in Colonial South Carolina from 1670 through the Stono Rebellion* (New York: W. W. Norton, 1974), 3–4; C. Duncan Rice, *The Rise and Fall of Black Slavery* (Baton Rouge: Louisiana State University Press, 1975), 102–03.

23. Wood, *Black Majority*, 111.

24. Ibid., 108–09.

25. Bernard E. Powers Jr. *Black Charlestonians: A Social History, 1822–1885* (Fayetteville: University of Arkansas Press, 1994), 10.

26. Ibid., 12.

27. Ibid., 15.

28. Wood, *Black Majority*, 30.

29. Ibid., 61–62.

30. Elizabeth Fox-Genovese *Within the Plantation Household: Black and White Women of the Old South* (Chapel Hill: University of North Carolina Press, 1988), 174.

31. Jacqueline Jones, *Labor of Love, Labor of Sorrow: Black Women, Work, and the Family from Slavery to the Present.* (New York: Basic Books, 1985), 15–16; Genovese, *Within the Plantation*, 391.

32. Charles B. Dew, "Sam Williams, Forgeman: The Life of an Industrial Slave in the Old South," in J. Morgan Kousser and James M. McPherson (eds.), *Region, Race, and Reconstruction* (New York: Oxford University Press, 1982), 206–09; William L. Van Deburg *The Slave Drivers: Black Agricultural Labor Supervisors in the Antebellum South* (New York: Oxford University Press, 1979), 3–25; Genovese *Roll, Jordan, Roll*, 327–394.

33. Jones, *Labor of Love*, 15–16.

34. Charles S. Johnson, *Shadow of the Plantation* (Chicago: University of Chicago Press, 1939), 2–3.

35. John W. Blassingame, *Slave Testimony: Two Centuries of Letters, Speeches, Interviews, and Autobiographies* (Baton Rouge: Louisiana State University Press, 1977), 186.

36. Ibid., 396.

37. Dew "Sam Williams," 206–09. See also Kenneth M. Stampp, *The Peculiar Institution: Slavery in the Antebellum South* (New York: Vintage Books, 1989), 65.

38. Jones, *Labor of Love*, 18.

39. Fox-Genovese, *Within the Plantation*, 172.

40. Jones, *Labor of Love*, 12.

41. Angela Y. Davis, *Women, Race and Class* (New York: Vintage Books, 1983), 11–12.

42. Robert William Fogel and Stanley L. Engerman, *Time on the Cross, vol. 1: The Economics of American Negro Slavery* (Boston: Little, Brown, 1974).

43. Van Deburg, *The Slave Drivers*, 7–9.

44. Ibid., 11.

45. Ibid., 50–51.

46. Winthrop D. Jordan, *White over Black: American Attitudes toward the Negro, 1550–1812* (Baltimore: Penguin Books, 1969); Theodore W. Allen, *The Invention of the White Race volume 2: The Origin of Racial Oppression in Anglo-America* (London: Verso, 1997).

47. Allen, *Invention*, 155–158.

48. Ibid., 84.

49. Ibid., 187.

50. Thomas Jefferson, "Notes on Virginia," in *The Writings of Thomas Jefferson vol. 2* (Washington, DC: Thomas Jefferson Memorial Association, 1903), 82.

51. Ibid., 193–94.

52. Ibid., 6.

53. Ibid., 195.

54. Van De Burg, *The Slave Drivers*, 32.

55. Edwin Morris Betts and James A. Bear Jr. (eds.), *The Family Letters of Thomas Jefferson* (Columbia, MO, 1966), 451–54.

56. Blassingame, *Slave Testimony*, 478.

57. John Chester Miller, *The Wolf by the Ears: Thomas Jefferson and Slavery* (New York: Free Press, 1977), 57.

58. Sidney Kaplan, *The Black Presence in the Era of the American Revolution, 1770-1800* (Washington, DC: National Portrait Gallery, Smithsonian Institution, 1973), 119.

59. Documentary Sources Database, "Copy of a Letter from Benjamin Banneker," in *Documenting the African American Experience* (Charlottesville: University of Virginia Library Electronic Text Center, 1996).

60. Ibid..

61. Thomas Jefferson, *Thomas Jefferson on Slavery* (Dep. Alfa: Informatica University of Groningen, 1996).

62. Miller, *The Wolf by the Ears*, 77.

63. Ibid., 1-5, 125-28.

64. Ronald Takaki, *Iron Cages: Race and Culture in 19th-Century America* (New York: Oxford University Press, 1990), 11, 29.

65. Jordan, *White over Black*, 23-27.

66. Larry E. Tise, *Proslavery: A History of the Defense of Slavery in America, 1701-1840.* (Athens: University of Georgia Press, 1987), 17-18.

67. David R. Roediger, *The Wages of Whiteness: Race and the Making of the American Working Class* (London: Verso, 1991), 142; Michael Goldfield *The Color of Politics: Race and the Mainsprings of American Politics* (New York: The New Press, 1997), 8, Allen, *Invention*, 161-162.

68. Bertram Wyatt-Brown, "Modernizing Southern Slavery: The Proslavery Argument Reinterpreted," in Kousser and McPherson, *Region, Race, and Reconstruction*, 30.

69. George M. Frederickson, *The Black Image in the White Mind: The Debate on Afro-American Character and Destiny, 1817-1914.* (New York: Harper and Row, 1971), 53.

70. Ibid., 53-54.

71. William W. Freehling, *The Road to Disunion, vol. 1: Secessionists at Bay, 1776-1854* (New York: Oxford University Press, 1990),191.

72. Jordan, *White over Black*, 23-27.

73. Freehling, *The Road to Disunion*, 180.

74. Wyatt-Brown, "Modernizing Southern Slavery," 32.

75. Ibid., 33. See also, N. B. De Saussure, *Old Plantation Days Being Recollections of Southern Life before the Civil War* (New York: Duffield, 1909) (Electronic Edition. Academic Affairs Library, University of North Carolina–Chapel Hill, 1997), 21.

76. Wyatt-Brown 35.

77. Genovese, *Roll, Jordan, Roll*, 299.

78. John C. Calhoun, "Slavery a Positive Good," 6 February 1837, in *Andrew C. McLaughlin's Readings in the History of the American Nation* (New York: D. Appleton, 1914), 206-212.

79. Tilden G. Edelstein, "Othello in America: The Drama of Racial Intermarriage" in Kousser and McPherson, *Region, Race, and Reconstruction*, 180.

80. Ibid., 182.

81. Ibid., 183.

82. Ibid., 183-84.

83. Ibid., 185.

84. F. G. De Fontaine, *History of American Abolitionism* (New York Herald, 1863). (http://www.loc.gov/ammem), 15.

85. Thomas P. Slaughter, *Bloody Dawn: The Christiana Riot and Racial Violence in the Antebellum North* (New York: Oxford University Press, 1991), 29–31.

86. Ibid., 33.

87. Stanley M. Elkins, *Slavery: A Problem in American Institutional and Intellectual Life* (Chicago: University of Chicago Press, 1959), 82.

88. Joseph Boskin, *Sambo: The Rise and Demise of an American Jester* (New York: Oxford University Press, 1986), 9; see also Patricia A. Turner *Ceramic Uncles and Celluloid Mammies: Black Images and Their Influence on Culture* (New York: Anchor Books, 1994), 73.

89. Boskin, *Sambo* ,74–75.

90. Robert C. Toll, *Blacking Up: The Minstrel Show in Nineteenth-Century America* (New York: Oxford University Press, 1974), 28.

91. Ibid., 55.

92. Ibid., 69–71.

93. Ibid., 81.

94. Eric Lott, *Love and Theft: Blackface Minstrelsy and the American Working Class* (New York: Oxford University Press, 1993), 6.

95. Ibid., 113.

96. Ibid., 27.

97. William L. Andrews, "The Black Male in American Literature," in Richard G. Majors and Jacob U. Gordon (eds.), *The American Black Male: His Present Status and His Future* (Chicago: Nelson-Hall, Inc., 1994), 62.

98. Mary Boykin Chesnut, *A Diary from Dixie* (Gloucester, MA: Peter Smith, 1961), 85.

99. Ibid., 284.

Chapter 2

The Context of Black Masculine Development during the Antebellum Era

> No man who has never been placed in such a situation can comprehend the thousand obstacles thrown in the way of the flying slave. Every white man's hand is raised against him—the patrollers are watching for him—the hounds are ready to follow on his track, and the nature of the country is such as renders it impossible to pass through it with any safety.
>
> —Solomon Northrup[1]

During the antebellum era, the lives of black men were conditioned by a wide variety of circumstances. This chapter discusses the typical problems, crises, and dilemmas faced by enslaved African American males and traces the responses they made to resolve them. Acquiescence and accommodation versus resistance and rebellion represented the two extreme poles in the continuum of responses to slavery. Responses to slavery can thus be grouped into a polarity pitting complete obeisance, servility, and acquiescence at one pole and total disobedience, rebelliousness, and contempt for authority at the other.

Docility, humility, silliness, and childishness were basic elements of personality demanded of black male slaves by owners and overseers. The elements of "irresponsibility," laziness, and lying clearly represent forms of resistance of the enslaved, forms that were difficult to punish due to both their subtleness and consistency with racist stereotypes.[2] John Blassingame found three primary characters within antebellum southern literature, not only "Sambo" but also "Nat" and "Jack." Nat stood at the opposite pole of the continuum from Sambo as an incorrigible slave rebel who, if given the opportunity, would burn the plantation, rape the white women, and slaughter the white men. Nat's obeisance was illusory, for he awaited only the time and circumstances to make his move; he was hard-core. Jack, too, obeyed, for the overwhelming firepower of white society made it rational to do so. Although not as rebellious as Nat, Jack would revolt if conditions suggested it was the appropriate action. More routinely, Jack took food from the slave master if hungry, shirked work when unwatched, and left the plantation to take care of his business when necessary. Jack engaged in a practical, day-to-day resistance and monitored closely the overall conditions that surrounded him and his fellow slaves.[3] Beyond these ideal types of African American male personalities, however, there was a nearly infinite variety of combinations of individual characters, all of whom were faced with limited options under slavery. By the time of the American Revolution, a distinct culture, re-created from an African basis, had already emerged within the slave quarters of the nation.[4] This process involved the creation of cultural standards and values that reflected the varied settings in which slaves found themselves. For the male field slave this meant forging ways of acting, thinking, and feeling suited to the uniquely harsh conditions. Undergoing arduous labor for the longest daily period that was humanly possible, upon pain of being lashed by a whip, was merely one aspect of their lives. To this excruciating physical pain amid toil, a form of social-psychological terror played itself out in his social relationships. This bred a hardness and routinized defiance, among other features, within a standard of behavior that forms the basis for the genesis of black masculinity. The historically evolving African American male gender-role ideal, in all of its complexity and diversity, was shaped by the battle to survive mentally, spiritually, culturally, and physically the rigors of slavery. This historic reality explains the fact that, as Horton and Horton point out, "among the slaves, men who refused to submit to the master's authority were accorded respect. Those who submitted too easily to the master's authority lost respect."[5] One particular type of black male personality was pointed to by many former slaves: the black man who refused to take a whipping.[6]

Frederick Douglass' well-known battle with overseer Edward Covey, reputed to be a "slave breaker," moved him to later write that his relationship with him depicted "how a slave was made a man." On a scorching day in August 1833, Douglass was apparently overcome with heatstroke and collapsed while fanning wheat. Covey, who had hired the young slave for the summer, kicked Douglass hard in the side and ordered him to get up and work. Douglass attempted to comply but again collapsed, prompting Covey to hit him with a hickory slat on the head. Douglass then decided to lodge a complaint with his slave master. To do this, however, he had to walk about seven miles through bush, bogs, and briar patches, a journey that consumed five hours. Shoeless and wounded, Douglass approached the slave master and related to him what had happened. The slave master dismissed Douglass' concerns and defended Covey and eventually threatened Douglass himself. Douglass walked back, but when greeted by the irate Covey, Douglass broke for the cornfield and hid.

Assisted by a slave who gave him a root that would purportedly protect him, he eventually returned to the plantation and was not immediately attacked by Covey, leading Douglass to begin to believe that the root was working. The next day, however, Douglass was startled by a lasso held by Covey. Their much-recounted battle resulted in Douglass' new sense of himself, as it "revived within me a sense of my own manhood," infusing him with self-confidence and a determination not to be bound by "slavery's chains."[7]

Efforts to maintain a high standard of nutrition, social status, material prosperity, and family stability almost always would end up involving acts deemed "criminal" under the system of slavery. For the enslaved black male, maintaining the persona of a thoughtful, intelligent, and curious individual was regarded as impudent, brash, and offensive.[8] Literacy itself was a crime, although many breaches in the total ban on reading and writing occurred. Recollections of slaves being "whipped like a thief" were common, as blacks determined to read had to engage in clandestine activity both to learn and to practice reading and writing. More than one slave found it necessary to venture deep into the woods in order to read.[9]

During the lengthy process of what Nathan Irvin Huggins has termed "Afro-Americanization," the family, friend, and quasi-kin networks of blacks congealed into informal institutions that anchored individuals and absorbed their loyalties.[10] The influence of this network, bound by emotion and mutual need, proved to be an important factor in shaping black male behavior. With almost all avenues of economic advancement barred to the slave, family and friend relationships assumed even greater importance. The male slave's relationships with the members of his family who had not been sold away or slain formed the most important part of his social world. The variety of individual circumstances and the constant shifting of the slave population meant that the proximity of the individuals dear to the slave varied considerably from individual to individual.

All of these males had to come to grips with the severe restrictions of their personal movements and the penalties for violating them, the violence meted out during the working day, the difficulty in developing families and maintaining them, and the decision whether to remain in slavery or flee it.

THE BATTLE OF THE BLACK MALE SLAVE FOR FREE MOVEMENT

With every act that the slave performed, the question of compliance or defiance confronted him. The right to travel freely from place to place was denied African Americans even in the rare case when an individual slave owner defied convention and permitted it. Yet, this right was routinely seized by black males and often by females, who were determined to wrest a measure of satisfaction from life in order to survive under these harsh circumstances. Due to the traditional male gender role, the ban on free movement was more irksome for males and provided an entire arena for struggle between slave owners, their staff, and authorities, on one hand, and individual slaves, the slave community, and their allies, on the other.

The antebellum American white male gender-role ideal put a premium on the capacity to move freely throughout the cities, towns, and countryside of the growing nation. In contrast, from the date of the earliest settlements, the average black male's freedom of movement was subject to severe limitations. Even so, male slaves typically left the plantation more than their female counterparts, most commonly during the course of their work or being hired out.[11] The American practice of severely limiting the freedom of African American geographic mobility, of the male in particular, was established during the initial decades of the American colonies. While much of the labor of bondsmen involved travel, and in certain areas slaves worked in key roles in the early transportation sector of the economy, when not traveling on behalf of the slave master's interests, the black male ran a gauntlet of dangers. On a regular basis, he was detained and subjected to various types of abuse, including torture and mutilation. In South Carolina restrictions on black mobility were codified into law with the passage of the 1690 Act for the Better Ordering of Slaves.[12] This law mandated that slaves carry tickets of permission to run errands or else face the pain of corporal punishments that included the branding of the skin, cutting off the nose, and castration. By 1722 South Carolina required that a runaway be castrated after the fourth escape.[13] In Georgia the slave code of 1755 required slaves to display passes when venturing off their home plantation. Two years later, the slave patrol system was instituted in Georgia, with patrollers empowered to administer 20 lashes to slaves caught without passes.[14]

The slave patrols, an obligation for white males between the ages of 18 and 45 in many areas, emerged early in colonial history. In South Carolina patrols consisting of ten men under a militia captain were mandated by law after 1690.[15] These armed entities were supplemented by the formally organized police forces in most areas. A small sector of employment for white males developed during slavery centered around the enforcement of the restrictions on African American mobility. Here the direct clash of white and black masculinities is evident as the great fear of black slave rebellion and the day-to-day battle to repress black resistance exerted a powerful formative influence to help shape white American masculinity. Michael Kimmel's comment that "manhood is less about the drive for domination and more about the fear of others dominating us, having power or control over us" accurately describes this imperative.[16]

Josephine Bacchus recalled that blacks would not dare "to go from one plantation to another" without a pass from the slave master. She said that being caught without the "walkin paper" from the slave owner meant being whipped "so hard with a "cat-'o-nine tails'" that the flesh would come "right off" the victim.[17] Benjamin Johnson commented that during slavery, when, "you go off to see somebody at night—jes' like you an' me want to laugh an' talk—an' if dey cetch you, an' you ain't got no pass, den dey gwine to whup you."[18]

Laws prohibiting the free movement of blacks and their enforcement meant that it was a crime for blacks to leave their home to visit friends, relatives, and others without permission. This criminalizing of what would be routine social life had far-reaching social, economic, psychological, and political implications for black males were compelled to travel to minimally satisfy physical, psychological, and social needs, and this imperative kept the slave patrols busy. A small cottage industry developed among blacks involving the production of forged passes. Since a realization of the injustice of the travel ban on African Americans formed a part of their common worldview, cooperative efforts to violate it were continually made.

Benjamin Johnson's visit to a neighboring plantation was discovered by the slave owner, who rejected his pleas of innocence and insisted that he should have been on his home plantation at work. Johnson, sensing impending violence directed at himself, threw the man into a puddle and escaped back to his home plantation, avoiding a beating.[19] Calvin Moye, a blacksmith, had a similar experience. After he had climbed up a pecan tree off his plantation, he encountered a group of slave patrollers. Finding him up the tree, they demanded to see his pass. Learning that he did not have it, they demanded that he come down to receive "a lesson" he would never forget and that would "make" him remember "to git it de next time." Aware that he would receive a horrible whipping, Moye waited there until the leader of the group ordered the others to "knock" the "coon" from the tree. They threw sticks, rocks, and other objects at him, forcing him down. Suddenly, however, he bolted and ran away, escaping back to the plantation.[20] Jacob Aldrich, a former Louisiana slave, recalled, "Dey didn't 'low you to go 'way from your plantation. If you go off, any 'peck' what find you catch you and whip you and carry you back."[21]

Another aspect of daily life forced the slaves to "steal away." Religious activity, when permitted, was generally heavily monitored and under authoritarian control. Christianity was a battleground for the slave's mind, with the slave master's handpicked preachers delivering messages reflecting the slave owner's concerns. Peter Randolph, who was a slave in Prince George's County, Virginia, wrote of the two types of preachers and versions of Christianity that the slaves encountered. The slave master's preacher, a "Brother Shell," exhorted "the poor, impenitent, hard-hearted, ungrateful slaves, so much beloved by their masters, to repentance and prayerfulness, while entreating them to lead good lives, that they might escape the wrath [of the lash] to come." The day following one sermon, Randolph wrote, Shell was "afflicted with his old malady, hardness of heart, so that he was obliged to catch one of the sisters by the throat, and give her a terrible flogging."[22] This type of brutal behavior, following bouts of piousness, fostered the growth of alternative underground churches among slaves. Dodging the slave patrols, they met in a log cabin, posting a lookout as a precaution. While they risked serious punishment for this crime, they were quite willing to take the chance, as the satisfaction and relief they gained from their worship helped them endure the pains of everyday existence.[23]

THE CRIMINALIZING OF DAILY EXISTENCE: THE MASCULINE DEVELOPMENT OF THE FIELD SLAVE

The relatively high cost of slaves helped give many slaveholders sufficient incentive to work their slaves to their physical limits while maintaining the levels of nutrition at a minimum. One estimate is that, during the 1850s, the average male slave yielded twice as much wealth as consumed by his purchase and maintenance.[24] This profit would have been impossible if the living conditions of the slaves had not been reduced to the barest minimum. These general conditions, coupled with the slaves' conscious and unconscious resistance to them, facilitated the practice of theft by slaves.

George Washington was puzzled by the little regard slaves displayed for slaveholder property, seemingly regarding any product as fair game.[25] Another American president, Thomas Jefferson, in contrast, reasoned that men "in whose favour no laws of property exist, probably feels himself less bound to respect those laws made in favour of others," and therefore could not the slave "justifiably take a little more from one, who has taken all from him?"[26]

The African American slaves rarely regarded this "theft" from the homes, kitchens, storerooms, and storehouses of slaveholders as a moral transgression. One "Uncle Billy" was caught by the slave master holding three "big fine collards" from his garden and was made to read the Bible's admonition not to steal. He countered this by pointing to a passage that read that, "you shall reap when you laboreth."[27] Other slaves, such as Shang Harris, pointed to the theft of a whole people from Africa.[28] John Brown recalled that slaves did not "see the wrong" of stealing from the slave owner. As long as "we were not acting against one another," the ethic against theft did not apply. "I am sure that, as a rule, any one of us who would have thought nothing of stealing a hog, or a sack of corn, from our master, would have allowed himself to be cut to pieces rather than betray the confidence of his fellow slave."[29]

Work and Whipping: the Daily Lives of the Field Slave
While systematic terror and regular violence were a staple of plantation life, a necessary feature utilized to enforce the harsh regimen of labor imposed on black men, women and children, methods of disciplining slaves varied from plantation to plantation. Thomas Cole, a former slave, referring to a neighboring plantation, said of the slave owner:

> After stripin' 'em off plum naked, he would have dem tied hand and foot, and bends dem ovah, and runs a pole 'tween de bend in de arms at de elbow and under de legs at de knees, and whip dem wid a cat-o'-nine tails till he bust he hide in lots of places 'cross deir backs, and he would put salt in dose raw places, especially iffen dey makes out lak dey wants ter fight or sasses him.[30]

These slaves would be whipped as they labored in the fields; thus, the violence extended to routine tasks.[31] Jack Maddox recalled that "life was pretty hard. There was a cowhide to get you every time you turned your head out of time."[32] Jack Walton said that during the phase of hoeing cotton, if he or other men got out of rhythm, the overseer would give them a bullwhip lash. If it persisted, the overseer would dismount his horse, obtain the assistance of two other slaves to hold the man down, and bullwhip him in a more vigorous manner.[33] It was literally a crime, one punishable by whipping, imprisonment, and, sometimes, death, for slaves not to fulfill their production quotas.[34] The penalty for picking "trashy cotton" on one plantation was 400 or 500 lashes.[35]

Slave driver George Skipwith's 1847 letter to his owner illustrates the routine nature of this brutality, and its thorough integration with the work process on his Hopewell, Virginia plantation. Suky was assigned to plant corn and was found to have shirked her tasks, and Skipwith "gave her four or five licks over her clothes" Isham covered up the cotton with the plow, and this act of resistance cost him two licks over his clothes; and Evally, Dinah, Jinny, Evaline, and Charlotte swept cotton far too slowly, earning them ten licks each. Shadrack, Robert, Armstead, and Frank were to cut oats, but instead they were apparently virtually idle. This angered Skipwith, as he wrote his owner that he told them that, "you do not intend to cut these oats untill i whip every one of you." Robert volunteered that "he knoed when he worked," prompting Skipwith to order him "to shut his lips," threatening him with a whipping if he failed to. Robert said that he was not afraid of being whipped by any man, and Skipwith lashed him with the whip, leading Robert to angrily throw down his tool and swear at him, expressing his disgust with the situation and vowing not to remain there. He then attempted to take the whip from Skipwith's hand but was unable to. Skipwith called for the assistance of other slaves, held the man down, and whipped him to his satisfaction. Interestingly, immediately following the whipping, Robert went to the plantation preacher to plead his case, for, in Skipwith's words, Robert had heard that the preachers had said "that they were worked to death and that they were lowed no more chance for liveing than they were dogs or hogs."[36]

Former slave James Curry recalled a slave hired for a summer by a neighboring slaveholder. At the end of the summer, the hired slave pointed to the neighboring fields where he once toiled and said, "I never saw blood flow any where as I've seen it flow in that field. It flows there like water. When I went there to work, I was a man, but now, I am a boy." His body had been broken by the arduous work pace there.[37] Curry explained one method, predating the "scientific management" theories of Frederick Winslow Taylor by decades, of determining the pace of work. Slaves were tested, one by one, for their speed of hoeing. The fastest worker was selected and placed at the head of the row, followed by the next fastest, until the slowest was placed at the end of the row. After hoeing began, however, all must keep up with the fastest worker, a rule enforced by the slave master's whip. He also occasionally would order slaves to "move your hoes," expecting a military-like response as he set the pace of work. He set the pace at the maximum possible rate, and when they faltered, he threatened them with violence, barking to them: "I told you to move your hoes, and you hav'nt moved them yet. I have twice to threat and once to fall."[38]

Flanders was an outstanding example of the black male whose personal creed was never to submit to a beating. Scarred heavily from having fought it out with upward of 15 different slave owners and their staffs, Flanders carried a reputation with him. Unfortunately, he was purchased by a white man who prided himself on being able to break any slave. An unfulfilled task led the slaveholder to assault Flanders with a hickory club while he was asleep. The defiant slave somehow got up and fought with the slave master. Although known as a strong man, the slave owner was overwhelmed by the indomitable Flanders and called for help and finally subdued him with the aid of slaves; the slave master had him carried to the smokehouse, where he was tied and hung from a crossbeam with his toes barely touching the ground. After some 400 lashes Flanders remained defiant, leading to his eventual murder by the angry slave owner.[39]

House slaves were not exempt from such cruelty. Louis Hughes "dreaded" beatings by the slave mistress. After one particular whipping, "after the first burst of tears, the feeling came over me that I was a man, and [that] it was an outrage to treat me so—to keep me under the lash day after day."[40] Hughes had come to his owners as a "Christmas gift" to the slave mistress, as at age 11 he had been torn from his loving mother to assume what was regarded as a "privileged" position for a male slave. This "elite" position hardly exempted Hughes from arbitrary whippings.[41]

Institutionalizing Theft

The harsh conditions of life on slave plantations often forced African Americans to "steal" to survive. Highly conscious of the injustice of their own enslavement and of the authoritarian system that attempted to regulate every aspect of their lives, including their diet, work rhythms, sexual relations, and bodily movements, African Americans responded creatively to the various quandaries they were daily confronted with. On many plantations, the effort to extract the maximum amount of labor ran up against the slave owner's determination to expend the minimum amount of resources on food for his laboring population. Although slaves raised food on their own patches after sundown and on Sundays, typically, their only day off, this was insufficient to compensate for a serious shortfall in rations. Former slave Betty Powers said that the food rations that were handed out on Sunday morning had to be measured out in minimal amounts to stretch them through the entire week. This could present a serious problem for families and households that included individuals with hardy appetites, quite common for those who perform heavy agricultural tasks from dawn to dusk. Situations such as these often presented slaves with a choice between risking being whipped due to poor work or being whipped for being caught stealing.[42] The body of slave narratives testifies to the widespread hunger slaves faced and their resort to theft to at least partially satisfy this hunger.

Frederick Douglass and his sister Eliza were among those slaves who were moved to steal from their hunger.[43] Another former slave stated that the slave master simply refused to give them any meat. "He would expect you to steal what you got at night." Apparently, these slaves had some success at this theft, for, as he lightheartedly noted, "[W]e stole so many chickens that if a chicken would see a darkey he'd run right straight to the house."[44] Madison Jefferson recalled that he had "cried for hunger after coming from work," as did his brothers and sisters, and, in his desperation, he had stolen food to stop this gnawing hunger.[45]

Isaac Throgmorton, who was enslaved in Louisiana and Kentucky before escaping to Canada, witnessed a horrible scene in Louisiana in which a slave accused of stealing a hog was taken by four men, stripped, and whipped. "One man had hold of each arm, and one hold of each leg, and the overseer whipped him" until he was tired and allowed the driver to whip him. They continued to alternate in whipping him before the slaves forced to witness the torture. Altogether, the slave took some 800 lashes, according to Throgmorton, while the driver and overseer smoked and drank. Throgmorton didn't believe the man stole the hog but knew there had been stealing, "for they had to steal, because they were pretty nearly starved out."[46]

Within the context of the field-slave brand of masculinity, the seizing of food and other property involved the fulfillment of a fundamental element of the male role. This routinized defiance, which also involved the saving of face, served to release aggressive feelings while allowing males to supplement their role as provider. To the extent that there was a consciousness of performing virtually all of the plantation's labor, that this is where the plantation's income was derived from, and that the gross exploitation of slavery was clear, the black man would not feel deficient as a provider. African American male and female involuntary labor was "providing" the plantation with whatever wealth it enjoyed. Beyond this, under such a general perspective, endeavoring, to all of his ability, to improve the lives of the community materially within the circumstances was all that his people could realistically expect.

To rebel during slavery was to achieve a fleeting "manhood" by forcibly seizing respect, a healing respect that could salvage a modicum of dignity from the generally bleak circumstance. Even the slave drivers, the African American supervisors charged with the task of waking, leading to the fields, managing, policing, and, often, rationing food to their fellow slaves, had few qualms about acquiring property outside the bounds of the law. At George Washington's Muddy Hole Farm, a black overseer, Davy, was suspected of pilfering lambs. The anxious Washington wrote, "[I]f the lambs had been poisoned, or had died a natural death, or their deaths had been occasioned by an accident, their bones would have been forth coming." Washington generally failed to comprehend why persons regarded as mere commodities and deprived of every human right would show little respect for the personal property of those who claimed ownership over them.[47]

The African American Slave Rebel

Although Gabriel, who led an abortive slave conspiracy in 1800 in Richmond, Virginia, thrived during his abbreviated life in an environment very different from that of most slaves, the process whereby he was criminalized was similar. The Henrico County area during the two decades following the American Revolution was the site of a thriving biracial artisan culture, while underground black-owned and black-operated shops and groggeries blossomed within a relatively cosmopolitan environment. Slave controls, notably those that hindered mobility, had loosened through the years. The rise of a free black community that blended seamlessly with the increasing numbers of slaves hired out in the Richmond area made for a growing ambiguity between the black free and black enslaved. Only a decade after the 1782 act that allowed the manumission or self-purchase of slaves, over 10,000 blacks had wrested free from the institution By

1800 the population of roughly 6,000 comprised a slight majority of blacks.[48] Born in 1776, six miles from Richmond, Gabriel, a literate blacksmith, married Nanny early in life. By the late 1790s Gabriel was accustomed to being hired out and enjoying relative freedom of movement in the city of Richmond. There he was part of a thriving artisan culture that was well aware of progressive democratic movements in several nations.[49] Nevertheless, Gabriel was thoroughly grounded in the realities of African American survival during the period and, in all likelihood, regularly stole pigs to supplement his diet and income. In September 1799 Gabriel was caught stealing a pig with his brother Solomon and another slave, Jupiter. Discovered by an overseer whose tongue-lashing prompted Gabriel to assault him, the three were tried, resulting in 39 lashes being administered to Jupiter at the public whipping post. A later conviction for the same offense of "Hogstealing" would result in the slave's ears being nailed to the pillory.[50] While the charges were dropped against Solomon, Gabriel was found guilty of what was possibly a capital crime, assaulting a white person. Under the "benefit of clergy" law, however, Gabriel was publicly branded and made to recite a verse from the Bible.[51]

The personal crisis faced by Gabriel apparently stimulated his political ambitions. Now aroused and criminalized, he joined with other slaves whose imaginations were fired by the ideologically stimulating artisan political culture. One of the men he conspired with, the massive Jack Ditcher, stood on the principle that African Americans had "as much right to fight for our liberty as any men."[52] The conspirators, except for Nanny, were all males. The scope of the plans for the uprising stunned whites, as it embraced several counties and had even enlisted the support of a seemingly improbable recruit, the nearly 100-year-old "mulatto" doorkeeper of the Virginia Capitol. His role, had the revolt progressed that far successfully, was to allow rebellious slaves entrance to the Capitol building in order to seize the direly needed arms housed there.[53]

Ultimately, the conspiracy spread itself too thin, spanning ten counties in Virginia and embracing at least 500 male recruits. By mid-August, Governor James Monroe heard rumors of a massive slave conspiracy. Despite the strengthening of slave patrols and other countermeasures taken by the authorities, the rebels were determined to push on with the plan and pronounced themselves five days before the planned uprising as ready "to do the business." Later, the hundreds of homemade swords made by Gabriel and other blacksmiths were distributed.[54]

A tremendous storm, washing out roads and isolating rural areas, swept Virginia on the day of the planned uprising. Too few men were able to assemble, and the rebellion was then postponed. During the succeeding hours, the leaders of the revolt were betrayed by a slave probably seeking to win favor from his slave master. The orgy of violence that followed included searches of black quarters, widespread torture, and scores of hangings by white authorities. One of the black rebels eloquently stated before being executed, "I have nothing more to offer than what General Washington would have had offer, had he been taken by the British and put to trial by them. I have adventured my life in endeavouring to obtain the liberty of my countrymen, and I am a willing sacrifice in their cause."[55]

On 2 October 1800, eight days before Gabriel's last request was granted—to be executed with his fellow rebels—Nat Turner was born on the plantation of Benjamin Turner. Throughout his life he stood out as an exceptional and gifted individual who enjoyed a reputation for extraordinary honesty, sobriety, and morality. The introspective Turner, on the strong advice of his grandmother, began preaching during his mid-20s. His black nationalism was shaped by the slave church, psychically far away from the center of plantation life, where the aspirations for freedom could be discussed among blacks.[56] While growing up, whites and blacks alike concluded that Turner "had too much sense to be raised [as a slave]; and, if he was, he would never be any use as a slave."[57] As a young man, Turner was caught away from the plantation without the necessary pass and was severely whipped. With the assistance of others, he retaliated by stringing a long rope across the road and seriously injuring the patrollers who were baited to ride into it.[58]

Intrigued by the passage "Seek ye the kingdom of Heaven, and all things shall be added unto you," Turner reflected on this passage as he toiled in the fields. Like Gabriel, a brutal whipping prodded him into taking the initiative.[59] The occasion of a new overseer, one of the common causes for increased master–slave conflict, ended in a brutal lashing of Turner. He responded by escaping to the Dismal Swamp, voluntarily returning a month later. Nat's father had escaped to freedom, and, undoubtedly, he himself could have, but, wanting to remain with his family and friends, he chose to return. Significantly, shortly after his return he married a woman named Cherry. The marriage, however, took a tragic turn, as they were separated at a slave auction when they were sold to different slaveholders. The ripping apart of Turner's young family must have weighed heavily on his mind as he continued to do hard labor. Not even being able to form a family or marry must have shaken Turner's psyche and pride the core. How could he have any future under slavery? If he married again, what was the guarantee that this would not happen again? Was he really a man if he allowed others to sell his wife away from him and callously deny him the right to a family?

Later, Turner organized a mass meeting at Pearson's Mill Pond deep in the woods. Crowds, lured by the promise that a miracle was going to take place, flocked to the pond, and the baptisms by Turner they witnessed further enhanced his local prestige. On 12 May 1828 Turner had a vision in which he heard a "loud noise in the heavens" and was told that "the Serpent was loosened," and the time was quickly coming "when the first should be last and the last should be first." This was interpreted by him as the sign that the time had come for blacks to revolt. "I should arise and prepare myself, and slay my enemies with their own weapons."[60] After the February 1831 eclipse of the sun, Turner felt that the time was ripe for the slave revolt he had been considering. He gathered his most trusted associates, Hark, Nelson, Henry, and Sam, reliable and staunch figures in the black slave community. All were field slaves who had "tasted the lash" and who participated in the slave church.[61] After the initial seven armed men raided the home of Joseph Travis, killing the first of 57 whites, their numbers grew. One of

Nat Turner's objectives, spreading "terror," was soon realized as whites fled to the swamps for safety. While the first real opposition fled after Turner and his men charged, they were soon defeated and dispersed by a sizable militia force. He retreated into the woods and waited for a day or so, hoping to regroup his men, but then dug a cave to hide in. Three thousand troops arrived to crush the revolt, and an all-out search for Turner was accompanied by a massacre of blacks. Turner was captured after two anxiety-ridden months for local whites. On 11 November 1831, Nat Turner, calm and unruffled, was hanged.[62]

The Black Male's Struggle for Family During Slavery
Practically all of the significant actions of African American males during slavery occurred within the social context of the family, the extended family, and the slave community. While the labor force demands of slavery did not necessitate two-parent families, the maintenance of labor discipline was generally enhanced by their predominance. Available evidence suggests that adult males exerted the decisive authority with respect to many aspects of family life, while women had a greater number of and more varied tasks.[63] According to historian Deborah Gray White, "slave women played important provider roles and . . . short of brute force, bondmen lacked the leverage by which to impose subordinate status on their wives," leading to an "equal" partnership with her enslaved spouse.[64] This stood in complete contrast to the hierarchical gender relationships prevailing among southern whites in the era that reinforced the "rule of men over women."[65]

While the early work of E. Franklin Frazier and, more recently, that of Daniel P. Moynihan disparaged the state of the black family during slavery and the male role within it, the path breaking work of Herbert Gutman refuted Frazier's notion of "semi-barbarous" field slaves who "seized upon the woman who happened to be at hand and with whom they had been thrown in closest contact."[66] Gutman's data on antebellum black families revealed that young, single mother-headed families were the exception, not the rule, among Virginia slaves. Despite the lack of legal sanction for slave marriage, upon emancipation most Virginia black families featured both a husband and a wife.[67]

Routine interference by the slave master, whippings, rapes, and the sudden loss of family members marked the life histories of slave families, of whom an estimated one-third were broken up by the slaveowner.[68] Yet the desire for stability and well-being on the part of the slaves often coincided with the desire for stability and abundant profits on the part of the slave master. When disruptions did occur, they hit slaves with terrible force and represented major losses in the lives of both black males and females.

The March 1859 sale of 436 African American slaves who had labored on the Butler plantation in St. Simons and Darien, Georgia, is representative of the general tragedy of family breakup during slavery. The massive nature of the sale revealed the dimensions of the tragedy of family and friend breakup by slave sales. A crowd described as "a rough breed, slangy, profane and bearish" came to bid on the Butler slaves, who were housed in horse stables at a racecourse for two drenching days of rain and gloom.[69] One after another, friends, kin, and loved ones were sold away—a tragedy of untold proportions for those victimized. One young couple saw their dreams of marriage shattered despite the best efforts of the young man involved. The 23-year-old Jeffrey, "chattel No. 319," was marked as a "prime cotton hand" and was sold for $1,310. The most pressing problem that weighed on Jeffrey was his love for a young female slave, Dorcas, "chattel No. 278." After he was sold, he begged and pleaded humbly for his new owner to purchase the love of his life, Dorcas.[70] Pleading that his new family would be a large one of loyal and hardworking slaves, he apparently won the man over. After the man examined Dorcas, he informed Jeffrey that he intended to purchase her. Jeffrey and Dorcas, their hopes reignited, quietly celebrated. The next day, however, when Dorcas was about to be sold, it was announced that she would not be sold alone but with a family of four. This ruled out her purchase by the man who had bought Jeffrey. Jeffrey immediately broke down in tears, crushed by the turn of events, and was consoled by his soon-to-be-departed old friends.[71]

Other plantations were marked by a routine interference in the sexual and romantic lives of slaves, both male and female. Historian John Blassingame wrote, "The black male frequently could do little to protect his wife from the sexual advances of whites. Most whites, however, realized that a liaison with a slave's wife could be dangerous. Occasionally, slaves killed white men for such acts."[72] On more than one plantation, white male overseers, slave masters, or family members physically intimidated slaves who sought to romance females on the plantation.[73] Frederick Douglass never forgot the whipping of his young aunt, Hester. The young woman's wrists were firmly secured with rope and attached to an above joist while the slave owner whipped her with a cow skin. Her crime was her romantic affection for another slave, an offense sufficient to incur the wrath of the man who claimed legal title to her.[74] The affectionate and intimate relationship that Sojourner Truth, who was then named Isabella, had with Robert, a slave from a neighboring farm, was brutally broken up by the man's owner. Having been warned not to visit Isabella, the men from the slave-owning Catton family learned that Robert had set out for a visit to her one Saturday afternoon. Isabella was ill and observed the scene from her window and later wrote that "they pounced on him in an animal-like manner bruising and mangling his head and face in the most awful manner, and causing the blood, which streamed from his wounds, to cover him like a slaughtered beast."[75] Robert's slave master had won the battle, and their romantic relationship was abruptly ended. Robert took a wife on his plantation, as his slavemaster had demanded. He died a few years later.[76]

Fatherhood for enslaved Africans took many forms and shapes, yielding a wide range of individual experiences that defy simple and general explanation. Although the slave master could arbitrarily intrude into the lives of a slave family, many black husbands found ways to limit this practice. While black males necessarily had to be cautious, circumspect, and deceptive with respect to whites, they were generally able to maintain their self-respect before their family and community. Black males performed what may be termed the "provider role" to a considerable extent under the slave system. By hunting, fishing, and raising gardens, black males helped supplement the meager diet provided by the slave masters. One former slave recalled that her father sold plantation goods to a hotel owner and would return with "sweet potatoes, watermelons, chickens, and turkeys." Georgia Baker had fond memories of her brothers' successful hunting trips. "George and Mack was de hunters. When dey went huntin' dey brough back jus' evvything: possums, rabbits, coons, squirrels, birds, and wild turkeys."[77] Former slave Frank Adamson, looking back on life at age 82, favorably recalled hunting possum with his father. He explained that his African-born father was definitely "a man" and chased away all of the other male competitors for his mother and married her without the permission of the slave master.[78] Robert Falls proudly remembered his father as a man who "was a fighter." The ex-slave lauded his father, a slave rebel, as a man "mean as a bear" and "troublesome" to slave owners.[79]

When a father was enslaved on another plantation away from his wife and children, it was often very difficult to make regular visits. Hannah Chapman's father was able to visit his children only under the cover of darkness. She recalled years later that "he missed us and us longed for him." Those precious few moments of joy remained with her the rest of her life. "Us would gather 'round him an' crawl up in his lap, tickled slap to death, but he give us dese pleasures at painful risk." When he would be discovered by the slave master, the family would "track him de nex' day by de blood stains."[80]

Prospects for individual freedom were often inextricably linked to personal romance and matrimony. Henry Bibb told his future wife that he had two conditions for marriage that she must agree to: to live according to the Bible and also to flee slavery for Canada later. Henry Bibb spoke for many other enslaved males when he spoke of the horror of living on the same plantation or close to his wife, where he would witness the "insults, scourgings, and abuses" to her. He lamented that the one phase of his life that he regretted was "that of being a father and a husband of slaves."[81]

William Wells Brown and Jermain Wesley Loguen were representative of black men who refused to marry while enslaved. Loguen declared, "I determined long ago never to marry until I was free. Slavery shall never own a wife or child of mine."[82]

Josiah Henson, born near Port Tobacco, Maryland, in 1789, recalled when his father had to be pulled off an overseer who had tried to rape his mother. The overseer saved himself by promising not to report the incident. Later, however, he broke this promise, making Henson's father a fugitive. For this act, described by Henson as "the sacrilegious act of lifting a hand" against a white, his father was forced to flee to the security of the woods. After being starved out, he endured a public lashing before the assembled slave workforce. Fifty lashes were directed to his back, making him scream in agonizing pain. What happened next seemed to anger, amaze, and sadden Henson: "His cries grew fainter and fainter, till a feeble groan was the only response to the final blows. His head was then thrust against the post, and his right ear fastened to it with a tack; a swift pass of the knife, and the bleeding members was left sticking to the place."[83] Henson's father changed, as he was no longer cheerful but turned sullen, depressed, and smoldering with anger before being sold off to an Alabama slaveholder.[84] The family's troubles had just begun, however, as it was soon shattered completely on the auction block where his mother was hit and kicked when she fell to her knees to implore the slave owners to purchase her baby with her. Henson witnessed her crawling away, moaning and sobbing, "Oh, Lord Jesus, how long shall I suffer this way?"[85]

Sella Martin, too, later recalled the trauma of family breakup on the auction block preceded by a long, seven-week journey in a slave coffle. Later, after he had heard his mother's and sister's screams as they were handcuffed and taken away, in his solitude, he for the first time realized the full meaning of being a slave for life. Although he had lost his mother and sister, he felt that this was "partially compensated, if not entirely overruled" by his solidarity with his "fellow bondsmen, and the hatred of the system that oppressed us." Later, this strength and spirit moved him to throw his energy into escaping slavery and to work to "overthrow oppression" in general.[86]

Anger was the reaction of Austin Steward, who recalled that he could have "wrung" the neck of the white man whipping his sister:

God knows that my will was good enough to have wrung his neck; or to have drained from his heartless system its last drop of blood! And yet I was obliged to turn a deaf ear to her cries for assistance, which to this day ring in my ears. Strong and athletic as I was, no hand of mine could be raised in her defence, but at the peril of both our lives.[87]

Jermain Wesley Loguen, too, endured a lifetime of agony after his family was shattered by the slave trade, an agony that fed an anger that fueled his later abolitionist activism.[88] Despite the liberal reputation of Thomas Jefferson, only seven slaves were manumitted upon his death, and the remainder's destiny was placed in the fate of the auction block in 1829, three years after the former president's death. Israel Jefferson, who served as a waiter in the dining room, experienced the family dispersing effects of slavery more than once, as the whereabouts of his children were unknown to him.[89]

African American parents counseled their male children on the best methods to use to negotiate and survive the emotional quandaries they would almost inevitably have to confront. Generally, they advised them not to attempt to retaliate after being whipped, but others took a very different approach. One slave father, for example, told his son to "die in defense of your mother."[90] Even unusually "kind" slave masters were "forced" by circumstances to break up enslaved black families. Lorenzo Ivy's family was sold by a man who had "caught the cotton fever" and sold off his property in order to move to better-suited soil.[91]

Resistance, Flight, and Freedom

For the African American male during the antebellum era, coming-of-age and personal development usually meant a clash with the slave system. For some, the approach of adulthood meant a trial by fire that would determine whether they would spend their lives as slaves or free men. From the colonial era until emancipation, the overwhelming majority of the slaves who ran away were young males unburdened by the childbearing and family-anchoring responsibilities borne by women.[92] One analysis of the advertisements in the *Richmond Enquirer* between 1804 and 1824 found that almost 85 percent of the runaways were male, while another of New Orleans newspapers found that 68 percent were male.[93] Another estimate is that 80 percent of the fugitives from slavery were males between the ages of 16 and 35.[94] The history-shaping impact of the continuous efforts of individuals, families, and small groups to flee from slavery should not be underestimated. Historian Mary Frances Berry stressed that the Fugitive Slave Clause was "used as a definite selling-point" for the approval of the Constitution in the South. The prospect of slave revolt, combined with the steady stream of fugitives, was a constant thorn in the sides of the South and North. Eventually, these pressures combined to polarize the American nation and lead to civil war.[95]

After young Frederick Douglass, taught by one of his slave mistresses to read, sharpened his literacy by assiduously studying the Columbian Orator textbook he purchased, he soon began plotting to escape to Pennsylvania with five other young men.[96] After one of their number dropped out, the group felt that to abandon their plan of escaping to freedom would be tantamount to admitting that they were "fit only to be slaves."[97] Unfortunately, their plot was discovered, and soon they were in the clutches of a heavily armed posse. When Douglass was ordered into a barn to be whipped, he heard his coconspirator, Henry Harris, refuse to cross his hands so they could be tied. The members of the posse drew their pistols and planted them against the young rebel's chest. Harris, still calm, dared them to shoot and then grabbed the guns, before being overcome and beaten. Throughout his long career Douglass would remember the sight of Henry Harris, tied up and bleeding, being dragged by horses for 15 miles to town.[98] Eventually, at age 20, aided by Anna Murray, his future wife, Douglass made a successful flight to the north from slavery. Having somehow obtained the papers of a seaman, on 3 September 1838, dressed as a sailor, Douglass boarded a train in Baltimore headed north toward the Susquehanna River. Although suffering through tense moments as the conductor considered whether to examine his seaman's papers more closely, he arrived in Wilmington, Delaware, and then Philadelphia and New York City, to the home of David Ruggles, the head of the local Vigilance Committee.[99]

Louis Talbert was another young man who could not take it any longer. The Kentucky slave, suffused with the sense of confidence resulting from an accumulation of knowledge of the forbidden world north of the Ohio River, and his friends shared an eagerness to escape and begin a life in relative freedom. The small group of 12 conspirators knew that they would have to first slip past the local patrollers and white civilians who would report their movements. They also knew they would have to make haste, for the slave owners were sure to put posses of experienced slave hunters on their trail, given the great loss of wealth they represented. Their most significant problem was crossing the Ohio River, which they resolved by building a raft under the cover of nightfall. Unfortunately, the rudimentary little raft, constructed by linking two logs together, could carry only two people at a time across the river. By daybreak only six had crossed, forcing those remaining on the Kentucky side to hide in vegetation during daylight hours.

Their slow progress only increased the odds of their capture. Not only had a large body of men left from Kentucky in pursuit of them, but local men on the north side of the river joined them as news of the valuable chattels' escape spread. The enticement of a generous reward for their capture was more than enough incentive for the scores of impoverished whites who hunted fugitive slaves for both sport and profit. Unfortunately, as was common among fugitives from slavery, their hunger led them to unwisely attempt to purchase food from a house, whose residents promptly alerted their pursuers to their whereabouts. Fleeing upon the approach of the slave catchers, the group split up, with most of them being captured. Louis Talbert and three others successfully eluded them to reach the Indiana home of the well-known Quaker abolitionist Levi Coffin, "President of the Underground Railroad."[100]

For some slaves, multiple attempts were necessary before they were able to escape bondage. During one of Moses Roper's escapes he was caught and beaten severely, tied to an axle of their chaise, and made to run behind it for eight miles back to the slave master, a common method of punishment employed by slaveholders.[101] The vengeful slaveholder gave Roper the best dinner he had ever had. After dinner he was stripped naked and given 50 lashes of the whip by each of four men. Later Roper was taken to a blacksmith, who outfitted him with a heavy chain around his neck and two huge iron bars on his feet. Chained to an enslaved woman, they were then paraded around the plantation as examples of the consequences of running away. Yet, he and the woman escaped again and hid in a stream, but due to hunger they were recaptured and whipped again. Months later, after enduring daily whippings and other torture, his irons were removed. On his next bid for freedom he was again caught. Angry, the slave master smeared Roper's face with tar and set it afire, burning the slave severely. Eventually, after many other beatings, Moses Roper's tenacity paid off, and he escaped slavery.[102]

The saga of William Parker began on a Maryland slave plantation owned by a man considered as a "kind" slave owner. Parker recalled that as he attained adulthood, he became aware that he would be compelled to break free from slavery at some point. Yet somehow he felt that "something besides the fact that I was a slave was necessary to exonerate me from blame in running away." What he needed was a direct stimulus to flee; a "cross word, a good fright, anything" would suffice. That "crooked word" never came, and finally the 16-year-old Parker told the slave master that he wasn't going to work on one particular day because he was tired, and it was raining. The slave owner picked up a stick and vowed to beat Parker until he began working. After tussling with the older man, Parker fled for the woods after the man called out for help. His brother Charles met him later, and together they crossed the Susquehanna River into Pennsylvania's Lancaster County.[103]

Parker settled into Lancaster County, Pennsylvania, where over 3,000 blacks lived under the constant threat of slave catchers. By the 1830s blacks had organized a self-defense group, the "Gap Gang," whose activism was directly aimed at the Fugitive Slave Law.[104] Prior to 1851 they had been involved in many episodes involving attempts to take blacks back to slavery in the South. On one occasion they pursued a captured black girl, tracking the slave catchers down, beating them, and rescuing the girl. Two of the offending slave catchers eventually died from their wounds.[105]

When Edward Gorsuch, the owner of the plantation near Baltimore, learned that grain was missing from his granary in 1849, the discovery set off a chain of events that impacted the course of U.S. history. After he learned that a free black tried to sell five bushels of wheat, the suspicion of theft began to be focused on four of Gorsuch's slaves, all of the adult males he owned. Learning that the slaveholder had been tipped off as to their theft and that a warrant had been put out for the arrest of the free black man, the four men fled for the North. Gorsuch, stunned by the loss of his four-man workforce, was determined to recapture them.[106]

Two of the fugitives found shelter in William Parker's house at Christiana, and when Gorsuch and his posse approached it, the occupants were warned by their sentry. The seven people inside carried their weapons to the second floor of the house. Gorsuch's posse positioned themselves on each side of the house to prevent any possible escape by the blacks. The six men were led by a U.S. marshal, who identified himself, leading Parker to firmly warn, "If you take another step, I'll break your neck." The marshal explained that he had warrants for the fugitives, but this failed to sway Parker, who replied that he "did not care for him nor the United States."[107]

After a prolonged argument and standoff, the blacks attempted to buy time, leading the slave owner's son to implore him to leave and the fugitives to sing hymns of their determination to remain free. Finally, Parker's wife, Eliza, blew the horn, a signal of crisis to the surrounding black families. Upon hearing the horn, the anxious posse fired shots at the garret of the house, setting off a gunfight. One posse member took a bullet above his right eye, and the fugitives stalled for time by asking for five minutes to surrender. Within minutes blacks from the surrounding rural neighborhood began to pour into the area. Gorsuch saw another former slave of his, Noah Buley, ride up on a horse among a score of others. Shotguns, pistols, scythes, and other weapons were carried by them to the site of the anticipated battle. Soon between 75 and 100 blacks were on the scene of the conflict. Samuel Thompson, another of the fugitives from Gorsuch's farm, told the slaveholder, "Old man, you had better go home to Maryland." Gorsuch urged the slave to give up but then was struck on the head by Thompson with a pistol, knocking him to his knees. Before he could get up, he was clubbed, then shot by Thompson. Other shots followed, and, with Gorsuch in all likelihood already dead, his head was torn to bits by the corn cutters many of the blacks carried. When Gorsuch's son came to his aid, he was shot at point blank range by a shotgun by Parker's brother-in-law but survived. Parker and the others fled.[108]

After a 500-mile journey, Parker finally reached the home of Frederick Douglass, a man he had known as a slave. Douglass accompanied Parker to the Genessee River, where they would depart. When they said farewell, Parker presented Douglass with a memento of the struggle: a pistol that he had seized from the slaveholder Edward Gorsuch, a symbolic gift that Douglass would treasure for the rest of his life.[109]

For African American male slaves, satisfying basic physiological, social, spiritual, and psychological needs was deemed to be "criminal" by the authorities, who egregiously meted out violence to enforce their rule. To make the African American "stand in fear" was the object in the effort to achieve the slaveholder's ideal master–slave relationship, as expressed by an antebellum southern judge: "'The power of the master must be absolute, to render the submission of the slave perfect."[110] This was the first phase of the criminalization of the black male, a key formative phase of the black presence in the United States. The next chapter discusses this criminalizing of daily existence in relation to the lives of the free, unenslaved African American male of the antebellum era.

NOTES

1. Eugene D. Genovese, *Roll, Jordan, Roll: The World the Slaves Made* (New York: Pantheon Books, 1974), 651. See also Raymond A. Bauer and Alice H. Bauer, "Day to Day Resistance to Slavery," *Journal of Negro History* 27, no. 4, (Oct 1942): 388–419.

2. Joel Williamson, *The Crucible of Race: Black–White Relations in the American South since Emancipation* (New York: Oxford University Press, 1984), 22–23.

3. John W. Blassingame, *The Slave Community: Plantation Life in the Antebellum South* (New York: Oxford University Press, 1972), 225.

4. Nathan Irvin Huggins, *Black Odyssey: The African American Ordeal in Slavery* (New York: Random House, 1977), 62; see also Sidney W. Mintz and Richard Price, *The Birth of African-American Culture* (Boston: Beacon Press, 1972); and Sterling Stuckey, *Slave Culture: Nationalist Theory and the Foundations of Black America* (New York: Oxford University Press, 1987).

5. James Oliver Horton and Lois E. Horton, *In Hope of Liberty* (New York: Oxford University Press, 1997), 83..

6. John W. Blassingame, *Slave Testimony: Two Centuries of Letters, Speeches, Interviews, and Autobiographies* (Baton Rouge: Louisiana State University Press, 1977), 717.

7. Frederick Douglass, *Narrative of the Life of Frederick Douglass* (Garden City, NY: Anchor, 1973), 58–78.

8. Williamson, *The Crucible of Race*, 23; Bertram Wyatt-Brown, *Southern Honor: Ethics and Behavior in the Old South* (New York: Oxford University Press, 1982), 412.

9. James Mellon (ed.), *Bullwhip Days: The Slaves Remember, an Oral History* (New York: Avon Books, 1988), 118–19.

10. Huggins, *Black Odyssey*, 62.

11. Deborah Gray White *Ar'n't I a Woman?: Female Slaves in the Plantation South* (New York: W. W. Norton, 1985), 76.

12. Peter H. Wood, *Black Majority: Negroes in Colonial South Carolina from 1670 through the Stono Rebellion* (New York: W. W. Norton, 1974), 52.

13. Winthrop D. Jordan, *White over Black: American Attitudes toward the Negro, 1550–1812* (Baltimore: Penguin Books, 1969), 155.

14. Donald L. Grant (ed.), *The Way It Was in the South* (Carol, 1981), 54.

15. John Hope Franklin, *Race and History: Selected Essays, 1938–1988* (Baton Rouge: Louisiana State University Press, 1989), 97.

16. Ibid. Michael Kimmel, *Manhood in America: A Cultural History* (New York: Free Press, 1996), 6–7.

17. George P. Rawick (ed.), *The American Slave: A Composite Autobiography,* Vol. 2: South Carolina Narratives (Westport, CT: Greenwood, 1972), 21.

18. Mellon *Bullwhip Days,* 140.

19. Ibid., 140–41.

20. Ibid., 166.

21. George P. Rawick (ed.), *The American Slave: A Composite Autobiography,* Vol. 1: Texas Narratives (Westport, CT: Greenwood, 1979), 24.

22. Peter Randolph, *Slave Cabin to the Pulpit* (Boston, 1893).

23. Ibid.

24. Grant, *The Way It Was in the South,* 39.

25. James Thomas Flexner, *George Washington, Anguish and Farewell (1793–1799)* (Boston: Little, Brown, 1972), 439.

26. Jordan, *White over Black,* 438.

27. Mellon, 48.

28. Ibid., 49.

29. Albert J. Raboteau, *Slave Religion: The "Invisible" Institution in the Ante-bellum South* (New York: Oxford University Press, 1978), 158.

30. Mellon, *Bullwhip Days,* 59; see also Wilma King, *Stolen Childhood: Slave Youth in Nineteenth-Century America* (Bloomington: Indiana University Press, 1995).

31. Mellon, *Bullwhip Days,* 60.

32. Ibid., 119.

33. Ibid., 138.

34. Ibid., 138.

35. Blassingame, *Slave Testimony,* 434.

36. Ibid., "Letter by George Skipwith Dated Hopewell July 8, 1847," 67–68.

37. Ibid., "Narrative of James Curry," 134–35.

38. Ibid., 135.

39. Ibid., "Sella Martin," 717–18.

40. Lester C. Lamon, *Blacks in Tennessee 1791–1970* (Knoxville: University of Tennessee Press, 1981), 19.

41. Ibid., 4.

42. Mellon, *Bullwhip Days,* 43.

43. William S. McFeeley, *Frederick Douglass* (New York: W. W. Norton, 1991), 44.

44. Mellon, *Bullwhip Days,* 45; Rawick, (ed.), Texas Narratives, 24.

45. Blassingame, *Slave Testimony,* "Madison Jefferson," 219.

46. Ibid., "Isaac Throgmorton," 433.

47. William L. Van Deburg, *The Slave Drivers: Black Agricultural Labor Supervisors in the Antebellum South* (New York: Oxford University Press, 1979), 55; Flexner, *George Washington*, 439.

48. Douglas R. Egerton, *Gabriel's Rebellion: The Virginia Slave Conspiracies of 1800 and 1802* (Chapel Hill: The University of North Carolina Press, 1993), 17.

49. Ibid., 21–24; Genovese, *Roll, Jordan, Roll*, (New York: Pantheon Books, 1974), 394.

50. Egerton, *Gabriel's Rebellion*, 31.

51. Ibid., 32.

52. Ibid., 40.

53. Ibid., 58.

54. Ibid., 67–68.

55. Ibid., 72; Gary B. Nash, *Race and Revolution* (Madison,WI: Madison House, 1990), 79.

56. S. B. Oakes, *The Fires of Jubilee: Nat Turner's Fierce Rebellion* (New York: Harper and Row, 1975), 23.

57. Eric E. Foner (ed.), *Nat Turner* (Englewood Cliffs, NJ: Prentice-Hall, 1971), 142.

58. William Wells Brown, "A Pioneer Black Historian and Nat Turner," in Foner, *Nat Turner*, 142.

59. Oakes, *The Fires of Jubilee*, 40.

60. Ibid., 41.

61. Ibid., 52.

62. Lerone Bennett Jr., *Before the Mayflower* (Baltimore: Penguin Books, 1966), 123–25.

63. Huggins, *Black Odyssey*, 168.

64. White, *Ar'n't I a Woman?*, 158.

65. Wyatt-Brown, *Southern Honor*, 402.

66. E. Franklin Frazier, *The Negro Family in the United States* (Chicago: University of Chicago Press, 1939), 19. See also E. Franklin Frazier, *The Free Negro Family*. (New York: Arno Press and the New York Times, 1968).

67. Herbert G. Gutman, *The Black Family in Slavery and Freedom, 1750–1925* (New York: Vintage Books, 1976), 9.

68. Blassingame, *The Slave Community*, 174.

69. Price M. Butler, *What Became of the Slaves on a Georgia Plantation?* (Washington, DC: Library of Congress, 1859).

70. Ibid., 16.

71. Ibid., 16–18.

72. Blassingame, *The Slave Community*, 172–73.

73. Rawick, Texas Narratives, 26.

74. McFeeley, *Frederick Douglass*, 17.

75. Carleton Mabee, *Sojourner Truth: Slave Prophet, Legend* (New York: New York University Press, 1993), 6.

76. Irvin Nell Painter, *Sojourner Truth: A Life, a Symbol* (New York: W. W. Norton, 1996), 19; Mabee, *Sojourner Truth*, 6.

77. Mellon, *Bullwhip Days*, 6.

78. Rawick, South Carolina Narratives, 14.

79. Leon F. Litwack, *Been in the Storm So Long: The Aftermath of Slavery* (New York: Vintage Books, 1980), 46.

80. Jacqueline Jones, *Labor of Love, Labor of Sorrow: Black Women, Work, and the Family from Slavery to the Present,* (New York: Basic Books, 1985), 37.

81. John F. Bayliss, *Black Slave Narratives,* (New York: Macmillan, 1970), 70; Blassingame, *The Slave Community,* 165.

82. White, *Ar'n't I a Woman?,* 147.

83. Bayliss, *Black Slave Narratives,* 103.

84. Ibid., 104.

85. Ibid., 106.

86. Blassingame, *Slave Testimony,* 705–08.

87. Austin Steward, *Twenty-two Years a Slave, and Forty Years a Freeman* (Rochester, NY, 1861), 97.

88. Van Deburg, *The Slave Drivers,* 18.

89. Blassingame, *Slave Testimony,* 481–83.

90. Blassingame, *The Slave Community,* 189.

91. Blassingame, *Slave Testimony,* 737.

92. White, *Ar'n't I a Woman?,* 70–76; Lathan A. Windley (ed.), *Runaway Slave Advertisements: A Documentary History from the 1730s to 1790s* (Westport, CT: Greenwood, 1983).

93. King, *Stolen Childhood,* 119.

94. Thomas P. Slaughter, *Bloody Dawn: The Christiana Riot and Racial Violence in the Antebellum North.* (New York: Oxford University Press, 1991), 18.

95. Mary Frances Berry, *Black Resistance, White Law: A History of Constitutional Racism in America* (New York: Allen Lane Penguin Press, 1994); see also Gerald W. Mullin, *Flight and Rebellion: Slave Resistance in Eighteenth-Century Virginia* (New York: Oxford University Press, 1974).

96. McFeeley, *Frederick Douglass,* 50.

97. Ibid., 53.

98. Ibid., 55.

99. Ibid., 73.

100. Levi Coffin, *Reminiscences of Levi Coffin* (New York: Arno Press, 1968), 209.

101. Ibid., 20.

102. Bayliss, *Black Slave Narratives,* 80–81.

103. Slaughter, *Bloody Dawn,* 48.

104. Ibid., 49.

105. Ibid., 50.

106. Ibid., 11.

107. Ibid., 60.

108. Ibid., 63–69.

109. Ibid., 78.

110. Kenneth M. Stampp, *The Peculiar Institution: Slavery in the Antebellum South* (New York: Vintage Books, 1989), 141.

Chapter 3

The Development of African American Masculinity among Free Black Males, 1619–1861

I cannot permit myself to believe that there is in either Asia or Africa a tribe or clan of heathen among whom a stranger would not be met with more civility than I received from Lloydsville to Zanesville. Aged men and women, young men and maidens, the mechanics in their shops, the farmers in the field, all, all hallowing, disparaging, pointing the finger full in one's face and even throwing stones and blocks. Respectable-looking women, standing in the doors of fine-looking houses call out, full in one's hearing, "Come, here goes a nigger!"[1]

—Martin Delany

Do not open your lips; die silent, as you shall see me do!

—Peter Poyas before his execution in the Denmark Vesey revolt[2]

The population growth of free blacks was robust during the post–American Revolution years, increasing from 60,000 in 1790, to 108,000 in 1800, to comprise some 11 percent of the national black population.[3] Little by little, African Americans, enslaved and free, chipped away at the pillars of slavery as the strength of the black impetus toward freedom combined with the complementary ideological thrusts of the first Great Awakening, and the American Revolution strengthened the beleaguered black communities in the North.[4]

This chapter traces the broad outline of the development of masculinity among the free black population prior to the Civil War. Black masculinity among unenslaved males in the northern cities took shape around the central thrust toward freedom shared by all Africans in American prior to emancipation. Its contours were shaped by responses to both the enslavement and the reality of the impenetrable web of oppression plaguing free blacks. During the first decades following the American Revolution, black community efforts were largely defensive battles involving the very survival of their small settlements and communities, which took precedence over the urgency of dismantling the structure of discrimination. During certain periods, such as the early 1830s, the chances of progressive change appeared increasingly remote or distant, helping foster the growth of self-improvement efforts. Although black males led the effort that exerted an important influence in shaping the African American male gender-role ideal, black women were more apt to participate in the activities of mutual aid, civic, and other social-political organizations.[5]

The 1830s emergence of the abolitionist movement was significant because it broke the sense of isolation and weakness felt by African American leaders in the North and opened a new front in the war against slavery, that of white public opinion. At the same time, the emergence, growth, and development of black institutions, as well as the absolute increases in population of northern black communities, added to this sense of power.[6] During the 1850s free blacks prospered in almost every city, including Charleston, strengthening black institutional power, as evidenced by a boom in the construction of African American churches.[7] Not only did this growing sense of power lead free blacks to increasingly resist demeaning customs, such as stepping aside for whites on the sidewalks, but more escaped slaves were able to find refuge in these growing communities.[8] With the growth of black institutional power, through the churches, fraternal organizations, and families, black patriarchy took definite form.[9]

While the leaders of the American Revolution skirted the issue of slavery and, ultimately, gave slaveholders assurances that their human property would be protected, the currents of freedom nevertheless had some positive ramifications in the northern states and set in motion the process of gradual abolition of slavery in some states and immediate emancipation in others. In Vermont, for example, slavery was abolished in its constitution of 1777. In Massachusetts slavery was declared unconstitutional, a violation of its promise that "all men are born free and equal, and have certain natural, essential, and unalienable rights." By 1780 the Pennsylvania legislature moved to abolish slavery, while in Rhode Island and Connecticut provisions were made in 1784 for gradual emancipation.[10] In 1799 the New York state legislature passed a gradual abolition act, and five years later, its neighbor, New Jersey, did likewise. The New York measure provided for the emancipation of those slaves born prior to 1799 on the Fourth of July 1827. For those born after 1799, the males would have as many as 28 years, and females as many as 25 additional years of slavery.[11] Liberalized laws of manumission were a result of the pervading atmosphere of liberty in the states of Maryland, Delaware, and Virginia. Notably, South Carolina and Georgia never considered making it easier for owners to emancipate their slaves.[12]

The 1793 invention of the cotton gin by Eli Whitney, however, dramatically changed the economic equation of slavery. Acreage began to be shifted from other crops to be put into the production of cotton. By 1800 the prices of slaves had doubled from what they had been ten years prior. Cotton and slavery appeared to be growth industries for decades to come. Slavery had a new lease on life.[13]

Ideologically, few white leaders during the era of the American Revolution could conceive of a future in which blacks would be both free and full-fledged citizens of the United States. Thomas Jefferson, for example, could not bear the thought of a free black community existing side by side with a free white community. For Jefferson, the emancipation of blacks from slavery was inconceivable unless it was accompanied by emigration. His stated reason for this insistence is that he believed that future Africans in America would be seek revenge upon realizing the full extent of slavery's cruelties. The well-rooted racial biases of the whites and the memory of the horrors of slavery by the blacks would doom any effort for the two to live peaceably side by side. In addition, fresh outrages, "new provocations," and what he felt were "the real distinctions which nature has made," as well as "many other circumstances," would produce a conflict ending in the "extermination of the one or the other race."[14]

John Saffin, the first person to deliver a public defense of the institution of slavery in America, viewed the emergence of a free black population as a distinct threat. Not only legal restrictions on their political, economic, and social liberties greeted the recognition of their growing numbers, but also occasional mob violence.[15]

Historian David Roediger points out that rather than merely perceived as "noncitizens," blacks were viewed as "anticitizens," as "enemies" in the white popular mind. Thus, they were violently attacked and driven from Independence Day celebrations in northern cities.[16] Roediger wrote that black Philadelphians' most common role prior to the Civil War in the Christmas masking traditions was "as victims of blackfaced mobs."[17]

While attending school in Cincinnati, John Mercer Langston witnessed the explosion of a growing hostility toward the city's emerging black middle class into an antiblack riot. The violence was preceded by the seizure and destruction of Dr. Gamaliel Bailey's abolitionist press, the *Philanthropist*. By the fall of 1840 tension continued to mount until mobs formed to attack the black community. Forewarned blacks rushed to mount a defense of their community in the strategically important city.[18] Following a night when an unknown number died in an all-night battle, black males were systematically rounded up by the police.[19]

Many black men hid to avoid arrest and in order to be on the scene to defend the community against the next assault. John Mercer Langston, only 11 years of age, living as a boarder in the "Germany" section of the city, witnessed two of his black male neighbors conceal themselves in chimneys of their homes. He himself had to flee across town to his brother's shop. Narrowly avoiding capture, he eluded pursuing whites to find his brother and five other men boarded up and hidden in their shop, hoping to avoid both notice and trouble. They were armed, however, fully prepared to defend the shop against the mob. They survived, although Gamaliel's press was destroyed, and the black community suffered a huge financial setback.[20]

Apart from the exceptional instances of collective violence targeting the free black communities of the North, a more pervasive and systematic bias occurred on a daily basis. Almost from the very emergence of the antebellum northern black communities, the black male population has suffered from disproportionate imprisonment. Lacking legal protections, as convenient targets of scapegoating, and economically disfranchised, it was almost inevitable that their involvement in the criminal justice system would be relatively extensive.[21] Blacks could be robbed, beaten, and murdered with impunity, as they lacked the right to be witnesses, jurors, or judges, leaving them deprived of legal protection. One study of the Massachusetts jail and prison population found that while the black population of the state was only 1/74th of the total, they made up fully one-sixth of the prisoners. In Pennsylvania a similar situation prevailed, blacks constituting only one 1/34th of the population but one-third of the prison inmates; and New York blacks were 1/35th of the population but one-sixth of the inmates.[22]

Chance encounters or inopportune arguments could disrupt the stability of whole families of free blacks. Martin Delany's mother, Pati, once received a threat from a merchant of selling "them brats of yours" into bondage. The incident made her hasten to register, as was the law, her two youngest children. Without this act, they indeed could have been legally sold into slavery.[23]

Early in Martin Delany's life he learned of the limits of freedom in Virginia. One night his father, Samuel Delany, didn't come home. In the middle of the night Martin was awakened to learn that his father had a fight with his employer after he had been threatened with a whipping. He had tried not to fight him but merely prevent the whipping, which he said he would not take from anyone. Soon sheriffs and their deputies were on the scene to help the man subdue Delany. However, Samuel Delany secured himself a position behind a wagon and held a heavy wooden bar as a weapon, cautioning his adversaries to stay away from him. Eventually, he was struck and immobilized by a rock thrown by one of the men, captured, and put in the Charles Town jail.[24]

The Delany family was petrified with fear that Samuel would be sold into slavery. They held a constant vigil outside the jail, hoping that he would somehow sense their presence and that this would strengthen him. Inside the court, the employer who had fought with the senior Delany now pleaded for him in court, arguing that he was the best carpenter in Martinsburg and completely reliable. He said that if Delany finished his house, he would not press charges. The judge, addressing Samuel Delany as "boy," asked him if he would behave himself. After a long silence and urging by the judge, he indicated that he would.[25]

Of paramount concern to the free blacks was the maintenance of themselves and their families in freedom. Vigilance, both personal and collective, had to be maintained to stay free of the clutches of the slave catchers. In 1829 George Garnet answered the door to a man who asked whether a "George Garnet" lived there. Not revealing that he was in fact the fugitive he sought, Garnet acted as if he was going to get him and jumped out of a second-story window, somehow not alarming a large, vicious dog, and escaped to the streets. To prevent capture by this slave catcher, a relative of the man who had formerly owned him, the family was forced to split up. His son, Henry Highland Garnet, was away at sea working as a cabin boy. When Henry returned to find his family dispersed by the hated slave catchers, already fired with a hatred of the slave system, he began walking armed with a clasp knife awaiting a confrontation with the slave catchers. Friends, eventually, spirited him away, and he hid on Long Island for a period.[26]

THE ECONOMIC PLIGHT OF FREE BLACK MALES IN THE CITIES

Eking out a living as a free black in the cities and towns was a difficult undertaking. In New York City, where four of ten black males were laborers or mariners, and in other locations, black males were forced to work two or three jobs to make ends meet.[27] Wives and other family members also were forced into the constricted labor market for blacks, working as domestics and laborers. The range of jobs open to blacks who were not enslaved narrowed even more during the years preceding the Civil War, spurred by white worker complaints of competition. Free blacks were forbidden to engage in a long list of occupations and trades.[28] Following the massive influx of European immigrants to southern cities, blacks were ousted from trades such as butcher and, even as servant.[29] In the northern cities also, black males were pushed out of numerous trades unfairly by employers, in favor of immigrants. At times, the employers would indicate that their hands were tied because the white employees would revolt against working alongside a black man. At other times, the employers would hire the black man, only to face a revolt by the workers. Black males were excluded from the status of cartman in New York City for decades, and it became expected that if a single black male was so employed, violence would be forthcoming.[30]

Throughout the colonial period, black slave labor competition with free white labor led to growing antiblack animosity on the part of white laborers and artisans. By 1707 white mechanics in Philadelphia bemoaned their "[w]ant of employment, and Lowness of wages, occasioned by the Number of Negroes . . . hired out to work by the Day."[31] At other times, it was not the laborers but the employers who acted to bar blacks from employment. The postmaster general, Gideon Granger, wrote to a Senate committee in 1802 that allowing blacks to be mail carriers would be disastrous for reasons of "a nature too delicate to engraft into a report which may become public, yet too important to be omitted over passed over without full consideration." Blacks working in such a capacity would constitute a distinct danger, according to Granger, for such employment was thought to provide them ample opportunity to foment a slave insurrection or merely pick up subversive ideas.[32] A few years later, Congress acted on the postmaster general's warning: it ruled in 1810 that "no other than a free white person shall be employed in conveying the mail."[33] There was a particular distaste for employing any black man in a position involving the wearing of a uniform, such as a conductor or watchman. Maryland lawmakers prohibited free blacks from engaging in the trade of agricultural produce without a special permit in 1796, while Virginia and Georgia ended the careers of free black river captains by banning them from the positions they had dominated for decades.[34]

By the mid-nineteenth century, Frederick Douglass complained that "every hour sees the black man elbowed out of employment by some newly arrived immigrant whose hunger and whose color are thought to give him a better title to the place."[35] The unfavorable image of the black male had taken on a life of its own, and association with blacks signified the loss of social status.[36] Free blacks had more success in the skilled trades in the lower southern cities than the upper southern cities. By 1860, for example, in the lower southern city of Mobile, 43 percent of the free black men worked at skilled trades, while in Charleston this figure reached 70 percent.[37]

Facing exclusion by the white labor unions and hostility from many white workers, blacks seized opportunities to work as strikebreakers. For over a century, use by employers of blacks as strikebreakers was a potent cause of interracial violence. In New York City in 1855, black strikebreakers took longshoreman jobs, causing violent clashes. Yet, there was little apology forthcoming from black leaders since it was well known that the unions involved excluded blacks from any opportunities to earn a living at those trades. *Frederick Douglass' Paper* commented: "Of course, colored men can feel no obligation to hold out in a 'strike' with the whites, as the latter never recognized them."[38]

CRIME, JUSTICE, AND REVOLT AND FREE AFRICAN AMERICAN MALES

The conditions facing free blacks in antebellum Charleston, South Carolina, shared some similarities with those facing their northern counterparts but were also distinct in many ways. Demographically, the conditions within the majority black city stood in sharp contrast to those of the northern cities, which were overwhelmingly white. In 1810, 53.2 percent of the population of Charleston was African American, and within this population the slaves outnumbered free blacks by an almost eight-to-one margin. The decade-by-decade changes in the number of free black Charlestonians are revealing. From 1810 to 1820, the number of free blacks in the city barely increased from 1,472 to 1,475. By 1830 it increased to 2,107 but still represented only 7.0 percent of the population. Following 1830 there was a precipitous decline, reflecting the white response to the Nat Turner rebellion. The number fell to only 1,558 in 1840. There was a marked increase during the decade of the 1840s to 3,441 in 1850, but it stagnated thereafter until the eve of the Civil War in 1860, when it stood at 3,219, representing 8.1 percent of the city's total population. This stagnation of the free black portion of the Charleston population is a testimony to the effectiveness of South Carolinian slaveholders's efforts to prevent manumissions.[39]

Whatever the special advantages enjoyed by the free African Americans by virtue of living in the city, their movement was hindered by the numerous prohibitions in antebellum Charleston. The slave patrols monitored their movements and subjected them occasionally to spasms of brutality, while in public spaces they faced prohibitions regarding restaurants, hotels, and transportation.[40] The few liberties they enjoyed were tenuous, yet the space afforded the lighter-skinned elite by the "borrowed ground"(crucial space with which to carve out a livable niche within Charlestonian social life) allowed them to respond creatively and constructively to new problems caused by racial repression. After a crackdown on black participation in the Methodist Church, an African Methodist Episcopal (AME) Church was established in 1815. Morris Brown and Henry Drayton traveled to Philadelphia, the seat of the AME Church, and returned to lead the Charleston branch. Institutionally, this massive exodus from the Methodist Church to the African Methodist Episcopal was a critical stage in the development of the city's black community. The leadership of Brown, who enjoyed a good reputation within the local black elite, helped to cement the growing unity of the city's black community, tearing down some of the obstacles that had prevented it. Battling elitism, the reality of the majority slave congregation ensured that no hard-and-fast lines could solidify as barriers to black unity. The Brown Fellowship Society led the effort of the lighter skinned elite to carve out "borrowed ground." For darker blacks who were free, the Free Dark Men of Color was formed, which, like the Brown Fellowship Society, served a variety of maintenance, social insurance, cultural, and political needs of the racial class segment.[41]

The slave population featured a significant segment that was, roughly, as "free" as the free blacks. Fifteen percent of enslaved Charlestonians lived apart from their slave masters and generally met the slave master only once a week to deliver their earnings. The reality of the blurred lines existing between hired-out slaves and propertyless free blacks illustrates the complexity of slave societies and the increasing difficulty of policing blacks as urban areas grew and modernized. This complex social structure was complemented by persons who were legally slaves but, in fact, family members "owned" by free black family heads.

The growing size and confidence of Charlestonian African Americans were reflected in the massive conspiracy led by Denmark Vesey, who with other leaders of the planned revolt enjoyed an unusual degree of freedom and independence. Monday Gell was a harness maker; Mingo Harth, a mechanic; Peter Poyas, a carpenter; and Tom Russell, a toolmaker, while Gullah Jack was a conjurer who had brought his bag of tools with him from Angola. While only 35 were hanged, the conspiracy embraced thousands of blacks, anticipated assistance from the black republic of Haiti, and shocked white South Carolinians out of a relative complacency.[42]

Even prior to the Denmark Vesey revolt, the free black population of Charleston faced restrictive measures.[43] In 1820 the state legislature passed a measure prohibiting manumission barring special legislative action, and imposed a special $50 per year tax on each person older than 15, and banned those who left from ever returning to the state.[44] For the free black, failure to pay the tax held the threat of being sold into slavery.[45]

Following the Vesey revolt, South Carolina's lawmakers passed a law banning free black seamen from leaving their ships when they were docked at the state's ports. The 1823 law stipulated that unless the captain of the vessel paid for the cost of imprisoning the black seamen, the individual seaman would be sold to recover the charges.[46] The South Carolina law was followed by those of other southern states.[47] After the revolt, an 1826 memorial to the state legislature deplored the increasing numbers of slaves employed as clerks and salesmen, as such work introduced them to "situations which are inconsistent with their condition."[48] They stressed that slaves should not be employed in any endeavor that involved "the exercise of greater intelligence & improvement," as this would eventually give rise to servile insurrection.[49] Despite these measures, Charleston, like Savannah and New Orleans, offered greater opportunities for blacks due to the relative anonymity, the nature of their labor, and their deliberate efforts to subvert the status quo.[50] The Charleston Neck area was notorious for the unchecked activities of the slaves who gathered there en masse.[51]

William Bryne's conclusions for antebellum Savannah ring true for many other urban areas heavily populated by African Americans:

To transcend legal restrictions is technically to break the law. Blacks were forced to accept illegal actions almost as a way of life, for, in a slave system which was theoretically extremely oppressive, virtually every normal human aspiration was in fact unlawful.[52]

Under these conditions the Denmark Vesey revolt seemed inevitable, as did its repressive aftermath. His use of the AME Church organization to recruit participants in the extensive slave conspiracy led to the church's burning by whites and the end of the antebellum AME presence in Charleston.[53] Free black churches were prohibited, while black slaves were no longer permitted to be hired out by slave owners.[54] The massive number of slaves to regulate and the constant fear of rebellion led to the establishment of a large municipal police force, which, by the onset of the Civil War, numbered some 250 officers. In 1842, in response to these fears, the South Carolina military academy, the Citadel, was established.[55]

In 1834 Charleston's whites' fears of revolt led to a measure banning all schools for blacks. In 1841 the "Act to Prevent the Emancipation of Slaves" was passed in an effort to reduce the number of slaves who behaved as if they were free, being owned by kin or white guardians.[56] In 1846 a law mandating all slaves to wear metal badges indicating their bondage was enacted in an effort to hinder the ability of slaves to pass as free.[57] By the eve of the Civil War, the small, free black population of Charleston was increasingly besieged. The web of restrictions on mobility grew more entrapping and intimidating as blacks were reenslaved under a variety of pretenses. Legislation was introduced to reenslave the entire free black population, including the self-consciously lighter-skinned elite.[58]

TROUBLED TRAVEL: BLACK MALE MOBILITY DURING THE ANTEBELLUM ERA

Travels by black men, for both short and long distances, were fraught with danger during the antebellum decades. Not only could individuals be illegally captured as fugitive slaves, but thieves and others could take advantage of their lack of legal protection. In many states the laws requiring free blacks to register upon entering a state were only loosely enforced, but individuals nevertheless had to be continually wary of the possibility of being ensnared by them. As early as 1726, the movements of unenslaved blacks in Pennsylvania were further circumscribed by new legislation. Basing the new laws on the premise that "free negroes are an idle, slothful people, and often burdensome to the neighborhood and afford ill examples to other negroes," it imposed a 20-pound indemnity on slave masters who freed their slaves.   To complete the threat to free blacks and underscore the tenuous nature of the freedom, a black who was regarded as not using his time productively in the opinion of a judge could be reenslaved.[59] In Virginia at the end of the eighteenth century free blacks were required to be registered in a special book in each municipality; however, these laws were widely disobeyed by free blacks.[60]

The early history of the District of Columbia provides an example of the webs of municipal legal restrictions entangling free blacks during the antebellum era. In 1808 a law was enacted that imposed a $5 fine on any black or "loose, idle, disorderly" individual out on the streets or found in a "tippling or other house" after 10 P.M. Slaves whose master did not pay were whipped. Four years later, in 1812, a law was enacted mandating free blacks "without visible means of support" to register and obtain papers certifying their free status. Slaves found in the District of Columbia's "nightly and disorderly meetings" were punished by 40 lashes, and free blacks were punished by a $20 fine which, if left unpaid, would become a six-month jail sentence.[61] Both slaves and free blacks were under the constant watch of the patrolling constable. If an African American resisted arrest, his ear was liable to be cropped upon order of the justice of the peace, although there is little evidence that this was regularly enforced.[62] Frederick Law Olmsted witnessed the arrest of 24 "genteel colored men" by raiding constables. They had gathered for "benevolent" purposes yet ended paying stiff fines and being flogged and jailed.   An 1835 citywide hunt for an individual guilty of distributing abolitionist material witnessed the emergence of a volunteer patrol. The patrol replaced a riotous mob whose actions included the burning of a home of a black female conjurer.[63]

To the west, in Ohio, in 1804 and 1807 the state legislature enacted measures to discourage black settlement. Blacks coming from outside the state were required to register in each county they entered. African Americans were required to carry passes at all times attesting to their freedom and, within the first three weeks of their arrival, were required to post a $500 bond. Whites who aided blacks were intimidated by heavy penalties for sheltering fugitive slaves or unregistered blacks. Whether these laws discouraged black settlement is open to dispute, but these laws proved to be excellent legal instruments of coercion during the occasional crackdowns and harassment of the state's black communities.[64]

Former slaves whose owners purchased land for them, fugitives who stole themselves and won their freedom, slaves who purchased themselves or their family members, and second-generation free blacks were all important elements of the early black population of Ohio, where slavery was prohibited in accordance with the Northwest Ordinance of 1787. An 1830s census of two southern Ohio communities found that almost 20 percent of the resident African Americans were free through self-purchase or as a result of friends or relatives purchasing their freedom.[65] In practice, the northern part of the state, particularly the Western Reserve, was much more hospitable to blacks than the southern part. Theaters and other public facilities were generally open to blacks, a fact that stunned antebellum visitors to Cleveland.[66]

Early in 1813, Pennsylvania lawmakers began considering legislation to limit the entry of African Americans into the state. The state was in the midst of a black population boom, as the approximately 6,500 African Americans in 1790 in the state grew to some 32,000 by 1820.[67] Charging blacks with being "nuisances," the measures were familiar ones, common to other states; mandatory registration, special taxes, and provisions for free blacks to be sold to compensate victims of crimes they commit. Often local authorities passed their own laws to restrict and control free blacks in their areas. In May 1820 Lancaster, Pennsylvania, adopted an ordinance that required free blacks to register in a "Negro Entry Book," a measure intended to enforce a tighter surveillance over a population blamed for multiple social ills. York, Pennsylvania, had passed a similar measure some 17 years earlier.[68]

Georgia demanded proof that free blacks entering the state were both hardworking and honest before six months elapsed—otherwise, they faced deportation from the state. North Carolina required entering free blacks to post a 200-pound bond. Violating this law meant arrest and sale at a slave auction. South Carolina and other states simply banned entry by blacks who were not enslaved.[69] Similarly, in Tennessee there was a severe curtailment of free black mobility, as one Tennessee lawmaker summed up the reigning sentiment: "Their mere presence, the simple act of walking our streets, and traveling our highways by the farms of the countryside is sufficient to incite insurrection in the slaves."[70]

The pattern of spatial off-limits or of a confined living space for unenslaved black Americans served to reinforce the severe limitations on opportunities for blacks of both genders. Alexander Crummell's, Henry Highland Garnet's, and Thomas Sidney's experience in New Hampshire illustrates how pervasive the denial of opportunities of education, free movement, and free speech was for African Americans in the antebellum north. Early in life, Alexander Crummell and his next-door neighbor Henry Highland Garnet attended the African Free School, whose alumni included Samuel Ringgold Ward, George Downing, Ira Aldridge, and James McCune Smith. In 1831 Boston Crummell, Alexander's father, helped found the Canal Street High School, which his son and Henry Highland Garnet attended. The younger Crummell vowed to mold himself into a top-flight intellectual after overhearing a conversation among white lawyers. One attorney quoted the pro-slavery senator John C. Calhoun as saying that, "if he could find a Negro, who knew the Greek syntax, he would then believe that the Negro was a human being and should be treated as a man." Crummell took that as a personal challenge and later seized an opportunity to attend the Noyes Academy in Canaan, New Hampshire, accompanied by his friends, Henry Highland Garnet and Thomas Sidney.

After enrollment and a nationally publicized appearance at an abolition meeting in July 1835 in Plymouth, New Hampshire, the youth became the target of whites determined to rid the area of their presence.[71] Soon the school became known as a "Nigger school," and a town meeting was held in Canaan, where it was decided to remove the blacks from the school and town. After oxen pulled the school building into a swamp, a mob threatened the black students, leading Garnet, at one point, to use a double-barreled shotgun to keep the attackers at bay.[72]

During his youth, John Mercer Langston learned to cope with, and occasionally challenge, the pervasive racial discrimination in the pre–Civil War North. Following an entire day's stagecoach travel trip in Oberlin, he was roughly informed, "We do not entertain niggers! You must find some nigger-boarding house." Suddenly, outside in a cold, pouring rain in a strange community, the young Langston was in a state of shock. Fortunately, a passing black man saw his distress and, learning of his dilemma, told him he would show him a place he could stay. The man, who was to become a lifelong friend of Langston's, allowed him to stay in his family's home.[73]

Later, after being ordered to ride outside the coach in the cold rain with the driver, he refused and fortunately found a key ally in a white man who came to his defense. He insisted that they sit in accordance with the regulations as the seating plan indicated, ending the dispute.[74]

Paul Cuffe's 1796 voyage to Vienna on the Eastern Shore of Maryland to pick up a large shipment of Indian corn astonished blacks and whites alike. The image of a black captain and all-black crew clashed with that of the slaves they passed toiling in the fields. After their shock wore off, white authorities grew anxious that the example of Cuffe might inspire slave rebellion. Earlier in the year, Maryland had passed a law enslaving free blacks suspected of being fugitives from slavery for six months. After the boat, docked the white crowd was anxious for the federal collector of customs to arrest Cuffe and his crew; however, he found that impossible, for Cuffe's credentials were in order. Nevertheless, Cuffe proceeded cautiously and was able to leave the port with the corn unmolested.[75] After Cuffe returned from Africa in 1812, his ship and its valuable commodities were seized by the U. S. Customs, forcing Cuffe to appeal to U. S. secretary of the treasury for its release.[76] With support from many influential individuals, Cuffe traveled to Washington to complete the appeal. He refused to dine separately from other travelers as instructed by a servant. "I told him as I rode with the company, I could eat with them. So we all sat down and ate at one table." Within the District of Columbia, a hotbed of slavery, it was deemed prudent that he travel with Samuel Hutchinson, a Quaker Friend. On the way home, following his successful meeting with President James Madison, who favored colonizing free blacks anywhere other than the United States, Cuffe headed home to Massachusetts. On the way he again refused to be forced to eat with the servants, "not as I thought myself better than the Servants, but from the nature of the Cause."[77] Although Cuffe initially worked with the American Colonization Society (ACS), he eventually distinguished his support for African emigration from theirs.

THE THRUST FOR MORAL REFORM AND THE AMERICAN
COLONIZATION SOCIETY

From their founding meeting in December 1816 in Washington, D.C., the ACS was a thorn in the side of free blacks. Founded by members of the American elite, including Francis Scott Key, Richard Rush, and John Randolph, the organization sought to rid North America of its free black population. A typical ACS tract described free blacks as "introduced among us by violence, notoriously ignorant, degraded and miserable, mentally diseased, brokenspirited, acted upon by no motive to honourable exertions." The colonizationists argued that the free blacks "wander unsettled and unbefriended through our land, or sit indolent, abject and sorrowful, by the streams which witness their captivity."[78] Education was to no avail but would merely "tease, frustrate, and finally disillusion him."[79] One ACS leader, Elias B. Caldwell, recommended maintaining free blacks "in the lowest state of degradation and ignorance," for to do otherwise was merely to promote a "higher relish for those privileges which they can never attain."[80]

A January 1818 meeting in Washington, D.C., gave thanks to the "opulent" slaveholders of Virginia who had generously filled their coffers and the political support they enjoyed from the House of Representatives. These statements served to underline the support the organization enjoyed at the highest level of political office in the United States. For the white colonizationists, it was clear that free blacks represented a "blot" on the American social landscape. Black rejection of their plans, in their perception, resulted entirely from "ignorance and misapprehension," as they made it clear that the opinion of this community was entirely irrelevant to the viability of their project.[81] Jefferson, too, commented in January 1811 that unenslaved blacks might object but that it was of little import.[82] African American communities were not slow to respond to the rising threat the colonizationists posed. By 1817 a black protest meeting at Philadelphia's Bethel Church resolved that since their "ancestors (not of choice) were the first successful cultivators of the wilds of America," they, "their descendants," felt "entitled to participate in the blessings of her luxuriant soil, which their blood and sweat enriched." They vowed "never [to] separate ourselves voluntarily from the slave population of this country," citing ties of blood, "suffering, and wrong," and later in the year led a 3,000-strong protest of the ACS effort to launch a Philadelphia branch.[83]

The transparent motives of the white colonizationists were apparent in their officials' discussion of the benefits of removing to West Africa slaves who would otherwise be manumitted. Removal of free blacks "who now corrupt them, and render them discontented" would also lend itself to greater social tranquillity, they reasoned, since the presence of free blacks exposed slaves to "harsher treatment and greater privations."[84]

The efforts of the white colonizationists bore some fruit but were unable to halt the growth of the unenslaved African American communities. Yet, the charges of degeneracy put blacks on the defensive and sparked a moral reform movement. William Whipper contended in 1837 that antiblack bias arose "not from the color of [black] skin, but from their condition." He felt that the most efficacious means of reducing white prejudice was to attain high standards by meeting and surpassing the contemporary values of whites by improving black mental, moral, and economic conditions.[85] Driven by the desire for black freedom in the North, Whipper and his contemporaries sought to reform everyday culture, evincing the seemingly eternal African American vacillation between self-improvement and radical structural reform. When one aim seems increasingly remote, the other gains favor as a general strategic thrust on the part of black leadership.

Contemporary whites allied to the cause of black liberty likewise counseled moral reform. The American Convention of Delegates from Abolition Societies advised blacks to collectively engage in regular work and education while maintaining a sober, frugal, and temperate demeanor. By avoiding alcohol, frivolous amusements, and assorted sins while building families within legal marriages and being industrious, blacks would eventually shake off their pariah status.[86] The American Moral Reform Society (AMRS) was an all-male organization dedicated to black collective self-improvement. An 1837 document, authored by William Whipper, identified two opposing political movements, one proposing "an indirect action on the sin of slavery, by removing the free to the land of their fathers." The other called for "a direct action" against slavery, a denunciation of slavery's guilt, while pleading "for the elevation of the free coloured man in the land of his nativity."[87] The organization strongly emphasized its ties to enslaved blacks in the South, stressing their unbreakable ties to the "land of our birth." Moreover, the assembled free blacks made it clear that they had no "desire to see our numbers decreased"; rather, they prayed for a multiplication of the number of blacks endowed with Christian morals and values in order to "warn this guilty nation of her injustice and cruelty to the descendants of Africa, until righteousness, justice, and truth, shall rise in their might and majesty, and proclaim from the halls of legislation that the chains of the bondsman have fallen."[88]

Another proponent of black moral reform, the influential Alexander Crummell, saw racial prejudice and the actual condition of African Americans as the two primary obstacles to black advancement. Viewing the black masses as largely "ignorant, unkempt, dirty, animal-like, repulsive, and half-heathen brutal, and degraded," and believing that nothing can be done to eradicate white racism and prejudice, Crummell felt that blacks alone could elevate themselves.[89] This implied that race progress was linked to progressive development of the individual black, intellectually and morally. Honesty, dignity, and self-discipline were highly valued by Crummell. He felt that "power" was what blacks needed and that power derived from personal character. When a high level of character was realized by blacks, then the race would enter the American mainstream.[90]

Another response to the repression faced by free blacks was a renewed interest in emigration. An address by Richard Allen in 1830 highlighted the resolution of blacks "to consider the propriety of forming a settlement in the province of Upper Canada." Securing this settlement would be designed to provide a refuge for those who were forced out of their homes, as well as those who favored emigration.[91]

THE FOUNDATIONS OF BLACK PATRIARCHY

The growing communities of free blacks in the northern and southern cities were hotbeds of energy, ambition, improvisation, and dedication. Many people within these communities had overcome considerable obstacles to become free of slavery and, despite the sea of prejudice, were determined to broaden their freedom for themselves and those still enslaved. Following the American Revolution into the early nineteenth century, free blacks were forced to both launch and develop the basic institutions necessary for a functioning community.

In Philadelphia the Free African Society, formed in 1787, was an important early achievement of its two principal leaders, Absalom Jones and Richard Allen. Heavily influenced by Quakers, the Free African Society urged blacks to abstain from "gaming and feasting" and to remember their counterparts in slavery. Wary of any shortcomings that would be used by their "enemies to declare that we are not fit for freedom," they counseled blacks to heed a strict, austere code of behavior.[92] This central aim pervaded virtually all of the subsequent organized and institutional activities of the national free black community and, surviving through the years of Emancipation and Reconstruction, continues to make its presence felt among contemporary African Americans.

Despite the determination of Philadelphia blacks led by Richard Allen to accommodate themselves to the racially biased practices in that city, they ended up in confrontation with white institutions. In 1792 the flagrant disrespect shown black worshipers at St. George's Methodist Church ended in a black walkout. Increasing black attendance and the new seats designated for blacks in a newly constructed gallery were the immediate causes of the confrontation. After Allen and other blacks took seats in the new gallery, they were rudely told to move. Instead of complying with their request to finish their prayer and then move, they were forcibly pulled up from their knees and ordered to move. They vowed never to return and set about the task of establishing their own church. In this endeavor, led by Absalom Jones, they were aided by Benjamin Rush, perhaps the leading scientist of the day. His influence was instrumental in the founding of St. Thomas' African Episcopal Church, obtaining a $2,000 loan from a local businessman.

After a decade of existence, a new head of the Philadelphia Conference of Methodists demanded the keys of the church and prohibited meetings except when he ordered them. He accepted no protests of this, noting that his word was law unless two-thirds of the church members voted to change the charter of incorporation. This they promptly did, removing their Bethel church from the Methodist conference. Yet, following this, the church was plagued with the insistence of many white ministers that they be allowed to preach. Finally, Allen and other black Methodist church leaders organized a conference in April 1816.[93] For Allen and other leaders this was a hard-won lesson in the value and necessity of independence.

Richard Allen's patriarchalism came to surface in the denial of evangelist Jarena Lee's ordination. According to Lee's account of a conversation with Allen after she told him of her calling to preach the gospel, Allen first asked Lee "in what sphere [she] wished to move in?" Determining that Methodism was the denomination she wanted to preach under, Allen related the story of a Mrs. Cook, who was allowed to preach only "by the verbal license of the preacher in charge at the time." However, with respect to women preaching, Allen indicated that "our Discipline knew nothing at all about it—that it did not call for women preachers."[94]

By the early nineteenth century African American values, attitudes, and behavior norms surrounding gender had taken a definite form. They had been shaped by early African American colonial traditions and African, Native American, and European cultural heritage.[95] Among other things, this synthesis of cultural influences reinforced the heavy female and minimal male role in child raising that characterizes African cultures.[96] The gender-role ideals of black males and females carried over into the emergent institutions of African Americans.

As a moral reform advocate, Alexander Crummell put forth, chiefly through his sermons, a philosophy of stringent self-discipline and restraint. He viewed blacks, as a race, to be vulnerable to excessive indulgence in sexual matters. A hedonistic lifestyle to Crummell was one of the greatest dangers confronting blacks. Ideally, black males and females would strive to fulfill the duties that accord with their place in society and exercise self-restraint in all things, especially sex. Flashiness and flamboyance were frowned upon, and a high standard of conduct was expected of both females and males. In particular, males' personal code of morality would operate in concert, as a kind of double safeguard against moral transgression.[97] Crummell wrote:

Take the sanctity of marriage, the facility of divorce, the chastity of woman, the shame, modesty and bashfulness of girlhood, the abhorrence of illegitimacy; and there is no people in this land who, in these regards, have received such deadly thrusts as this race of ours. And these qualities are the grandest qualities of all superior people.[98]

Crummell felt that a lack of African civilization and American slavery had impaired the moral development of black women. The duty of the black male leadership, to Crummell, was to establish the general conditions for the realization of "the delicate tenderness of her sex."[99]

Although Crummell professed a belief in sexual equality, he felt that "the man by the sanction of nature and revelation, by law and custom, by reason and instance, has the precedency."[100] The proper functioning of the black family, for Crummell, was key to the ability of blacks to progress in American society. Virtually every person should be married, and the male role was as a protector and provider. His belief that the female role in marriage ideally centered on the domestic duties as housewives and mothers was consistent with the mainstream of black opinion during this period.[101]

During the first quarter of the nineteenth century the new institutional life of black Americans was dominated by males.[102] The middle-class black male of the North exerted a heavy influence on the shaping of gender-role ideals via black newspapers, organizational bylaws, and the pulpit. To a considerable extent, this more organized and formal body of values conformed to the popular American gender-role ideals.[103] The *Aliened American* newspaper, for example, advised black males to do more than just "bow and tip" the hat in the company of women. The man must be the protector of his wife and children, be independent, and be involved in the affairs of the wider society. Hard work was manly, as was skill acquisition, learning a trade, and entrepreneurship. This advice was inextricably tied to the overall welfare of blacks as a race.[104] The particular role of mothers was to inculcate these values in the young with the explicit message that it was not only for their own good but for the good of the entire race. Fathers, on the other hand, were to lead by setting an example of hard work and sobriety and in other ways behaving as a positive role model.[105] Black male leaders accepted the notion that, ideally, men should be able to earn sufficient income to support their wives and children without their wives' entering the workforce. This would allow their women to become true ladies, with all the traditional femininity this implies.[106]

Well-acquainted with the shortcomings or faults of their own people, black newspapers chided their readers to dress decently in public, never forget their manners, and treat others with respect. Public displays of sexuality, lewdness, or drunkenness were particularly frowned upon. Modest and simple clothing was favored as opposed to the wild, flamboyant, and outlandish.[107]

All-male formal and informal associations arose addressing issues of manhood and offering opportunities for political competition. The ceremonial "governor" elections, extending almost until emancipation, offered opportunities to demonstrate athletic, oratorical, and other talents. The Prince Hall Masons and other lodges, as well as organizations of black workers, seamen, and businessmen, began to create a rich organizational life for free black males.[108]

Organizations that included both black males and black females were generally dominated by males, and the lack of sexual equality was a problem that diminished and distorted the organizational contribution of women. Both genders overwhelmingly accepted the notion that males should occupy the overwhelming bulk of the leadership roles. Women were encouraged by both men and women to take a more passive, but supportive, role. In many circles, the opinion was that women should accept a secondary role and avoid intimidating the male with superior knowledge or logic in conversation, allowing him to feel superior and "be a man."[109]

At the 1848 Colored National Convention, women, disgusted with the total male domination of the proceedings, resolved:

Whereas we the ladies have been invited to attend the Convention, and have been deprived of a voice, which we the ladies deem wrong and shameful. Therefore . . . we will attend no more after tonight, unless the privilege is granted.[110]

Despite their general acceptance of the dominant organizational role of males, the antebellum free black male leadership accepted female leadership to a considerably greater extent than did the contemporary white male leaders. With Frederick Douglass setting an important example as a progressive role model with respect to the struggle for sexual equality, other black male leaders endorsed important leadership roles for black women.[111]

Sojourner Truth's statement that if "colored men get their rights, and not colored women theirs, you see the colored men will be masters over the women, and it will be just as bad as it was before" has been distorted to place her in opposition to the black male franchise.[112] When Truth pointed to the weaknesses of black men as an argument for black women's rights, she focused on the issue of control over a family's money rather than on violence. Truth said that she wanted to keep agitating for woman suffrage before federal policy hardened. White women needed the vote, but black women needed it even more, having less education and a more limited choice of jobs. "[W[ashing," she said, "is about as high as a colored women gets."[113] The increasing awareness of the need for women's equality accompanied the increased militancy of black antislavery activists during the eventful 1850s. The next section discusses the rise of this more proactive form of antebellum black masculinity.

THE RISE OF AN ASSERTIVE BLACK MASCULINITY AMONG FREE BLACKS

By the 1850s the power of the northern black community had grown into a significant political factor, and it existed in a shaky alliance with a slowly growing abolitionist movement. The Fugitive Slave Act of 1850 was a catalyst for political mobilization of Africans in America as a dormant black convention movement was reawakened by the passage of the Fugitive Slave Act.[114] Some 140 delegates met in Rochester, New York, in July 1853 to hammer out a program to oppose this new measure.[115]

One issue that galvanized these activists arose after President Franklin Pierce vigorously enforced the Fugitive Slave Act in 1854, vowing to "incur any expense" to return fugitive slave Anthony Burns to Virginia, and dispatched a ship to Boston. Treating Burns as a criminal moved Charlotte Forten to deplore this effort "to prevent a man, whom God has created in his own image, from regaining that freedom with which, he, in common with every other human being, is endowed."[116]

The dramatic events of the 1850s energized black activists and propelled a change in consciousness. Boldness, assertiveness, and direct action became more valued as attributes of black masculinity than previously. With a new frankness, William Whipper argued that racism stems from "man's selfish nature, pride and ambition" and is learned by both the "ignorant" and "learned." He maintained that if slavery was abolished immediately, racism would still be alive and well in the nation.[117]

Jermain Wesley Loguen is representative of the new stridency of the 1850s brand of black masculinity. Touring the North for the antislavery cause, Loguen complained of those who were "very willing to work in the name of the slave, if the thing pays, and the pay goes directly to their pockets."

The colored man is "all right"; he is a "good nigger" so long as he will worship at their shrine, and pour money into their coffers; but let him only presume to think and act for himself, like an independent and accountable being, and above all to put his own penny into his own pocket, and he is no longer a "good nigger"! Away with such arrant hypocrisy, that would save a man from the clutches of the slavedriver only to fasten upon him the shackles of another dependent despotism! I am sick of all such friends of the slave.[118]

William Watkins shared the view that the times called for an aggressive type of manhood. Writing in 1854, he contended that a "timid man" was not the stuff of the reformer. "Moral courage" as opposed to "physical courage" was demanded in this new era. Scorning the "spaniel-like obsequiousness, and lick-the-dust servility" of those "unmanly" "cowards," he contemptuously told them to move out of the path of the true reformer who would "most assuredly crush them." The determination and energy Watkins expressed pervaded the era.[119]

While Watkins called for more "living men," he said there were too many "dead men" already. Loguen called for "more true soldiers in the field, who are not afraid to die." His fervent cries to "fight on and ever, and not quit the field" reverberated in the years to come, in the battles of the Civil War, in the struggles of Reconstruction, against the lynch mobs and Jim Crow, and into the tumultuous turmoil of the 1960s and 1970s. A self-made man, Loguen typifies an exceptional personality born of rare circumstances that shines during periods of crisis and change.[120] The value of independence he manifests is reflective both of his own personal development and of the collective experiences of black males of the era, particularly black abolitionist males. "For myself," Loguen wrote, "I am willing to cooperate with others, so long as I can do so and maintain my manhood. Beyond that I will not go."[121]

Henry Highland Garnet presaged the increasing impatience of free blacks, who, over the long course of the nineteenth century, were gradually increasing in demographic presence and potential power. This could be sensed in their growing stridency. At the 1843 Buffalo meeting of the National Negro Convention, Garnet harangued the assembled black men: "You act as though your daughters were born to pamper the lusts of your masters and overseers." He added, "And worst of all, you timidly submit while your lords tear your wives from your embraces and defile them before your eyes. In the name of God, we ask, are you men?"[122]

Independence as an ideal gender-role value adhered to by black males appeared to be in vogue, spurred on by the quickened pace of national events involving slavery. A black convention in 1848 equated dependence with degradation and stated, "Men may indeed pity us, but they cannot respect us" without the attainment of black independence economically. The fact, as one leader put it, that "our fathers are their coachmen, our brothers their cookmen, ourselves their waiting-men, [o]ur mothers their nurse-women, and our wives their washer women" meant that social and political equality should not be expected. Two decades earlier, David Walker, in his *Appeal*, similarly expressed the sentiment that menial service occupations, such as bootblacking, waiting, and barbering for whites, were inherently degrading and indicative of a state of dependence.[123]

Following the Civil War, black masculinity would undergo dramatic changes, and lose its contrasting and overlapping forms represented in a northern free black variety and a southern field slave variety, and then merge into a masculinity shaped by class, region, culture, and other factors. The Civil War would provide an arena for many to transcend by leaps and bounds the limited horizons that the shackles of slavery confined them to. Suddenly, African Americans were swept up in the tidal wave of history, and the old slavery times were no more.

NOTES

1. Dorothy Sterling, *The Making of an Afro-American: Martin Robison Delany, 1812–1885* (Garden City, NY: Doubleday, 1971), 44.

2. Sterling Stuckey, *Slave Culture: Nationalist Theory and the Foundations of Black America* (New York: Oxford University Press, 1987).

3. Mary Beth Norton et al., *A People and a Nation: A History of the United States* (Boston: Houghton Mifflin, 1990), 166.

4. Ira Berlin, *Slaves without Masters: The Free Negro in the Antebellum South* (New York: New Press, 1974), 16–41.

5. Willi Coleman, "Architects of a Vision: Black Women and Their Antebellum Quest for Political and Social Equality," in Ann D. Gordon (ed.), *African American Women and the Vote, 1837–1965* (Amherst: University of Massachusetts Press, 1997), 26.

6. Berlin, *Slaves without Masters*, 41, 346.

7. Ibid., 345; Bernard E. Powers Jr., *Black Charlestonians: A Social History, 1822–1885* (Fayetteville: University of Arkansas Press, 1994); see also Jason Poole, "On Borrowed Ground: Free African-American Life in Charleston, South Carolina 1810–61," *Essays in History* 36 (1994): 4; Michael P. Johnson and James L. Roark *Black Masters: A Free Family of Color in the Old South.* (New York: W. W. Norton, 1984).

8. Poole, "On Borrowed Ground," 4.

9. Nick Salvatore, *We All Got History: The Memory Books of Amos Webber* (New York: Random House, 1996), 57–66. See also James Oliver Horton and Lois E. Horton, *In Hope of Liberty: Culture, Community, and Protest among Northern Free Blacks, 1700–1860.* (New York: Oxford University Press, 1997).

10. Norton et al., *A People and a Nation*, 165.

11. Irvin Nell Painter, *Sojourner Truth: A Life, a Symbol* (New York: W. W. Norton, 1996), 23; Kathryn Grover, *Make a Way Somehow: African-American Life in a Northern Community, 1790–1965* (Syracuse, NY: Syracuse University Press, 1994).

12. Norton et al., *A People and a Nation*, 166; Berlin 29–31; Edgar J. McManus, *Black Bondage in the North.* (Syracuse, NY: Syracuse University Press, 1973), 161, 181.

13. Philip S. Foner, *Organized Labor and the Black Worker, 1619–1981* (New York: International, 1981), 4.

14. Thomas Jefferson, *The Writings of Thomas Jefferson* (Washington, DC: Thomas Jefferson Memorial Association, 1903), 193.

15. Larry E. Tise, *Proslavery: A History of the Defense of Slavery in America, 1701–1840* (Athens: University of Georgia Press, 1987), 18.

16. David R. Roediger, *The Wages of Whiteness: Race and the Making of the American Working Class* (London: Verso, 1991), 57.

17. Ibid., 106.

18. John Mercer Langston, *From the Virginia Plantation to the National Capital*

(Hartford, CT: American, 1894), 64.

   19. Ibid., 65.

   20. Ibid., 66.

   21. Randall Kennedy, *Race, Crime, and the Law* (New York: Pantheon Books, 1997), 40.

   22. Leon F. Litwack, *North of Slavery: The Negro in the Free States, 1790–1860* (Chicago: University of Chicago Press, 1961), 93–95.

   23. Sterling, *The Making of an Afro-American*, 11.

   24. Ibid., 12.

   25. Ibid., 13.

   26. William J. Moses, *Alexander Crummell: A Study of Civilization and Discontent* (New York: Oxford University Press, 1989), 17.

   27. Shane White, *Somewhat More Independent: The End of Slavery in New York City, 1770–1810* (Athens: University of Georgia Press, 1991), 159; Mary Frances Berry and John W. Blassingame, *Long Memory: The Black Experience in America* (New York: Oxford University Press, 1992), 39.

   28. Berry and Blassingame, *Long Memory*, 40.

   29. Bernard E. Powers, Jr., *Black Charlestonians: A Social History, 1822–1885* (Fayetteville: University of Arkansas Press, 1994); Berlin, *Slaves without Masters*, 97.

   30. Roediger, *The Wages of Whiteness*, 58.

   31. Foner, *Organized Labor*, 4.

   32. Litwack, *North of Slavery*, 57–58.

   33. Ibid., 58

   34. Roger Lane, *Roots of Violence in Black Philadelphia, 1860–1900* (Cambridge: Harvard University Press, 1986), 19–29; Berlin, *Slaves without Masters*, 97.

   35. Foner, *Organized Labor*, 6.

   36. Ibid., 10.

   37. Berry and Blassingame, *Long Memory*, 39.

   38. Litwack, *North of Slavery*, 160.

   39. Poole, "On Borrowed Ground," 4.

   40. Powers, *Black Charlestonians*, 56.

   41. Poole, "On Borrowed Ground," 6–7.

   42. Stuckey, *Slave Culture*, 50–52; Powers, *Black Charlestonians*, 30; see also Bertram Wyatt-Brown, *Southern Honor: Ethics and Behavior in the Old South* (New York: Oxford University Press, 1982), 409–10.

   43. Poole, "On Borrowed Ground," 14.

   44. Ibid., 12.

   45. Powers, *Black Charlestonians*, 56.

   46. Ibid., 32.

   47. Litwack, *North of Slavery*, 51; Randall Kennedy, *Race, Crime, and the Law* (New York: Pantheon Books, 1997), 80.

   48. Powers, *Black Charlestonians*, 15.

   49. Ibid., 15.

   50. William A. Bryne, "Slave Crime in Savannah, Georgia," *Journal of Negro History* 79, no. 4, (Fall 1994): 353; see also John W. Blassingame, *Black New Orleans, 1860–1880* (Chicago: University of Chicago Press, 1973).

   51. Powers, *Black Charlestonians*, 23.

   52. Bryne, "Slave Crime," 33.

   53. Poole, "On Borrowed Ground," 12.

54. Ibid., 14.

55. Power, *Black Charlestonians*, 33.

56. Poole, "On Borrowed Ground," 18.

57. Ibid., 19.

58. Ibid., 30.

59. Thomas P. Slaughter, *Bloody Dawn: The Christiana Riot and Racial Violence in the Antebellum North* (New York: Oxford University Press, 1991), 22.

60. Douglas R. Egerton, *Gabriel's Rebellion: The Virginia Slave Conspiracies of 1800 and 1802* (Chapel Hill: University of North Carolina Press, 1993), 29.

61. Constance McLaughlin Green, *The Secret City: A History of Race Relations in the Nation's Capital* (Princeton: Princeton University Press, 1967), 18.

62. Gladys-Marie Fry, *Night Riders in Black Folk History* (Knoxville: University of Tennessee Press, 1975), 90.

63. Ibid., 90.

64. David A. Gerber, *Black Ohio and the Color Line, 1860–1915* (Chicago: University of Illinois Press, 1976), 3; Kenneth L. Kusmer, *A Ghetto Takes Shape: Black Cleveland, 1870–1930* (Chicago: University of Illinois Press, 1976), 5.

65. Gerber, *Black Ohio*, 19.

66. Kusmer, *A Ghetto Takes Shape*, 6–7.

67. Julie Winch, *Philadelphia's Black Elite: Activism, Accommodation, and the Struggle for Autonomy, 1787–1848* (Philadelphia: Temple University Press, 1988), 17.

68. Slaughter, *Bloody Dawn*, 37.

69. Berlin, *Slaves without Masters*, 92.

70. Lester C. Lamon, *Blacks in Tennessee 1791–1970* (Knoxville: University of Tennessee Press, 1981), 20.

71. William J. Moses, *Alexander Crummell: A Study of Civilization and Discontent* (New York: Oxford University Press, 1989), 17.

72. Ibid., 23.

73. Langston, *From the Virginia Plantation*, 91.

74. Ibid., 91–92.

75. Lamont D. Thomas, *Rise to Be a People: A Biography of Paul Cuffe* (Urbana: University of Illinois Press, 1986), 17.

76. Ibid., 73.

77. Ibid., 75.

78. Litwack, *North of Slavery*, 21; Thomas, *Rise to be a People*, 110.

79. Litwack, *North of Slavery*, 23.

80. Ibid., 23.

81. American Society for Colonizing the Free People of Color, *The First Annual Report* (Washington, DC: Library of Congress, 1818), 7.

82. Ibid., 13–14.

83. Charlotte L. Forten, *The Journal of Charlotte Forten* (New York: Dryden Press, 1953), 9.

84. American Society, *The First Annual Report*, 39.

85. American Moral Reform Society, *The Minutes and Proceedings of the First Annual Meeting of the American Moral Reform Society* (Washington, DC: Library of Congress, 1837). 4.

86. Ibid., 5.

87. Ibid., 5.

88. Ibid., 5.

89. Moses, *Alexander Crummell*, 210.

90. Ibid., 210.

91. Ibid., 210–11.

92. Winch, *Philadelphia's Black Elite*, 5–7.

93. Gary B. Nash, *Forging Freedom: The Formation of Philadelphia's Black Community, 1720–1840* (Cambridge: Harvard University Press, 1988), 118–19; Winch, *Philadelphia's Black Elite*, 14.

94. Jacquelyn Grant, "Black Theology and the Black Woman," in Beverly Guy-Sheftall, *Words of Fire: An Anthology of African-American Feminist Thought* (New York: New Press, 1995), 326.

95. James Oliver Horton (ed.), *Free People of Color: Inside the African American Community* (Washington, DC: Smithsonian Institution Press, 1993), 99; see also Lawrence W. Levine, *Black Culture And Black Consciousness: Afro-American Folk Thought from Slavery to Freedom* (New York: Oxford University Press, 1977).

96. Horton, *Free People*, 100; Deborah Gray White, *Ar'n't I a Woman?: Female Slaves in the Plantation South.* (New York: W. W. Norton, 1985), 106–08.

97. Moses, *Alexander Crummell*, 217.

98. Ibid., 218.

99. Alexander Crummell, *The Black Woman of the South: Her Neglects and Her Needs.* (Washington, DC: Library of Congress, n.d.), 7.

100. Moses, *Alexander Crummell*, 219.

101. Horton, *Free People*, 102.

102. Ibid., 102–03.

103. Coleman, "Architects," 29.

104. Horton, *Free People*, 102–04.

105. Ibid., 104.

106. Painter, *Sojourner Truth*, 71–72.

107. Horton, *Free People*, 105.

108. Ibid., 111; Salvatore, *We All Got History*, 60–66.

109. Horton, *Free People*, 117.

110. Coleman, "Architects," 30.

111. Ibid., 29–30;

112. Painter, *Sojourner Truth*, 220.

113. Ibid., 227.

114. Kennedy, *Race, Crime, and the Law*, 84.

115. Phillip S. Foner and George E. Walker (eds.), *Proceedings of the Black National and State Conventions, 1865–1900* (Philadelphia: Temple University Press, 1986), xix.

116. Forten, *The Journal*, 34; Roy Franklin Nichols, *Franklin Pierce: Young Hickory of Granite Hills* (Norwalk, CT: Easton Press, 1969), 361.

117. William Whipper, "William Whipper to Frederick Douglass [October 1854]," in Peter Ripley et al. (eds.), *The Black Abolitionist Papers* (New York: Microfilm Corporation of America, 1981), 243–44.

118. Jermain Wesley Loguen, "Jermain Wesley Loguen to Frederick Douglass [March 1855]," in Ripley et al., *The Black Abolitionist Papers*, 271.

119. William J. Watkins, "Editorial by William J. Watkins 7 April 1854," in Ripley et al., *The Black Abolitionist Papers*, 213.

120. Loguen, "Jermain Wesley Loguen," 272.

121. Ibid., 272.

122. James Oliver Horton and Lois E. Horton, "Violence, Protest, and Identity: Black

Manhood in Antebellum America," in James Oliver Horton (ed.), *Free People of Color: Inside the African American Community* (Washington, DC: Smithsonian Institution Press, 1993), 80–97.

123. Litwack, *North of Slavery*, 174.

Chapter 4

The Civil War and the Black Male

Fondly do we hope, fervently do we pray, that this mighty scourge of war may speedily pass away. Yet, if God wills that it continue until all the wealth piled by the bondsman's two hundred and fifty years of unrequited toil shall be sunk, and until every drop of blood drawn with the lash shall be paid by another drawn with the sword, as was said three thousand years ago, so still it must be said "the judgments of the Lord are true and righteous altogether."

—President Abraham Lincoln

How extraordinary, and what a tribute to ignorance and religious hypocrisy, is the fact that in the minds of most people, even those of liberals, only murder makes men. The slave pleaded; he was humble; he protected the women of the South, and the world ignored him. The slave killed white men; and behold, he was a man.

—W.E.B. Du Bois[1]

On 12 April 1861 Fort Sumter, South Carolina, was attacked by southern forces marking the beginning of the U.S. Civil War. The war raged for almost four solid years, until the formal surrender of Confederate forces at Appomattox Court House in Virginia on 9 April 1865. These were fateful years for the future of blacks in the United States, presenting the most favorable opportunity for the achievement of black liberty in the history of the African presence on the American continent. For individuals, it represented the best chance for manumission en masse since the War of 1812, when the British invaded the South. This Civil War among whites featured one side determined to expand and perpetuate slavery against another side determined to merely perpetuate slavery. At the outset of the conflict, President Lincoln sought to guarantee slavery where it then existed, while halting its expansion. This chapter provides an overview of the participation of black males in the Civil War, both as soldiers and as civilians, and discusses its impact on their social, psychological, and political status.

Following the beginning of the Civil War, many blacks in America rejoiced at this historic rupture of national white unity. Frederick Douglass placed himself squarely on the side of disunion: "I am for a dissolution of the Union—decidedly for a dissolution of the Union!"[2] Douglass declared, "God be praised!" upon hearing that Fort Sumter had surrendered. He vowed that during the war he would "stand up for the downtrodden, to open my mouth for the dumb, to remember those in bonds as bound with them."[3] He warned that "any attempt now to separate the freedom of the slave from the victory of the Government . . . any attempt to secure peace to the whites while leaving the blacks in chains . . . will be labor lost." He was supremely confident that the "logic of events" would make abolition of slavery a reality. The Union could not be saved without black emancipation. Until this, he warned, the rebellion could "never be effectually put down."[4]

Yet for American whites, north and south, arming blacks was, at the war's outset, out of the question, for slavery was not to be jeopardized for what was thought to be a brief, but bloody, affair. Both the South and the North believed that the war would not be a long one.[5] Yet, by the end of the war, President Lincoln himself would wonder aloud whether the war was God's punishment of America for two and one-half centuries of black bondage.[6]

WINNING THE RIGHT TO FIGHT FOR FREEDOM

The inauspicious beginning of the Civil War for the North signaled immediately that the war would not be the brief affair both sides anticipated. The first battle of Bull Run, 21 July 1861, pitted 30,000 federal troops under General Irvin McDowell against 22,000 Confederate troops of General P.G.T. Beauregard. The battle near Manassas Junction, Virginia earned General Thomas Jackson his nickname "Stonewall," for the rebels' defensive stand. With 9,000 southern reinforcements turning the tide of the battle against ill-trained northern troops, the pitiful scenes of routed northern troops straggling back to the District of Columbia were witnessed by many of the nation's budding press corps.[7]

During the initial weeks of the war, the questions within the white American mind concerning the intelligence, common sense, and humanity of blacks led to doubt as to which side the enslaved African Americans would take in the conflict. Most white Americans, north and south, felt that blacks could scarcely comprehend the nature of the conflict and that, at any rate, their thoroughly ingrained loyalty to their slave masters would render them irrelevant to the outcome of the conflict. Early in the war these questions were answered in an unambiguous manner with the Union occupation of the South Carolina sea islands off Port Royal, after the summer of 1861. Roughly a month after Fort Sumter, slaves began to arrive at the lines of the Union army.[8] Enslaved blacks immediately fled the plantations upon the approach of the Union forces.[9] Sam Mitchell, for example, witnessed the slave master order his father to help move his family and the slaves they owned to the mainland as the Union army approached.

Sam's father, a carpenter, at his mother's insistence defied the slaveholder and hid until the master was forced to flee the oncoming northern troops.[10] From the beginning, Douglass advocated that the Lincoln administration emancipate blacks from slavery and enlist them in the fight to save the Union. Since the Confederacy used blacks in factories, plantations, and other supportive roles, the Union army would also find it necessary to do so, Douglass maintained. Douglass prophetically asserted that the "Negro is the key of the situation—the pivot upon which the whole rebellion turns."[11] Douglass wrote that merely the first thrust of one black regiment would qualitatively alter the situation in the North's favor.[12]

Douglass also felt that it was important for the black slaves to play the key part in their own emancipation. He not only expected that they would fight harder, but that their participation itself would be empowering, impelling them to an accelerated personal development. In this way, it would prepare the former slave for a free life. In addition, the collective weight of hundreds of thousands of black men capable of being soldiers would likely be of political significance. Finally, in both the spiritual and psychological sense, the status of a soldier would be liberating for the black male. Douglass maintained: "Once let the black man get upon his person the brass letters, U.S., let him get an eagle on his button, and a musket on his shoulder and bullets in his pocket, and there is no power on earth which can deny that he has earned the right to citizenship in the United States."[13]

The eagerness of many free blacks to fight in the Union army could not be denied. From the war's outset, black men tried to enlist in the Union army. On 23 April 1861, Jacob Dobson, a black man who worked in the U.S. Senate, wrote a letter to the Secretary of War expressing his and 300 other African Americans' determination to play a part in the defense of the capital.[14] In Boston a rally in April 1861 urged the lifting of the prohibition on blacks serving in the U.S. Army.[15] In New York City black men went as far as organizing drilling sessions on their own to prepare for combat until the city's authorities forced them to halt.[16] In two other major centers of free black population, Philadelphia and Cleveland, black leaders announced their readiness to engage the slaveholders in direct combat.[17] In Cleveland blacks resolved at a meeting in April 1861 that they were ready "to go forth and do battle" as blacks did in the American Revolution and the War of 1812. Yet the Ohio Constitution also forbade their entry into the military.[18] Nevertheless, President Lincoln expressed profound doubts as to the character of black males. "If we were to arm them, I fear that in a few weeks the arms would be in the hands of the rebels," Lincoln stated. On another occasion, Lincoln pointed to the political realities of employing black troops. He said, "To arm the negroes would turn 50,000 bayonets from the loyal Border States against us that were for us."[19] Popular white sentiment maintained that this was "a White Man's war." Others feared the success of the black man would force a new respect upon him, one that they had no desire to extend to him. A common feeling among white Union army soldiers was that it would be degrading to fight the South alongside an inferior black man. "We don't want to fight side and side with the niggers. We think we are a too superior race for that," one Union soldier wrote.[20] The image of the black male among white Americans during this period as a cowardly and unthinking menial also led to the conclusion that he would make a poor soldier. One man opined, "I don't believe you could make soldiers of these men at all, they are afraid, and they know it."[21] One editorial by Douglass, "Fighting Rebels with Only One Hand," noted that the cry "Men! men! send us men!" was increasingly heard, but, nevertheless, black enlistment was rejected. He complained of the government's unwillingness, even in this dire hour, of receiving men who have the most at stake in the defeat of the Confederates.[22]

Indeed, from the outset of the war, being highly conscious of the political situation, General Ben Butler, having been already taken to task in his home state for offering to crush a rumored slave rebellion in Maryland, coined the term "contraband" for the blacks who escaped slavery by reaching Union lines. Butler's refusal to deliver escaped slaves back to a Confederate general who had come under a flag of truce to recapture them was based on international legal reality governing "contraband of war." The new label of "contraband," which was to be applied to hundreds of thousands of African Americans in the next four years, had the ideological advantage of allowing the Union forces to shelter the escaped slaves while still not according them the status of humans. The implied recognition of the property rights of southern slave owners also appealed to the influential merchants and bankers whose support for the war effort was of critical importance.[23] President Abraham Lincoln responded to the reality of the "contrabands" by asking Congress to begin to consider practical steps for mass colonization—or expulsion, of most contemporary African Americans—to a land outside the borders of the United States.[24]

"The Port Royal experiment" was regarded as one in which the nation would learn whether blacks would work without the compulsion of the lash. Such was the state of the African American image that this was considered a legitimate question for the era's most prominent intellectuals. This was accompanied by a second question, Would blacks fight for their freedom?[25] The underlying assumption of most commentators was that blacks were, according to their nature, childlike. Even whites dedicated to improving opportunities for African Americans shared this assumption.[26]

Before the North would make use of black men as soldiers, they were relied on as laborers. General William Tecumseh Sherman's war strategy stressed destroying anything of value to the Confederacy. In this he relied on black laborers often traveling with the Union army. Systematically, he employed them in tearing apart the southern railway system. They would line up on each side of the track and lift it in coordination, and then drop it. They would pry apart the spikes holding the cross ties so that any train would derail when attempting to cross the tracks.[27] Blacks played other supplementary roles in support of the northern forces. Acting as teamsters, porters, and pioneers, many black males played valuable roles in this manner.

Dealing roughly and rudely with black males, however, was a matter of tradition and custom that would not be changed quickly. In September 1862 the city of Cincinnati faced an imminent invasion of the city by the Confederate troops led by John Morgan. On 2 September 1862 Mayor George Hatch issued a proclamation that all business in the city be suspended and that residents assemble at voting sites to organize themselves for the defense of the city.[28] Black males were not allowed to vote and had been recently roughly rejected after they volunteered for the local defense force. Black males were not sure how to respond to the call; one hesitantly asked a policeman whether the mayor's proclamation applied to them and received the reply, "You know damned well he doesn't mean you. Niggers ain't citizens." All the mayor wanted, the officer said, was for "you niggers to keep quiet." [29] The military, however, had decided to impress black men into service to work on the fortifications. William Wells Brown wrote: "The privilege of volunteering, extended to others, was to be denied to them. Permission to volunteer would imply some freedom, some dignity, some independent manhood."[30] Instead, gangs of toughs went from house to house rudely seizing the males. Often, they cursed the family and conducted unwarranted searches. Brown wrote:

They went from house to house, followed by a gang of rude, foul-mouthed boys. Closets, cellars, and garrets were searched; bayonets were thrust into beds and bedding; old and young, sick and well, were dragged out, and, amidst shouts and jeers, marched like felons to the pen on Plum Street, opposite the Cathedral. No time was given to prepare for camplife; in most cases no information was given to the purpose for which the men were impressed. The only answers to questions were curses, and a brutal "Come along now; you will find out time enough."[31]

They were hauled to camps where, for little cause, they were reportedly threatened with being shot. Following the appointment of a more liberal white as commander of the "Black Brigade," conditions improved considerably. The men were allowed to return home to obtain necessary items to make their stay at the camps more bearable. For three weeks they labored on the fortifications, at the end of which their antislavery commander addressed them, admitting that they were subjected to indignities and applauding them that these failed to dampen their zeal. They were thanked for the hard labor of cutting down trees, building roads, and constructing forts. Attributing their perseverance to "the accustomed patience" of their "race," it was admitted that:

a portion of the police, ruffians in character, early learning that your services were accepted, and seeking to deprive you of the honor of voluntary labor, before opportunity was given you to proceed to the field, rudely seized you in the streets, in your places of business, in your homes, everywhere, hurried you into filthy pens, thence across the river to the fortifications, not permitting you to make any preparation for camp-life.[32]

Other black males found unique ways to make a contribution to the war effort against the South. Arriving at Union lines 13 May 1862 aboard the *Planter* with his wife, relatives, and black crew members, Robert Smalls said, "I thought the *Planter* might be of some use to Uncle Abe." Smalls, a 23-year-old slave, had been forced to work as an assistant pilot for the Confederate army on the cotton steamboat. Smalls had planned for some time to escape in this manner and was greeted by all as a hero.[33]

In March 1862 a change in command resulted in Major General David Hunter's becoming the commander of the Department of the South.   An abolitionist in conviction, Hunter declared "contrabands" in this district "free" and quietly began to recruit troops from black slave communities on the islands. His initial efforts met with little success, as blacks were suspicious of the sudden opportunity to don a uniform and arms to go to battle. He later instituted a draft of all able-bodied black men between 18 and 45 in the states of South Carolina, Georgia, and Florida.[34] Later, however, he used his troops to roughly round up 500 male ex-slaves to be transformed into soldiers. But, by mid-May, the Lincoln administration revoked Hunter's mandates, restoring the slave status of the blacks within Hunter's administrative area.[35]

This policy was soon reversed with aid from the celebrated Robert Smalls. General Saxon's aide Mansfield French recruited Smalls to travel with him to Washington, where he related the thrilling story of his escape to Secretary of the Treasury Salmon P. Chase. Smalls symbolized the energy emancipated slaves would bring to the war effort, as his liberation of a $60,000 steamer made good copy in the northern press and was a shot in the arm for the black male image early during the war. His discussion with Chase, in all likelihood, played a part in the decision to begin recruiting black men once again. Soon the newly recruited black troops were fighting small skirmishes and acquitting themselves well.[36]

As the war dragged on, Lincoln's attitude toward the participation of black troops evolved. White morale in the North was ebbing as over 100,000 desertions by late 1862 drained the strength of the Union army while a string of midsummer 1862 military defeats further demoralized the North. These factors provided sufficient incentive for the measures passed by Congress in July 1862 giving the go-ahead for the recruitment of black soldiers into the Union army. President Lincoln wrote to Andrew Johnson, then War Governor of Tennessee, on the subject of "raising a negro military force":

The colored population is the great available and yet unavailed of force for restoring the Union. The bare sight of 50,000 armed and drilled black soldiers upon the banks of the Mississippi would end the rebellion at once. And who doubts that we can present that sight if we but take hold in earnest?[37]

THE CIVIL WAR: A WAR OF LIBERATION FOR THE BLACK MALE SOLDIER

Following the decision to enlist black troops in the Union army, the recruiting campaign was not entirely smooth. Not only did hostile slave owners hamper recruiting efforts, but many blacks, especially slaves, were skeptical of the army's promises. There was more success in recruiting among those who had fled to Union lines.   Prominent in their minds were the recent assurances to the Confederacy that the abolition of slavery was not the issue. In addition, there had been over a year of repeated statements that the civil conflict was "a white man's war."[38]

In Massachusetts Governor John A. Andrews relied on the well-known figures of the national black community to recruit blacks into army. Frederick Douglass, Charles Lenox Remond, Martin R. Delany, John Mercer Langston, and Henry Highland Garnet all pushed for black men to enlist in the Union army.[39] Among the recruits were Lewis and Charles Douglass, sons of the famed abolitionist. They and hundreds of other black men proudly paraded by 20,000 citizens of Boston in the 54th Massachusetts Regiment in May 1863.[40]

The AME Church's *Christian Recorder* urged black men to enlist. "Go with the view that you will return freemen. And if you should never return, you will die with the satisfaction of knowing that you have struck a blow for freedom, and assisted in giving liberty to our race in the land of our birth."[41] Sayles Bowen of Washington, DC, said: "When we show that we are men, we can then demand our liberty, . . . peaceably if we can, forcibly if we must. If we do not fight, we are traitors to our God, traitors to our country, traitors to our race, and traitors to ourselves."[42]

In some areas, the black recruits faced taunts and harassment from local whites.[43] In Washington, DC, a reporter for the *Christian Recorder* witnessed "an excited rabble" chasing a black soldier, John Ross. Included among the pursuers was a U. S. police officer. Captured and while being taken away, Ross told the officer he would go peacefully with him. While the officer obligingly arrested him, he allowed the mob to brutalize him prior to taking him in.[44]

Off-duty black soldiers suffered harassment often. Another such incident occurred in Zanesville, Ohio, in February 1864, when a black soldier, a recruiter, was verbally assaulted in a barbershop by Confederate sympathizers. He left the shop, complying with the request of the frightened barber, but was then surrounded by a crowd. The soldier was hit with a stick and responded by knocking his assailant down, which set the mob upon him, pummeling him as they yelled, "Kill the nigger." He tried to flee into the Zane House but was met there by additional hostility. He was stoned until the police finally protected him until other soldiers arrived.[45] Even among black soldiers themselves, racial bias created considerable stress. At a camp in Jacksonville, Florida, housing troops that fought at Fort Wagner, violence erupted after a black soldier was arrested for theft and strung up by his thumbs in the parade grounds. Arguing that white soldiers were not treated this way, a crowd of black soldiers acted to cut him down and exchanged gunfire with a 23-year-old white officer. Six black soldiers were executed as a result of these events—the last servicemen to be executed in the American armed forces for mutiny.[46]

This wariness of blacks of the promises of the Union government recruiters was displayed during the drive to enlist black males. Recruiters repeatedly guaranteed to black male audiences that they would enlist in the U.S. Army on the basis of equality. Massachusetts governor John A. Andrews promised the black recruits "the same treatment, in every respect, as the white volunteers receive." As soldiers, they were told they would receive equal payment, food, protection, and other rights as whites. Douglass, a recruiter for the armed forces, calmed the anxieties of prospective black male recruits with the words, "I have assured myself on these points and we can speak with authority," citing his long experience for the cause of emancipation.[47]

The volunteer regiments of blacks in South Carolina and Massachusetts, nevertheless, chafed under the unequal pay they received. Comprising unenslaved blacks, they received only $10 per month, of which $3 could be spent on clothing. The white soldiers' pay was $13 per month and a $3.50 for clothing.[48] While Douglass, no doubt feeling embarrassed and abused because he had personally guaranteed their equal treatment, met with President Lincoln on 10 August 1863 to attempt to resolve the problem. One soldier said, "We were promised three hundred dollars bounty and thirteen dollars a month, or whatever the white soldiers got." He complained that now that they were in the army, the promises to them were forgotten.[49] Douglass himself admitted candidly that he, in his "humble way," had "contributed somewhat to that false estimate."[50] Martin Delany refused to continue to recruit in Rhode Island in protest over the unequal pay and bounties for black soldiers. He lamented the sense of betrayal that now filled the minds of young men "taught to hold his name sacred."

Although there are reports that the military units of ex-slaves were puzzled and angered by the principled stance of the Massachusetts and South Carolina black soldiers, the latter felt adamantly that equality of treatment was a life-or-death issue not to be compromised away. What gnawed away at them was the prospect of their wives and children suffering from shortages of money, while they, charged with their support, were sacrificing their lives on the battlefield. They made it clear that they were willing to bear the sacrifice if white soldiers were made to equally bear it. Even as they went into combat, they resisted this discrimination by the refusal on the part of several units to accept any pay at all.[51] In the Massachusetts 55th Regiment soldiers nearly reached the point of stacking their arms. In the Third South Carolina Volunteers Sergeant William Walker led a rebellion of black soldiers that did just that and led to his own court-martial and execution for mutiny.[52]

Yet, it remained an issue until June 1864, when the equal-pay measures finally passed Congress.[53] Unfortunately for the ex-slave, retroactive pay extended back only until 1 January 1864, whereas for the other blacks, unenslaved prior to 19 April 1861, it extended to the latter date.[54] In all, some 186,000 black men, over 134,000 of whom had been recruited or drafted from the Confederate states, participated in the Civil War. While they constituted only 10 percent of the Union army manpower, they played a decisive role in the outcome, changing the balance of the war.[55]

BLACK CIVIL WAR RESISTANCE BEHIND THE LINES

The longer the war went on, the more conscious blacks became of their interest in it. Booker T. Washington recalled his mother's awakening him before dawn on his "bundle of rags in the corner." He heard her praying to God that "Abraham Lincoln and his soldiers might be successful and that she and I might some day be free."[56] African slaves had always been attuned to the trends and developments that affected their welfare. Via conversations overheard in the "Big House," the slave community's "grapevine," and through newspapers and magazines, slaves learned of the current news. That it was a grave crime to read a newspaper, magazine, or book did not deter many slaves, who would escape to secluded areas to do their reading. Despite attempts to disguise the meaning of the unprecedented mobilization of the South, the meaning of the great conflict was soon widely understood among those in bondage. Early on, the attitude was one of "wait-and-see"; later, more active attempts to escape slavery or help destroy the institution that had meant so much misery to them were made.

The South depended on the faithful labor of Africans to sustain its war effort. The depleted white manpower in the southern heartland would ideally be compensated for by loyal slaves who worked harder than ever for their masters. One southern newspaper felt that the Confederacy's advantage stemmed from its reliance on slave labor. Whereas in the North "the men who join the army" "are the producers, and the factory operatives," in the South, the slaves "can go on undisturbed in their usual labors."[57] Black men and women were forced into service of the Confederacy by means of impressment. They were used for the construction of the Confederate defenses, and, if more than 20 were required, the state would hire an overseer. The nightmare of the impressed black male was the service at the behest of the Confederate army, as this involved direct risk and support of a recognized force opposed to black life and liberty.[58]

All of the time-honored methods of resistance that slaves utilized were made use of during the period of the Civil War. Maroon colonies in outlying areas multiplied as slaves used the new opportunities to escape from the hard conditions of plantation labor and discipline.[59] Anna Miller recalled that, "my sis and nigger Horace runs off. Dey don't go far, and stay in de dugout Ev'ry night dey'd sneak in and [get] 'lasses and milk and what food dey could."[60] The gradual thinning of the number of physically able white males, resulting in a diminishing number of slave patrols, undoubtedly was immediately noticed by black slaves. Moreover, the balance of intimidation, relied on by slave drivers and overseers, tipped back in the slave's favor, so a new hesitancy and fear crept into whippings and other physical means of coercing labor. There were efforts, therefore, to restore the previously existing balance of terror that served to inhibit the black community. In Mississippi, for example, older men and younger males formed "home guards" to attempt to continue the prewar system of slave patrols.[61]

In Louisiana slaveholders appealed to the Union army commander of the Department of the Gulf for aid to restore their plantation's productive capacity. In a January 1863 letter, the planters of Terrebone Parish complained that not only did the Union army seize almost all of their horses, mules, carts, and wagons, but the blacks were openly defiant. The planters complained that:

many of the negroes led astray by designing persons, believe that the plantations & everything on them belong to them, the negroes— They quit work, go & come when they see fit—Ride off at night the mules that have been at work all day—Fences are pulled down gates & bars are left open— Cattle, & sheep hogs & poultry are killed or carried off & sold—Negroes in numbers from one plantation to an other at all hours night &

day—They travel on the rail road—They congregate in large numbers on deserted plantations. In Some instances negro Soldiers partially armed have been allowed to visit the plantations from which they inlisted. In a word we are in a State of anarchy.[62]

The committee of planter representatives implored the Union authorities for aid in order to plant corn and sugarcane warning that "without bread the negroes must Starve, revolt," and become dependent on government relief. With a "prompt & decided course" that necessitated "obedience & work from our Slaves," the "country & especially the poor negroes" can be saved. In pleading for relief to stave off starvation, slaveholder James Taylor complained that his sole support during the early years of the war was through the income earned from hiring out his two slave carpenters, but, after refusing to work, they escaped to Union army lines.[63]

Another manifestation of the decline in the sense of intimidation that slaves felt was displayed in the streets of Jackson, Mississippi. There slaves were said to have increasingly filled the streets, dressed in their best clothes, smoking cigars, and behaving in what was regarded as an insolent manner.[64] More terrifying were the mysterious deaths that occurred on the unmanned plantations. Increasingly, isolated slave mistresses reflected upon how they had treated their slaves and wondered how their slaves regarded them. In a few cases, slave mistresses were murdered by discontented slaves.[65]

Plots by blacks to rise in arms were discovered by southern authorities during the war, although none were successfully executed. Far from the loyal support the white southerners boasted of early on, increasingly, fears rose of a "new front" of rearguard military activity by black insurrectionists.[66] Discoveries of weapon caches within the slave quarters gave credence to what was hoped was paranoia. Soon after Fort Sumter fell, slave uprising alerts plagued a half-dozen southern states. In Bossier Parish, Louisiana, slaves were reported to be forming a military organization.[67] There is evidence that this rearguard threat distracted, Southern soldiers from their Confederate army duties. One Mississippi unit requested permission to be able to return home to prevent an expected Christmas slave uprising.[68]

The close proximity of Union lines meant, in effect, that the North was now closer to many who had been previously cut off from this avenue of escape. One black escapee observed, "It used to be five hundred miles to git to Canada from Lexington, but not it's only eighteen miles! *Camp Nelson* is now *our* Canada."[69] Octave Johnson, who was a soldier in the Louisiana Corps D'Afrique, was awakened to work one morning so early he could not see. Not rising properly, the overseers intended to whip him, prompting him to run away to the woods. He remained there a year and a half during the war, surviving from stealing "turkeys, chickens and pigs" and living in a small, but growing, maroon colony. Hunted by one Eugene Jardeau, "master of hounds," the fugitives ended up killing eight bloodhounds. Eventually, they escaped to Union lines and Johnson joined the Union army. Yet, the failure rate for slaves who took flight was often high. While one Affy escaped to Union lines, her former slave master recaptured and hanged several young black males also trying to escape slavery in this manner.[70] In another case, after being caught, a black man was shot and badly wounded by the slave master on his way to Union lines. Nevertheless, he managed to thrash his pursuer in a swamp and successfully escape.[71] During the war approximately .5 million slaves successfully reached Union lines, self-emancipating themselves. In July 1862 a Confederate official complained of the tendency of blacks "to be insubordinate" and to flee to Union forces, leading his forces to administer some 40 hangings for "insurrection" in the prior year.[72] This and the recruitment of blacks into the Union army provided a safety valve, forestalling armed rebellion during the years the South was most vulnerable to it.

THE BLACK MALE AS LIBERATOR

The Civil War was a grueling brutal, nasty affair that led to battle fatigue, rampant diseases, and massive death. One black soldier wrote, "I prayed on the battle field some of the best prayers I ever prayed in my life, made God some of the finest promises that ever were made."[73] Throughout it all, however, black men won praise from both their friends and enemies for their actions on the battlefield. One Wisconsin officer said he "never believed in niggers before, but by Jasus, they are hell in fighting."[74] Defenders of the black man's claim to courage were heartened by the actions of the 54th Massachusetts Regiment at Fort Wagner. The assault received widespread coverage in the press and was one of the first national boosts in collective prestige enjoyed by the black male.[75] The spirit of bravery and self-sacrifice for the cause of black emancipation was a motivating force for these men, many of whom died never tasted freedom. Lewis Douglass' letter to his future wife, Amelia, exemplified this spirit. "Remember if I die," he wrote, "I die in a good cause."[76]

In August 1862 the War Department gave approval to the formation of a regiment of slaves in South Carolina—the First South Carolina Volunteers. Thomas Wentworth Higginson, a New England abolitionist and friend of the late John Brown, was appointed commander.[77] Standing out from his contemporaries by his high moral and social principles, Higginson was nevertheless influenced by the prevailing racial sentiment. Speaking of his fondness for the black soldiers he commanded, he said: "I think it is partly from my own notorious love of children that I like these people so well." He felt blacks were "perpetual children, docile, gay, and lovable."[78] Nevertheless, the black troops quickly registered successes. In one raid by the South Carolina black troops in early June 1863, they drove off Confederate pickets, torched six rice mills and several buildings on five plantations, and liberated 725 African American slaves.[79]

Colonel Robert Gould Shaw, who shared similar abolitionist sentiments with his new friend Higginson, had earlier deplored the use of the black 54th Massachusetts regiment on missions to burn and loot Confederate property. This he understood was detrimental to the image of black troops and awaited an opportunity to erase this memory. The objective of putting more pressure on Fort Sumter by capturing the batteries on James and Morris Islands was decided upon, and Shaw fought to have the 54th Massachusetts involved in the action.[80] In a diversionary action, the black troops charged into a withering fire in an effort to seize Fort Wagner but ultimately failed. Despite their failure to seize the fortress, their willingness to sacrifice their lives en masse began a transformation of the image of the black soldier that was to continue through the entire course of the war.[81] With the regiment's casualties amounting to almost one-half of its soldiers, it paid a frightful price to earn "his full right to manhood," as one historian described it.[82] Edgar Dinsmore wrote Carrie Drayton, with whom he was not previously acquainted, letters from Morris Island, South Carolina, in 1864, proudly stating that victory is close at hand. He beamed when describing his own role: "I was one of the first of the despised race to leave the free North with rifle on my shoulder and give the lie to the old story that the black man will not fight."[83]

The men of the 54th and 55th Massachusetts, however, paid a psychic cost even prior to their battlefield sacrifices. The men who would soon become martyrs and heroes, had only weeks before, been humiliated by the discriminatory pay they were offered. As free blacks from the North they had been recruited with the promise that they would be paid at the rate volunteers were. Instead, they were paid at a rate considerably below that of the white volunteers. On principle they refused to accept the paychecks, going over four months without pay. On seven occasions they were lined up to receive their pay but refused on principle to accept it. Most of the families of the men suffered from their lack of income, more than one having to turn to the almshouse for relief.[84] Later, when in an effort to quell the controversy Governor Andrews of Massachusetts offered to make up the difference in pay, they rejected that effort on principle. Adding to their anger, one white officer berated them, declaring, "You must remember you have not proved yourselves soldiers. You must take notice that the Government has virtually paid you a thousand dollars apiece for setting you free," apparently not knowing that they had been free prior to the war. He angered them by stating that "any one listening to your shouting and singing can see how grotesquely ignorant you are."[85]

Even more demoralizing for these black soldiers were events on the home front. On Monday, 13 July 1863, the New York Draft Riots exploded in a frenzied attack on African Americans, particularly males. By evening, rioters had set the Colored Orphan Asylum afire, with its residents narrowly escaping death. Black males especially were sought out by the rioters for attack, as they blamed them for the horrible and seemingly endless specter of war they were confronted with.[86] On the first day of the riot William Jones was lynched and hanged, and his corpse was set afire.[87] Black shoemaker James Costello got off one shot before a white mob pummeled him, tortured him, and then hanged him.[88]

Immediately prior to their historic assault on Fort Wagner, the men of the 54th Massachusetts learned of the massive antiblack riots sweeping New York City. Sergeant Robert J. Simmons' home was burned in New York City by rioters three days before the assault, and his 17-year-old nephew was slain during the riot. Simmons was wounded and then captured by the Confederates. He died only weeks later in a jail cell in Charleston, South Carolina, and was later cited for his exceptional bravery.[89]   Lieutenant Colonel Edward N. Hallowell, who reached the parapet of Fort Wagner, later wrote in his account of the battle:

Yes, the colored troops fought well. That is not the most that may be said for men . . . It is all very well of course to praise the bravery of these men as soldiers, but with what words may we express our admiration of the dignity, self-respect, self-control, they showed in their conduct as men as well as soldiers in the matter of pay? They were promised the same pay, and, in general, the same treatment, as white soldiers. No one expected the same treatment in the sense of courtesy, but every one believed a great nation would keep faith with its soldiers in the beggarly matter of pay. They were promised thirteen dollars per month. They were insulted with an offer of seven dollars.[90]

The battle for Fort Wagner was perhaps the pivotal event in the changing northern white opinion as to the wisdom of relying on black troop, and, as such, was an event of signal importance to the history of the black male image.[91]

At Port Hudson on 26 May 1863, similar scenes of sacrifice and heroism occurred as thousands of brave soldiers charged repeatedly against withering Confederate gunfire. The charismatic Captain Andre Callioux died with the flag in his hands.[92] His inspired leadership drove the men under him to risks they would not have otherwise taken. The athletic Callioux's death in battle resulted in a massive funeral in New Orleans and moved William Wells Brown to write of Callioux and the black troops at Port Hudson that, "the self-forgetfulness, the undaunted heroism, and the great endurance of the negro, as exhibited that day, created a new chapter in American history for the colored man." Unfortunately, Callioux, whose heroic acts were carried out while his wounded left arm hung uselessly at his side, was undermined by incompetent leadership. Brigadier General William Dwight, Jr., a hard drinking man, had earlier written his mother of the "experiment" he was conducting with black troops. For Dwight, who was reportedly drunk on the day of the Port Hudson battle, this was test of whether black troops would stay and fight or run away. Not bothering to carefully reconnoiter the area, Dwight also refused to allow his troops to surrender once it was clear that they were being cut to shreds by the withering Confederate fire. Dwight ordered the African Americans to "keep charging as long as there is a corporal's guard left." "When there is only one man left, let him come to me and report," he said.[93]

Despite often being led into battle with only a few days training, African American soldiers were often motivated by very personal concerns. Private Spotswood Rice wrote to his children in order to assure them of his determination to rescue them from his former slave owners. Soon, he wrote, some 800 white and 800 black Union soldiers were going to converge on his old plantation. This would lead to their rescue, he assured them. He wrote that the slave mistress accused him of trying to "steal" his children. Rice wrote, however, that soon he would "let her know that god never intended for a man to steal his own flesh and blood." He wrote that he once "had some respect for them but now my respects is worn out and have no sympathy for Slaveholders." He questioned the slave mistress' brand of Christianity, comparing it to the Devil's in Hell. "You tell her from me that She is the frist [sic] Christian that I ever heard say that a man could Steal his own child especially out of human bondage." He ended his letter with, "Oh! My Dear children how I do want to see you."[94] On the same day, Rice penned an angry letter to Kitty Diggs, the slave mistress, threatening her for holding his children, telling her to expect no mercy when he came with the troops to rescue his children. In other cases, enslaved spouses described their struggle to leave the plantation in letters to their soldier husbands; in one incident the slave master angrily rejected offers of money for a wife's release.[95]

Confederate troops, however, doubly angry at the black soldier, disregarded the established, time-honored international rules of warfare in their treatment of black prisoners. At a battle at Marks Mill, Arkansas, described by an observer as "sickening to behold," a massacre of black soldiers who had surrendered took place. These atrocities were repeated again and again, as the Confederate troops made clear their disrespect for both black troops and the norms of warfare.[96] The civilian black population spoke out against these mounting atrocities and violations of the rules of international warfare, many urging a policy of an "eye-for-an-eye." Frederick Douglass criticized Lincoln for not speaking on this issue early on. When Lincoln finally did, in July 1863, he termed the southern policies "a relapse into barbarism" and established a policy of executing a Confederate prisoner for each Union soldier killed in violation of the rules of international warfare. Similarly, for every captured Union soldier placed at hard labor, the North would commit a Confederate soldier to hard labor.[97]

This policy did not prevent the Fort Pillow, Tennessee, massacre from occurring on 12 April 1864. Following their surrender, approximately 300 black Union soldiers were massacred. The commander of the southern forces was General Nathan Bedford Forrest, who said the wholesale killing signified that "negro soldiers cannot cope with Southerners."[98] Later, a similar atrocity occurred in Petersburg and at the Battle of Poison Spring where men of the First Kansas Colored Regiment were taken prisoner and summarily executed.[99] William Wells Brown, a former recruiter, was so upset at the treatment of black soldiers that he stated: "Our people have been so cheated, robbed, deceived, and outraged everywhere, that I cannot urge them to go," citing "an imbecile administration" as the reason.[100]

The massacres of black prisoners by Confederate forces served to spur on blacks in the Union army to fight even harder. Many of them vowed to treat their Confederate prisoners in a similar manner, while "Remember Fort Pillow" became an energizing slogan. From the point of view of the white South, the North had committed the vilest treachery conceivable in employing black ex-slaves as soldiers against them. Those whom they sincerely regarded as their property and whom they claimed lacked the character and capacity to make good soldiers were trained and armed against them. They also reasoned that since black males were "spoiled" forever, being unfit to be slaves, atrocities were justified.[101] Officially, the Confederacy regarded black soldiers as "slaves in arms" who, whether officers or not, did not enjoy the internationally accepted protection accorded prisoners of war. In practice, some black prisoners of war were executed, others were given to state authorities, and others were put to work at hard labor. Some were also sold as slaves; however, the majority were imprisoned and used as laborers. The South refused to exchange black prisoners, since they regarded them as property belonging to Confederate citizens.

Black males played important roles in the Civil War as spies for the North. General McClellan relied heavily on black intelligence for information on Confederate positions. After the arrival of Jefferson Davis' coachman, William A. Jackson, at the Fredericksburg camp, considerable attention was focused on him. Thirty-one years old, Jackson provided Union army officers with abundant information. He reported on the strained and difficult conversations that Jefferson Davis had with a Confederate general concerning the retreat from Manassas and described Davis' panic upon learning of a military setback and of contingency plans to evacuate the Confederate capital of Richmond, Virginia.[102] Nathaniel Evans gave the Union army brain trust invaluable information on the besieged capital of the Confederacy, Richmond, Virginia. Most importantly, he described the earthworks and fortifications with sufficient detail as to be useful to Union generals. Union success in innumerable battles, including the "great battle of the West," Chickamauga, was paved by the knowledge local blacks gave them of roads, terrain, and strategic sites.[103] George Scott, another escapee, provided information that led to the Battle at Big Bethel.[104] Black males, as well as females, including Harriet Tubman, often played key roles as scouts and spies. "Uncle Jim" Williams, escaped from slavery and joined the 95th Illinois and later directed Union troops to his former plantation home in Carroll Parish, Louisiana, and resulting in the defeat of a body of 250 Confederate troops.[105]

Only on rare occasion did slaves have the opportunity to exact vengeance or retribution from the slave masters. Some black troops were reported to survey an area's slaves as to who was the most disagreeable overseer in the vicinity. When they apprehended him they would strap him on a horse backward, before taking him to their superiors. Occasionally slave masters and overseers were whipped and the "Big House" looted and wrecked.[106] Union army chaplain Henry McNeal Turner witnessed such an action highlighted by a black soldier's blow to the mouth of the slave master. Turner recalled, that "When the rich owners would use insulting language we let fire do its work of destruction. A few hours only are necessary to turn what costs years of toil into smoke and ashes."[107]

As many of the soon-to-be-victorious black troops passed the areas where only three or four years before they had labored as slaves, they must have savored this progress. One letter from the field reported that recently escaped slaves then in the employ of the federal government requested permission for a leave of absence to attempt to rescue their families and wives being held in slavery. The commander was unable to offer them boats but offered 15 soldiers to aid their bold endeavor. The attempt when awry, however, when they met larger irregular and regular Confederate forces than expected, scattering the blacks and leading to a number of deaths. On another occasion, black soldiers encountered a well-known slave owner in Virginia and had the opportunity to physically discipline him before an appreciative black slave audience. One William Harris bloodied his former slave owner with two dozen lashes from a whip. When he finished, he handed his whip to an African American woman who, upon finishing, gave it to another.[108]

Occasionally, in a small world, blacks experienced joys they never dreamed of during the military conflict. In Wilmington, North Carolina, a black woman in the crowd watching the victorious troops march through town saw her own son. She caught the man, who knew only that his mother was living when he entered the service, and hugged him madly.[109]

Chaplain Garland H. White of the 28th U. S. Colored Infantry had undreamed-of pleasure on 12 April 1865 after he entered the devastated former Confederate capital, Richmond. Early in the day White made a speech to a massive crowd of freed African Americans, who exulted over their victory. Then, the slave pens, holding cells for blacks convicted of no crime but that of being enslaved, were broken open, and the liberated people poured out, praising God. So intense were the emotions by the collective throng of African Americans that White wrote, "[I] n this mighty consternation I became so overcome with tears that I could not stand up under the pressure of such fullness of joy in my own heart," and he had to rest for a period. Later, as he moved down Broad Street to the army camp, a woman approached him and, after pumping him with questions, announced, "This is your mother, Garland, whom you are now talking to, who has spent twenty years of grief about her son."[110] "I cannot express the joy I felt at this happy meeting of my mother and other friends," Garland wrote. Through the celebration's giddiness, however, White complained that some "people do not seem to believe that the colored troops were the first that entered Richmond." He stated that these soldiers were with the Army of the James "I was with them, and am still with them." [111]

As Frederick Douglass had hoped at the outset of the war, black males often experienced enormous personal development as a result of their participation in the war. The social mobility of these soldiers, if they survived— for one in three died as a result of participation in the conflict—was dramatic. From slaves who were not legally entitled to any ownership, in a few short years they had the opportunity to purchase property, some freedom of movement, and other opportunities. The bounty that was promised was one of the primary means by which, following the war, they could realize dreams that had been completely unforeseen earlier.

One middle-aged sergeant in a black Louisiana regiment said that as a slave back on the plantation he had felt himself to be an old man. But now in his new Union army uniform he felt young and full of energy for the "cause."[112] Corporal Thomas Long felt that if black men had not become soldiers en masse, freedom would have been insecure and might have slipped out of their grasp. In addition, there was the threat that their children would say, "Your fader never fought for he own freedom." Pounding the table for emphasis, he stressed that no one could utter such a statement any more.[113]

Black aspirations generally and those of the male particularly were fired by the victory of emancipation and the participation of black men in the Civil War.

While still not highly esteemed by the great masses of white Americans, the overall image of the black male improved significantly as a result of his role in the northern victory. The still-powerful "Sambo" image was briefly negated and replaced by one of heroism, bravery, and ability. Genuine heroes, such as South Carolina's Robert Smalls, as well as a new class of leaders emerged from the Civil War, and this image of a tested and victorious U. S. soldier represented a marked advance over that of the docile and ignorant slave. Many felt that they had attained a true sense of "manhood" on the battlefield. As they demobilized and returned to civilian life, thousands of black soldiers shared a desire to maintain this status and carve out a stable, prosperous existence as free workers in a democratic society. They had high expectations for themselves, their families, and their society. They were fully prepared to invest their energy, emotions, resources, and hopes in the effort to construct a wholesome black community in America.

NOTES

1. W.E.B. Du Bois, *Black Reconstruction in America* (New York: Atheneum, 1983).

2. James M. McPherson, *The Negro's Civil War: How American Blacks Felt and Acted during the War for the Union* (New York: Ballantine Books, 1991), 12; Ira Berlin, Barbara J. Fields, Thavolia Glymph, Joseph P. Reidy, and Leslie S. Rowland (eds.), *Freedom: A Documentary History of Emancipation, 1861—1867* (Cambridge: Cambridge University Press, 1985), 4.

3. Phillip S. Foner (ed.), *The Life and Writings of Frederick Douglass* (New York: International Publishers, 1952), 13.

4. McPherson, *The Negro's Civil War*, 17.

5. Bruce Catton, *This Hallowed Ground: The Story of the Union Side of the Civil War* (New York: Pocket Books, 1961), 51.

6. Abraham Lincoln, *Second Inaugural Address* Saturday, 4 March 1865 (University of Kansas, Department of History).

7. Mary Beth Norton et al., *A People and a Nation: A History of the United States* (Boston: Houghton Mifflin, 1990), 403.

8. Willie Lee Rose, *Rehearsal for Reconstruction: The Port Royal Experiment* (New York: Oxford University Press, 1962), 14.

9. Norton, *A People & a Nation*, 403; Joel Williamson, *After Slavery: The Negro in South Carolina during Reconstruction, 1861–1877.* (Hanover, NH: University Press of New England, 1965), 5.

10. Rose, *Rehearsal*, 12.

11. Foner, *The Life and Writings of Frederick Douglass*, 13; Edward A. Miller, Jr., *Gullah Statesman: Robert Smalls from Slavery to Congress, 1839–1915* (Columbia: University of South Carolina Press, 1995), 1–3.

12. Foner, *The Life and Writings of Frederick Douglass*, 15.

13. W. J. Moses, *The Golden Age of Black Nationalism, 1850–1925* (New York: Oxford University Press, 1978), 52.

14. McPherson, *The Negro's Civil War*, 19.

15. Ibid., 20.

16. Ibid., 22.

17. Ibid., 29.

18. Kenneth L Kusmer, *A Ghetto Takes Shape: Black Cleveland, 1870–1930*

(Chicago: University of Illinois Press, 1976) 25–26.

19. McPherson, *The Negro's Civil War*, 166.

20. Ibid., 165.

21. Ibid., 165.

22. Ibid., 164.

23. Rose, *Rehearsal*, 15.

24. Ibid., 19.

25. Ibid., 31.

26. Ibid., 129.

27. Benjamin Quarles, *The Negro in the Civil War* (Boston: Little, Brown, 1969), 320.

28. William Wells Brown, *The Negro in the American Rebellion: His Heroism and His Fidelity* (New York: Citadel Press, 1971), 100-01.

29. Ibid., 101.

30. Ibid., 102.

31. Ibid., 102–03.

32. Ibid., 106.

33. Leon F. Litwack, *Been in the Storm So Long* (New York: Vintage Books, 1980), 51; Willamson, *After Slavery*, 7.

34. Rose, *Rehearsal*, 144–46; Williamson, *After Slavery*, 14.

35. Rose, *Rehearsal*, 150.

36. Ibid., 192–94; Williamson, *After Slavery*, 7.

37. McPherson, *The Negro's Civil War*, 171.

38. Litwack, *Been in the Storm*, 76.

39. Ibid., 77.

40. Ibid., 78.

41. Ibid., 77.

42. McPherson, *The Negro's Civil War*, 181.

43. Roger Lane, *Roots of Violence in Black Philadelphia, 1860–1900* (Cambridge: Harvard University Press, 1986), 20; Litwack, *Been in the Storm*, 70.

44. McPherson, *The Negro's Civil War*, 181.

45. Ibid., 197–98.

46. B. Kevin Bennett, "The Jacksonville Mutiny," *Civil War History* 38, no. 1 (March1992), 40–50.

47. Litwack, *Been in the Storm*, 80.

48. McPherson, *The Negro's Civil War*, 200.

49. Litwack, *Been in the Storm*, 80.

50. Ibid., 80.

51. Ibid., 80–81.

52. Ibid., 83.

53. McPherson, *The Negro's Civil War*, 206.

54. Litwack, *Been in the Storm*, 85.

55. Ibid., 97.

56. Booker T. Washington, *The Story of the Negro: The Rise of the Race from Slavery* (New York: Negro Universities Press, 1969), 5.

57. McPherson, *The Negro's Civil War*, 39; Berlin et al., *Freedom*, 4–5.

58. Quarles, *The Negro*, 47; see also Winthrop Jordan, *Tumult and Silence at Second Creek: An Inquiry into a Civil War Slave Conspiracy.* (Baton Rouge: Louisiana State University Press, 1993).

59. Quarles, *The Negro*, 47.

60. Litwack, *Been in the Storm*, 57.

61. Ibid, 57; see, for example, Berlin et al., *Freedom*, 60.

62. Vernon Lane Wharton, *The Negro in Mississippi, 1865–1890* (New York: Harper and Row, 1965), 18; see also James L. Roark, *Masters without Slaves: Southern Planters in the Civil War and Reconstruction* (New York: W. W. Norton, 1977).

63. "Louisiana Planters to the Commander of the Department of the Gulf Terrebonne Parish, Louisiana, January 14th 1862," *The Black Military Experience*, 532–34. (http://www.coax.net/people/lwf/default.htm), "North Carolina Slaveholder to the Commander of the Department of North Carolina," 8 October 1862, in Berlin et al., *Freedom*, 86; see also John W. Blassingame, *Slave Testimony: Two Centuries of Letters, Speeches, Interviews, and Autobiographies* (Baton Rouge: Louisiana State University Press, 1977), 449–50.

64. "Louisiana Planters," n.p.

65. Wharton, *The Negro*, 17.

66. Litwack, *Been in the Storm*, 61; see also Jordan, *Tumult and Silence at Second Creek*.

67. Litwack, *Been in the Storm*, 46–47.

68. Ibid., 47.

69. Ibid., 51.

70. Ibid., 56; "Testimony by a Corporal in a Louisiana Black Regiment before the American Freedmen's Inquiry Commission," in Berlin et al., *Freedom*, 217.

71. Litwack, *Been in the Storm*, 56.

72. McPherson, *The Negro's Civil War*, 60–61.

73. Litwack, *Been in the Storm*, 100.

74. Ibid., 101.

75. McPherson, *The Negro's Civil War*, 195.

76. Ibid., 194–95.

77. Litwack, *Been in the Storm*, 69.

78. Ibid., 69.

79. Williamson, *After Slavery*, 21.

80. Noah Andre Trudeau, *Like Men of War: Black Troops in the Civil War, 1862–1865* (New York: Little, Brown, 1998), 63; Rose, *Rehearsal*, 255.

81. Ibid., 255–57.

82. Ibid., 258.

83. "Edgar Dinsmore Letters," *Journal of Negro History* 25, no. 3 (July 1940): 363–71.

84. Norwood P. Hallowell, *The Negro as a Soldier in the War of the Rebellion* (Boston: Little, Brown, 1897), 17.

85. Rose, *Rehearsal*, 261–62.

86. Iver Bernstein, *The New York City Draft Riots: Their Significance for American Society and Politics in the Age of the Civil War* (New York: Oxford University Press, 1990), 21.

87. Ibid., 27.

88. Ibid., 29.

89. Edwin S. Redkey (ed.), *A Grand Army of Black Men: Letters from African-American Soldiers in the Union Army, 1861–1865* (Cambridge: Cambridge University Press, 1992), 28.

90. Hallowell, *The Negro*, 16–17.

91. Williamson, *After Slavery*, 20.

92. Joseph T. Wilson, *The Black Phalanx* (Hartford CT: American, 1892).

93. Brown, *The Negro,* 172; Trudeau, *Like Men of War*, 43.

94. Spotswood Rice, "Spotswood Rice to My Children," 3 September 1864, in F. W. Diggs to General Rosecrans, 10 September 1864, D-296 1864, Letters Received, ser. 2593, Department of the MO, U.S. Army Continental Commands, Record Group 393 Pt. 1, National Archives.

95. Spotswood Rice, "Spotswood Rice to Kittey Diggs," 3 September 1864, in F. W. Diggs to General Rosecrans, 10 Sept. 1864, D-296 1864, Letters Received, ser. 2593, Department of the MO, U.S. Army Continental Commands, Record Group 393 Pt. 1, National Archives; Blassingame; *Slave Testimony* 119.

96. Litwack, *Been in the Storm*, 89.

97. Ibid., 90.

98. Ibid., 91. See also Anne J. Bailey, "A Texas Cavalry Raid: Reaction to Black Soldiers and Contrabands," *Civil War History* 35, no. 2 (June 1989): 138–152.

99. Litwack, *Been in the Storm*, 92.

100. Ibid., 91–92.

101. Ibid., 88.

102. Quarles, *The Negro*, 81–82.

103. Ibid., 83.

104. Ibid., 79.

105. Ibid., 84.

106. Litwack, *Been in the Storm*, 94.

107. Ibid., 95.

108. "Commander of a Black Brigade to the Commander of the District of Eastern Virginia," 1 September 1864, in Berlin et al., *Freedom*, 98–99; Litwack, *Been in the Storm*, 65.

109. Redkey, *A Grand Army*, 167.

110. Ibid., 177.

111. Ibid., 178.

112. McPherson, *The Negro's Civil War*, 191–92.

113. Ibid., 217.

Chapter 5

African American Males and the Challenge of Emancipation, 1865–1895

A million of men using proper efforts cannot be overlooked in a nation like this, and as American Slavery is to be abolished as the friends of freedom shortly hope, and its enemies fear, then our population will be sufficiently great to set at defiance every attempt to crowd us out of respectable employment, and to compel those who would succeed in business to court our patronage.

—George S. Massey, Sergeant-Major,
43d U.S. Colored Infantry, March 1865[1]

The Reverend Henry McNeal Turner grabbed anxiously at the paper only to have a young man snatch the first sheet before he was able to. The second sheet was torn to bits by several of the outstretched hands of the crowd in front of the *Washington Evening Star*. Turner successfully outfought the others for the third and then battled his way out of the pressing crowd and made his way down Pennsylvania Avenue. With this copy of the Emancipation Proclamation in hand, he was soon swallowed up by an enthusiastic mob near the White House and lifted up and carried to a platform. He began reading the document before the animated mass, and soon President Abraham Lincoln appeared at a window in the White House and bowed for the crowd while celebratory cannon blasts were heard in the distance.[2] Across the river in one of the Washington, D.C.'s, "contraband" camps of escaped slaves, George Payne, a former Virginia bondsman, said that, the "Lord has heard" the black "groans" and "has come down to deliver!"[3]

While Richmond, the capital of the Confederacy, featured exuberant celebrations by African Americans, these were tame compared to what might have been had the black troops been allowed to enter the city first. Later, many African Americans would criticize the decision forcing them to wait on the outskirts and allow white troops to reap the credit as liberators. Despite this refusal to allow the African American soldier to occupy center stage in a struggle in which he had played such a critical role and that meant everything to him, it was a moment of unprecedented happiness and celebration among a people that had known little else than bondage and the struggle against it since being brought to America. Africans in America had never known such collective joy, and little could dampen this moment. The slave jails where innocent blacks awaited resale to the highest bidder, the slave auctions where families had been routinely shattered for centuries, and the slave owners, slave traders, and slave drivers who profited from systematic black degradation were all instantly made relics of the past. At Lumpkin's Jail, where Robert Lumpkin deposited his slaves for sale, a crowd of blacks gathered. As its inmates surged out of their cells, they heard the improvised chant:

> Slavery chain done broke at last!
> Broke at last! Broke at last!
> Slavery chain done broke at last!
> Gonna praise God till I die! [4]

As the cells were opened by black soldiers, its inmates poured out, continuing to give thanks for their abrupt change in fortune.

Lieutenant Colonel A. G. Bennett, 21st U.S. Colored Troops, had the honor of personally demanding that the mayor of Charleston, South Carolina, surrender. Black troops of both Bennett's unit and the 54th Massachusetts then entered the city victoriously. There were also elements of the former Third and Fourth South Carolina regiments, many of whom had been slaves in this very area. Later, another black unit, the Massachusetts 55th penetrated the city borders.[5] The arrival of Major Martin R. Delany, the veteran black nationalist, was cause for considerable excitement among the African Americans in the city. Never had such a prominent role been played by a black man, legally, in South Carolina. African Americans greeted Delany with a huge rally at the Zion Church and later a massive parade featuring rows of black clergymen, children, fishermen, teamsters, coopers, bakers, blacksmiths, and members of other trades—all celebrating black emancipation.[6] This seemed like a truly revolutionary change for black South Carolinians, empowering them to a new outlook on their ideals, aspirations, and actions.

Some 68,178 African American men were dead or missing in the wake of the Civil War, amounting to one of three of those who had served.[7] Black people had won their freedom from slavery, but it remained for them to win equal rights and social justice. With the leap forward from the status of chattel property, they set about doing the many things denied to them. Now their underground meetings, before held in the obscure bush or swamps, were held in the open. These meetings could now be larger, now that they were not hampered by the constant surveillance of the slave patrols and the restrictions on movement. Now firearms could be acquired; dogs and other animals could be owned; property could be legally possessed; and marriages could be legalized. Black women now were able to wear their finest clothes in the towns and cities—offending the sensibilities of whites who considered them as "playing the lady," which would soon become de facto crime for black women and, indirectly, for their men.[8]

Reconstruction of the lives of black men and women during the postwar period began with a profound sense of optimism and confidence. The steady increase in social consciousness, spurred, in part, by the pivotal role played by black males during the Civil War and the other upheavals; the migratory movements; the disruption of the antebellum routine; and displacement of the old slave elite stimulated consciousness and collective self-confidence. Yet, African Americans faced the hard realities that the white North only grudgingly accepted the view that emancipation was a desirable measure, that pervasive and deeply rooted racial biases against blacks remained despite a temporary surge in liberal sentiment, that an economy built on slavery would be a challenge to transform into one of a more humane orientation, and that their former adversaries, slaveholders, their staffs, and the institution's sundry defenders, temporarily weak and demoralized, were determined not only to prevent black progress but also to resume their ability to earn money by means of unfree black labor. This chapter traces the transformation of the black male slave into the free black hamstrung by economic, social, and political webs fashioned largely by the former slave elite in order to replicate the antebellum social order.

THE POSTWAR SOUTH: POLITICAL, ECONOMIC, AND SOCIAL CONDITIONS

The black celebrations of the victory of emancipation sent a cold chill through the bones of white southerners. The decision of poor and working-class whites to "cling frantically" to the former slave masters helped constrict the choices for black people.[9] They aspired not to create a democratic and egalitarian South but rather to occupy the roles and replicate the prestige of the planters who controlled African Americans. The prospect of actually competing with the former slaves was the nightmare of the poor and working-class whites. After all, the "dreaded" specter of social equality would likely mean that a significant portion, if not the majority, of African Americans would soon be accorded more social status and enjoy more material prosperity and political power than they. Their acceptance of the hegemonic racial myths of black inferiority made the prospect of equality in any form repugnant. For this reason they came to form the storm troops of the southern resistance against efforts aimed at racial equality mounted by blacks. W.E.B. Du Bois estimated that not one in ten whites supported the notion of black equality, emancipation, or any serious attempt to rein in the white South.[10]

Unfortunately, a key condition for the dramatic transformation of the prewar social system of the South was the existence of an influential force of northern whites sympathetic to their cause. But, by the mid-1870s, the wave of racial liberalism that peaked during the Civil War was largely a thing of the past, as Horace Greeley could declare: "I was, in the days of slavery, an enemy of slavery, because I thought slavery inconsistent with the rights, the dignity, the highest well-being of free labor. That might have been a mistake."[11] The vacillation of former northern liberals, the leadership of President Andrew

Johnson, and the unreformed and embittered southern whites mitigated against the likelihood of a peaceful solution to the question of the postwar social order. In Natchez, Mississippi, a newspaper wrote: "The true station of the negro is that of a servant. The wants and state of our country demand that he should remain a servant."[12] The key to achieving this was, for the planters, to maintain control and ownership of the most important agricultural land.[13] This meant that blacks would have to remain shut out from opportunities to acquire ownership of significant amounts of land.

The antebellum, pro-slavery views of southerners were transformed in accordance with the altered political economy of the postbellum South. Their outlook, the perspective of those who esteemed themselves as the region's "natural leaders," was heavily impacted by the events immediately following the war. The assassination of President Abraham Lincoln and the accession to the presidency of Andrew Johnson had an impact that is difficult to estimate. Johnson's legacy, however, was marked by his consistent pattern of actions counter to black interests.

The presidency of Andrew Johnson proved to be an important early source of comfort and support for the crushed slaveocracy of the South. The ease with which southern land barons gained pardons provided an early boost to their confidence that they could succeed in reconstructing southern society to closely resemble that of the antebellum period. The mass of rank-and-file Confederate southerners who joined the rebel army or supported it were required only to pledge allegiance in order to gain a pardon and fully restore their American citizenship. The leaders of the rebellion, those who played key roles by holding high offices and military positions, some of whom had resigned from the U.S. Army to become Confederate officers, were merely paroled and allowed to go where they wished. There were no massive jailings, no trials or executions. While one Confederate officer was arrested and tried and executed, his offenses were "war crimes," not treason. General Robert E. Lee left the war a heroic figure in the eyes of millions of Americans and, following his surrender at Appomattox, rode to his home and lived out his remaining years at peace. Jefferson Davis, the president of the Confederacy, was imprisoned for two years. Only the temporary political disfranchisement of the Confederate leaders was endured by them, aside from a few who suffered property losses. The myth of the "brutality" inflicted upon the white South in the postbellum period stemmed from the reality that they suffered the loss of their human property, black slaves, the military occupation, and the gross exaggeration of the political disabilities imposed upon them.[14]

In his message accompanying his veto of the Civil Rights Bill of 1866, President Andrew Johnson registered his objection to the proposed citizenship of African Americans complaining that the measure discriminated against "large numbers of intelligent, worthy, and patriotic foreigners, and in favor of the negro."[15] Johnson also raised, in this connection, the "revolting" specter of black–white intermarriage, which was, in his opinion, just one of the dire consequences of such legislation.[16] He concluded that the bill constituted discrimination against whites, as it established "for the security of the colored race safeguards which go infinitely beyond any that the General Government has ever provided for the white race."[17]

Fused to the generally low opinion of black capacity was an active hostility toward the entire spectrum of black aspiration. The defeated whites, with destruction and embittered amputees surrounding them, with blacks seemingly more "impudent," "uppity," and "insolent" than ever before, focused their anger on these blacks. Their determination and anger ran headlong against the brimming optimism and aspirations held by African Americans. Samuel Thomas, an assistant commissioner of the Bureau of Refugees, Freedmen and Abandoned Lands, felt that that "whites esteem the blacks [as] their property by natural right."[18] He noted that the white southerners "boast that when they get freedmen affairs in their own hands, 'the niggers will catch hell.'" [19]

THE STRUGGLE TO ACQUIRE LAND IN THE POSTBELLUM SOUTH

The black soldiers were termed by one observer "apostles of black equality" for their efforts to defend black rights during the immediate postwar period.[20] Empowered by their common experiences of enslavement and redemption through the armed struggle against the South, many had educated themselves. During a period of experimentation and moving about, the black soldiers helped to spread a gospel of land acquisition and political rights in the areas they traveled. They helped build many nascent African American institutions, such as schools, churches, and orphanages, while helping mobilize blacks for political involvement through the initiation of political clubs and societies.[21] Many individual soldiers purchased land for themselves by means of the bounty and savings derived from participation in the Civil War. Their political influence helped to spread this fever for land acquisition among blacks. The recognition that independence, one of the most cherished values of black males emerging from servitude, was of critical importance to their overall personal and collective development made it, even more than other forms of material acquisition, the most important black masculine value. The former slave owners themselves, from the opposite perspective, seeking to continue to earn substantial profits from a command of black labor, sought to prevent black land acquisition in order to maintain control over masses of black males and, through them, entire families.

Indeed, the returning black soldiers themselves had to immediately struggle to keep from being entrapped in a slavery-like situation. The head of the Louisiana Freedmen's Bureau in 1865 refused to provide aid to evicted families of black soldiers if the soldier failed to sign a contract to labor for the plantation owner in a timely fashion. Near Port Hudson, ex-slaveholders evicted newly emancipated black women and children, leaving them starving on a levee for a week, yet the Freedmen's Bureau refused to intervene, placing more pressure on the black soldiers to contract with men whom, only months before, they had defeated on the battlefield.[22]

There is ample evidence of a short period during which the image of the black male was at a historic high point due to his performance in the Civil War. For example, an 1864 report to the Secretary of War, Edwin M. Stanton, read:

It is hardly necessary for me to speak of the character of the colored man as a soldier, as presented here in the Valley of the Mississippi. The universal official attestation to his soldierly bearing and true valor under the severest trials, has put that beyond question. Nor are his sobriety, orderliness, and willing submission to discipline, less conspicuous.[23]

Soon, however, many of the returning soldiers would be embroiled in the everyday disputes that were to decide the future status of African Americans in the South.[24]

The high energy that the returning black male soldiers brought to their communities encouraged a willingness to protest and sacrifice for the cause of equally accessible services for blacks. For example, with initiation of horse-drawn railway service on the streets of Savannah, Georgia, in January 1869, a policy of segregation was instituted. Separate black cars, running one-third as frequent as the white, were provided by the municipal authorities. In May 1870 James Habersham, an activist and constable of a militia district, refused to leave a white streetcar and was arrested.[25] Thousands of similar incidents marked the phase of popular black mobilization during the first years following the Civil War.[26] Land was the key prize of the battles during this period, as the extent to which former slaves could obtain signficant amounts of land would largely determine whether, during the decades to come, they would constitute a budding yeoman farmer sector or a landless agricultural mass mired in tenancy and peonage.

Countering these aspirations, George Fitzhugh contended that without close tutelage, the black race would die out in the foreseeable future. He advocated the establishment of a "Black Code," including a number of "severe" laws to "compel" blacks to work for planters.[27] Planters remained absolutely convinced that the constant threat of the lash during the work process was a necessity.[28] This was tied to a strategy of keeping blacks landless—a valuable lesson they learned from the history of slavery's abolition in the Caribbean.[29] If the freed slaves succeeded in acquiring ample amounts of land, it would then be especially difficult to force them to work on the plantations. In Mississippi the thoroughness of the measures to prevent black acquisition of land was shown by the laws prohibiting the renting or leasing of lands during this period.[30] In addition, at public gatherings the planters jointly vowed never to sell or lease lands to blacks.[31] The Black Code's vagrancy law amendments in Mississippi stipulated that "all freedmen, free negroes and mulattoes in this State" over 18 who had "no lawful employment or business, or found unlawfully assembling themselves together, either in the day or night time, and all white persons assembling themselves with freedmen, free negroes or mulattoes, on terms of equality, or living in adultery or fornication with a free woman, free negro or mulatto, shall be deemed vagrants." The penalty was life imprisonment for the crime of racial intermarriage.[32] Especially damaging for black males and their families was the accusation of "indolence," directed specifically at those males who sought to earn a living outside of the prescribed plantation "hand" role. The trait of independence was regarded as "indolence," and this was generally regarded as a crime.[33] Social historian Kevin Gaines concluded that a distinct form of repressive violence awaited those black males who were able to maneuver through the minefield to own businesses, work as professionals, or somehow achieve financial independence. Men such as Arna Bontemps' father, a well-dressed, independent businessman, upset the delicate psychological balance of many whites. To avoid succumbing to the provocations of hostile whites, black males were forced to exercise a disciplined self-restraint. Often this was not sufficient to forestall the formation of a lynch mob. With often no hiatus in the effective coverage of slavery and the new Black Code, free black male economic activity was again proscribed. Again, one or more routine and normal acts of earning a living, satisfying a human need, or performing a routine activity were defined as crimes. Violence was closely associated with these "crimes"; indeed, the post–Civil War southern social structure rested as much on violence as did its predecessor.[34] Historian Leon Litwack stressed that to seek to achieve or accumulate wealth, or attain social prestige or any other effort to break out of the narrow and humiliating roles southern whites designed for blacks was tantamount to an insurrectionary act. Violence threatened any individual or group of blacks who crossed these lines, which surrounded every aspect of life. The active hostility of white society to the "uppity" educated black was hardly a secret during that era. Charles Holcombe's son was murdered after disagreeing over crop production figures with a white man. His illiterate father was not exposed to this risk, and the systematic cheating of him went uncontested, allowing "harmony" to prevail. In retrospect he realized that his son "had stepped outen his place when he got dat eddycation."[35]

In Mississippi a new law stipulated that after the second Monday in 1866, all blacks either must have signed contracts or must have a license for other work.[36] In addition, blacks were prohibited from possessing guns, ammunition, dirks, and bowie knives.[37] A further catchall clause in the measure hampering almost every conceivable black initiative stated that any black "committing riots, routes, affrays, trespasses, malicious mischief, cruel treatment to animals, seditious speeches, insulting gestures, language of acts, or assaults on any person, disturbance of the peace, exercising the function of a minister of the Gospel, without license" would be subject to a fine and a maximum prison term of 30 days.[38] In June 1870, however, the Reconstruction-era state legislature repealed these measures.[39]

The profitability of convict-leasing encouraged the criminalization of an ever-larger number of offenses. By 1876 thefts valued at more than ten dollars were deemed grand larceny punishable by imprisonment. Thus, the system aimed to foster a dependence of the black male laborer and, through him, the entire black population on the planters. If a black man exercised his rights and broke a contract, there would be no other employment opportunities. Without the contract, he was effectively a "criminal," and soon he would be imprisoned and forced to labor for the harshest plantation owners.[40] African American males, many only children, were arrested on a variety of charges, mostly bogus and petty, often in wholesale "sweeps," imprisoned, and then basically sold to cotton planters, railroad operators, road builders, and other employers. Those who purchased the laborers had little incentive to care about their health, much less provide adequate health care. Instead, they worked them harder than slaves had been worked, often starved them, and provided the worst shelter and clothing. Sky-high death rates followed, as in 1870, for example, 41 percent of Alabama convicts died.[41] For the black males involved in the convict-leasing system, the system meant a psychically and spiritually numbing return to slavery. A report by the U.S. commissioner of labor found that the inmates "worked to the utmost and [were] barbarously treated," resulting in an "appalling death rate."[42] While the prisoner mortality rate for the United States as a whole stood at 25 per 1,000, for those leased out in Texas plantations it was 49 per 1,000. Convicts leased to the timber camps in east Texas swamps suffered from a frightful mortality rate of 250 per 1,000.[43]

The criminalization of black men, in this instance through the convict-lease system, reaped tremendous profits for some people. The high mortality rate resulted from convicts being worked to their physical limit in a system Edward Ayers has described as "tailor-made for capitalists concerned only with making money fast."[44] By 1882 fully 43 percent of the male workers of the Pratt Coal and Iron Company were employed via the convict-lease system. Joseph E. Brown, a former Georgia governor, had a direct interest in black labor. His coal mines reached an agreement with the state for 300 "able-bodied" men, at the price of eight cents per day, for 20 years.[45]

For their part, African Americans sought to secure an equal and valued place in a biracial community. Having many personal, family, and community decisions to make and weighing several options, blacks unsurprisingly enjoyed a new sense of responsibility. In June 1865 Petersburg, Virginia blacks collectively stressed their understanding of emancipation as making it incumbent upon them to be industrious, not idle. Prior to this, blacks on the South Carolina Sea Islands had given ample proof to the skeptical that they would work hard without the compulsion of the whip.[46] Yet, in other parts of South Carolina, the exhilaration of emancipation, anger and resentment toward the ex-slave owners, and the need for continuing hard labor proved a volatile mixture, aggravating both land-hungry blacks and land-possessing whites. The manager of a plantation near Orangeburg, South Carolina, wrote of his labor troubles to his mother:

The poor negro, besotted with ignorance, & so full of freedom, looking forward to January as to some day of Jubilee approaching, . . . thinking only that freedom confers the privilege of going where & doing as they please, work when they wish, or stop if they feel disposed, & yet be fed, supported & cared for by his Master, lazy, trifling, impertinent! Mother, they are awful![47]

Beyond the racial perceptions of the planters, there were the sheer demands for labor discipline demanded by the plantation economy.[48] For the planters, the desire was to restore a social situation for blacks as closely resembling slavery as possible within the new order. For that to occur, blacks had to have little or no choice as to whom they would work for and what circumstances they would work under. They would need to lack physical and social mobility, lack political or social rights, be obligated to labor to the capacity that their physical being could endure, and face severe penalties for violating this new slavelike order. Hence, criminal penalties would need to be in place for labor disputes, violations of social etiquette, and attempts to exert political power.

Edmund Rhett, the South Carolina "fire-eater" who encouraged southern secession, and other leaders saw their opportunity to recast Southern society in a neoslave mold with the design of a new "Black Code." Rhett contended that the "general interest both of the white man and of the negroes requires that he should be kept as near to the condition of slavery as possible, and as far from the condition of the white man as is practicable." This was crucial, for "negroes must be made to work, or else cotton and rice must cease to be raised for export."[49] In fashioning the new code to regulate black life and labor, Rhett stipulated four key aspects that it should encompass: not allowing blacks to acquire ownership of land; requiring that African Americans have a fixed place of residence (under penalty of hard labor on a chain gang); regarding violations of contracts by laborers as criminal, and resulting in bonding the laborer to an employer; and giving employers power to whip laborers.[50] Not surprisingly, the black community of South Carolina was united in its denunciation of the legislation.[51]

Alabama's Hugh J. Davis Jr. summed up the feeling of the leading southern thinkers: "Negroes will not work for pay, the lash is all I feel that will make them."[52] In Mississippi, Governor Benjamin Humphreys summed up his sense of the crisis in the state's agricultural labor force. Prioritizing white supremacy and stressing the necessity of racial purity and for blacks to perform hard labor, Humphreys declared that "[t]o work is the law of God" and that "the cultivation of the great staples of the South require[s] continuous labor from January to January," and so blacks must be compelled to work. By this means not only blacks' happiness would be secured, but white homes would once again "become the abode of plenty."[53]

For the governor and the planters the first step in the return of "plenty" involved the restriction of black liberty. For the black male particularly, now officially "the head of household," for tax, political, and other legal purposes, this meant a serious infringement upon his rights. The initial measures of what were to be known as the "Black Code" provided for the apprenticing of black children without the consent of black parents. In addition, the measure stipulated that the former slave owner would enjoy an advantage in obtaining the "apprentice."[54]

The planters' desires ran headlong into those of the mass of freed slaves; whose desires seemed, at the superficial level, to confirm their views. A common attitude of those emerging from lives full of unrewarded, arduous, and involuntary labor, often supplemented by a constant lash from a whip, was expressed by one black South Carolinian: "I's want to be a free man, cum when I please, and nobody say nuffin to me, not order me roun'."[55] Black males, in particular, desired the physical mobility denied them during slavery. Yet, this was frequently frustrated by an opposing determination on the part of the planters, Freedmen's

Bureau agents, and others to force them to remain on the plantation, often with no choice of employers. Freedmen's Bureau agents often initiated or gave their blessing to roundups of black males in urban areas, who were labeled "idlers and vagrants" and shipped en masse to plantations.[56]

The fervent hopes of African Americans for land-ownership on which to establish stable, prosperous, and happy families received a boost by a June 1865 announcement by General Rufus Saxon, an opponent of slavery prior to the Civil War. Having already supervised the distribution of land to thousands of blacks under the field orders of General Sherman, Saxon announced that blacks would be provided with bureau-controlled land in 40-acre plots. In July the head of the Freedmen's Bureau, General O. O. Howard, issued Circular 13, providing for the setting aside of additional 40-acre plots for black families. However, the opposition, led by President Andrew Johnson, largely negated these measures. President Johnson's policy, reflected in the issuance of Circular 15 by the Freedmen's Bureau, restored the land of planters to whom Johnson was busily handing out generous pardons. In the end, blacks received almost none of the Bureau lands, as they generally reverted to their previous owners.[57]

When General Howard later toured the South Carolina Sea Islands and announced the new policy of returning the land to the former slave owners, it was poorly received. The pain and anger were visible when he advised the former slaves to "lay aside their bitter feelings, and to become reconciled to their old masters."[58] A committee formed on Edisto Island condemned the government for allying with its former enemy against them, which created "a more unpleasant condition" than slavery. One man explained that while "you only lost your right arm in war and might forgive them," the "man who tied me to a tree and gave me thirty-nine lashes and who stripped and flogged my mother and my sister and who will not let me stay in his empty hut" without laboring for him unconditionally was beyond any question of forgiveness.[59]

After Major General Daniel Sickles was named commander of the occupation forces in South Carolina, a massive restoration of the land to the former slave owners occurred through the insistence upon the possession of a signed warrant as proof of land-ownership for those who had obtained their land under the provisions of the Sherman grants. Later, Sickles ordered blacks in South Carolina to contract for the coming year with the planter on whose land they resided or to move. This measure was later enforced by soldiers who scoured the plantations and evicted those who disobeyed the order.[60]

The planters insisted upon the signing of long-term contracts with blacks, with Freedmen's Bureau agents supporting this effort.[61] Following President Johnson's directive to the Freedmen's Bureau to restore the lands of pardoned ex-slave-owning Confederates, the agency embarked upon a policy of encouraging, often coercing blacks to enter into long-term contracts with planters.[62] In Mississippi, for example, the bureau assistant commissioner compelled blacks to sign long-term contracts by threatening them with arrest.[63] Louisiana required that black males enter into contracts the first ten days of the year, committing them to labor for the entire year. Once signed, the black was forbidden to leave the plantation without permission during the term of the contract and a refusal to work would result in forced labor on public projects.[64] Blacks criticized this policy, which often involved deporting blacks from urban areas back to the countryside, maintaining that the insistence that all blacks enter contracts was blatantly discriminatory. In some places, black men refused to sign labor contracts and went as far as asserting their own ownership of the property.[65] Another tactic was tried by a group of blacks in Cherokee County, Alabama, who made a pact among themselves not to contract for less than two dollars a day during that season. The penalty for violation of this agreement, enforced by themselves, would be 50 lashes on the back.[66]

Coupled with the demand that black males sign long-term contracts were antienticement measures that forbade an employer to hire someone wh was still under contract to another employer. This meant that a black male who left employment before the end of his contract would be frozen out altogether and be vulnerable to the web of vagrancy laws. For the offenses of unemployment, whether through lack of decent job offers or from angering the employer, imprisonment and forced labor were the consequence.[67] This systematic practice severely impaired the ability of black males to take advantage of an emergent free market in labor by preventing them from selecting the employer who offered the most favorable terms.[68] This was in order to avoid a situation such as that in Mississippi, where the competition over the labor of blacks, planters complained, had reached intolerable levels. The wages of blacks rose with this competition, as many blacks had moved into the towns, draining them of their previous source of labor.[69]

In a large proportion of the South's sugar and cotton agricultural areas planters attempted to use the gang system of labor as was practiced during slavery. Generally contracting with a large group of black males as plantation laborers, remuneration was withheld until the end of the year. "Full hands," men with the largest capacity for work, were rewarded with more, either in cash or agricultural produce, than "half" or "three-quarter" hands.[70] Former slave skilled workers and craftsmen received more than did the ordinary full hand.[71] The squad system of labor that evolved from this consisted of perhaps a dozen self-selected black males who chose to work together as a unit. Often, they worked under a supervisor or overseer chosen directly by themselves. As usual, the black laborers and the plantation owners sharply contrasted in their preference for labor systems. Former slaves refused to work under the gang system, which had so much of the feel of slavery about it. The squad system was preferred by them, as its equalitarian, self-selecting characteristics held more appeal to ex-slaves.[72]

Another common new labor relationship, sharecropping, involved the signing of contracts binding the family to work on a section of land in exchange for either one-third or one-half of the crop, depending on whether the tools, seed, and other items needed for production were provided.[73] Sharecropping represented a distinct advance over the squad system of labor in that it allowed blacks critical physical and psychological distance from white oversight. For the planter, sharecropping offered the advantages of the steady labor of entire families. Under the sharecropping arrangement the level of black food consumption was increased, an important quality-of-life feature. However, it was characterized by a relatively low level of productivity, which aggravated the continual conflict revolving around the planters attempts to implement a slavery-like supervision over black laborers.[74] One area of conflict revolved around the continual renegotiation of the tasks and scope of the plantation work, as jobs, such as weeding in the rain or repairing fences, that were over and above what they were being compensated for, went undone by blacks refusing to perform them.[75] Under these arrangements disputing the landowner's word could be dangerous, as Cane Cook of Americus, Georgia learned when he gently disagreed with the account book. Asked if he was disputing the white man's word, Cook denied that he was. Despite this and all of his attempts to avoid conflict with the large, brutal man, he was struck with a large stick. Paralyzed, he had to be carried home by friends; later, he lamented that he had "to be fed like a baby."[76]

RECONSTRUCTION AND THE URBAN BLACK MALE

President Andrew Johnson reflected a pervasive sentiment in his view that white labor should receive priority over black. After taking office as president and finding six "stout negroes" at work on the White House grounds, Johnson immediately inquired as to whether white men had been replaced by these black men.[77] Later, during the 1870s, black males were ousted from many trades and occupations to be replaced by whites. In Vicksburg, Mississippi, white porters replaced black ones at retail enterprises, as did the Vicksburg & Meridian Railroad for all of its mail agents. In late summer 1865 white caulkers in Baltimore demanded that black caulkers employed at a city shipyard be summarily dismissed and replaced by whites. After the owner refused their demand, they led a strike of Baltimore shipyard white workers eventually prevailed, as their drive to oust blacks from the shipyards gained the support of many of the city's white workers.[78] The black caulkers, led by Isaac Myers, fought back by raising $10,000 to invest in a black-owned shipyard company. Myers was later president of the Colored National Labor Union, which fought for the rights of black male laborers.[79]

In North Carolina black males were excluded from employment in the state's cotton mills, which employed 30,000 whites, mostly women. The mill owners argued that this exclusion was necessary to guard against race mixing and the unnecessary construction of housing, since segregation was mandatory.[80] By the 1890s there were occasional cracks in the exclusion, as one mill hired black women and a black male supervisor in the wake of firing 300 white women. In demanding their jobs back, the white women's male relatives circulated a petition that focused its ire on the black male supervisor, citing his "dangerous proximity with our maidens," holding that he should be ousted lest their daughters be deprived of opportunities.[81]

As representatives of white workers, unions played their part in the historical degradation of black males in the workforce. At the time of the founding of the American Federation of Labor (AFL) in 1881, Samuel Gompers said that the union did "not want to exclude any workingman who believes in and belongs to organized labor." The founding convention included at least four representatives of black organizations and a few black delegates.[82] Following a warning from an African American delegate of the dire consequences of excluding blacks who might later be hired as replacement workers during a strike, the workers' convention resolved that the federation would be inclusive of "the whole laboring element of this country no matter of what calling." Prospective affiliates were required to pledge "never to discriminate against a fellow worker on account of color, creed or nationality."[83] Later, in 1890, when requested to organize the primarily southern National Association of Machinists, which was founded on a racially exclusionary principle, the union's leadership voted it down until its racially discriminatory clause was deleted from its constitution, and when the integrated International Machinists Union of America was formed, the AFL quickly extended recognition to the organization.[84] Gompers' racial liberalism, however, was short-lived. By the 1890s, however, the union leader had capitulated to racism and ignored the issue of segregation in unions. By the turn of the century, Gompers could say with perfect seriousness, seemingly a difficult task given his intimate knowledge of the exclusion of blacks from unions, that they "so conducted themselves as to be a continuous convenient whip placed in the hands of the employers to cow the white men and to compel them to accept abject conditions of labor." Somehow, to Gompers, black exclusion from labor unions was the fault of blacks themselves.[85]

White unions in the railroad industry proved detrimental to the blacks in the industry. Prior to the formation of the initial railroad brotherhoods, blacks could be found in key positions. As the unions organized through the nation, all jobs for blacks within the industry, except for porter and waiter, were threatened. The position of fireman had long been regarded as a black job since the work was so unpleasant. Since the experience as a fireman often enabled African Americans to rise to the position of engineer, many were African American. Eligible only to white males between the ages of 18 and 45, the unions served their members by seeking the firing of blacks and the hiring of whites to replace them.[86] In 1890 in Texas, the Brotherhood of Locomotive Trainmen went out on strike in an effort to force the Texas Central Railroad to fire its black workers. When this tactic failed, the white union relied on racial stereotypes, charging in a lawsuit that blacks lacked the mental capacity to work on the railroads. This, however, failed also.[87] In the aftermath of the abortive strike launched by the American Railway Union in 1894, a concerted campaign was launched labeling blacks "immoral, untrustworthy, inherently vicious and indolent by nature." Union literature charged that blacks were unable to perform satisfactorily due to a propensity to sleep on the job and panic in emergencies. "Their stupidity caused many accidents" and "I think it almost as well to educate a hog, for the animal can not accomplish any harm with his education, while the negro can" are two representative statements of the type of racial sentiment that the turn-of-the-century union contained.[88]

In Cleveland the percentage of black males in the skilled trades dropped precipitously from 1870, when it stood at 31.7 percent, to 1910, when it was only 11.1 percent. The skilled trades that had formed the backbone of the city's relatively large black middle class, including blacksmith, shoemaker, and painter, registered the largest declines.[89]   The boom in unskilled employment accompanying Cleveland's initial industrialization bypassed African Americans, as by 1890, for example, only three blacks worked in the city's steel industry.[90] Heavy European immigration, employers who felt blacks were ill suited to perform industrial labor, and trade union exclusion all contributed to the dearth of blacks in early Cleveland industry.[91] As blacks lost status, white worker organizations were increasingly driven to demonstrate their contempt out of a fear of being identified with blacks and thereby losing social status.[92] This state of affairs left blacks with little reason to heed pleas not to break strikes by becoming replacement workers.[93]

An array of laws, customs, values, and attitudes blocked black male entry to most trades and professions. The consequences of this dearth of opportunity on the family and the individual were profound. For the family, the lack of economic anchoring led to more instability than would have been the case. For the individual, despite the knowledge that an enveloping atmosphere of racial discrimination stood in the way of black progress, the sheer fact of financial instability, the gradual discouragement of individual aspiration and ambition, and the lack of viable options inevitably wrought damaging psychological consequences. Most blacks, individuals as well as families, emerged from slavery with virtually no resources. However, even those comparatively advantaged suffered from the universal discrimination and prejudice they met with in striving to get ahead.

Frederick Douglass' daughter Rosetta married Nathan Sprague, for example, who had served in the famed Massachusetts 54th in South Carolina. He moved to Rochester, New York, following the war and lived in the Douglass' home with his wife and daughter, Anne. After giving up farming on the outskirts of Rochester, he, with his father-in-law's assistance, obtained his hack license. While he had a hack described by his wife as "the finest that can be found" and excellent horses, he found little success. The white hackmen were hostile to his attempt to work in the city. They threatened his hack, while the local police told him to move on when he tried to take his place at the hack stand. He stood his ground as, through Douglass, he had connections in high places. Unfortunately, he couldn't last two weeks, as his hack was destroyed by his white competitors.[94]

Discouraged in his attempts to find work, Nathan Sprague left for Nebraska. He was determined to make it on his own, after having received ample assistance from Frederick Douglass. He wrote to his father-in-law, "[I]f I do not make it is not because you have not did all you could to help me." A few months later, however, he returned home penniless. His relations with both his wife and his father-in-law deteriorated. He continued to have difficulty maintaining regular employment when Douglass helped him obtain a job at the post office. He reached rock bottom within a year when he was caught and convicted of opening mail and stealing valuables from it. He was sentenced to a year in the Monroe County

Penitentiary.[95] After he was released and joined his wife in Washington, DC, he quietly lived out the rest of his life.[96]

THE RECONSTRUCTION OF THE BLACK FAMILY ALONG PATRIARCHAL LINES

At the beginning of Reconstruction, the black male was the dominant gender in black social, economic, and political life. Economically, he was the central figure, both as, ideally, the principal earner and worker and as the head of the household. Socially, within the family he was generally the primary decision maker, despite being often removed from child raising. Politically, he soon became enfranchised and, often, politically involved, while the black female remained disfranchised and generally barred, by custom and law, from political involvement. During Reconstruction northern missionaries socialized their students into gender-role ideals characterized, as in the white mainstream, into "separate spheres" for females and males, but roles were distinctly different. Glenda Gilmore explains that black women were socialized into "an evangelically driven ethos of 'usefulness'" that allowed them entry into the "business of the race." As the perquisites of "ladyhood" were denied to black females by the white masses, Gilmore concludes that "African Americans of both sexes entered Reconstruction valuing strength, initiative, and practicality."[97] Notwithstanding this, Cain Hope Felder concludes that historically, African Americans have "uncritically" bought into "a socialization that tolerates and accepts the patriarchal model of male control and supremacy that typifies the Eurocentric, Western, Protestant tradition in general." This

patriarchal emphasis that inhibits the advancement of women in the socio-political and ecclesiastical spheres has often been mirrored by African American male culture as more normative than exceptional. Assumptions that men have the right and duty to dominate and to shape all dimensions of discourse in social and especially religious institutions and structures are easily documented in African American social and cultural history.[98]

Economically, both black males and females supported the withdrawal, when possible, of females from the paid workforce. Not only would the black female be afforded a greater degree of safety from the attacks, but at home she could enhance the independence of the entire family and foster its personal development. The desire to put the intruding former white slave owners and staff at a safe distance, minimizing the chances of dangerous incidents occurring, and the desire for general peace of mind also enhanced the attractiveness of this. Yet, it was a difficult achievement given the determination of the white political elite during Reconstruction to make it a necessity, as during slavery, for the black female, indeed, the entire black family to be devoted to hard labor during the entirety of every working day. Jacqueline Jones points out that:

the withdrawal of black females from wage—labor-a major theme in both contemporary and secondary accounts of Reconstruction—occurred primarily among the wives and daughters of able-bodied men. (Women who served as the sole support for their children or other family members had to take work wherever they could find it.). [99]

A black woman removed from the workforce was able to enhance the standard of living for her family. Not only could she grow crops vital to their sustenance, but she could raise her children better, maintain the household, and make clothes and, often, herbal remedies. Jones points out that black woman's work occurred within two vastly different settings, outside the home, on one hand, and within the home, on the other. In the society at large she suffered from having the lowest sex-race status in society and being confined to "women's work" at times and "nigger work," the dirtiest and most arduous "men's work." Work in the home, however arduous it might have been, offered possibilities for more satisfaction, in meeting the needs and desires of her husband, children, and other kin, than the paid labor force.[100] In this sense, the family's welfare depended, in large part, on the extent to which black women were free of obligations to labor outside the home. However, the precarious and meager nature of the income, lives, and work careers of most black males in the South made two incomes or more per household necessary for survival generally. As in slavery, black women's domestic duties allowed them critical space for appropriating needed resources for the black family. Generally, each day the black women servants in the old "Big House" would bring home food in the "service pan," which was crucial to the survival of many black families.[101]

An important motive for the desire for black females to withdraw from the labor force was that of protection. By the prevention of abusive incidents perpetrated by white men, violent and family-shattering situations could be better avoided. The effort of whites to replicate the slavery situation clashed with black aspirations for independence and autonomy, creating a volatile matrix of conflict. The rape of black women, what an Alabama white physician termed "splitting a nigger woman," was considered custom by many white males during the post–Civil War period. Many varieties of sexual assault threatened black females of all ages, creating a profound anxiety among African Americans of both genders.[102] No wonder a black convention in 1869 advised black men in Georgia to "take their wives from the drudgery and exposure of plantation soil" "as soon as it is in their power to do so."[103]

The ability of the black family to provide effective protection for black women varied to some extent by social class. The small black elite was generally afforded more options and could afford more physical distance and security from human predators. However, avoiding or preventing incidents was quite important due to its capacity to lead to a chain of events, dragging down the males into a cycle of violence, sometimes leading to deaths and other times leading to flight north or imprisonment.

The patriarchal ideal of the family during this period went virtually unquestioned. Following the war the Freedmen's Bureau officially dealt with the black husband as head of the family unit. Bureau agents counseled ex-slaves on the proper gender ideals. "Be a Man," the head of the Freedmen's Bureau in

Tennessee, General Clinton B. Fisk, counseled. Fisk lectured:

Husbands must provide for their families. Your wives will not love you if you do not provide bread and clothes for them. They cannot be happy and greet you with a kiss, when you come home, if they are hungry, ragged, and cold. By industry and economy you can soon provide a real good home, and plenty of food and clothing for your family; and you should not rest until this is done.[104]

Fisk had complementary advice for black women, advising them to be of pleasant appearance, clean, "neat," and "tidy." Their activities should include mending clothes, housekeeping, and tending a garden.[105]

Black patriarchalism was reinforced during the initial years of Reconstruction by the Freedmen's Bureau's utilization of the black husband as the family head for purposes of contracts, as well as through its policy of paying black males more regardless of the relative productive capacities of the individuals concerned. When women were not in the workforce, pressure was generally placed on black men to influence them to get back out into the fields. Merchants, too, generally dealt with the black male as the representative for the family. The surrounding community, to a considerable extent, held the black male family head responsible for the social behavior of the entire family. This increasing postbellum division of labor based on gender moved the black family away from the makeshift egalitarianism that had characterized its social relationships during slavery.[106]

The conventions of blacks held following the Civil War charted an ambitious course of progress to be led by the black male. Women played little role in these conventions as they were politically disfranchised, and emphasis was placed on the empowerment of black males within the black community. The ideal black male personality implied by the resolutions of the conventions embodied notions of well-balanced, well-rounded men of action. There was a consciousness of both the enormity of work that needed to be done and the scarcity of resources with which to accomplish it. There was a strong element of self-criticism in the resolutions. One, for example, derided black men who engaged in "vagrancy and pauperism." The convention urged black men, in this light, to remain on the land, work hard, and save their money to buy land.[107]

Politically, the official enfranchisement of the black male after 1867 allowed him to serve on juries, hold political office, and exercise voting rights. Politics being the exclusive province of the black male and with predominant influence in the black church, patriarchalism became firmly entrenched within the black community. With first military and then official political involvement and economic life designated as male spheres, black males were clearly the dominant gender among African Americans. Consistent with this growing separation between a public male sphere and a private female sphere, the ideology surrounding the family increasingly stressed a new, more submissive and segmented, ideal black female gender role. Community leaders stressed the need for women to make home a comfortable sanctuary and for obedient submission to the husband's guidance. One black Virginian activist, Thomas Bayne, declared,

"It is a woman's right to raise and bear children, and to train them for the future duties in life."[108]

The male-only suffrage carved out electoral politics as the almost exclusive sphere of males. The black male, like males of other American ethnicities, was dubbed the head of the household. Ideally, his earnings would provide the crucial, if not sole, support of the family. He was the official representative and leader of the family, the extended family, church, community, and almost every other institution in civil society.[109] Laura Townes, commenting on St. Helena Island, complained that the "notion of being bigger than woman" was "inflating the conceit of the males to an amazing degree."[110] In her journal she described a scene in church where it was announced that an upcoming meeting was for male voters.   "The females can come or not as they choose, but the meeting is for men voters." Another male declared, then, that "the women will stay at home and work in the fields hoeing corn and weeding."[111]   Glenda Gilmore, however, notes that black male voters often saw themselves as representing their wives and families, as "delegate-husbands."[112]

Many black women supported the female franchise. Harriet Tubman was convinced that the male-only vote was an injustice. During her last years she joined a woman suffrage organization. In reply to a question asking whether she believed women should have the right to vote, she replied, "I suffered enough to believe it."[113]

Susan B. Anthony and Elizabeth Cady Stanton, pioneer white feminists, warned that African American men were socialized by their masters into behavior norms of "tyranny and despotism" and argued that women—read as white women—deserved the ballot more than "ignorant" black males. Stanton declared, "It would be better to be the slave of an educated white man than of an ignorant black one."   The former antislavery allies of Frederick Douglass aligned themselves with Negrophobic Democrat George Train, who financed their feminist newspaper, *The Revolution*.[114] Susan B. Anthony wrote within its pages:

While the dominant party have with one hand lifted up TWO MILLION BLACK MEN and crowned them with the honor and dignity of citizenship, with the other they have dethroned FIFTEEN MILLION WHITE WOMEN—and cast them under the heel of the lowest orders of manhood.[115]

Stooping even lower, Stanton related an incident in which a black man was lynched in Tennessee for the alleged rape of a white woman. Astoundingly, Stanton found a causal connection between black males' winning the right to vote and this alleged criminal act. She wrote, "The Republican cry of 'Manhood Suffrage' creates an antagonism between black men and all women that will culminate in fearful outrages on womanhood, especially in the southern states."[116] In 1869 Frederick Douglass addressed an American Equal Rights Association meeting and pleaded the logic of the black male's obtaining of the vote then and later working for the winning of the female franchise. Together, the black male and female franchise legislation was doomed to failure; practical politics dictated that separately the black male franchise was likely to pass. Douglass urged his audience to try to understand why the vote was so urgent for black males:

When women, because they are women, are hunted down through the cities of New York and New Orleans, when they are dragged from their houses and hung upon lamp posts; when their children are torn from their arms, and their brains dashed upon the pavement; when they are objects of insult and outrage at every turn. . . . when their children are not allowed to enter schools; then they will have an urgency to obtain the ballot equal to our own.[117]

The winning of the franchise for black males cemented their political and familial dominance of the black community following the Civil War. Whereas the antebellum black family in slavery was more egalitarian in character, with the effective male role being diminished by both absence and the status of the man as husband, the postemancipation black family tended to be more patriarchal.

The minuscule African American middle-class elite faced problems of a different character than that of the more numerous, subsistence-level masses. Assertive women with a drive to have fulfilling careers were hampered by the prevailing, lingering Victorianism. During the 1880s Fannie Jackson was forced, for example, while teaching at the Philadelphia Institute for Colored Youth, to hire a janitor in order to have him escort her home for reasons of both propriety and safety. Lucy Ellen Moten apparently was too attractive to be principal of the Washington Minor Normal School and was forced to obtain Frederick Douglass' assistance to win the position. Douglass, one of the earliest prominent male supporters of women's rights in the nation, committed her to renouncing cardplaying, dating, dancing, and certain articles of clothing in order for him to intervene on her behalf.[118]

For the black woman at the apex of the black social structure, the domination by males of the most important social institutions in African American life was readily apparent. Anna Cooper, born Annie Julia Haywood in 1858 in Raleigh, North Carolina, protested against gender oppression as a teenager at a religious school. She complained that male candidates for the ministry received advantages, while women were discouraged from studying theology. Cooper protested that "the only mission open before a girl. . . . was to marry one of" the ministerial candidates.[119] Mary Helen Washington notes that Du Bois, in an essay on women, quotes Cooper's observation that "only the black woman can say 'when and where I enter'" but attributes the statement not to her but anonymously to "one of *our* women" despite his personal friendship with her.[120]

Washington, however, laments that Cooper is "never able to discard totally the ethics of true womanhood" and gives short shrift to the lives of black women lower on the socioeconomic ladder. Cooper, according to Washington, admitted that women were an "unacknowledged factor" in both the African American and women's struggle but maintained that women's "quiet and unobserved presence as they stand 'aloof from the heated scramble'" of political life would register some impact. Notwithstanding the limitations of this strategy for women married to men wielding substantial political power, for most black women, the lack of black male power and influence would mitigate against this form of political participation.[121] However, for Cooper and other prominent turn-of-the-century female figures such as Fannie Jackson Coppin, Frances Harper, Mary Church Terrell, and Josephine St. Pierre Ruffin, the cult of true womanhood, influenced their perception of female gender-role ideals.[122]

In an 1898 speech, Mary Church Terrell discussed the work of the National Association of Colored Women and stressed the domesticity of the ideal black woman. Terrell said, "Believing that it is only through the home that a people can become really good and truly great," the organization was to focus its work on "that sacred domain."[123] The organization planned to develop "mothers Congresses" in black communities across the nation that would focus on child-raising strategies and housewife strategies.[124] Similarly, Cooper explained that the clubs her organization planned to establish across the nation would offer instruction on "the best way to sweep, dust, cook, wash and iron, together with the information concerning household affairs." In addition, presentations on "social purity" and child raising were made to impoverished African American woman of the South.

While Anna Cooper advocated the universal pursuit of careers as a method to dramatically improve the overall status of the African American woman, she nevertheless accepted the overall logic of black male patriarchy. Within this framework the "loose woman" was a key negative gender role for women, and a strict adherence to moral standards was more important for females than for males. The values of self-discipline, abstinence, sexual purity, and service to society were important within this moral framework. For outstanding achievers and activists such as Terrell, Cooper, and Wells, however, independence was a major gender-role ideal.[125] Wells wrote approvingly of "the patriarchal demeanor" of two leaders of the Holly Springs, Mississippi, community who were "endeavoring to put their thoughts into action." She favored a stereotypically masculine personality eager for action, adventure, and race progress; however, this was also her ideal for feminine gender roles.[126] Her well-known statement that "A Winchester rifle should have a place of honor in every home" predates later statements by Malcolm X and others. Her self-defense posture was of a firmness that few men of the era dared verbally express: "When the white man. . . knows he runs as great a risk of biting the dust every time his Afro-American victims does, he will have greater respect for Afro-American life."[127] She had the highest respect for strong, active, and ambitious men, not "miserable excuses for men" or "weak, deceitful creatures." Her assertiveness, independence, wit, and refusal to totally conform to traditional gender standards made her early relationships somewhat problematic.[128]

Anna Cooper was clear in the kind of man she viewed as meeting the demands of the age:

We need men who can let their interest and gallantry extend outside the circle of their aesthetic appreciation; men who can be a father, a brother, a friend to every weak, struggling unshielded girl.[129]

The opinions expressed by prominent black female achievers were not always gently expressed. For example, Washington, D.C.'s, Nannie Helen Burroughs asserted, "Whenever the men of any race defiantly stand up for the protection of their women, . . . the women will. . . . be saved from the hands of the most vile," and she complained, "White men offer more protection to their prostitutes than many Black men offer to their best women."[130] While perhaps unfair in her harshness toward black men, Burroughs nevertheless points to her expectations of protection, evidence of the acceptance of the basic tenets of black patriarchy by virtually every segment of the black community. At the opposite end of the socioeconomic continuum, Angela Davis' study of three women blues performers finds that "black women were able to autonomously work out—as audiences and performers—a working-class model of womanhood."[131]

THE BLACK MALE ELECTED OFFICIAL DURING RECONSTRUCTION: IMAGE VERSUS REALITY

What, in a society moving toward social justice, would have been one of the most positive images of black males in the history of the United States, that of their progressive roles in Reconstruction-era southern governments, has been transformed into one most damaging to the black male image historically. The image of the black male in Reconstruction is often portrayed as one of greedy, ignorant, semisimian creatures, aided by unthinking and corrupt northern whites legislating ridiculous and unfair laws in the Congress and state houses of the South. The unreconstructed view of Reconstruction, captured in movie classics like *Gone with the Wind* and *Birth of a Nation*, which portrayed African American males as drunken, ignorant, incompetent, and lustful savages, exercised a sway over virtually all thinking white Americans. These images have been powerful and enduring ones, accepted by such intellectually endowed presidents as Theodore Roosevelt, Woodrow Wilson, and John F. Kennedy, as well as the less endowed presidents, including Lyndon B. Johnson, who once spoke frankly of his anxiety that blacks would end up "pissing" again in the halls of Congress as in Reconstruction.[132]

Yet, for politicians and leaders who did not enjoy the luxury of extensive political experience, the first generation of black elected officials in the post–Civil War era fared extremely well. The first black man to gain a seat in the U.S. Senate, Hiram R. Revels of Mississippi, is representative of a generation of pioneering black male elected officials that had to contend with resistance, at first, to their very presence and, later, to the generally progressive, pro-black legislation they introduced. Revels himself saw resistance to his Senate swearing in at every step of the way. An ordained A.M.E. minister and educator, he was involved in the recruitment of Maryland blacks for the Union army during the Civil War.[133] Following the war, Revels was assigned to Natchez, Mississippi, where in the fall of 1869 he became a compromise candidate for a seat in the state Senate. This

Reconstruction Mississippi government registered important, if rather temporary, achievements. With black men constituting 40 of the 140-man body, in short order they eliminated the Black Codes, banned racial discrimination, filled vacancies for the U.S. Senate, and ratified the Fourteenth and Fifteenth Amendments.[134]

In the U.S. Senate, however, during the swearing-in process, Revels' credentials were immediately challenged by a Delaware congressman who asserted that they had not been certified by the state's military governor but admitted soon afterward that he opposed Revels because he was black.[135] Later, another congressman objected to his seating by charging that Revels had not been a citizen the required nine years. In fact, he could not have, since blacks could not be citizens until the Civil Rights Act of 1866.[136] Racially prejudiced comments and humor flew freely during these sessions. This was, after all, a quite emotional occasion, as Revels was replacing the Senate seat of none other than the former President of the Confederacy, Jefferson Davis.[137]

The record of Congressman Joseph H. Rainey of South Carolina provides a good example of the type of legislation that the initial generation of black elected officials supported. As the first black to hold a seat in the U.S. House of Representatives, Rainey, in April 1871, delivered his maiden speech to the Congress. Speaking in favor of the passage of the "KKK Act," which proposed to make it a federal crime for persons to conspire to try to prevent an officeholder from taking or executing his duties, Rainey later supported measures to provide for equality of treatment for blacks in public spaces, in the areas of public accommodations, entertainment, education, and travel.[138] Rainey commented that as long as black men were passive, taking what the powers-that-be thought they should receive, "we are good, clever fellows." But, "just as soon as we begin to assert our manhood and demand our rights we are looked upon as men not worthy to be recognized, . . . we become obnoxious, and we hear this howl about social equality."[139]

The initial black national and state legislators keenly felt the pervasive discrimination in public accommodations and conveyances. Alabama-born James T. Rapier, born in 1837 and educated at law schools in Canada and Scotland, was elected in 1872 to the U.S. House of Representatives. His speech on 9 June 1874 honed in on this web of discrimination.[140] He noted the paradox that black legislators were supposed to be representatives "for a free people," yet "his own chains hang about him" and that his "position [was] no mantle of protection in our 'land of the free and home of the brave'" complaining that he was "subjected to far more outrages and indignities in coming to and going from this capital in discharge of my public duties than any criminal" who was white. He noted that instead of his lofty position's providing him a shield from "insult," "it too often invites it."[141] He deplored the recent denial of a first-class seat, not to mention a sleeping berth, to the treasurer of the state of South Carolina, Francis L. Cardozo. Threatened with death, he "was compelled, a most elegant and accomplished gentleman, to take a seat in a dirty smoking-car, along with the traveling rabble." Rapier went on to note that, in his own case, he was unable to obtain a meal or room in a single inn from Washington, D.C., to Montgomery, Alabama.[142]

Congressman Rainey also complained about the discrimination he faced in the nation's capital, asking:

Do you think it is right that when I go forth from this capital as an honored member of Congress that I should be subjected to insults from the lowest fellow in the street if he should happen to feel so inclined?[143]

Rainey's discussion on the floor of the House of his treatment while traveling was revealing. He was able to obtain first-class status on the train from Charleston to Savannah, but on the way back he could not. Traveling by boat from the nation's capital to Norfolk, Virginia, he was forced to eat with the servants despite paying a full fare. He noted that despite being denied use of the public schools, blacks paid the taxes that funded them.[144] His colleague, Congressman Richard H. Cain of South Carolina, also had a rough time traveling from South Carolina to Washington by train; to avoid trouble, he refrained from eating food in the diner and ordered it brought to his car. Despite this, the whites operating the railroad felt that this was "putting on airs" and rejected his request.[145]

Other Reconstruction-era African American legislators fought for the rights of a people who had recently emerged from centuries of slavery. Their anger in lodging demands for, at least, equal treatment was based on a keen sense of past injustice. Cain, also reminded his congressional colleagues of the freedman's perspective on current events. Cain told them, "You robbed us for 200 years." He described the work blacks performed as "toiling without pay."[146] When another congressman suggested blacks consider emigrating to another country, Cain replied that, "you have brought us here, and here we are going to stay." The black stake in the country, Cain felt, was based on his people's long experience in America. "Our mothers and our fathers and our grandfathers and great-grandfathers have died here. Here we have sweated. Here we have toiled. Here we have made this country great and rich."[147]

Considering the pioneer black lawmakers' contributions to the founding of modern education, public health, and other vital structures in post–Civil War southern states during their brief tenure, their accomplishments are hardly outshone by those of their white predecessors, who plunged their region into a losing war. Finding corruption among the generation of politicians, black and white, was hardly difficult, and political motives go quite far in accounting for the debased image of the black male politician during the Reconstruction era. Historian Benjamin Quarles concluded, "Without doubt, . . . there were among Negro officeholders those with itching palms and a limited sense of their public responsibility. But an even larger number were just the reverse."[148]

George White's speech in the U.S. House of Representatives on 7 March 1898 on the gross inequities within the American armed forces reflected the "accommodationist" ideological trend of the era coming three years after the Atlanta Compromise speech of Booker T. Washington. As the last African

American congressman for an extended period, for George White merely to prod the federal government for black rights reflected positively upon his store of courage. Yet, the acquiescence, the constant professions of loyalty that African American men, including Frederick Douglass and many other Reconstruction and post-Reconstruction leaders, proclaimed, noting often that the black man protected the white woman of the South during slavery and the Civil War, must be considered as one component of the black masculinity in an era where African Americans were on the defensive.

We have always endeavored to be loyal to every trust imposed in us. In our Southland, when the master and son went forth to battle to perpetuate our bonds, we protected, revered, and held intact the honor of the wife and daughter who remained at home, and history fails to record a single instance where that trust was betrayed.[149]

On the defensive, Congressman White pointed to continued evidence of loyalty and servility that made African Americans attractive as workers and neighbors.

As laborers our places can not be filled in the South by any class of people. Among us there are no strikes; no tumults or riots; no labor organizations to bar the white man from making an honest living; no tramps; but humble, faithful citizens, ever true to the trust imposed in us by the proclamation of the lamented Lincoln. We are grateful to all benefactors.[150]

Fearful of insulting the South, White trod gently over the description of the crimes committed daily against blacks and, in attacking a double standard, evinced a lack of principle himself referring to "half-breed foreigners" who held themselves up as U.S. allies and who could gain a hearing while the federal government lamely denied it had the power to intervene in state affairs to uphold black human rights. Yet, White was a paragon of excellence when he, on behalf of African Americans, virtually disfranchised, bade farewell to Congress:

This, Mr. Chairman, is perhaps the Negroes' temporary farewell to the American Congress; but let me say, Phoenix-like he will rise up some day and come again. These parting words are in behalf of an outraged, heart-broken, bruised and bleeding, but God-fearing people, faithful, industrious, loyal, rising people full of potential force.[151]

By 1895 African Americans had experienced many ups and downs since their first intoxicating days of emancipation. From the utopian-like hopes that full citizenship could be attained for the first generation following emancipation, black hopes plummeted after being dampened by the blood and gore of Reconstruction's violence and the rise of lynching during the post-Reconstruction era. As the last vestiges of Reconstruction-era political power were being whittled away with no easy path of progress obvious, the black mood at the turn of the century was defensive, bleak, and limited.[152] The following chapter discusses the problem of anti-African American violence in relation to accommodationist thought and its implications for the development of black masculinity in the twentieth century.

NOTES

1. Edwin S. Redkey (ed.), *A Grand Army of Black Men: Letters from African-American Soldiers in the Union Army, 1861–1865* (Cambridge: Cambridge University Press, 1992), 220.

2. J. M. McPherson, *The Negro's Civil War: How American Blacks Felt and Acted during the War for the Union* (New York: Ballantine Books, 1991), 50.

3. Ibid., 63.

4. Leon F. Litwack, *Been in the Storm So Long: The Aftermath of Slavery* (New York: Vintage, 1980), 168.

5. Benjamin Quarles, *The Negro in the Civil War* (Boston: Little, Brown, 1969), 325–28.

6. Dorothy Sterling (ed.), *The Trouble They Seen: The Story of Reconstruction in the Words of African Americans* (New York: Da Capo Press, 1994), 2.

7. Litwack, *Been in the Storm*, 98.

8. Eric Foner, *Reconstruction: America's Unfinished Revolution, 1863–1877* (New York: Harper Row, 1988), 79.

9. W.E.B. Du Bois, *Black Reconstruction in America* (New York: Atheneum, 1983), 131.

10. Ibid., 131.

11. Irvin Nell Painter, *Standing at Armageddon: The United States 1877–1919* (New York: W. W. Norton, 1987), 1; C. Vann Woodward, *The Strange Career of Jim Crow* (New York: Oxford University Press, 1974), 70.

12. Foner, *Reconstruction*, 133.

13. Ibid., 135.

14. Kenneth M. Stampp, *The Era of Reconstruction, 1865–1877* (New York: Alfred A. Knopf, 1965), 11.

15. Andrew Johnson, "The Civil Rights Bill of 1866 Should Not Be Enacted," in Brenda Stalcup, (ed.), *Reconstruction: Opposing Viewpoints* (San Diego: Greenhaven Press, 1995), 66.

16. Ibid., 67–68.

17. Ibid., 70.

18. Samuel Thomas, *Samuel Thomas, Assistant Commissioner, Bureau of Refugees, Freedmen and Abandoned Lands* (WPA Archives Web Site, 1995).

19. Thomas, *Samuel Thomas*, n.p.

20. Foner, *Reconstruction*, 80.

21. Ibid., 80.

22. Jacqueline Jones, *Labor of Love, Labor of Sorrow* (New York: Basic Books, 1985), 44.

23. James McKaye, *The Mastership and Its Fruits* (New York: Loyal Publication Society, 1864), 20.

24. Sterling, *The Trouble They Seen*, 168–69.

25. August Meier and Elliott Rudwick, "A Strange Chapter in the Career of Jim Crow," in August Meier and Elliott Rudwick (eds.), *The Making of Black America: Essays in Negro Life & History*, (New York: Atheneum, 1973), 15.

26. Sterling, *The Trouble They Seen*, 63.

27. Gerald D. Jaynes, *Branches without Roots: Genesis of the Black Working-class in the American South, 1862–1882* (New York: Oxford University Press, 1986) 58–59.

28. Foner, *Reconstruction*, 156.

29. Ibid., 34.

30. Vernon Lane Wharton, *The Negro in Mississippi, 1865–1890* (New York: Harper and Row, 1965), 87; see also Neil R. McMillen, *Dark Journey: Black Mississippians in the Age of Jim Crow* (Urbana: University of Illinois Press, 1989).

31. Foner, *Reconstruction,* 134.

32. Ibid., 133.

33. Ibid., 133.

34. Kevin K.Gaines, *Uplifting the Race: Black Leadership, Politics, and Culture in the Twentieth Century* (Chapel Hill: University of North Carolina Press, 1996), 53.

35. Leon F. Litwack, *Trouble in Mind: Black Southerners in the Age of Jim Crow* (New York: Alfred A. Knopf, 1998), 60.

36. Wharton, *The Negro,* 87.

37. Ibid., 88.

38. Ibid., 88.

39. Ibid., 93.

40. Jaynes, *Branches without Roots,* 306–07; William Cohen, *At Freedom's Edge: Black Mobility and the Southern White Quest for Racial Control, 1861–1915* (Baton Rouge: Louisiana State University Press, 1991), 29.

41. Litwack, *Trouble in Mind,* 274.

42. Jaynes, *Branches without Roots,* 272.

43. Joel Williamson, *The Crucible of Race: Black–White Relations in the American South since Emancipation* (New York: Oxford University Press, 1984), 58.

44. Edward L. Ayers, *Vengeance and Justice: Crime and Punishment in the 19th Century American South,* (New York: Oxford University Press, 1984), 193.

45. Foner, *Reconstruction,* 179–80.

46. Benjamin Quarles, *The Negro in the Making of America* (New York: Collier Books, 1964), 127.

47. Joel Williamson, *After Slavery: The Negro in South Carolina during Reconstruction, 1861–1877* (Hanover, NH: University Press of New England, 1965), 38–39. See also Thomas Holt, *Black over White: Negro Political Leadership in South Carolina during Reconstruction* (Urbana: University of Illinois Press, 1977).

48. George L. Beckford, *Persistent Poverty: Underdevelopment in Plantation Economies of the Third World.* (New York: Oxford University Press, 1972), 51–54.

49. Williamson, *After Slavery,* 75.

50. Ibid., 75.

51. Ibid., 77; Holt, *Black over White,* 23.

52. James L. Roark, *Masters without Slaves: Southern Planters in the Civil War and Reconstruction* (New York: W. W. Norton, 1977), 107.

53. Wharton, *The Negro,* 83; see also Thomas C. Holt, "'An Empire over the Mind': Emancipation, Race, and Ideology in the British West Indies and the American South," in J. Morgan Kousser and James M. McPherson (eds.), *Region, Race, and Reconstruction* (New York: Oxford University Press, 1982).

54. Wharton, *The Negro,* 84.

55. Jaynes, *Branches without Roots,* 73.

56. Foner, *Reconstruction,* 157.

57. Ibid., 158–59. A similar process occurred in Alabama; see Peter Kolchin, *First Freedom: The Responses of Alabama's Blacks to Emancipation and Reconstruction* (Westport, CT: Greenwood Press, 1972), 36.

58. Foner, *Reconstruction*, 158–60.

59. Ibid., 160.

60. Ibid., 160.

61. Williamson, *After Slavery*, 84.

62. Jaynes, *Branches without Roots*, 73.

63. Foner, *Reconstruction*, 161.

64. Ibid., 160.

65. Stampp, *The Era of Reconstruction*, 80.

66. Foner, *Reconstruction*, 105.

67. Jaynes, *Branches without Roots*, 118.

68. Ibid., 306.

69. Foner, *Reconstruction*, 132.

70. Wharton, *The Negro*, 82–83.

71. Foner, *Reconstruction*, 171–72; see also Charles S. Johnson, *Shadow of the Plantation* (Chicago: University of Chicago Press, 1939).

72. Foner, *Reconstruction*, 172.

73. Jones, *Labor of Love*, 61–62.

74. Foner, *Reconstruction*, 173.

75. Ibid., 174.

76. Ibid., 136.

77. Sterling, *The Trouble They Seen*, 268.

78. Foner, *Reconstruction*, 179–80.

79. Jaynes, *Branches without Roots*, 263–64.

80. Ibid., 276.

81. Gilmore, Glenda Elizabeth, *Gender and Jim Crow: Women and the Politics of White Supremacy in North Carolina, 1896–1920* (Chapel Hill: University of North Carolina Press, 1996), 23.

82. Ibid., 24.

83. Philip S. Foner, *Organized Labor and the Black Worker, 1619–1981* (New York: International, 1981), 64.

84. Ibid., 64.

85. Ibid., 65.

86. Ibid., 76.

87. Ibid., 103–04.

88. Ibid., 104–05.

89. Kenneth L. Kusmer, *A Ghetto Takes Shape: Black Cleveland, 1870–1930* (Chicago: University of Illinois Press, 1976), 73.

90. Ibid., 66–67.

91. Ibid., 67–68.

92. Ibid., 69.

93. Ibid., 69.

94. Dorothy Sterling (ed.), *We Are Your Sisters: Black Women in the Nineteenth Century* (New York: W. W. Norton, 1984), 419–20.

95. Ibid., 419–21.

96. Ibid., 422.

97. Gilmore, *Gender and Jim Crow*, 36. On the development of the African American family during slavery, see Herbert Gutman, *The Black Family in Slavery and Freedom, 1750–1925* (New York: Vintage Books, 1976).

98. Cain Hope Felder, *Stony the Road We Trod: African American Biblical Interpretation* (Minneapolis: Augsburg Fortress, 1991), 227.

99. Jones, *Labor of Love*, 58.

100. Ibid., 78.

101. Sterling, *We Are Your Sisters*, 353.

102. Jaynes, *Branches without Roots*, 230.

103. Ibid., 230.

104. Sterling, *We Are Your Sisters*, 320.

105. Ibid., 320.

106. Jones, *Labor of Love*, 61–63.

107. Foner, *Reconstruction*, 116.

108. Ibid., 87.

109. Sterling, *We Are Your Sisters*, 318.

110. Ibid.

111. Ibid.

112. Gilmore, *Gender and Jim Crow*, 18.

113. Sterling, *We Are Your Sisters*, 411.

114. Irvin Nell Painter, *Sojourner Truth: A Life, a Symbol* (New York: W. W. Norton, 1996), 227.

115. Paula Giddings, *When and Where I Enter: The Impact of Black Women on Race and Sex in America* (New York: William Morrow, 1984), 66.

116. Ibid., 66.

117. Ibid.

118. Anna Julia Cooper, *A Voice from the South* (New York: Oxford University Press, 1988), xxxvi.

119. Ibid., xxxi

120. Ibid., xlii.

121. Ibid., xlvi; see also Kevin K. Gaines *Uplifting the Race: Black Leadership, Politics, and Culture in the Twentieth Century* (Chapel Hill: University of North Carolina Press, 1996); Joy James, *Transcending the Talented Tenth: Black Leaders and American Intellectuals* (New York: Routledge, 1997).

122. Cooper, *A Voice from the South*, xlvii.

123. Mary Church Terrell, *The Progress of Colored Women* (Washington, DC: Library of Congress, 1996).

124. Ibid., 11.

125. Mariam Da Costa, *The Memphis Diary of Ida B. Wells* (Boston: Beacon, 1995), 6; Gilmore, *Gender and Jim Crow*, 44.

126. Da Costa, *The Memphis Diary*, 7.

127. Giddings, *Where and When I Enter*, 20.

128. Da Costa, *The Memphis Diary*, 10.

129. Cooper, *A Voice from the South*, 33.

130. Giddings, *Where and When I Enter*, 113.

131. Angela Y. Davis, *Blues Legacies and Black Feminism: Gertrude "Ma" Rainey, Bessie Smith, and Billie Holiday* (New York: Pantheon Books, 1998), 46.

132. Stampp, *The Era of Reconstruction*, 4–13.

133. Maurine Christopher, *America's Black Congressmen* (New York: Thomas Y. Crowell, 1971), 2.

134. Ibid., 3.

135. Ibid., 4.

136. Ibid., 4–5.

137. Ibid., 5.

138. Ibid., 29–31.

139. Ibid., 31–32.

140. James T. Rapier, "Segregation Should Be Abolished," in Brenda Stalcup

(ed.), *Reconstruction: Opposing Viewpoints* (San Diego: Greenhaven Press, 1995), 187.

141. Rapier, "Segregation," 189; Sterling, *The Trouble They Seen*, 181.

142. Rapier, "Segregation," 190.

143. Christopher, *America's Black Congressmen*, 32–33.

144. Ibid., 34.

145. Ibid., 37.

146. Ibid., 92.

147. Christopher, *America's Black Congressmen,* 92–93.

148. Quarles, *The Negro in the Making of America*, 137.

149. George White, "Additional Regiments of Artillery" (Washington, DC: Library of Congress, 1996), 3–4.

150. Ibid., 4.

151. Rayford W. Logan, *The Betrayal of the Negro: From Rutherford B. Hayes to Woodrow Wilson* (New York: Collier, 1954), 100.

152. John Edward Bruce, *The Blood Red Record: Review of the Horrible Lynchings and Burning of Negroes by Civilized White Men in the United States: As Taken from the Records: With Comments by John Edward Bruce* (Albany, NY: Argus, 1901), n.p.

Chapter 6

Booker T. Washington, Accommodationism, and Black Masculinity

> [I]t must be confessed the colored soldier is much more aggressive in his attitude on the [question of] social equality than he used to be.
> —Major August P. Blocksom [1]

> If colored men elect to stand by criminals of their own race because they are of their own race, they assuredly lay up for themselves the most dreadful day of reckoning.
> —President Theodore Roosevelt[2]

Around 9 P.M., 19 March 1911, Booker T. Washington emerged from a Manhattan subway station and made his way to an apartment building just south of Central Park on West Sixty-Third Street. Entering the exclusively white building, Washington repeatedly rang the bell to no avail. While he waited, two young female residents passed him before he finally gave up. After a short period, Washington returned to the apartment to try again, but this time a white man, Henry Albert Ulrich, who had seen him earlier, came from his apartment to ask him what he was doing there while simultaneously accusing him of burglarizing his home. Before Washington could reply, the man began delivering punches to the side of his head. Vainly trying to explain why he was there, the man continued to savagely beat him. Desperate, the 55-year-old Washington tried to fight back, but the younger man prevailed, reducing the Wizard of Tuskegee to pleading for mercy. According to the perpetrator of the assault, Washington, bleeding, pleaded again for the man to let him go: "I know I have done wrong. Let me go."[3]

Washington somehow escaped to the street, but the white man, using a heavy cane that a fellow citizen lent him to beat the black leader, whaled away on Washington, who pleaded, "Don't beat me this way," urging him now to call the police. Washington began running again, fearing for his life. The white man beat him as he ran, with the owner of the weapon running beside him. Washington caught his foot in the trolley tracks. Stumbling and falling, he landed at the feet of a plainclothes policeman, whom his pursuer told that Washington was a thief. He told the officer that he had caught Washington looking through a keyhole and fiddling with the doorknob. Washington's assailant told the police officer that "if you hadn't shown up I'd [have] knocked that black man's head off." They considered charging the man, widely known as the most influential black man in America, with rape since they felt he was stalking the two white women whom he had encountered in the building.[4]

The bloodied, battered, and thoroughly beaten Washington could not initially convince the officer that he was indeed the famous Booker T. Washington. After he did, the charges were dropped, and Ulrich himself was charged with felonious assault and jailed until he could raise bail. Washington received 16 stitches and a bandage that covered almost his entire head.[5]

It was an ironic twist of fate for a man who had come so far to end up close to becoming what many a black male of the era feared: a victim of white violence. Only one short decade previous to this incident, Washington had had one of his most glorious personal achievements, being a luncheon guest of President Theodore Roosevelt. This event capped Washington's gradual emergence to the status as the chief spokesman for his people. During this period Washington elaborated his philosophy and strategies for black progress in America. The practical consequences of this strategy and outlook had important implications for the shaping and molding of black manhood during this period.

Washington's nightmare ended where those of other black males would only be beginning. Realizing that he was indeed the renowned educator, the situation reversed itself as the man being pursued became the victim, and his pursuer became the victimizer, and the legal case against Washington was dismissed. Despite this, Washington had experienced the initial stages of the criminalization process. Knocking on a door in an all-white building was a crime in the de facto sense for black males during the era. The de facto prohibition of the black male presence in many areas of public space represents the modern urban equivalent of the restriction on black geographic mobility experienced during slavery and its Jim Crow aftermath. Exercising a bit of freedom in New York, Washington made a wrong move and paid a fearsome price for it. For practically any other black man of the era, this would have meant almost certain imprisonment. For many, Washington's status was no excuse for this breach of racial etiquette. Senator "Pitchfork" Ben Tillman of South Carolina, whom the Tuskegean had tried to woo, rejected Washington's excuses and defended the educator's attacker as being justified because he "had made goo-goo eyes" at a white man's spouse.[6]

This chapter discusses the events that shaped black masculinity at the dawn of the twentieth century. It was an era during which Ida B. Wells led a national campaign against lynching, which was aimed chiefly at African American males. Wells-Barnett pointed out that the United States was the only nation that "burns its criminals." It was a "human holocaust" possible only in the United States, she stressed. Not only men were victims, but women, even when pregnant, and children were also murdered by white mobs during the era. Wells sought to refute the charge that black male rape of white women gave rise to the custom of lynching. Wells-Barnett charged that the "cowardly lyncher revels in murder, then seeks to shield himself from public execration by claiming devotion to woman."[7] Wells-Barnett listed the wide range of reported direct causes of lynching murders as well as the wide range of remedies for the practice of lynching that had been proposed, including "education," but noted that "it is as grave a crime to murder an ignorant man as it is a scholar."[8] Following the 1891 lynching of 11 Italians in Tallulah, Louisiana, in which an embarrassed U.S. government compensated the families of the victims, an outcry concerning the barbarity of the crime was heard for a period.[9] For this reason, Wells-Barnett asserted that it is the responsibility of the federal government to ensure that the practice of lynching be eliminated as soon as possible.[10]

The new era was launched on 18 September 1895, when Booker T. Washington addressed a large crowd of blacks and whites at the opening of the Cotton States Exposition. "Cast down your buckets where you are," Washington implored African Americans. Work for good, "friendly" relationships with the "southern white man," who, echoing decades of white pundits, was the best ally of the recently enslaved people. Washington also worked another favorite theme—the loyalty of black people to the southern white man. Addressing the "white man" directly, he stressed that these 8 million blacks had, "without strikes and labor wars, tilled your fields, cleared your forests, builded your railroads and cities." A big selling point was the black character, which Washington described as "the most patient, faithful, law-abiding, and unresentful people that the world has seen."[11]

Clark Howell, the editor of the *Atlanta Constitution*, hailed the speech as "epoch-making" and "one of the most notable speeches, both as to character and the warmth of its reception, ever delivered to a Southern audience."[12] Most importantly, for Howell, this "representative Negro" gave the white South a "full vindication" of their policy that "the Negro" must turn to "his best friend," the "white people of the South," for progress. The best feature of the address for Howell was that the nettlesome "question of social equality" was eliminated as an issue. Washington, crowned the African American's negotiator, had given up the quest for full civil rights in the South and accepted an inferior place in the social order for the foreseeable future.[13] Du Bois, writing in 1923 in *Century* magazine, later described the "deal" Washington negotiated for blacks: "Let politics alone, keep in your place, work hard, and do not complain."[14]

The long-lasting appeal of Washington's speech, however, lay in the "compromise" portion of it. Stretching his hand in the air, with fingers extended, he proposed, "In all things that are purely social, we can be as separate as the fingers, yet one as the hand in all things essential to mutual progress," as he closed his fingers into a fist. Washington then termed "social equality" "the extremest folly," cementing his God-like status in the hearts of those fervently opposed to

black civil rights.[15]   One year later, the Supreme Court's *Plessy v. Ferguson*
decision found that "separate but equal" accommodations for African Americans
were "reasonable" applications of state power.[16] Clearly, for both black males and
black females, things would get worse before they would get better. During his
speech Booker T. Washington declared that "when it comes to business, pure and
simple, it is in the South that the Negro is given a man's chance in the commercial
world."[17] What the Tuskegee educator was referring to was, in all likelihood, a
mystery to most of his fellow African Americans, some of whom were found in
tears in the crowd following his speech. Only three years before, in Memphis,
Tennessee, Ida Wells' young life was changed forever after three young
businessmen friends of hers were lynched for the apparent crime of being
successful in the grocery business. Thomas Moss, Calvin McDowell, and Henry
Stewart didn't die without a struggle but were slain after opening the People's
Grocery across from a white grocery. With his last words, Moss advised his
people to "go west," for "[T]here is no justice for them here."[18] Despite the regular
occurrence of lynchings, Washington's Atlanta speech set the tone for the era until
its influence began to slowly decline in the wake of the 1906 Brownsville affair
and the Atlanta riots.

AN ACCOMMODATIVE BLACK MASCULINITY

Booker T. Washington's accommodationist philosophy was an important
element in the development of the black masculinity prevalent at the turn of the
century. The end of black resistance to Jim Crow and the promise of subservience
were embraced as a "historic" compromise. No longer would the small white
merchants or workers find it necessary to worry about the emergence of black
competitors, as the majority of trades, occupations, and careers would be left to
whites. Opportunities for blacks would be confined to marginal and undesirable
areas that did not pose a challenge to the immutable racial hierarchy that dictated
that no black could occupy a higher position than any white. The element of black
loyalty to whites was a basic component of accommodationism, as well as the
admission by blacks that, as a backward race, they were, in general, decades away
from the attainment of the capacity to independently survive, much less thrive.

While Booker T. Washington discouraged any protest or complaint,
occasionally terming it "whining," he urged blacks to put their noses to the
grindstone and work harder.[19] Washington's overall philosophy inevitably made
him a strong supporter of the emerging all-black towns in the South, Midwest, and
Southwest. This was especially true of Mound Bayou, Mississippi, founded in
1887 by Isiah Montgomery, a man who shared Washington's faith in economic
progress as the path of black advancement. Mound Bayou enjoyed some economic
success but, notably, became a place to which black men too ambitious to live
safely elsewhere in Mississippi flocked. "Whitecapping," the practice of driving
upwardly mobile blacks from town, acted to maintain the exclusion of blacks from
the vast majority of occupations, trades, and retail opportunities.[20] Black male
owners of groceries, hacks, and print shops were forced out of business by whites

determined not to allow any breach in the servile and menial jobs they desired blacks to be confined to.[21]

Accommodationism's political consequences went far beyond the denial of political representation for African Americans at the levels of local, state, and federal executive, legislative, or judicial branches. This disfranchisement also resulted in the de facto white selection of black political representatives. Politically, black males were to accept that they were not fit to participate in the political process. The unconstitutionality of their disfranchisement was ignored, as stress was placed on working hard and financial status, despite the disadvantages inherent in acceptance of the status quo. Washington advised young men to steer clear from involvement in "mere political activity."[22] In general, Washington's politics boiled down to accepting whatever the white power structure, locally, regionally, and nationally, imposed upon African Americans. It represented the surrender of the black vote and legitimate political power during a period when only males had the franchise.

Educator Kelly Miller summed up his view of the differences in leadership style and content between Washington and Frederick Douglass, who died in 1895, the same year Washington's star rose. Miller compared Douglass to a "lion," "bold and fearless," whereas Washington was "lamblike, meek, and submissive." While Douglass "held up to public scorn the sins of the white race," Washington focused on the "faults of his own race."[23]

Despite the horrors of slavery, contemporary racial prejudice, and discrimination, one of Booker T. Washington's key personal values was his sense of personal loyalty to whites, painting in his *The Story of the Negro* a portrait of racial harmony in the South.[24] The "fidelity" and "harmony" about which Washington writes contrasts with the bitter anger that Du Bois observed during a casual survey of black opinion in the rural South. One man told him candidly, "Let a white man touch me, and he dies; I don't boast this, I don't say it loud, or before the children, but I mean it." He continued to tell Du Bois of witnessing the whipping of his father and mother while they picked cotton "till the blood ran."[25]

In W.E.B. Du Bois' famous essay "Of Mr. Booker T. Washington and Others," the scholar took the Tuskegean to task for a program and outlook that ignored the "manhood" needs of African Americans. Noting that Washington's "counsels of submission overlooked certain elements of true manhood,"[26] Du Bois complained that Washington's program was transformed into a philosophy and "a veritable Way of Life" of "submission and silence."[27] Washington was the embodiment of the "old attitude of adjustment and submission," and his acceptance of the doctrine of black inferiority at a critical juncture in national history was an unprecedented event for African Americans. Prior to this when white racism "intensified," black "self-assertion" did likewise. Now, for the first time, according to Du Bois, "a policy of submission is advocated." Throughout world history, it has been generally concluded, Du Bois asserted, that those who "voluntarily surrender" "manly self-respect" have been considered "not worth civilizing." For Du Bois, black politics of the era should have, at a minimum, pushed for "manhood" rights of voting rights, civil equality, and full educational opportunity.[28]

Consistently, Washington pinned the blames for blacks' plight on themselves. In 1904, speaking to black farmers, he suggested that black progress could be achieved "if you would take some of the money you spend in candy and help the school—that is build a schoolhouse for your children. I say candy, because one of the most disgusting sights to me is to see a man, a great big man going around the streets eating a red stick of candy on Saturdays."[29] The same year Ida Wells-Barnett criticized Washington for relating a story to a "cultured" black women's club in Chicago that implied blacks regularly stole hogs prior to the emergence of Tuskegee.[30]

Washington asserted that blacks "disfranchise ourselves in nine cases out of ten because we do not exercise enough forethought to pay our polltax. We should pay our polltax whether under the law we are allowed to vote or not." Few voices of dissent were heard during the Washington-organized Negro Conference of farmers, as complaints or protests were frowned upon.[31] In addition, whites, such as Benjamin F. Riley were allowed to speak. Riley told one gathering in 1910 that the whites who were "favorable to your race are the original slave owners and their descendants."[32] In his book, *The White Man's Burden*, he wrote of the childlike blacks: "[W]here others would resist, he tamely submits, and where others would cherish malice and hatred, he returns to a quiet good humor."[33]

The element of racial dignity, consciousness, and pride was distorted by Washington's deference to whites. Unable, perhaps by personal constitution and upbringing, to voice a serious objection to any proposal, however antiblack, put forth by the white South, Washington was reduced to servile flattery to reach his objectives.[34] In autumn 1906 Washington wrote his white friend, Charles A. Wickersham, in order to try to temporarily moderate some of the rules of the segregated Atlanta railroad terminal that he managed. The National Negro Businessmen's League was holding a national meeting in Atlanta, where African Americans from over 30 states would be arriving.[35]

Writing with characteristic meekness when addressing whites, Washington asked if there was "some action" to "modify," "if possible," "the rule . . . which requires colored people to enter and leave the depot at a side door." He explained that the men, not having lived in Atlanta, would not think of "going to the side door." Wickersham replied that it was not a question of a side or a front entrance but of a "White Entrance" and a "Negro Entrance." He did offer to put up another sign to direct the blacks to "the Main Colored Entrance." The prospect of another sign frightened Washington to an even greater extent, and he pleaded with Wickersham to leave the signs as they were. He volunteered that he would try to discourage any criticism of the Atlanta terminal practices in the black newspapers.[36]

With regard to Washington's program for black education, Du Bois warned that the "Talented Tenth" would not "lightly lay aside their yearning and contentedly become hewers of wood and drawers of water."[37] Another critic of accommodation, William H. Ferris, a Yale graduate, scathingly ridiculed the program, pointing to its implications for black manhood and maintaining that "Booker Washington's propaganda has given color to the opinion that the negro is mentally inferior."[38] Chicago attorney Edward H. Morris, another critic, held the Tuskegean was "largely responsible for the lynching in this country."[39]

Opposition to Washington surfaced at the 30 July 1903 meeting in Boston, where 2,000 people packed a sweltering church. Upon the introduction of the Tuskegee educator-politician, scuffles broke out in the crowd between opponents and supporters of Washington. The leader of the opposition to Washington in Boston was William Monroe Trotter, the Harvard-educated editor of the militantly integrationist *Boston Guardian*, who was arrested with his sister. Trotter had tried to read the nine questions that had been prepared to confront Washington with. Arrested on a charge of disturbing the peace, Washington gleefully pressed charges, and Trotter was convicted and sentenced to 30 days in jail.

Du Bois was perhaps most critical of Washington's "hushing of the criticism of honest opponents," terming it "a dangerous thing."[40] Hubert H. Harrison, a leftist intellectual of such repute that the *New York Times* once described his corner orations as one of the must-see sites in the city, was dismissed from his post office position following the publication of two of his articles criticizing the Tuskegee educator.[41] Washington, in turn, dismissed his critics as "simply spoiled young men who had been educated beyond their intelligence."[42]

Socially, the accommodationist philosophy represented a surrender of the principles of equality, fairness, and freedom of choice for African Americans. Washington's critics clearly felt that full "manhood" rights were inseparable from voting rights, social equality, and a minimum of economic justice. Fighting for these objectives and failing to achieve them, despite a valiant effort, were one thing: the voluntary surrender of these essentials, an "unmanly" act, was quite another. Accommodationism was, at best, a detour on the path of black progress in the spiritual, psychological, and social-psychological sense and fostered a limited, self-conscious, defensive, and intellectually underconfident black male personality. Accepting an inferior role in society, replete with a scripted code of deference backed by custom and law, the inherent sense of human dignity was eroded and, sometimes, irretrievably lost for the individual. The essential spirit of efficacy, the feeling that the individual can rise according to his or her talents, skills, knowledge, or business acumen, was largely shattered by the knowledge, almost from birth, that rigid barriers existed barring the way to success. Accommodationism, as practiced by Washington, sought to formalize this distinctly inferior status, orienting black socialization, education, and training to conform to the "reality" of the needs of the social system.

THE ERA OF ACCOMMODATIONISM AND THE BLACK MALE IMAGE

The atmosphere that marked the emergence of accommodationism not only as a philosophy but also, in Du Bois' term, as "a veritable Way of Life" was characterized by distinctly derogatory images of the African American male.[43] The publication of *The Complete Tales of Uncle Remus* by Joel Chandler Harris in the decade of the 1880s presented the narrator, black Uncle Remus, as faring poorly in his new status as a freedman.[44] Uncle Remus' folksy humor conveyed Harris' conviction that higher levels of education were unsuited to the limited intellectual capacities of the African. The African folktales faithfully rendered by Harris, however, show a Br'er Rabbit as a clever, improvising character who survived despite his small size by means of his wits.[45] Frederickson points out, however, that Br'er Rabbit, following the Civil War, having migrated to the city, has harsh words for freedmen who believed the system owed them something. Expecting something for nothing, they couldn't keep out of "udder foke's chick'n coops." But, Br'er Rabbit knew how to deal with these individuals: "You slap de law onter a nigger a time or two."[46]

The "Negro as a beast" theories that denied that blacks were human formed a part of the atmosphere conducive to lynching. According to this logic, all discussion on black education and rights was meaningless, as the limited intellectual capacity of blacks would make freedom amid naturally superior whites impossible. Black education was a complete waste of taxpayers' money or, even worse, counterproductive, as its effect on feeble black male minds was thought to produce hordes of savage rapists.[47] Popular magazines routinely coupled the Sambo images with those they termed "darky," "nigger," "pickaninny," "coon," and worse. These magazines of wide circulation regularly cited their perceived fondness for watermelons, chickens, theft, and liquor.[48]

The nineteenth century ended with the black male face of Sambo appearing in virtually every public setting in America. Projecting a smiling, empty-headed, primitive, and innocent persona, this image could be found in advertising, works of art, magazines, books, and calendars.[49] The Milton Bradley Company produced the Darky's Coon Game and the Jolly Darkie Target Game, the object of which was to throw a wooden ball at Sambo's face, aiming for the mouth.[50]

During the 1890s the American media hammered away at the theme of the black male as an incurable chicken thief. By 1905 the image of the black male as a chicken thief became predominant in films, including *Chicken Thieves*, *Interrupted Crap Game*, and *Prize Fight in Coon Town*.[51] At least one movie graphically depicted a brutal lynching of a black male for an alleged attack on a white woman.[52] Still worse, one New York City theater advertised a movie on the subject of lynching with lobby posters that read, "Hear His Moans and Groans."[53]

D. W. Griffith's *Birth of a Nation* exerted a significant influence on the subsequent depictions of blacks in American film. The film, which premiered in early February 1915, depicted black males as rapists, drunkards, and corrupt Reconstruction-era politicians. Black protesters are depicted with picket signs demanding "equal marriage" and as celebrating wildly upon the enactment of legislation allowing interracial marriage.[54] The play upon which the film was based was intended, according to its author, to evoke a feeling of revulsion on the part of whites, especially women, in relation to black men. It is written within a tradition of melodrama that identifies virtue with the virgin and evil with the rapist.[55] Gus, the black man, foaming at the mouth, pursues the white woman, Flora, so intensely that she leaps from a cliff in her revulsion at this creature.[56] Gus is merely lynched, as censors excised his castration from the film.[57] During the decades of the 1920s four of five black roles were servile ones, most often maids and butlers. The loyal slave who cared more for his master's happiness than his own was a theme that was adopted by subsequent productions. Later, Stepin Fetchit-type roles became standard portrayals of the black male in film.[58] During this period portrayals of Africa were dominated by Tarzan movies featuring swarms of identity-less, half-clad, semiwild, and voiceless Africans dominated by low-achieving white male adventurers.[59]

THEODORE ROOSEVELT'S ASSAULT ON BLACK MASCULINITY

Theodore Roosevelt, perhaps the most important individual influence on American masculinity during the early decades of the twentieth century, proved to be an important factor in the era's black masculinity also. Roosevelt influenced American masculinity in several ways, including his own maturation and toughening as a male, which was capped by an experience in the West as a cowboy and encapsulated into a veritable philosophy in *The Strenuous Life: Essays and Addresses*. Yet, while encouraging an aggressive and venturesome masculinity for American whites, Roosevelt's message for black males was quite the opposite.[60] It was a message heavily influenced by the realpolitik of the era, which dictated that black males be kept at arm's length, even if they formed an important bloc of voters who consistently voted for his Republican Party.

In October 1901 Roosevelt invited Booker T. Washington to dine with him at the White House. This token, symbolic gesture by the Republican Roosevelt raised a firestorm of controversy among whites, north and south. The president, however, had no intention of challenging the Jim Crow system of segregation by his invitation to the educator.[61] Indeed, Roosevelt had been supported by the "lily-white" Republicans, who had purged African Americans from the ranks of their southern state parties, and by Democrats committed to white supremacy. In defense, the president stressed afterward that women in the Roosevelt family did not sit down and dine with the black educator.[62]

While the invitation to Booker T. Washington only one month into the new administration served to raise black hopes, the publicity resulting from the invitation revealed the depths of white opposition to "social equality." One Memphis newspaper deplored the dinner as "the most damnable outrage that has ever been perpetrated by any citizen of the United States." A Richmond newspaper accused Roosevelt of favoring "that white women may receive attentions from negro men."[63] Later, Roosevelt complained that a Maryland senator was conducting a campaign based largely on race by using a campaign button showing Booker T. Washington and Roosevelt dining.[64]

In 1904 a loyal Booker T. Washington greeted Roosevelt's victory in the presidential election that year with great enthusiasm, promising to urge his "people" to show their "gratitude" by "showing a spirit of meekness and added usefulness."[65]

Despite his enthusiasm for the administration of President Theodore Roosevelt, the scourge of antiblack lynchings persisted. When the president did address the subject of lynchings, it hardly served to soothe the anger of African Americans. Roosevelt stressed the horror of the alleged crime committed rather than condemn the practice of lynching. In an August 1903 letter, Roosevelt discussed the perceived problem of black male rape of white women. After mildly chiding whites for lynching blacks, Roosevelt wrote that the black man "in a certain proportion" of the cases was "guilty of a crime horrible beyond description; a crime so horrible that . . . he has forfeited the right to any kind of sympathy whatsoever."[66] Roosevelt maintained that "the criminal not merely sins against humanity in inexpiable and unpardonable fashion, but sins particularly against his own race," a theme at which he was to repeatedly hammer away before African American audiences.[67]

In a speech to the Lincoln Day dinner in New York in February 1905, Roosevelt conceded the need to have fairness and equal justice for men of all races. Later, however, he shifted into the theme of the blacks' responsibility for their own condition. "Every vicious, venal, or ignorant colored man is an even greater foe to his own race than to the community as a whole," Roosevelt declared. He placed the onus of responsibility for condemning black crime on black people: "The colored man who fails to condemn crime in another colored man, who fails to co-operate in all lawful ways in bringing colored criminals to justice, is the worst enemy of his own people, as well as an enemy to all the people."[68]

Viewing lynchings as brought on by black savagery, Roosevelt urged that "the colored people throughout the land . . . in every possible way show their belief that they, more than all others in the community, are horrified at the commission of such a crime and are peculiarly concerned in taking every possible measure to prevent its recurrence."[69] For the record, Roosevelt did urge a halt to illegal, unsanctioned lynchings and their replacement by "swift vengeance" through legal means.[70]

For the black veterans of the Spanish-American War disappointment marked their hopes that their participation in the war would validate black demands for equality. Not only had hundreds of black troops been harassed and repeatedly threatened with violence as they traveled south to leave for Cuba, but the War Department continued to refuse to commission black officers. On the way south, black troops passing through Lakeland, Florida, pistol-whipped a store owner who refused to serve them and killed a white mob member, apparently by mistake.[71] On another occasion black troops liberated their comrade from jail after he was unjustly imprisoned.[72] Following the war, black troops were again the recipients of violence, as many in uniform were assaulted as they returned home.

Although President Theodore Roosevelt enjoyed a relatively high level of popularity in black America, he disparaged African intelligence, courage, and military prowess. While Roosevelt wrote in a letter to an associate that African American troops under his command in Cuba performed "well," he believed they lacked ability in comparison to their white counterparts.[73] Roosevelt was adamant in his conviction that a white must serve as an officer above African American troops. Once he reported that he "witnessed an extraordinary panic among the colored troopers" who were ordered to dig a trench. Roosevelt said that when he attempted to lead a march of the African American troops back to the trenches, "the rearmost men grew nervous, jumped forward and in a few seconds the whole body broke and came in like so many stampeded buffaloes, racing and jumping over the trench."[74] Roosevelt wrote that he "attributed the trouble to the superstition and fear of the darkey," who was only "a few generations removed from the wildest savagery."[75] In an magazine article authored in early 1899, Roosevelt wrote that he had fired his pistol to halt this frantic retreat to the rear by frightened black troops, immediately infuriating the national black community. Presley Holliday, an eyewitness to the events Roosevelt described, felt especially betrayed by the remarks, which he felt would give "the wrong impression of colored men as soldiers, and hurt them for many a day to come." Holliday recalled that Roosevelt's own soldiers told him that the men were merely rushing to the rear to retrieve ammunition and medical supplies to take back to the front.[76] The next day, Roosevelt gave the impression of apologizing to the black unit for his drawing and firing his pistol mistakenly. Holliday's frustration undoubtedly reflects the sentiment of many black soldiers who were initially so hopeful that the outcome of war would bolster black progress:

I could give many other incidents of our men's devotion to duty, of their determination to stay until the death, but what's the use? Colonel Roosevelt has said they shirked, and the reading public will take the Colonel at his word and go on thinking they shirked.[77]

Apparently, however, shortly after the exhilaration of combat, Colonel Theodore Roosevelt thought better of the black troops' fighting capacity. In a private letter to John E. Bruce, Roosevelt, referring to the Ninth and Tenth Cavalries, wrote: "I wish no better men beside me in battle than these colored troops showed themselves to be. Later on, when I come to write of the campaign, I shall have much to say about them."[78] Following the Spanish-American War, the much-admired General Joe Wheeler, a conservative southerner celebrated by Roosevelt, poured praise upon the black troops, writing that their "unfaltering courage" led them to participate in the charge of the cavalry at Las Guasimas. He wrote that "under murderous fire" they "gained the crest of San Juan Hill and captured the formidable intrenchments of the Spaniards," noting that the "reports of all their commanders unite in commending the Negro soldier," and pointed to "their brave and good conduct, their obedience, efficiency and coolness under a galling fire."[79]

Sergeant Horace Wayman Bivins from Puntoteague, Virginia, played a prominent role in these important battles. He recalled later that the black troops were hailed by enthusiastic crowds all the way south and given flowers and other gifts. In Illinois schoolgirls presented the African American soldiers with flags and flowers. Bivins later planted one of the flags at the top of the San Juan Hill on 1 July 1898.[80] The Hampton graduate's account of the taking of San Juan Hill highlights the key role of the black troops. After his unit trained their guns on the Spanish blockhouses on San Juan Hill, they charged and captured the initial entrenchments. Later, elements of his Tenth Cavalry charged up the hill and successfully seized the blockhouse, thereby capturing San Juan Hill. The white Rough Riders and the black Tenth Cavalry captured the Hill, according to Bivins.[81] Other lore from the war stresses the role the black troops played in rescuing the Rough Riders from defeat at Las Guasimas. The Rough Riders, after setting out for battle "in great glee," confidently predicting victory, soon found that they were in the middle of an ambush. The Rough Riders were in deep trouble. Not only were they trapped, but their mules had been shot, and several officers had been killed or wounded. The Tenth Cavalry's entry into the battle, however, made the Spanish flee immediately, as they feared being outflanked. Without this aid, the Rough Riders "would have been exterminated," in the opinion of the black soldiers at the scene of battle.[82] General John J. Pershing was among those with lavish praise for the performance of the black troops. For a few brief weeks during the summer of 1898, the black Cuba campaign veterans were heroes to both blacks and whites.[83]

When the troops were mustered out, Theodore Roosevelt addressed the black troops and gave them glowing praise for rescuing the Rough Riders from ambush. With the glorious battle still ringing in his ears, flush in the enthusiasm of the fight for his cause, Roosevelt felt a debt of gratitude to the heroism coming from unexpected quarters. After returning to the United States and immersing himself in the realities of political life, Roosevelt's battlefield euphoria quickly wore off. The rough treatment given Rough Rider veteran Mason Mitchell before a white audience after he praised the heroism of the black troops of the Tenth Cavalry signaled a white determination not to alter the traditional attitude toward black troops, in general, and the black male, in particular. The hostility of white audiences, especially in the South, to praise of the black troops was hard for astute politicians to ignore.[84] Black soldiers were not popular with the white public, as evidenced from the difficulty finding communities willing to tolerate their presence.   Within this political context, Michael Lanning concludes that, motivated "by a desire not to alienate white voters and a crusade to make the Rough Riders the absolute heroes of the war, Roosevelt began to downplay the performance of the black regiments and ultimately challenge their bravery and loyalty."[85]

The black soldiers and Roosevelt parted ways to separate fates. With his enshrinement as a war hero, one willing to lead his troops into the most withering fire of the enemy, Roosevelt's legend grew. Some of the black troops became victims of the antiblack riots in Wilmington, North Carolina, and other violence at the end of the century, and all faced the identical social barriers that had been in place when they departed American shores.[86]

THE BROWNSVILLE AFFAIR, BLACK CRIME, AND THE BLACK MALE IMAGE

On 13 August 1906 the wild shooting by an unknown group of men in the Texas town of Brownsville took the life of a bartender while wounding a police officer who encountered the men. This ten-minute outburst of random shooting in the streets, a fairly common occurrence during the period in Texas, mushroomed into one of the more important events impacting the image of the black male during the early years of the twentieth century.[87]

The Brownsville events took place amid a period of racial tension in the Texas community that included whites, Mexican Americans, and blacks. Three companies, B, C, and D of the First Battalion of the U.S. Infantry, were involved in several incidents during a two-week period illustrating the hostility that local whites and Mexican-Americans felt toward the troops.

The status of soldier for the black males, falling outside the dominance of the local whites, placing them on a equal or superior footing in some ways, was unacceptable for whites. The black soldier, while subjected to clearly unequal treatment, nevertheless posed a very real challenge to the Jim Crow system and threatened the norms of deference imposed by local whites.

Following the stationing of black troops in Brownsville, local whites immediately complained to federal authorities and the White House. The secretary of war, future president William H. Taft, wrote back, noting the almost universal objection to the presence of black troops. He pointed out that their records revealed that black soldiers were as disciplined as white soldiers and that the latter "average a greater degree of intemperance than colored ones." Taft expected the "good conduct" of the black soldiers, in time, to change the attitude of the community.[88] However, the white community in Brownsville was determined to rid the town of the black military presence, as tensions were increasing exponentially by the day. On the day of the shooting a black soldier was also accused of raping a white woman in Brownsville.[89]

Following the shooting, rumors among whites pinning it on the despised black troops spread rapidly. The townspeople organized themselves into a "Citizen's Committee" and telegraphed President Roosevelt concerning their plight. They wrote that due to the presence of the African American soldiers "our women and children are terrorized and our men are practically under constant alarm and watchfulness."[90] They requested the replacement of the black troops with white troops immediately. Roosevelt responded by ordering an immediate investigation and then removing the African American troops. Abandoning any commitment to the principle of due process, Roosevelt's chief investigator, Major August P. Blocksom, recommended that if the guilty men among the troops were not identified within a short period, the entire battalion be dishonorably discharged. Blocksom, agreeing with the white citizens of Brownsville, said, "[I]t must be confessed the colored soldier is much more aggressive in his attitude on the [question of] social equality than he used to be."[91]

Accepting his investigator's conclusions, President Roosevelt ordered another investigator to interrogate 12 "suspects," directing him to find evidence proving their guilt. Considerable pressure was placed on all of the men to "confess" to having participated in the raid. President Roosevelt's threat—dishonorable discharge of every man in the three companies—served to intimidate the men. Roosevelt decided early on to dismiss the black troops en masse but delayed his action until following the elections. His caution was fully justified since the African American vote was important in his victory. The African American community was quickly angered by the summary dismissal without honor of troops that enjoyed considerable respect and prestige among them.[92]

As the facts seeped out to the black community, their anger grew more intense. An independent investigation conducted by the Constitution League revealed evidence suggesting the impossibility of the men's being at the scene of the shooting. A routine call-to-arms happened to be issued simultaneously to the sounds of the firing of the guns, and all of the men were accounted for. The Constitution's League's investigation indicated that the inquiry ordered by President Roosevelt erred on several counts.[93] Subsequent investigations by the Brownsville local government and the Roosevelt administration were based on the assumed guilt of the black soldiers as the investigators only sought to determine whom of the soldiers participated.

Not one to back down from a fight, Roosevelt vigorously defended his actions. On 19 December 1906 Roosevelt responded to Senator Benjamin Foraker's criticism by terming the Brownsville violence an act "of horrible atrocity, and, so far as I am aware, unparalleled for infamy in the annals of the United States Army." He claimed that a "blacker crime never stained the annals of our Army." [94]

In stridently defending his actions, Roosevelt threatened blacks who disagreed with his actions. "If colored men elect to stand by criminals of their own race because they are of their own race, they assuredly lay up for themselves the most dreadful day of reckoning."[95] Given the lynchings that were then occurring with frightful regularity, Roosevelt's warning of a "most dreadful day" might not have seemed an idle threat. Indeed, it is testimony to the official nod given to mob violence against African Americans during the early part of the twentieth century. Following a roast of Roosevelt at the Gridiron Club's annual dinner, he later engaged in a heated exchange with Senator Foraker, who hit back hard after the president criticized him.[96] During Foraker's reply President Roosevelt had to be restrained from retaking the floor. During the heat of the exchange Roosevelt exclaimed that "some of the men were bloody butchers they ought to be hung."[97]

One notable aspect of the Brownsville affair and its aftermath was the use President Roosevelt made of his relationship with Booker T. Washington. Through Washington, Roosevelt attempted to placate the African American community's anger at the mass dismissal of the Brownsville soldiers. This anger was reflected in the columns of black newspapers, in the pulpits of the black church, and in daily conversations. Soon, African American Methodist bishops issued a statement citing the "monstrous injustices" inflicted upon the black troops by the Roosevelt administration.[98] In 1906 the national African American community was stunned by the words of Roosevelt once more. President Roosevelt once again held up the black male as a bogeyman as he discussed the antiblack mob violence in Atlanta, Georgia:

> The white people of the South indict the whole colored race on the ground that even the better elements lend no assistance whatever in ferreting out criminals of their own color. The respectable colored people must learn not to harbor their criminals, but to assist the officers in bringing them to justice. This is the larger crime, and it provokes such atrocious offenses as the one at Atlanta.[99]

This statement within the annual message of President Roosevelt in 1906 was a harsh indictment of the black community. Yet, it was not as harsh as he had originally planned. Booker T. Washington reviewed the statement prior to its delivery and influenced Roosevelt to moderate its antiblack sentiment somewhat.[100] Kelly Miller, writing to Washington, felt that the statement would further tarnish the black image, damaging it more than the combined impact of the era's most die-hard racists.[101]

Miller concluded that African Americans would "be branded as a lecherous race, with the authority of the President of the United States."[102] Roosevelt did just that, and his comments served to further cement the historical association tying the black male to crime and for this to be used as a justification for violence and racial discriminatory measures. Washington's reply asserted that Miller misassessed the probable impact of the president's message on black male rape and the lynching. Washington defended President Roosevelt, writing that "he had for his object the saying of something that will help to make life and property for the Negro in the South safer, and in order to do this he has, in a measure, placed himself in touch with the Southern people."[103]

The chorus of black critics of Washington's accommodationism steadily grew, and by late 1899, blacks in Boston, led by Archibald H. Grimke, sent an open letter to President William McKinley. From the outset the letter takes a quiet un-Washingtonian tone, noting the president's "extraordinary" and "incomprehensible silence on the subject of our wrongs." Aware of the perception of blacks in the public mind as wards and dependents, the Bostonians declared that they were addressing the letter to him "not as suppliants, but as of right, as American citizens, whose servant you are, and to whom you are bound to listen, and for whom you are equally bound to speak, and upon occasion to act, as for any other body of your fellow-countrymen in like circumstances."[104] The effort of blacks to improve their condition, they suggest, "has been met everywhere in the South by the active ill-will and determined race-hatred and opposition of the white people of that section. Turn where he will, he encounters this cruel and implacable spirit. He dare not speak openly the thoughts which rise in his breast."[105] Washington himself admitted to Grimke that this letter was a "straightforward and manly" one.[106]

By the end of the nineteenth century William Monroe Trotter and a wider circle of middle-class Boston blacks began to openly attack Washingtonianism. As a member of the Massachusetts Racial Protective Association, Trotter criticized Washington's meekness, complaining that Washington's "attitude has ever been one of servility."[107]   In Boston, as in the rest of the nation, segregation was increasing during the first decade of the century, propelling blacks into activism. As Trotter witnessed the regular lynchings and the silence of traditional white politicians, Washington's counsels of passivity and inaction drew the ire of one who termed himself constitutionally "unsuited to playing the part of the timid, or the cowardly," invoking the "spirit of protest, of independence, of revolt." Trotter declared the "policy of compromise" to be a failure and asserted that the "policy of resistance and aggression deserves a trial."[108]

THE WILLIAM MONROE TROTTER–WOODROW WILSON CONFRONTATION

In November 1914 an African American delegation led by William Monroe Trotter met at the White House with President Woodrow Wilson. Trotter reminded the president of his delegation's appeal to him the previous year concerning the increasing racial discrimination in all areas of American life, notably in the federal government itself. Trotter reiterated the delegation's view that "such segregation was a public humiliation and degradation, entirely unmerited, and far-reaching in its injurious effects."[109]   Moreover, the Boston editor reminded the president of his promise to investigate these charges. Despite Wilson's reassuring words, a full year later, segregation in the Treasury and Post Office departments, among others, remained in full force, and, in some cases, actually increased.

In a distinct contrast to the policy of "meekness" followed by his arch enemy, Booker T. Washington, Trotter forthrightly presented Wilson with a detailed portrait of the segregation within the departments of the Treasury and Post Office. He described segregated rest rooms, lunchrooms, dressing rooms, and working areas.   Trotter stressed that the "lavatory segregation is the most degrading, most insulting of all. Afro-American employees who use the regular public lavatories on the floors where they work are cautioned and then warned by superior officers against insubordination." Black people realized, the black leader continued, that if "they can be segregated and thus humiliated by the national government" in the nation's capital, "the foundation of the whole fabric of their citizenship is unsettled."   Trotter asked Wilson rhetorically: "Have you a 'new freedom' for white Americans and a new slavery for your Afro-American fellow citizens? God forbid!"[110] These were bold words to President Wilson, a man who approvingly reviewed the infamous antiblack film classic *Birth of a Nation*. Trotter's demeanor was completely at odds with that expected of a black man or woman in the presence of a white superior, much less the president of the United States. That a black man would address the chief executive eye-to-eye, man-to-man constituted a flagrant breach of racial etiquette.

Trotter then presented a demand that the president issue an executive order banning segregation in the federal government on the basis of race or color."[111] This seemed to irritate Wilson, who quickly responded, "Let us leave politics out of it. If the colored people made a mistake voting for me, they ought to correct it and vote against me if they think so. I don't want politics brought into it at all," showing open disdain for the black vote. Counterposing the "American people" to "the Negro race," Wilson stated that the "American people sincerely desire and wish to support" black progress and rejoice in "evidences" of black advancement. "But," he added, "we are all practical men" and could expect "friction" between races. The "best way" to "help the Negro" was to foster his "independence." He defended the segregation of the departments, saying that his administration was not "seeking" to put black employees at a "disadvantage" but merely attempting to arrive at arrangements that would relieve tension.[112]

President Wilson told the delegation that, "it takes the world generations to outlive all its prejudices." His administration merely "did not want any white man made uncomfortable by anything that any colored man did, or a colored man made uncomfortable by anything that a white man did." "It works both ways," the president concluded, denying that there was any discrimination in this arrangement. Wilson said that he had been assured that genuinely "separate but equal" facilities were provided the black employees.[113]

Trotter angrily replied, "We are not here as wards. We are not here as dependents. We are not here looking for charity or help. We are full-fledged American citizens vouchsafed equality of citizenship by the federal Constitution." Making a logical argument for basic decency, Trotter urged that Wilson consider that black employees had used the public toilets for the 50 years prior to his administration's actions. President Wilson's anger at being spoken to in such a manner then boiled over, and he complained that Trotter's "tone" offended him. He said that the organization must "choose another spokesman" if the organization wanted another meeting with him. Trotter, according to the president, was "the only American citizen that has ever come into this office who has talked to me in a tone with a background of passion that was evident." Unawed by this demand by Wilson, Trotter replied, "I am from a part of the people, Mr. President," to which Wilson observed, "You have spoiled the whole cause for which you came."[114] Trotter replied that he was "pleading for simple justice," adding that if he seemed "contentious," he was simply attempting to represent the feelings of his people. He explained that the members of the delegation were "branded as traitors to our race on segregation" by supporting Wilson's campaign for president. Cutting off the president's attempt to interrupt him, Trotter stressed how deeply African Americans felt about these issues.[115]

Following the meeting, President Wilson admitted that he regretted his emotional outburst during the meeting. "Never raise an incident into an issue. When the negro delegate threatened me, I was a damn fool to lose my temper and to point them to the door" instead of listening and merely telling them he would consider their petition.[116] President Wilson's perception of being "threatened" is revealing. The condition the president imposed upon any dialogue with African Americans was that they speak from a position of complete powerlessness. The very idea of a "negro" threatening to harm Wilson politically could not be tolerated, since Wilson did not clearly concede the black right to vote in any area of the nation. Trotter's eloquence and sophistication, as well as his respectfully aggressive manner, in all probability offended the racial sensibilities of the president as they would have offended whites with far less status than he.

The impact of this meeting perhaps halted the spread of segregation within the federal bureaucracy. William Monroe Trotter's courage to stand firm for racial justice in an era of rampant antiblack violence and political repression reflected both an increasing collective self-confidence as well as an increasing sense of political desperation. Unbeknownst to Trotter and the other delegates but surely suspected was that Wilson had already promised southerners such as arch racist Thomas Dixon that he would take care of the problem of the black presence in the federal government. He vowed to deal with "the force of colored people who are now in the departments in just the way in which they ought to be handled."[117]

The acquiescent accommodationism inculcated by Booker T. Washington marked an era of self-doubt for African American males. This accommodationism peaked during this era, when an all-out assault on the black male's character had been in progress for several decades. The structural and institutional racism, coupled with the range of racially prejudiced individuals functioning within the logic of these overarching systems, served to reinforce black self-doubt. With the funneling of money and influence through Booker T. Washington coupled with the disfranchisement of the masses of black males, a new leader was created. With his talent for sensing the desires of both southern and northern white political, cultural, and economic leaders, it is not surprising that his stated views dovetailed with theirs. As Washington's policy took concrete form, and he grew more powerful, an increasingly insistent criticism of his strategy and example began to be heard. William Monroe Trotter's example of an assertive masculinity continued a traditional of black middle-class behavior aided, in a new era, by a more powerful black community. While Booker T. Washington's visit to the White House caused a furor at the turn of the century, the Sage of Tuskegee was on his very best manners and merely elated to be there. Fifteen years later Trotter went toe-to-toe with President Woodrow Wilson, not waiting passively for respect, but rather demanding it.

The overwhelmingly male character of black politics was reflected in the formation of the all-male American Negro Academy in 1897 and the Niagara Movement in 1905. Patriarchalism reigned in politics and ideology among African American males, reflected in the presumption of male leadership and dominance by leaders such as Alexander Crummell, W.E.B. Du Bois, and William Monroe Trotter. Yet, as the next chapter discusses, it was a woman who led the battle against the scourge of lynching.

NOTES

1. A. J. Lane, *The Brownsville Affair: National Crisis and Black Reaction* (Port Washington, NY: Kennikat Press, 1971), 21.

2. Ibid., 241.

3. Louis R. Harlan, *Booker T. Washington: The Wizard of Tuskegee, 1901–1915* (New York: Oxford University Press, 1983), 380.

4. Ibid., 381.

5. Ibid., 382.

6. Willard B. Gatewood, Jr. "Booker T. Washington and the Ulrich Affair," *The Journal of Negro History* 55 (January 1970), 29–44.

7. Ida M. Wells-Barnett, "Lynching Our National Crime," in Phillip S. Foner (ed.), *The Voice of Black America: Major Speeches by Blacks in the United States, 1797–1973* (New York: Capricorn Books, 1975), 72; Alfreda Duster (ed.), *Crusade for Justice: The Autobiography of Ida B. Wells* (Chicago: University of Chicago Press, 1970), 71, 181–200.

8. Wells-Barnett, "Lynching," 73.

9. Walter White, *Rope and Faggot* (New York: Arno Press and the New York Times, 1969), 223; Wells-Barnett, "Lynching," 74.

10. Wells-Barnett, "Lynching," 74–75.

11. Lerone Bennett, Jr., *Before the Mayflower* (Baltimore: Penguin Books, 1966), 228–29.

12. Booker T. Washington, "Address of Booker T. Washington . . . Delivered at the Opening of the Cotton States and International Exposition, at Atlanta, Ga., September 18, 1895" (Washington, DC: Library of Congress, 1895).

13. John Henrik Clarke (ed.), *Marcus Garvey and the Vision of Africa* (New York: Vintage Books, 1974), xxxi; Washington, "Address," 5.

14. W.E.B. Du Bois, "Back to Africa," in Clarke, (ed.), *Marcus Garvey*, 116.

15. Bennett, *Before the Mayflower*, 228–29.

16. Ibid., 232.

17. Washington, "Address," 5.

18. Paula Giddings, *When and Where I Enter: The Impact of Black Women on Race and Sex in America* (New York: William Morrow, 1984), 17.

19. Harlan, *Booker T. Washington*, 213.

20. Ibid., 226.

21. Ibid.

22. Ibid., 10.

23. Kelly Miller, *Radicals and Conservatives and Other Essays on the Negro in America* (New York: Schocken Books, 1968), 32.

24. Booker T. Washington, *The Story of the Negro: The Rise of the Race from Slavery* (New York: Negro Universities Press, 1969), 32–33.

25. W.E.B. Du Bois, "Of the Training of Black Men," *Atlantic Monthly* 90 (1902): 289–97.

26. W.E.B. Du Bois, "Of Mr. Booker T. Washington and Others," in *The Souls of Black Folk* (New York, Fawcett, 1961), 44.

27. Ibid., 42–43.

28. Ibid., 48.

29. Harlan, *Booker T. Washington*, 206.

30. Ida M. Wells-Barnett, "Booker T. Washington and His Critics," in Mildred I. Thompson (ed.), *Ida B. Wells-Barnett: An Exploratory Study of an American Black Woman, 1893–1930* (Brooklyn, NY: Carlson, 1990), 256.

31. Harlan, *Booker T. Washington*, 206.

32. Ibid., 206.

33. Ibid., 256–57.

34. Ibid., 244.

35. Ibid., 297.

36. Ibid.

37. Du Bois, "Training of Black Men," 295.

38. Harlan, *Booker T. Washington*, 42.

39. Allan H. Spear, *Black Chicago: The Making of a Negro Ghetto, 1890–1920* (Chicago: University of Chicago Press, 1967), 61.

40. Du Bois, "Of Mr. Booker T. Washington," 45; Harlan, *Booker T. Washington*, 50–51; Stephen R. Fox, *The Guardian of Boston: William Monroe Trotter* (New York: Atheneum, 1970), 27–33

41. Portia P. James, "Hubert H. Harrison and the New Negro Movement," *The Western Journal of Black Studies* 13 (1989): 83–84.

42. Harlan, *Booker T. Washington*, 62.

43. Du Bois, "Of Mr. Booker T. Washington," 42–43.

44. Joel Chandler Harris, *The Complete Tales of Uncle Remus* (Boston: Houghton Mifflin, 1955).

45. Joseph Boskin, *Sambo: The Rise & Demise of an American Jester* (New York: Oxford University Press, 1986), 104.

46. George M. Frederickson, *The Black Image in the White Mind: The Debate on Afro-American Character and Destiny, 1817–1914* (New York: Harper and Row, 1971), 211.

47. Gilbert Osofsky (ed.), "A View of the Negro as a Beast," in *The Burden of Race: A Documentary History of Negro–White Relations in America* (New York: Harper Torchbooks, 1967), 184–87.

48. Boskin, *Sambo*, 108.

49. Ibid., 122.

50. Ibid., 142; Patricia A. Turner, *Ceramic Uncles & Celluloid Mammies: Black Images and Their Influence on Culture* (New York: Anchor Books, 1994), 11.

51. Thomas Cripps, *Slow Fade to Black* (New York: Oxford University Press, 1977), 14; Boskin, *Sambo*, 144.

52. Cripps, *Slow Fade to Black*, 14.

53. Ibid., 25.

54. Ibid., 48

55. Robert Lang (ed.), *The Birth of a Nation* (New Brunswick, NJ: Rutgers University Press, 1994), 12–18.

56. Ibid., 121.

57. Michael Rogin, "'The Sword Became a Flashing Vision,'"in Robert Lang (ed.), *The Birth of a Nation*, 277.

58. Cripps, *Slow Fade to Black*, 108; Turner, *Ceramic Uncles*, 163.

59. Cripps, *Slow Fade to Black*, 112.

60. Arnaldo Testi, "The Gender of Reform Politics: Theodore Roosevelt and the Culture of Masculinity," *The Journal of American History* 81, no. 4 (March 1995): 1509–33; Kenneth O'Reilly, *Nixon's Piano: Presidents and Racial Politics from Washington to Clinton.* (New York: Free Press, 1995), 66–81. Theodore Roosevelt, *The Strenuous Life: Essays and Addresses* (New York: Century, 1904).

61. L. L. Gould, *The Presidency of William McKinley* (Lawrence: Regents Press of Kansas, 1980), 23.

62. Rayford W. Logan, *The Betrayal of the Negro* (New York: Collier, 1954),

347–48; Willard B. Gatewood Jr., *Theodore Roosevelt and the Art of Controversy* (Baton Rouge: Lousiana State University Press, 1970), 35–36.

63. Gould, *The Presidency*, 23.

64. Theodore Roosevelt, "Letter to Dr. Lyman Abbott,"29 October 1903, in E. E. Morison (ed.), *The Letters of Theodore Roosevelt* (Cambridge: Harvard University Press, 1951), 639.

65. H. Garfinkel, *When Negroes March* (New York: Atheneum, 1969), 28.

66. Theodore Roosevelt, "Letter to Governor Winfield T. Durbin," 6 August 1903 in Morison, *The Letters*, 540–43.

67. Roosevelt, "Letter to Durbin," 541.

68. Gould, *The Presidency*, 237–38.

69. Roosevelt, "Letter to Durbin," 541.

70. Ibid.

71. Willard B. Gatewood Jr., *"Smoked Yankees" and the Struggle for Empire: Letters from Negro Soldiers, 1898–1902* (Fayetteville: University of Arkansas Press, 1987), 24. See also Willlard B. Gatewood Jr., *Black Americans and the White Man's Burden, 1898–1903* (Chicago: University of Illinois Press, 1975).

72. Gatewood, *"Smoked Yankees,"* 63.

73. Elting E. Morison, *The Letters of Theodore Roosevelt* (Cambridge: Harvard University Press, 1951), 1304.

74. Ibid., 1305.

75. Ibid..

76. Gatewood, *"Smoked Yankees,"* 92.

77. Ibid., 96.

78. Herschel V. Cashin, et al., *Under Fire with the Tenth U.S. Cavalry* (New York: Arno Press and the New York Times, 1969), 147.

79. Ibid., xiv.

80. Ibid., 61.

81. Ibid., 93–96.

82. Ibid., 124.

83. Gatewood, *"Smoked Yankees,"* 8–9.

84. Michael Lee Lanning, *The African American Soldier: From Crispus Attucks to Colin Powell* (Secaucus, NJ: Carol,1997), 93.

85. Ibid., 94.

86. Glenda Elizabeth Gilmore, *Gender and Jim Crow: Women and the Politics of White Supremacy in North Carolina, 1896–1920* (Chapel Hill: University of North Carolina Press, 1996), 105–113.

87. John D. Weaver, *The Brownsville Raid* (New York: W. W. Norton, 1970), 15–16.

88. A. J. Lane, *The Brownsville Affair: National Crisis and Black Reaction* (Port Washington, NY: Kennikat Press, 1971), 14.

89. Ibid., 5; Weaver, *The Brownsville Raid*, 29.

90. Lane, *The Brownsville Affair*, 19.

91. Ibid., 21.

92. Ibid., 80.

93. Ibid., 28; Weaver, *The Brownsville Raid*, 39.

94. Lane, *The Brownsville Affair*, 137.

95. Ibid., 241.

96. Gould, *The Presidency*, 242.

        97. Nathan Miller, *Theodore Roosevelt: A Life* (New York: William Morrow, 1992), 468.

        98. Lane, *The Brownsville Affair*, 71.

        99. Ibid., 104.

        100. Ibid.

        101. Ibid., 106.

        102. Ibid.

        103. Ibid.

        104. Colored People of Massachusetts, "Open Letter to President McKinley by Colored People of Massachusetts," *Anniversary of Emancipation in the District of Columbia* (Washington, DC: Library of Congress, 1889), 1–2.

        105. Colored People of Massachusetts, 4.

        106. Stephen R. Fox, *The Guardian of Boston: William Monroe Trotter* (New York: Atheneum, 1970), 27–33.

        107. Ibid., 29.

        108. Fox, 33.

        109. C. Lunardini, "Standing Firm: William Monroe Trotter's Meetings with Woodrow Wilson, 1913–1914," *Journal of Negro History* 64 (Summer 1979): 255.

        110. Ibid., 256.

        111. Ibid.

        112. Ibid.

        113. Ibid., 257.

        114. Ibid., 260.

        115. Ibid., 262; O'Reilly, *Nixon's Piano*, 88.

        116. Kendrick A. Clements, *Woodrow Wilson: World Statesman* (Boston: Twayne, 1987), 99–100; Lunardini, "Standing Firm," 262.

        117. O'Reilly, *Nixon's Piano*, 89.

Chapter 7

Black Males, Race Riots, and the Scourge of Lynching

> What shall we say of a nation of more than 76,000,000 people, with courts of law, school-houses on every hilltop, churches on almost every other corner in the cities, towns and villages of this great country, with a powerful and influential press, which goes into paroxysms when an American citizen is murdered in a foreign land—that quietly and complacently winks at the foul and disgraceful saturnalia of crime within their own borders, when the victim of these crimes are Negroes?
>
> —John Edward Bruce, 1900[1]

By 1913, on the 50th anniversary of their emancipation from slavery, black Americans looked back and surveyed their progress as a people. One-half century removed from the chains of slavery had meant the purchase of over a half million homes, the management of a million farms, and the ownership of tens of thousands of small businesses. Over 40,000 black churches, some owners of considerable property, were available to worshipers. Literacy was at a relatively high level compared to that of the rest of the world and to blacks themselves a half century earlier. A vibrant press arose to meet this demand for reading material, adding to the dynamism of growing communities across the nation.[2] Yet, persistent poverty, the chains of peonage and tenancy, poor education, poor health care, deficient housing, and myriad social problems beset African Americans. Topping the list of concerns was the problem of lynching, which had in common with slavery the fact that it was perpetuated, at least partly, by a professed federal constitutional inability to intervene to halt or discourage the practice. By virtue of the "gentlemen's agreement" enshrined in the Compromise of 1877, American presidents remained silent while African Americans were slain in a variety of ways, including roasting, hanging, and slower, more tortuous methods.

By April 1917, however, war was declared on Germany, and soon leaders such as W.E.B. Du Bois were calling on African Americans to "close ranks" to fight alongside white citizens for democracy and freedom. Not all blacks agreed that this was a wise course; the *Pittsburgh Courier*, for example, pointed to the impossibility of ignoring the grievances of blacks during the course of the war. After all, "the lyncher won't let us. The Jim-Crower won't let us."[3] A. Phillip Randolph asserted that blacks "would rather make Georgia safe for the Negro" and that "no intelligent Negro is willing to lay down his life for the United States as it now exists."[4] Hubert H. Harrison wrote:

> Du Bois, of all Negroes, knows best that our "special grievances,". . . consist of lynching, segregation and disfranchisement, and that the Negroes of America can not preserve either their lives, their manhood or their vote (which is their political life and liberties) with these things in existence.[5]

There was opposition to subjecting black males to the draft, from both the Right and the Left. From the Right, figures such as Mississippi senator James K. Vardaman, argued that the induction of black soldiers would introduce "arrogant, strutting representatives of black soldiery in every community," perhaps remembering the recent experiences at Brownsville and elsewhere and, also that of the post–Civil War era.[6] At the time of the outbreak of war, no training camps for black officers were established, while 14 for whites were. At this time, there was only one black West Point graduate, Charles Young. Following black protest, a reserve officers' training camp for blacks was established in May 1917. By October 1917 over 600 were commissioned as officers in the army.[7] Some 400,000 black men served in World War I, with the overwhelming majority of black soldiers performing supportive, supply, and service roles rather than combat. This chapter discusses the challenges of the World War I, antiblack race riots, and the phenomenon of lynching, a practice that was aimed chiefly at African American males.

THE CHALLENGE OF LYNCHING AND THE AFRICAN AMERICAN MALE

The images of black males hanging from ancient southern trees, "the strange fruit" of a democracy, provided an apt symbol of how elusive freedom and equality were for African Americans in the postslavery order. Although lynch mob victims included black men, women, and children, as well as whites, and foreigners, black males were its primary targets. Unrelated to real or alleged sexual crimes of black males, lynching emerged in the aftermath of the Civil War as a principal weapon in the effort to retard, halt, and reverse black progress. Lynching had a policing function that brought together the threads of the contemporary racial image of black males into a paradigmatic justification for routinized barbarity.

Harvard graduate Phillip A. Bruce, scion of the owner of 500 slaves, wrote an 1889 book that held that blacks, "cut off from the spirit of White society," had regressed to a state of primitivism.[8] This resulted in a wave of rapes of white women, according to Bruce, as the black primitives "found something strangely alluring and seductive in the appearance of White women." Bruce concluded that higher socioeconomic-status African American males, including preachers, teachers, and attorneys, were just as likely as common laborers to commit rape upon white women.[9] *Harper's Weekly* called this the "New Negro Crime" as white society mobilized against this perceived, growing threat.

The patterns of lynchings changed over time and varied by region of the South. In Virginia lynchings for real or alleged trivial offenses decreased during the 50-year period of 1880 to 1930, whereas in Georgia it rose markedly. These minor offenses included the common allegation of brushing a white, especially a white woman, from the sidewalk and "insolence."[10] Lynchings for alleged "sexual offenses" decreased in Georgia from over 60 percent of all lynchings in the 1880s in the state, to roughly 20 percent in the 1920s. In Virginia lynchings for sexual offenses increased from an already high 50 percent of all lynchings in the 1880s, to almost 70 percent in the 1920s.[11] According to Arthur Raper, author of an early study on lynching, 16.7 percent of the 3,693 victims between 1889 and 1929 were alleged to have committed rape, while another 6.7 percent were accused of attempted rape.[12]

According to Joel Williamson, during Reconstruction whipping, as a hangover from the tradition during slavery, was more likely to be the chosen form of punishment for such offenses, rather than lynching, which first emerged in the South in the 1830s. With the demise of the old generation of whites raised in the antebellum era, the new generation, who seized the reins of power as "radicals," quickly popularized the practice of lynching.[13] Lynching came into vogue in 1889, and its new respectability among the southern political elite is perhaps epitomized by the sudden change from a declared opposition to it by "Pitchfork" Ben Tillman in 1891, to his vow to lead a lynch mob to murder an alleged rapist the succeeding year.[14] On the same theme of generational change, Glenda Gilmore writes that in North Carolina by the 1890s, the rise of the "New White Man" was accompanied by a stress on how the previous generation had neglected to protect and provide for southern white women of all classes. No longer would they be exposed to the perils of working alongside the bestial black males, all classes of whom would inevitably rape and ravish all classes of white females.[15] At the same time the purity of white women was proclaimed, the New White Man voiced his determination to prohibit all interracial sexual relationships. Assuming the purity of white women, then, made it easy to detect any transgressions sexually across racial lines. Either a white woman herself was guilty of a grave crime, or a black man was forcibly imposing himself on her. Gilmore writes, "Henceforth, there could be no consensual interracial sex between white women and black men. White women would be incapable of it."[16] Via this assumption, the black elite of the period, the "Black Best Men," were assumed to have high economic and political ambitions solely due to a motivation to get close to the white woman. Relatedly, the rapes committed by poor black men were assumed to have been inspired by the ambitions of the Black Best Men. "Social equality" came to imply black male–white female sexual relations and was used as a convenient theme to mobilize white voters. Lynching functioned to make it clear to youth such as young Elijah Poole, later known as Elijah Muhammad, that there was no hope of individual development in the area for African Americans. After he witnessed a lynching in Cordele, Georgia, he left home to find work elsewhere, to seek to avoid becoming a victim. "Whitecapping" was a particular form of lynching perpetrated by whites resentful of black competition. Sterling Thompson was lynched in January 1901 after having had some success at farming. The politically prominent Republican lived on the outskirts of Atlanta in Campbellton, where his white neighbors coveted his land and property. He refused to sell, and whites planned to murder him and force his widow to sell the farm. Although he resisted, he was slain in a shootout at his home.[17] At the height of the wave of lynching, black males were the favorite victim. As a form of entertainment, lynching drew thousands of spectators, often from distant places. Occasionally, the railroad would sanction the process by running a special "excursion" train to the site of the lynching. The burned to a crisp, tortured, mutilated body would be torn apart by the crowd, which included women and children in abundance, and the mob battled over body parts as souvenirs. After Sam Hose was lynched, his bones were sold for 25 cents, and part of his crispy liver was sold for 10 cents.[18] The fascination with the body parts of the victim by broad segments of white southern society cries out for analysis. Cole Blese, a South Carolina governor who favored lynching blacks, once received the gift of a severed finger of a lynching victim in the mail. So delighted was he that he planted it in the gubernatorial garden.[19]

IDA B. WELLS AND THE ANTILYNCHING MOVEMENT

By 1892 Ida B. Wells had already published her pamphlet *Southern Horror: Lynch Law in All Its Phases*. In an unprecedented gathering, 250 prominent black women united to help Wells raise funds to publish the booklet in October 1892. Early on, Wells formulated a strategy, relying on the undermining of the stereotype as rapist that the black male was saddled with by media that often advertised their lynchings, giving time and place.[20] That year the numbers of lynchings increased to a recorded high, 241, the most in Louisiana, Tennessee, and Arkansas.[21] The horror of lynching, touching Wells-Barnett personally, inspired her to analyze carefully the cause of lynching and to utilize that analysis in leading a decades-long campaign against this form of systematic murder.

Wells-Barnett smashed the myth and defense that the white community simply "went mad" upon the discovery of some outrage, usually rape, perpetrated by an African American, usually male.[22] Wells-Barnett wrote at the very dawn of the new century in January 1900 that lynching "represents the cool, calculating deliberation of intelligent people" to violate every legal right of its victims. Following the war, first "red-shirt" gangs and then the Ku Klux Klan began to make use of lynching to "intimidate, suppress, and nullify the negro's right to vote," thus inaugurating the modern era of lynching.[23] As Wells-Barnett noted, after the "alleged menace of universal suffrage" was eliminated as a threat to white domination, lynching continued nevertheless. Lynching was a response to threat to the white domination of society. Any dispute between black and white, with or without violence, was influenced by the specter of a possible lynching. "Saucy," "insolent," and "uppity" blacks were lynched for being so perceived.[24]

The infamous lynching of Sam Hose is a case in point. Sam Hose, prior to the fateful dispute with his employer, was known as an intelligent, responsible, and capable man. After his employer drew his gun on him, Hose threw an ax that instantly killed the man.[25] Yet, rumor among whites inflated Hose's crime to murdering his employer from behind while he sat at his dinner table and then raping his wife.[26] Not only the lynchers but both northern and southern newspapers accepted these rumors at face value, while one noted that the employer's wife was not permitted to identify Hose for fear the trauma would be too great for her fragile health. The mob was content to allow her mother, who did not witness the alleged crime, to identify Hose. A crowd of roughly 2,000 went to Newman, Georgia, and cheerfully watched Sam Hose burned at the stake. A poster pinned on a tree proclaimed the theme of the event, "We Must Protect Our Southern Women."[27] Later, Lije Strickland, mentioned by the tortured Hose while he was in agonizing pain, was taken from his home before his wife and five children, strung up, and hanged. After his ears were cut off, and a finger was amputated, a note was finally pinned to his body reading: "We Must Protect Our Ladies." Revealingly, after Strickland's employer temporarily halted the mob's progress and extracted a promise from them to deliver the victim to the local jail, the mob was reignited by arguments that Strickland had stirred up other blacks and had run away years ago.[28]

The practice of lynching persisted from decade to decade due to the effective intimidation and forced unity of local whites and the hands-off attitude on the part of the federal government. Hortense Powdermaker, who studied racial relations in Indianola, Mississippi, during the 1930s, asserted that, with the exception of "poor Whites," few whites would state their support of lynchings, observing that "very few white men would try to halt one," as many agreed that occasionally lynchings were needed to "keep the Negro in his place."[29] Presidents from the Reconstruction to the Depression ignored pleas to intervene to halt the bloodshed caused by lynching. Most were like Benjamin Harrison, who proposed an antilynching bill not on behalf of African Americans who were being regularly lynched but in the aftermath of the lynching murders of 11 Italian nationals.[30] President William H. Taft's statement typified the presidential response over the decades: "It is not the disposition or within the province of the Federal Government, 'to interfere with the regulation by the Southern states of their domestic affairs.'" Holding to a position so eerily close to that which tolerated slavery for decades after the American Revolution, the official representatives of the white North turned their eyes from the weekly carnage that served to repress the aspirations and hope of millions of African Americans.[31]

Lynching faded gradually as the twentieth century progressed, declining more quickly in some states than others. In Kentucky, for example, lynching peaked during the 1890s and declined sharply after 1910.[32] The increasing urbanization of African Americans, changes in the southern economy, the development of more sophisticated communication infrastructures, and black community defenses against lynching helped foster its demise.[33]   When the National Association for the Advancement of Colored People launched a major campaign to end the practice in 1919, support began to build for the Dyer Anti-Lynching bill. African American organizations, newspapers, and activists mobilized to push for the bill's passage. After debate began on the bill in January 1922, despite arguments from southern lawmakers defending lynching as a response to the rape of white women, the bill passed the House but eventually succumbed to a southern filibuster in the Senate. Nevertheless, the national campaign for the bill's passage in all likelihood helped gradually reduce the number of lynchings.[34]

WORLD WAR I AND THE BLACK MALE

World War I had a radicalizing impact on black consciousness in general and on black male consciousness in particular. W.E.B. Du Bois wrote in June 1919 that for African Americans:

[T]his double experience of deliberate and devilish persecution from their own countrymen, coupled with a taste of real democracy and world-old culture, was revolutionizing. They began to hate prejudice and discrimination as they had never hated it before. . . . A new, radical Negro spirit has been born in France.[35]

Black youth such as Harry Haywood were inspired to be soldiers after they read of the exploits of the black Tenth Cavalry Regiment, which helped pursue Mexican revolutionary Pancho Villa. This romantic image of the black soldier helped influence young Haywood to sign up in 1917 with the Eighth Illinois Regiment, a black National Guard unit. This unit was federalized in July 1917, and, with them, Haywood was shipped to basic training at a camp near Houston, Texas. Haywood and no doubt many others recalled Woodrow Wilson's promises of black equality as a motivating factor as he trained to fight in World War I. Wilson had promised, "Out of this conflict you must expect nothing less than the enjoyment of full citizenship rights."[36]

Before being shipped to France in April 1918, Harry Haywood's unit almost replicated the angry behavior of the Houston mutineers. The hostility of local whites in Newport News, Virginia, gave rise to a fight with the black troops. Haywood admitted that his fellow soldiers had defiantly smashed local customs wherever they went, at times in a flagrant, reckless manner. In Newport News, Haywood recalled that, at one point, the men in his unit had picked up their guns and headed to the center city to confront the local police but were dissuaded from doing so by their officers.[37]   One morning, the black troops were ordered to "forward march" toward a fence. Between the troops and the fence were local whites who appeared hostile. Since the captain neglected to order a halt to the march, the troops "marched directly into the whites, closing in on them, cursing and cuffing them with fists and rifle butts, kicking and kneeing them. . . . Of course, we didn't want to kill anybody, we just wanted to rough them up a bit."[38]

In France in 1918, Haywood and the other black soldiers faced a chilly reception. The black soldiers were not privy to a secret bulletin that betrayed a racial discrimination in even harsher terms than what was immediately apparent. The document, the *Secret Information Bulletin concerning Black American Troops*, warned that the increase of blacks in the United States had created the "menace of degeneracy," which necessitated segregation:

> Although a citizen of the United States, the black man is regarded by the white American as an inferior being with whom relations of business or service only are possible. The black is constantly being censured for his want of intelligence and discretion, his lack of civic and professional conscience, and for his tendency toward undue familiarity [39]

The document seems to refer to the practice of lynching in its reference to the need to "sternly" "repress" the "vices of the Negro," specifically mentioning rape as one of them. It suggested an increase in "intimacy between French officers and black officers" had occurred. It allowed white officers to "be courteous and amiable" with their African American counterparts but made it clear that they were not to be dealt with equally as American white officers, for this would deeply insult the latter. "We must not eat with them, must not shake hands or seek to talk or meet with them outside the requirements of military service."

Also ruled out was commending "too highly the black American troops, particularly in the presence of [white] Americans." The American bulletin advised the French to:

> Make a point of keeping the native cantonment population from "spoiling" the Negroes. [White] Americans become greatly incensed at any public expression of intimacy between white women with black men. . . . Familiarity on the part of white women with black men is furthermore a source of profound regret to our experienced colonials, who see in it an overweening menace to the prestige of the white race. [40]

Harry Haywood reported that his black unit had been treated well by the French but that these men were stunned to learn that a town they entered was the site of a court-martial and hanging of a black soldier for the alleged crime of rape. The African American's body was left hanging for a full day as "a demonstration of American justice," in Haywood's words. [41]

The especially harsh and humiliating conditions encountered by black soldiers during the period occasionally gave rise to conflict, even violence. In August 1917 African American soldiers of the 24th Infantry revolted after being subjected to abusive treatment from Houston police and civilians for months. Earlier, local race relations were inflamed in the city of 130,000, 30,000 of whom were African American, by a campaign by the Anti-Saloon League of Texas. The day prior to an election the organization ran an ad in the daily newspaper sounding an alarm that some 3,000 black troops were to be stationed in the city within a month. The advertisement asked whether the "men of Harris County" could "afford to continue the saloon in face of this." [42] The Houston business sector had arduously campaigned for Camp Logan to be located in the city, as it would be a boost to the local economy, but balked when they learned that black troops would be stationed at the camp. The army refused to budge but assured the municipal leaders that black troops would remain in the area for no longer than seven weeks. Immediately, the black soldiers met barriers of discrimination.[43]

More than once black soldiers tore the "colored" signs from streetcars and threw them out of the window and sat in areas designated as "white."[44] On one occasion, when the number of black soldiers exceeded the capacity of the black section of the streetcar, and they sat in the forbidden section, the conductor ordered them off, leading to some violent incidents.[45] The soldiers' commanders then agreed to restrict the behavior of out-of-camp black soldiers. Special military police were to patrol the black communities considered hot spots. Black soldiers were ordered not to gather in groups of more than three. For men who were veterans of wars in Cuba and the Philippines, these restrictions smacked of rank insults.

The unit's African American military police were disarmed and given orders to call the Houston police if an arrest or any force was necessary.[46] The notion of blacks in positions of authority, even that of military police, violated the strict standards governing the extant white supremacist values of the region. After being disarmed, the black military police were verbally and physically harassed by the local police in front of black Houstonians, proud of the soldiers' accomplishments and bearing.

After two white police officers broke up a crap game and then chased the black teenage suspects through the neighborhood, the fatal chain of events was set off. The police later invaded the home of a black woman and insulted her, referring to the problems of "[Y]ou all God damn nigger bitches." The officer berated her for objecting to the invasion of her home, telling her that where he was from "we don't allow niggers to talk back to us. We generally whip them down there," slapping the woman after he finished his statement. He then told his partner, who had been drawn by the woman's screams, that they should send her to the "Pea Farm" for 90 days "cause she's one of the biggety nigger women." They dragged her from the house and arrested her. A crowd gathered when a black soldier, Private Alonzo Edwards, interceded, offering to pay her fine, whatever it was. This further irritated the police officer, who pulled out his gun and pistol-whipped Edwards. "I wasn't going to wrestle with a big nigger like that," he later said.[47]

Corporal Charles W. Baltimore heard of the beating and arrest of Edwards and, doing his job, visited him in order to interview him as well as the two police officers, who immediately displayed their hostility. Like Edwards, he was hit with the officer's gun and, being unarmed, was unable to respond. He fled to a house and hid under a bed: the officers followed him, shooting, catching up to him, and pistol-whipping him again, finally arresting him. Later, the officer said that he was confronted with an irate black soldier, Baltimore, who forcefully inquired as to "who whipped that soldier," leading to his retort, "I don't report to no niggers." He claimed that when Baltimore went into his own pocket, he hit him. Soon, rumors spread that Corporal Baltimore had been killed.[48]

Their white officer, fearing revolt, disarmed the men, stacking up their arms. The sergeant guarding the arms, however, was killed, and the weapons were seized after rumors that a white mob was approaching the camp. Private Albert D. Wright, who had been beaten by the same officer who assaulted Baltimore, angrily vowed to "shoot up every white son-of-a-bitch on Washington Street. We will show these damn sons-of-bitches who we are."[49] Angry and ready to die, one participant said, "Well, if we die," "we will die like men."[50] Led by Sergeant Vida Henry, a veteran of 18 years, roughly 100 men marched from the camp to confront the police. Along the way they were enthusiastically cheered by local blacks, longtime victims of the Houston police. When they eventually engaged the police, a fierce battle resulted, ending in 17 whites being slain. After an entire division of white troops was dispatched, the men dropped their arms and surrendered. The leader of the mutineers, Sergeant Vida Henry, took his own life, 13 others were subsequently executed, and 41 sentenced to life in prison.[51] African Americans were shocked to learn that the men were secretly hanged even prior to the public notice that a verdict had been reached. Thousands of white Houstonians, however, reportedly rejoiced.[52]

BESIEGED BLACK COMMUNITIES AND BLACK MALE DEFENSE EFFORTS

Ida Wells-Barnett's antilynching campaign's literature focused on the consequences of the abandonment of the rule of law and its replacement by mob rule. Many African American males, such as Robert Charles of New Orleans, had no faith in an unjust legal system. Many were determined that their communities would not continue to be victimized by this form of antiblack violence.

During the summer of 1900 the Louisiana lawmakers considered imposing the type of Jim Crow segregation on New Orleans streetcars that was the rule elsewhere. Their objective was not the physical separation of the races, according to the bill's sponsor, but rather the "demonstration of the superiority of the white man over the negro."[53] Increasingly, concern among whites rose about alleged remarks made by black male youth to passing white females. The city's media were stridently racist in both their news stories and editorials. One series, "The Negro Problem," ran during the months of June and July 1900.[54]

Robert Charles and a friend were stopped by a trio of white policemen, and soon scuffling broke out. One officer drew his gun, prompting Charles to draw his. Charles fired and fled but discovered he had been wounded. One officer was hit and wounded by Charles' fire, and from his hospital bed he commented, "For a nigger such as Charles   a club is the only effective weapon" contending that had he struck the African American man with his club, the gunfight might not have taken place.[55]

Robert Charles, now the subject of a large-scale manhunt, finally got back to his room, in all likelihood intending to tend his wound and get his Winchester ready. Before he could do this and leave the room, it was surrounded by the police. When a police captain broke into his room, Charles fatally shot him. Charles issued a verbal challenge to his attackers, saying he had something for all of them. Soon another officer was shot in the head, and the other three terrified officers took refuge nearby in a black woman's room, only to be taunted and cursed by the defiant Charles. "Those white men were scared," the black woman told a reporter the following day.

The manhunt grew in scope, as did white anger as word spread of the shootings. All during the day clashes that could possibly ignite violence occurred. Crowds gathered crying for Lenard Pierce, Charles' companion, to be lynched after he was jailed. Mobs of whites formed and began hunting down blacks to beat or kill. The next day mobs carrying shotguns and rifles formed, while the media railed against "Negro criminals." A meeting was held at the Robert E. Lee monument, where 2,000 white males gathered armed with guns, clubs, and assorted weaponry. After speeches, they set off to march to the jail, with the objective of lynching the jailed Pierce.[56] At the jail, shots by a determined policeman kept them at bay, and they confined themselves to beating or killing any blacks they chanced upon.[57]

A day later they finally located Charles hiding in a house near his. He killed two white officers when he was discovered there and then, under siege and facing death, fired on as many whites as he could. Soon over 1,000 men surrounded the house with weapons. They fired wildly, hitting the room with over 5,000 shots. Yet, Charles would stick his head out occasionally and fire back. Finally, the mob, including city officials, police, and firemen, decided to burn Charles out. Fleeing the heat, Charles was shot by the police 34 times.[58] Rioting continued, to include the burning of the Lafon School, the primary educational institution for blacks in the area.[59] Charles became a legend among the impoverished African Americans of the area. Jelly Roll Morton admitted that he once knew "the Robert Charles song," but he "found that it was best" for him to forget it.[60] During the week Charles had shot 27 whites, including seven dead, of whom 4 were police officers.

White emotion came to a boil by this series of events. Newspapers subsequently termed Charles a "monster," "bad nigger," "worthless, crapshooting Negro," and "ruthless black butcher," among other things. He was accused of being a "devil" who sought "African supremacy." Charles, however, had been a political activist who looked to the Pan-Africanist leadership of Bishop Henry McNeal Turner of the African Methodist Episcopal Church. Born around the time of emancipation to Jasper and Mariah Charles, both enslaved in the cotton area along Bayou Pierre, Copiah County, Mississippi, in May 1896, Charles joined the International Migration Society. This was a white-founded, for-profit operation that recruited African Americans with the promise of transport to the African continent. It took 197 blacks to Liberia in 1895 and 321 in 1896. Many perished once in Liberia, and others were disillusioned with the venture and sought to return home. Charles himself had made a down payment on a trip to Liberia.[61]

On 22 September 1906 the Atlanta riot broke out after whites began assaulting blacks. Despite five days of violence, perhaps two dozen deaths, and considerable black loss of property, it could have been worse. Black armed force was used to check the incursions of the mob in some areas. In the Brownsville suburb of Atlanta, gunfire from residents of the stable black community was necessary to keep the rioters at bay, and near Atlanta University a Professor Du Bois did guard duty with a shotgun in his arms.[62]

In Springfield, Illinois, almost two years later, in August 1908, a false accusation of rape victimizing George Richardson, an African American male, led to an orgy of looting, arson, and murder by a huge white mob. The white woman later admitted that Richardson did not rape her. She later committed suicide, but the damage had been done. The underlying cause of the riot was simply stated repeatedly by white residents of Springfield: "Why, the niggers came to think they were as good as we are!"[63] The direct spark was a false accusation of rape, but the underlying cause was the perception that Springfield blacks were getting too numerous and didn't "know their place." Some 6,000 blacks fled Springfield, some of whom had lived there for generations. One black man was lynched after he fired on whites who were attempting to set his house afire.[64]

Sociologist Allen Grimshaw counted 33 "major interracial disturbances" in the United States during the first half of the twentieth century, 18 of these between 1915 and 1919. Grimshaw has suggested that the riots such as Springfield in 1908 and Atlanta in 1906 bore similarity to "pogroms." Many of these riots stemmed from the manipulation of labor disputes by employers and other pillars of the Establishment. The racial prejudices of the white workers could readily be used to redirect their anger from the employers to blacks. It was not unusual for the police and the National Guard to join in the attack on the black community. For blacks it was necessary to retreat and set up some means of defense in order to survive the onslaught. Arms were by necessity used to prevent the murder, rape, arson, and looting that typically accompanied this violence. In East St. Louis in 1917, racial tensions had been strained to the utmost shortly after white workers won a key strike. The employers' determination to break the new momentum on the part of the white workers played a key role in the generation and perpetuation of conflict. Other key factors included a heavy black in-migration, racial union-busting tactics, wily politicians, and, most importantly, racially inflammatory newspaper practices. Several prominent, white, upper-class figures attempted to use the race issue to their own advantage and, in doing so, irresponsibly inflamed the white public. Labor leaders campaigned against "wholesale importation" of blacks and gained the support of realtors who alleged that blacks were causing property values to fall. The newspapers publicized the white "indignation meetings" against the black population, exaggerating the weapons that the blacks possessed. The police, for their part, focused on blacks and, whenever they had the opportunity, searched and disarmed them.[65]

President Wilson fanned flames leading to the 1917 East St. Louis riot by lending credence to the black "colonization" scare. His Democratic Party found political advantage in charging their Republican opponents with importing blacks to vote Republican in order to swing the state in the close 1916 election.[66] Local white leaders echoed Wilson's charge of colonization. Prior to the July riot, in mid-May, a committee of the white workers of the Central Trades and Labor Union, of the AFL, requested that East St. Louis' mayor, Fred Mollman, communicate to southern blacks that there were no jobs for them in East St. Louis.

They warned, ominously, that if present conditions persisted, there would be violence to the extent that the 1908 Springfield violence would look like "a tame affair."[67] Mayor Mollman later announced that he had requested that southern governors convince blacks not to migrate to East St. Louis.

White workers and their allies' objectives were to restrict and reduce the number of blacks, specifically black males, who could compete with them for jobs. These workers' own power was undermined by their exclusion of blacks from their labor unions, leaving no reason for the blacks not to participate in strikebreaking actions. For black males, this wholesale discrimination, in residency, settlement and employment, reinforced the existing de facto restriction of their freedom of movement. Whole towns, regions, and cities were closed off to African American settlement, with even travel through them being hazardous. Lacking this freedom of mobility, they were less able to take advantage of propitious opportunities.

The labor leaders viewed a rapid influx of blacks through the prism of racist ideology and saw a move to foster black domination. They began to speak of drastic measures to eliminate the black presence. The newspapers fanned the flames leading to a crisis atmosphere. The newspapers stressed black aggression and weapon possession and warned that a riot might erupt, pointing to the increase in black crime and to black insults to whites. The stereotype of the "gun-toting" black male was stressed; it was commonly remarked that the first thing a black male did when he arrived in East St. Louis was buy a gun. One letter to the editor said that black males bought guns for a dual purpose, first to defend themselves against white adversaries and, second, "as a meal ticket when they get hungry."[68]

In May there was a rehearsal of sorts for the full-scale violence two months later. A 28 May meeting led by labor leaders and the mayor featured opportunist politicians working the crowd's emotions with images of blacks moving in white neighborhoods and taking white jobs. The cry went up, "East St. Louis must remain a white man's town."[69] As the emotionally aroused crowd left City Hall, a rumor swept the crowd that a black man had shot a white man in a robbery. Other rumors involving white women being insulted and shot swirled, and soon there were the traditional shouts of "Lynch him!," "Get a rope!"

Blacks were then summarily attacked while the police force limited itself to ensuring that blacks remained weaponless and taking wounded to the hospital.[70] African American males reportedly were busy buying or otherwise obtaining weapons for what was clearly to be a battle for survival. Although police searched African American cars coming from across the bridge from St. Louis for weapons, seizing large amounts occasionally, light-skinned blacks were used to shuttle the weapons into the black community of East St. Louis. Blacks nevertheless expressed confidence: "As long as the state or United States troops do not disarm us, we are able to take care of ourselves."[71]

The National Guard and mobilized black community stabilized the situation for the time being. Systematic searches of black homes for weapons drew more black anger.[72] Meanwhile black workers were attacked as they left work by striking white workers. In mid-June, a 66-year-old black man was beaten severely for, according to a local newspaper, refusing "to give his seat on a Collinsville streetcar to an elderly [white] lady."[73]

Following the beating of a black woman and her emotional recounting of it to a group of black men, the conflict heated up.[74] Drive-by shootings by whites on black homes prompted the first serious black counterattack. The police, receiving reports of armed blacks, sent a patrol to investigate. According to a reporter, the police ran into a crowd of 200 blacks, some of whom opened fire immediately. Two men died, one then and the other the next day. The bullet-riddled car was left in the path of white workers, stoking their anger and providing convincing evidence to them of black savagery.[75]

By the time the July riot began, blacks had received considerable warning of the impending attack. Blacks were again assaulted at random on the street. Rudwick wrote, "By the early afternoon, when several Negroes were beaten and lay bloodied in the street, mob leaders calmly shot and killed them. After victims were placed in an ambulance, 'there was cheering and hand-clapping.'"[76] Houses were burned, and blacks were shot as they fled them. The National Guard, unfortunately, did not stand by idly as it had before in May. This time it took an active part in assisting the white mob.[77] Whites gathered en masse and before their attack marched in military formation. A carnival-like atmosphere prevailed when the first African American was shot. Indiscriminately, blacks of any gender, age, color, or character were attacked. White dissenters against the mob's actions were themselves physically intimidated by the mob.

After blacks were beaten and lay injured often they were then fatally shot. Increasingly, isolated blacks were beaten and lynched as the day wore on. Finally, some of the leaders of the mob reached the areas where the two white officers had been slain only two months earlier. They burned black homes and shot the residents as they fled. Screams of horror filled the air as the white rioters sought to terrorize blacks into fleeing the city en masse. The brutality and sadism of the mob were chilling, and the torture was sickening to reporters who witnessed the scenes, which included the throwing of a small boy into a burning house. Gun battles raged in parts of the black community, a cease-fire was arranged by the militia, and some of the black combatants were escorted to St. Louis. The reaction of blacks across the nation to the events in East St. Louis was a renewed spirit of militance and racial consciousness. The editor of the black *Atlanta Independent* pointed to a dilemma: "If we don't work South we are jailed; if we do work North we are mobbed."[78]

Following the riot, trials of the blacks arrested for the murder of the white detectives took place. Dr. Leroy Bundy, a prominent local black leader, was charged as the leader of a planned insurrection. The prosecution presented evidence that, at the time the police were slain, there were some 75 to 100 armed blacks on the scene.[79] Bundy was said by the newspapers to have targeted certain white leaders for assassination and to have been an "aggressive political agitator."[80] Indeed, Bundy was the epitome of the "aggressive Negro," as he was a former member of the St. Clair County Board of Supervisors. He was a political leader in addition to his business activities, making him a target of the opponents of African Americans.[81] Dr. Bundy was convicted, and the prosecution requested

life in prison for the dentist. Fortunately, a defense committee led by Chicago's
Oscar De Priest, appealed the case to the Illinois Supreme Court, which reversed
the conviction. The prosecution, feeling it had a weak case, decided not to retry
Dr. Bundy.[82]

Following the East St. Louis turmoil, a silent march of 5,000-strong took
place on Fifth Avenue in New York City.[83] At one of Marcus Garvey's regular
Sunday afternoon meetings held at Harlem's Lafayette Hall, on 8 July 1917, the
"Conspiracy of the East St. Louis Riots" was the subject. An irate Marcus Garvey
addressed the crowd, describing the orgy of antiblack violence as a "crime against
the laws of humanity," a "crime against the laws of the nation," and a "crime
against the God of all mankind."[84]

The year 1919 witnessed over 20 violent mass conflicts between blacks
and whites, including cities such as Omaha, Nebraska; Longview, Texas; and
Washington, D.C. The riot that occurred in Chicago was sparked 27 July 1919
after a black boy was stoned while he was drifting on a raft. The drowning of this
teenager after he breached the boundary of the beach reserved for whites, set off
the racial disorder. By crossing the unofficial Jim Crow line on the beach, 15
whites and 23 blacks perished. Prior to this wave of conflict, it was difficult to
defend the black community, but with the massive migration of southern blacks
into the city and hundreds of black veterans demobilized, this was no longer the
case.[85]

As in St. Louis, blacks were attacked by white mobs as they left their
workplaces, in this case, primarily the stockyards. Oscar Dozier had the
misfortune of leaving work on the afternoon shift and, after being chased for four
blocks, being fatally stabbed in the chest several times. When Harry Haywood
returned to Chicago following World War I, he obtained a job as a waiter on the
Michigan Central Railroad. On 28 July 1919 the bloody Chicago riot began. After
Haywood had returned from a run to Michigan, he found that his friends were
actively involved in designing a strategy to defend the black community from an
anticipated invasion by "Irishmen from west of Wentworth Avenue."[86] This was
not the first time that they had clashed with white "athletic" clubs that were
instruments of the city's ward bosses.[87] They positioned a submachine gun in a
strategically situated apartment, overlooking the expected point of entry into the
black turf.[88] Other black veterans of World War I were also involved in a
mobilization for the defense of the black community. Many soldiers had vowed
that after risking their lives for their country, they would no longer accept
humiliating, second-class treatment. One ambush of whites involved in drive-by
shootings in the black community reportedly resulted in the wounding of many
whites in a truck, several of whom were off-duty police officers.[89] There is no
reason to believe that Harry Haywood was unique in his assessment that the
Chicago riot marked "a pivotal point" in his life. Following this, he was even less
likely to take "any insults lying down," leading him to walk out of several jobs.[90]

The summer of 1919 witnessed rallies, demonstrations, and protests
mobilizing African Americans to voice a determination to halt the white mob
violence. Marcus Garvey declared at one such rally that "the best thing the Negro

of all countries can do is to prepare to match fire with hell-fire. No African is going to allow the Caucasian to trample eternally upon his rights."[91] Garvey told blacks to prepare for "the new emancipation" that would take place after Europe or Asia sparked a new worldwide conflagration. "Black men shall die then and black women shall succor them, but in the end there shall be a crowning victory for the soldiers of Ethiopia on the African battleground," Garvey confidently predicted.[92]

The "red summer" conflicts, like the 1960 rebellions, heavily impacted contemporary black consciousness. More than one analyst has drawn the connection between these events and the Garvey and Harlem Renaissance movements of the 1920s. It is significant that following the race riots of the 1919–1921 period, in which black males mounted determined effort for defense of the black communities against the violent incursions by whites, the pattern of interracial violence was transformed permanently. Mass attacks by whites on black communities never again assumed the same proportions.

The first two decades of the twentieth century marked the progress of a difficult transition of the black male from the rural setting to the urban one. Progress was never smooth, however, as war, depression, and other crises awaited him. His ability to adapt to new circumstances would again be tested amid the backdrop of a changing racial order.

NOTES

1. John Edward Bruce, *The Blood Red Record: Review of the Horrible Lynchings and Burning of Negroes by Civilized White Men in the United States: As Taken from the Records: With Comments by John Edward Bruce* (Albany, NY: Argus,1901), 12.

2. Lerone Bennett, Jr., *Before the Mayflower* (Baltimore: Penguin Books, 1966), 287.

3. Benjamin Quarles, *The Negro in the Making of America* (New York: Collier Books, 1964), 187.

4. Sally Hanley, *A. Phillip Randolph* (New York: Chelsea House, 1989), 46.

5. Hubert H. Harrison, *When Africa Awakes* (New York: Poro Press, 1920), 67.

6. Mary Beth Norton et al., *A People and a Nation: A History of United States* (Boston: Houghton Mifflin, 1990), 675.

7. Quarles, *The Negro*, 182–83.

8. Paula Giddings, *When and Where I Enter: The Impact of Black Women on Race and Sex in America* (New York: William Morrow, 1984), 27.

9. Ibid.

10. Joel Williamson, *The Crucible of Race: Black–White Relations in the American South since Emancipation* (New York: Oxford University Press, 1984), 187.

11. W. Fitzhugh Brundage, *Lynching in the New South: Georgia and Virginia, 1880–1930* (Urbana: University of Illinois Press, 1993), 51.

12. Arthur F. Raper, *The Tragedy of Lynching* (New York: Dover, 1933), 32; see also James Cameron, *A Time of Terror: A Survivor's Story* (Baltimore: Black Classic Press, 1994); and George C. White, *Racial Violence in Kentucky, 1865–1940: Lynchings, Mob Rule and "Legal Lynchings"* (Baton Rouge: Louisiana State University Press, 1990).

13. Williamson, *The Crucible of Race*, 183.

14. Ibid., 185.

15. Glenda Elizabeth Gilmore, *Gender and Jim Crow: Women and the Politics of White Supremacy in North Carolina, 1896–1920* (Chapel Hill: University of North Carolina Press, 1996) 67.

16. Ibid., 72.

17. Claude Andrew Clegg, *An Original Man: The Life and Times of Elijah Muhammad* (New York: St. Martin's Press, 1997), 11; Brundage, *Lynching*, 24.

18. Ralph Ginzburg, *100 Years of Lynchings* (Baltimore: Black Classic Press, 1988), 13.

19. Williamson, *The Crucible of Race*, 188.

20. Giddings, *Where and When I Enter*, 31.

21. Ida B. Wells-Barnett, "Lynch Law in America," in Mildred I. Thompson (ed.), *Ida B. Wells-Barnett: An Exploratory Study of an American Black Woman, 1893–1930* (Brooklyn, NY: Carlson, 1990), 239.

22. James Weldon Johnson, *Along This Way: The Autobiography of James Weldon Johnson* (New York: Penguin Books, 1993), 366.

23. Ibid., 236.

24. Wells-Barnett, "Lynch Law," 239.

25. Brundage, *Lynching*, 83.

26. Ibid., 85.

27. Ginzburg, *100 Years*, 10–11.

28. Ibid., 15.

29. Hortense Powdermaker, *After Freedom: A Cultural Study in the Deep South* (New York: Atheneum, 1969), 52.

30. Kenneth O'Reilly, *Nixon's Piano: Presidents and Racial Politics from Washington to Clinton* (New York: Free Press, 1995), 59.

31. Ibid., 78.

32. White, *Racial Violence*; Raper, *The Tragedy*, 25.

33. Brundage, *Lynching*, 85.

34. Johnson, *Along This Way*, 365–66; Sondra Kathryn Wilson (ed.), *The Selected Writings of James Weldon Johnson. Volume One, The New York Age Editorials (1914–1923)* (New York: Oxford University Press, 1995), 54.

35. W.E.B. Du Bois, "An History toward a History of the Black Man in the Great War," in Julius Lester (ed.), *The Seventh Son: The Thought and Writings of W.E.B. Du Bois, Volume Two* (New York: Random House, 1971), 131.

36. Harry Haywood, *Black Bolshevik: Autobiography of an Afro-American Communist* (Chicago: Liberator Press, 1978), 43.

37. Ibid., 52.

38. Ibid., 53.

39. "Secret Information Concerning Black American Troops," in Bernard C. Nalty and Morris J. MacGregor (eds.), *Blacks in the Military: Essential Documents* (Wilmington, DE: Scholarly Resources, 1981), 88–89.

40. Haywood, *Black Bolshevik*, 55.

41. Ibid., 66.

42. Robert V. Haynes, *A Night of Violence: The Houston Riot of 1917* (Baton Rouge: Louisiana State University Press, 1976), 23.

43. Ibid., 57.

44. Ibid., 64.

45. Ibid., 65.

46. Ibid., 71.

47. Ibid., 95.

48. Ibid., 97.

49. Ibid., 130.

50. Ibid., 158.

51. Ibid., 130; Haywood, *Black Bolshevik*, 44–45.

52. Haynes, *A Night of Violence*, 7.

53. William Ivy Hair, *Carnival of Fury: Robert Charles and the New Orleans Race Riot of 1900* (Baton Rouge: Louisiana State University Press, 1976), 139.

54. Ibid., 141.

55. Ibid., 120.

56. Ibid., 149–50.

57. Ibid., 152–53.

58. Ibid., 173–74.

59. Ibid., 177.

60. Ibid., 179.

61. Ibid., 68.

62. David Levering Lewis, *W.E.B. Du Bois: Biography of a Race, 1868–1919* (New York: Henry Holt, 1993), 334–35.

63. William English Walling, "A Description of Racial Violence in the North," in Gilbert Osofsky (ed.), *The Burden of Race: A Documentary History of Negro–White Relations in America* (New York: Harper, 1967), 204.

64. Ibid., 204.

65. Elliot Rudwick, *Race Riot at East St. Louis* (Urbana: University of Illinois Press, 1982), 31.

66. Ibid., 13.

67. Ibid., 23.

68. Ibid., 25–26.

69. Ibid., 28.

70. Ibid., 31.

71. Ibid., 33.

72. Ibid., 36.

73. Ibid., 38

74. Ibid., 38.

75. Ibid., 40.

76. Ibid., 45.

77. Ibid., 55.

78. Ibid., 64.

79. Ibid., 113.

80. Ibid., 119.

81. Ibid., 121.

82. Ibid., 131.

83. Johnson, *Along This Way*, 320.

84. Tony Martin, *Marcus Garvey, Hero: A First Biography* (Dover, MA: Majority Press, 1983), 45.

85. Quarles, *The Negro*, 192; Allan H. Spear, *Black Chicago: The Making of a Negro Ghetto, 1890–1920* (Chicago: University of Chicago Press, 1967), vii.

86. Haywood, *Black Bolshevik*, 81; William M. Tuttle, *Race Riot: Chicago in the Red Summer of 1919* (Chicago: University of Chicago Press, 1996), 37–40.

87. Haywood, *Black Bolshevik*, 80–81.

88. Ibid., 82.

89. Ibid.
90. Ibid., 83.
91. Theodore G. Vincent, *Black Power and the Garvey Movement* (Berkeley, CA: The Ramparts Press, n.d.), 43.
92. Ibid., 43.

Chapter 8

Marcus Garvey and the New Negro Man

Going giggling, prancing and jumping about like a child stamps you as
a clown. A man must be a man, a woman must be a woman, whilst a
child must be a child.

— Marcus Garvey[1]

On 30 October 1919 at Madison Square Garden, Marcus Mosiah Garvey of the
powerful Universal Negro Improvement Association (UNIA) declared, "It will be
a terrible day when the blacks draw the sword and fight for their liberty. I call
upon you 400,000,000 blacks to give the blood you have shed for the white man
to make Africa a republic for the Negro."[2]

Only four years after the death of Booker T. Washington, Garvey, a man
who admired much of the Tuskegean's work, established a very different standard
for black manhood. Gone was the deliberate political and social passivity
encouraged by Washington's accommodationist philosophy. In its place Garvey
stressed independently financed projects and programs aimed at black self-
reliance. In contrast to the restricted vision of the self-doubting, self-blaming
philosophy of Washington, an expansive, even bombastic vision was substituted.
This chapter traces and analyzes the forms of masculinity that were prevalent in
the post-Washington era, particularly those associated with the UNIA and its
leader, Marcus Garvey.

Malcus Mosiah ("Marcus") Garvey Jr. was born in St. Ann's Bay,
Jamaica, on 17 August 1887 to Malcus Mosiah Garvey Sr. and Sarah Jane
Richards. Malcus Mosiah Garvey Sr., a stonemason, provided strong guidance as
well as an example of striving and achievement for young Marcus   build upon
and was a man who not only was skilled at his trade but was active in the church
and community. He was a "village lawyer" who mediated conflicts among the
country people. A highly literate man, his library and newspaper subscriptions
helped young Marcus gain an appreciation for both the written word and the world

beyond St. Ann parish.[3] After Marcus' active, challenging, and adventurous boyhood in St. Ann's Bay, his father obtained an apprenticeship for his son as a printer with one of his best friends.[4] By 18 Garvey was a foreman, a considerable personal achievement.[5] Marcus' political awareness grew, and he became a leader in the Printer's Union. He also began speaking about one of his lifelong passions, the conditions of his fellow Jamaicans. Garvey studied elocution under Dr. J. Robert Love, the most prominent contemporary black Jamaican politician. The Bahamas-born Love's Pan-Africanist leanings and social conscience both impressed and influenced Garvey. Soon, as Love had done before him, Garvey founded a newspaper, *Garvey's Watchman*.[6]

Marcus Garvey traveled extensively in Latin America and Europe between 1910 and 1914 in order to learn as much as possible about conditions in the African diaspora. In Costa Rica he worked as a timekeeper on a banana plantation and on the docks at Port Limón.[7] Soon, Garvey founded a newspaper, in Spanish, *La Prensa*. Later, he went to England, where he worked on the docks of London, Liverpool, and Cardiff. All the while he was educating himself, reading voraciously.[8] Traveling to France, Italy, Spain, Austria, Hungary, and Germany, he arrived back in London destitute landing a position with the *Africa Times and Orient Review*, edited by Duse Mohamed Ali.[9]

In July 1914 Garvey returned to Jamaica to found the UNIA and the African Communities Imperial League (ACL) in Kingston almost immediately upon his arrival. The UNIA's motto, "One God! One Aim! One Destiny!," would soon be the slogan of millions of Africans worldwide. In 1916 Garvey returned to the United States and in New York City delivered his first American lecture. He soon left on a 38-state national tour that sharpened his already formidable speaking abilities and, once again, allowed him to learn about conditions in another part of the African diaspora.

After launching the New York branch of the UNIA in 1918, within a year Garvey's organization had grown to such an extent that the First International Convention of the Negro Peoples of the World drew 25,000 at Madison Square Garden, the largest convention ever in African American history.[10] The parade sponsored by the convention was truly awe-inspiring, as it stretched ten full miles. Marcus Garvey sported an imperial-looking military uniform leading the Universal African Legions' cavalry and infantry units, the African Motor Corps, and the Black Cross Nurses.[11] Posters, banners, and signs displayed slogans that included, "Down with Lynching" and "Negroes Fought in Europe and Can Fight in Africa."[12] For those individuals searching for an organization that had the potential to develop a military capacity, the UNIA, like several other black nationalist groups, included a paramilitary wing that served a security and self-defense function.[13] The delegates to the convention resolved: "With the help of Almighty God, we declare ourselves sworn protectors of the honor and virtue of our women and children, and pledge our lives for their protection and defense everywhere, and under all circumstances from wrongs and outrages."[14] Garvey took full advantage of the ripe conditions for black radical organizing. Beginning in July 1918, when the UNIA was legally incorporated in New York, hundreds of branches were formed, with over 50 being established in Cuba, over 30 in Trinidad and Tobago, and over 700 in the United States by the middle of the decade.[15] In New York, UNIA membership peaked at 35,000.[16]

For a period after the UNIA elected Garvey the provisional president of Africa, there was much to base this optimism upon. When Garvey arrived in Costa Rica in 1921, 15,000 enthusiastic supporters met him at the docks in Port Limón, forcing the management of the United Fruit Company to provide a VIP train for Garvey in order to get workers to load three ships with bananas. By taking Garvey to San José for three days, the workers would have time to perform labor they were prepared to ignore in order to greet Garvey. Even so, they delayed Garvey's boarding of the special train because there were some spots on the outside of it.[17] In San José, the UNIA leader was welcomed by the president of Costa Rica, repeating a similar welcome from Cuba's president the previous year.[18] Garvey's leadership helped increase the sense of power and pride felt by African peoples worldwide.

Two ingredients were key to the phenomenal emergence of Garvey and his UNIA: first, the charismatic, energetic, and organizational genius of Marcus Garvey and second, the general conditions facing African, Afro-Caribbean, and African American people in the historical conjuncture of the post–World War I period. The oratorical talents of Garvey are the stuff of legend. In his first public speech following his speaking tour, on 12 July 1917, he captured the hearts of many of the 2,000 people in the audience. Invited by Hubert H. Harrison to speak at the founding meeting of the Liberty League of Negro Americans, Garvey upstaged the Virgin Island-born Harrison, regarded by many as the foremost intellectual in Harlem.[19] Harrison, Garvey, and many others gained a measure of fame and notoriety speaking on Harlem's soapboxes, emblematic of the vibrant intellectual atmosphere there at the time.[20]

The international atmosphere was one of rapid change as the Bolshevik revolution, the Irish Easter uprising, and West Indian revolts signaled the arrival of a new era of social and political change. While the United States experienced a "red summer" in 1919, the Caribbean witnessed unrest among the colonized in Jamaica, Grenada, Trinidad, and other nations. [21]

On the national level, Harlem led a wholesale renaissance in black American culture, termed a "spiritual emancipation" by Alain Locke, who wrote in his essay "The New Negro" that "the Old Negro had long become more of a myth than a man."[22]   This figure was more an object rather than an active historical subject, determining his destiny himself. With a "renewed" sense of "self-respect," the new African American viewed the future with optimism, determined to fuel progress from internal resources whatever the obstacle. Clearly, the mythical "day of 'aunties,' 'uncles,' and 'mammies'" had passed, if it had ever truly existed.   "Uncle Tom and Sambo have passed on," Locke commented.[23] Feeling more empowered than ever, this "New Negro" felt confident that the obstacles of the past would soon melt away in a bright future.[24]

African Americans were in the midst of rapid growth and development within urban areas, propelling cultural, social, economic, and political transformation. The percentage of blacks living in urban areas rose from only 20 percent in 1890, to 27 percent in 1910, to 44 percent in 1930.[25] The black urban growth rate was most rapid during the decade of the 1920s, when it increased by 3.8 percent.[26] Especially significant with regard to the historical analysis of black masculinity was the increasing diversity within black America. The late 1910s and the early 1920s witnessed a huge influx of black immigration from the Caribbean, especially significant in Harlem.[27] By 1920 over 80,000 blacks lived north of 125th Street in Harlem. Within one decade this number had more than doubled to almost 200,000, with foreign-born blacks representing approximately 18 percent of Manhattan's population by the latter year.[28]

Accompanying this increasing urbanization was a lengthening expectancy of black life. While black male life expectancy stood at 32.5 years at birth during the 1900–1902 period, by 1919–1921 it had risen to 47.1years. Black female life expectancy increased from 35.0 years at birth during the 1900–1902 period, to 46.9 years in the 1919–1921 period.[29]

Marcus Garvey himself was initially impressed at what he saw as the progress of Afro-America, writing in November 1917 of the powerful impression black-owned enterprises, including banks, stores, cafés, and restaurants in Washington and Chicago, made on him. He felt satisfied that in at least one part of the African diaspora, "sufficient pride" existed for blacks to "do things for themselves," comparing this initiative to what he felt was a Rip Van Winkle-like slumber among blacks in the West Indies.[30]

GARVEY'S BLACK MALE SOCIALIZATION PROGRAM

Marcus Mosiah Garvey's perspective on black manhood reflected the currents of the era he lived in. The stress on individual success, reflecting the contemporary popular culture, was manifested in his presentation of "rags-to-riches" stories. Garvey believed in the power of an individual and a people collectively to undergo rapid and continuous development, sufficient to emerge as world-historical forces in a single generation. Much of Garvey's advice flowed from his embrace of the ethic of success so much in vogue during the era. In striving for success, Garvey emphasized, one should never "expect others to pave the way for us with a pathway of roses."[31] In order to arrive at this state of success, personal discipline, self-control, and a powerful will to achieve were necessary elements of individual character.

Marcus Garvey geared his message to the transformation of both the consciousness and the behavior of the millions of Africans worldwide who were his constituency. Garvey used various devices to get his message across, including "dialogues." In "A Dialogue: What's the Difference," for example, a son asks his father why he sees "people speaking and acting disrespectfully toward the Negro." The father explains that this is "only because" "the economic condition of the blackman is so low today."[32] The son remarks that he has been "made to feel that the Negro was never anybody and could never be anybody."[33] Near the end of the dialogue between the father and son, the son asks, "So there is no need, father, for me to hold down my head any longer?" The father replies, "No, my son, you should hold up your head and be as proud as any other boy in the world."[34]

For Garvey, the importance of the recovery of the African "mind," the ability to perceive and conceive independently, was key to individual and collective success in the future. Garvey held that under the "white man's civilization," black people had been "humiliated" and denied any opportunity for "initiative." However, Garvey maintained, "when the Negro recovers himself and starts to think independently, . . . he will find that there is absolutely no difference between him and the white man."[35]

One problem was that the African Americans were "satisfied to be subservient" compared with white Americans, according to the UNIA leader. The "white man" is "not afraid of responsibility, he is not afraid of any risk, he is adventurous, he is bold, he has daring in his blood."[36] He approvingly added that this "character" "gave us discoverers like Columbus, Raleigh, Drake and great conquerors like Napoleon, . . . and warriors like Charlemagne, Attila."[37] Garvey's critical view of the contemporary black character also included the notion that blacks have "been too lazy and careless" with their lives in contrast to whites, who have "been builders for the last one thousand years at least." Ignoring Egypt and other black civilizations momentarily, Garvey continued to assert that blacks had not "built any nation, kingdom or empire" and must "start where the white man started hundreds of years ago."[38] On other occasions Garvey pointed to the achievements of ancient African civilizations.

Marcus Garvey was a proponent of having programs of both home training and "public training" of black people. He deplored what he viewed as the lack of "home training" among American blacks. His middle-class "Talented Tenth" rivals for political leadership would no doubt have strongly disagreed, but Garvey held that "the home-training of the Negro is as bad as his public training." He maintained, in fact, that the African American had "very little of home-training."[39] He complained:

[U]nlike the Jew, there is no family Creed into which the Negro youth are inducted. There is no guiding policy or principle in which he is trained . . . even in the home, hence the youth goes out into manhood without an objective or a set purpose. That is why nearly every Negro thinks differently on racial matters.[40]

Thus, Garvey would view the fostering of a homogeneity and unity of thought as one positive attribute of such manhood socialization programs.

Garvey and Garveyism, however, were concerned with the defense and protection of black families, communities, nations, and continents. The "father" in Garvey's dialogue devotes some energy to explaining to the "son" the need to engage in energetic defense of black life, individually and collectively. The father states that the black "has been too lazy and careless with his own life." The father continues to say that it "is the duty of man not only to protect his own life but to protect the existence of his tribe, his clan or his race" since "mankind has always been in universal warfare against each other."[41]

Garvey's concept of black manhood demanded an independence of thought, especially with respect to the demands of the overall society. Bowing blindly to the dictates of white society, culture, or standards would violate this general standard of independence of thought and action. Both genders of African Americans should be "self-reliant, self-expressive and self-willed," Garvey maintained, for the person who "is dependent upon someone else to do something for him never gets anything done."[42] Perhaps, for this and other reasons, the UNIA held that Africans should not fight in white wars.[43]

Marcus Mosiah Garvey's independence of thought was perhaps the key factor in both provoking the wrath of the federal government and, not coincidentally, stimulating black interest in the organization. J. Edgar Hoover and the Federal Bureau of Investigation (FBI) and General Intelligence Division (GID) by 1919 had instituted a heavy surveillance of black organizations of all types.[44] Hoover described Marcus Garvey as "the foremost radical among his race" and vowed "once and for all" to "put" him "where he can peruse his past activities behind the four walls of the Atlanta clime." In order to fulfill his vision, Hoover assigned James W. Jones, an African American, to penetrate the UNIA and watch Garvey. The agency considered using the Mann Act, the same "White Slave Traffic" law that was successfully used against boxer Jack Johnson, to jail Garvey. In 1923, however, the agency obtained an indictment of Garvey on mail fraud for his efforts to finance the Black Star Steamship Line.[45]

Marcus Garvey's masculine gender ideal dictated an assertive political and economic posture for African American males. Garvey's "father" taught his "son" that it "is not what the other fellow will give you—you must take; it is what you want that you must have. The white man has no more right of interfering with the black man's progress than the black man has to interfere with the white man."[46]

MARCUS GARVEY'S "NEW NEGRO" MAN

Marcus Garvey and the UNIA had a detailed program for personal development of the African American male. This program was embodied in the "Lessons from the School of African Philosophy, the New Way to Education." The first lesson, "Intelligence, Education, Universal Knowledge and How to Get It," answers many basic questions that might emerge to interfere with the process of individual learning. Garvey maintained that one must "never stop learning" and "never stop reading." It was also important to be wary of "trashy literature" and focus on acquiring "standard knowledge." Good novels were seen as convenient means of "getting information on human nature" since "personal experience is not enough," the "individual life" being very short, and novels allow one to "feed on the experience of others." In particular, Garvey recommended studying the autobiographies and biographies of people who have achieved greatness in some aspect of life.[47]

Aware of the contemporary shortage of quality education, Garvey sought to instruct the African American masses, his followers in particular, on "How to

Read." Garvey advised African Americans to try to read as much as possible, at least four hours a day, and to take advantage of situations where there is an opportunity to read. "Don't waste time," Garvey counseled students. "Any time you think you have to waste put it in reading something." A minimum of one book a week over and above the routine reading of newspapers and journals should be covered. "After five years you will have read over two hundred and fifty books." During this time the difference between one who has not read a single book and that person will be enormous. "You will be considered intelligent and the other person be considered ignorant."[48]

The UNIA leader especially emphasized the study of history.[49] According to Garvey, "knowledge is power."[50] He related that the "greatest men and women in the world burn the midnight lamp" after others have retired to bed. Repetition of that one action on a daily basis propels them further than their counterparts, as it is a cumulative process. It is worth stressing that Garvey recommended that the masses of black Americans follow this program, not solely a "Talented Tenth." This is profoundly assertive in this sense, when one compares the objections against a "liberal arts" education for African Americans from some proponents of industrial education. Garvey assured African Americans, so confident was he of their capacity for education, that if they practiced his method, "week after week, month after month, year after year," they would be "so learned in the liberal arts as to make you ready and fit for your place in the affairs of the world."[51] Persistence, consistency, economy of time, a focused effort would yield the desired results, allowing individuals themselves to forge a course of development and change in a direction of their own choosing.

Marcus Garvey's educational program stressed the achievements of blacks throughout history. He insisted that his students never "yield to any statement in history or made by any individual [,] caring not how great, that the Negro was nobody in history. Even if you cannot prove it always claim that the Negro was great," Garvey urged. He stressed that each of the pharaohs was black and advised that when "you are dealing with Jews let them know that they were once your slaves in Egypt if you have to say so."[52]

Garvey offered detailed advice on the subject of black leadership, particularly concerning the ethics of leadership and leadership development.[53] In particular, he offered advice designed to maintain the unity of blacks, advice that he himself had difficulty heeding.

Never divide or create confusion between the different colours in the Negro race, but always try to prove that the standard Negro is the African and all Negroes should be proud of their black blood without insulting any colour within the race. This is very, very important.[54]

In stark contrast to other contemporary black leaders, Garvey eschewed integration, particularly interracial marriage. Garvey wrote that for "a Negro man to marry someone who does not look like his mother or [is] not a member of his race is to insult his mother, insult nature and insult God who made his father."[55]

He called for a "campaign of race purity" and for blacks to "close ranks." Yet, he desired that blacks "respect all shades of their own race" and be without prejudice with regard to different skin tones and shades of blacks.[56] He advised that blacks never "admit that the Negro is more immoral than the white man but try to prove the contrary." He pointed to the "bastard children" left by the white man "everywhere he has been," making him "not competent to say that he is socially and morally purer than any other race."[57]

Garvey offered an abundance of advice on the subject of ideal black masculine demeanor. "Lesson 7, Character" stresses "honesty" as the most important element of character. Stressing the need for the highest moral standards, Garvey advised steady and consistent relationships between males and females. "Don't run around always with different people of the opposite sex." In particular, he advised leaders, "never flirt or indicate that you are a flirt [.] Never try to make love to two persons in the same organization."[58]

Marcus Garvey recommended that alcohol be used temperately, as "self-control" was a basic component of a positive black masculinity, in his view. Other aspects of the ideal masculine demeanor involved proper hygiene, good verbal skills, good dress, proper table manners, proper public manners, and general courtesy. In particular, it was important to be nice and kind to children. Eating in public was also bad form, according to Garvey, as were "eating and chewing gum in people's faces," for it was "an ugly sight and shows gross disrespect."[59] The manner of public behavior was also important, for example, frivolity in public, for it sent a direct message to the world about one's personality. Instead of behaving "frivolously" in public, a serious demeanor encouraged people to believe that the individual has "dignity."[60]

It was also important, in Garvey's view, to understand ways of defusing interpersonal conflict and avoiding needless involvement with violence. Garvey recommended counting to ten when angry and stressed developing a capacity for "self control" as one of the key African American male gender-role ideals. Extended to male–female relationships, this suggested that a man should never "fall in love to the point of losing control." Moreover, this love should not derive from the "personal appearance" of the person but should have a lot to do with the person's "character, disposition, temperament, and behaviour."[61] He counseled patience in waiting to find the mate who is compatible with an individual. In general, he felt that the ages of 30 to 35 were ideal for people to get married. He also cautioned against adulterous relationships and excessive numbers of children.[62]

A key to Garveyism was the emphasis on racial purity. This had special significance in development of the movement's views of gender equality and women. Women were seen as the mothers of the race, and, as one prominent Garvey official wrote, "if you find any woman—especially a black woman—who does not want to be a mother, you may rest assured she is not a true woman."[63] A primary task of black men was to protect black females, ensuring racial purity by throwing "our protecting arms around our women," which would foster a return to the mythical "days of true manhood when women truly reverenced us," and women were placed upon the pedestal from which they have been forced."[64]

Yet, in practical terms those women who attempted to emulate the ideal "New Negro Woman" ended up working a double or triple shift as their roles in organizations, and as homemakers, mother, and, often, income earners stretched their physical and emotional selves to the maximum.[65] Amy Jacques Garvey was forced to quit her political work during a hectic period when her husband, Marcus, was constantly traveling. She received little financial assistance from her husband and had to struggle to feed, house, and provide an education for her children. She harshly judged Marcus Garvey for his behavior during their relationship: "What did he ever give in return? The value of a wife to him was like a gold coin—expendable, to get what he wanted, and hard enough to withstand rough usage in the process."[66]

The political aims of the UNIA reflect the new assertiveness and determination of the Garveyite man and woman. The ultimate goal of UNIA efforts was the founding of a black nation. Thus, standing apart from the accommodationism of Booker T. Washington and from the efforts aiming at "social equality" of the National Association for the Advancement of Colored People (NAACP) and others, Garvey set the UNIA's sight on an independent black nation. Garvey told Africans worldwide, "Never be satisfied to always live under the government of other people because you shall ever be at their mercy."[67]

One of the key aspects of Marcus Garvey's legacy is that he put forth an urban model of assertive, race-conscious, and militant manhood to masses of African Americans. It was as much an attitude and perspective as it was a specific ideology. Clearly, had such an attitude or perspective been implemented consistently in the Jim Crow South of the era, violence would have been the inevitable outcome. It was clearly a product of the new urban milieu, with its cosmopolitan influences, its accelerating sense of empowerment and confidence. The formal ideology of Garvey and the ideology and practice of Garveyites must be clearly distinguished. A wide range of individuals embraced Garveyism, as its general program struck a responsive chord in millions of African Americans, West Indians, Central Americans, and Africans. The editors of the *Messenger*, hardly allies of Garvey, fairly summed up Garvey's contribution:

Garvey has done much good work in putting into many Negroes a backbone where for years they have had only a wishbone. He has stimulated race pride. He has instilled a feeling into Negroes that they are as good as anybody else. He has inspired an interest in Negro traditions, Negro history, Negro literature, Negro art and culture. He has stressed the international aspect of the Negro problem.[68]

Yet, Garvey presented the black man as the embodiment of black humanity, glorifying him and projecting him to greatness as a leader, ruler, or commander. While men within the organization often held titles deriving from Garvey's himself, the Knight Commander of the Nile, women within the organization were organized into supportive roles such as within the Black Cross Nurses.[69] Men were thus the movement's external leaders, its would-be diplomats and statesmen, relegating women to various social, cultural, and financial support activities. UNIA divisions each featured both a male and a female president. However, the male president managed the entire division, while the female president administered only the women's work and organization of the local group.[70] Despite this, women did play a variety of roles within the organization.

To a considerable extent, the "New Negro" of the 1920s was influenced by Garvey and Garveyism.[71] It is also true that ordinary Garveyites, involved in a diverse set of activities across the United States, made the Garvey movement what it was. The Reverend Earl Little, the father of Malcolm X, for example, was described by his son as a "dedicated organizer" for Garvey's UNIA.[72] Malcolm X proudly recalled his father's activism for the UNIA:

As young as I was then, I knew from what I overheard that my father was saying something that made him a "tough" man. I remember an old lady, grinning and saying to my father, "You're scaring these white folks to death!"[73]

Earl Little's uncompromising ways, however, in all likelihood cost him his life. During a period marked by threats by the white supremacist Black Legion and in an area where blacks were not allowed on the streets of the small towns at night, Earl Little was found on streetcar tracks, dead.[74]

Ironically, despite Marcus Garvey's emphasis on black unity, a fissure developed between him and other important African American leaders. In reaction to Garvey's meeting with the Ku Klux Klan, several black leaders, including A. Phillip Randolph, wrote the attorney general of the United States seeking Garvey's arrest and deportation. The "Garvey Must Go" campaign fed conveniently into the federal government's efforts to jail Marcus Garvey and destroy the UNIA movement. In what was perhaps the "nadir" for black leadership, these leaders wrote: "The UNIA is composed chiefly of the most primitive and ignorant element of West Indian and American Negroes." Marcus Garvey termed this effort on behalf on the "Marcus Garvey Must Go" campaign "the greatest bit of treachery and wickedness that any group of Negroes could be capable of." He described their behavior as akin to that of the "good old darkey."[75]

Ultimately, after his conviction Garvey was jailed in February 1925 in the Atlanta penitentiary, as J. Edgar Hoover had planned. Later, an international campaign and a massive Harlem rally, had sufficient impact to induce President Calvin Coolidge to commute Garvey's sentence and deported him.[76] Speaking from the docks of New Orleans in November 1927, Garvey vowed to remain in service of African redemption, saying, "The greatest work is yet to be done. I shall with God's help do it."[77]

INCREASING BLACK MALE INVOLVEMENT IN INDUSTRY

In 1924 Joseph Hill wrote in *Opportunity Magazine* that in 1880 the geographical center of the African American population was in the northwestern corner of Georgia. By the 1920s it had moved northward to northeastern Alabama, a shift caused by the massive migration northward due to an unprecedented northern demand for black labor.[78] The beginnings of World War I served to spur the massive migration of African Americans from the South. Cleveland's black population grew 300 percent during the decade following 1910, Chicago's 150 percent, and Detroit's by 600 percent.[79] In Chicago by 1920, some 5,300 black workers labored in the stockyards, over 3,200 in the iron and steel factories, over 1,200 in the packing houses, and thousands in other industries.[80]

By 1914, on the eve of World War I, over 80 percent of blacks were gainfully employed toiled in agriculture, domestic work, or personal services. African Americans remained trapped in tenancy, sharecropping, and debt peonage within the Jim Crow South. The surge of industrial development in the South, beginning in the 1880s, largely bypassed blacks as jobs went to whites. Black males were shut out of nearly all of the industrial occupations that were not very difficult or unpleasant. The sooty and dangerous work of coal mining, for example, actively sought blacks to assume the most hazardous positions. In 1889, for example, 46.2 percent of the coal miners were black.[81]

Trade and transportation positions that were considered "Negro work" included teamsters, hackmen, and chauffeurs. Between 1890 and 1910, the number of blacks in these occupations more than doubled. Even greater numbers of black men were employed by the railroads, another magnet for black male employment. However, only about 4 percent of the blacks involved in the railroad were considered skilled employees,[82] for example, firemen, brakemen, and locomotive engineers. The overwhelming majority of the African American males employed by the railroad company were porters or waiters.

The number of African Americans in the iron and steel industries more than quadrupled between 1890 and 1910, totaling 36,646 by the end of the period. This influx into these industries occurred almost wholly in southern factories as Andrew Carnegie exclusively relied on European immigrant laborers.[83] Blacks remained shut out of the southern textile industry as white workers adamantly refused to work alongside them. Under the Jim Crow system, employers had an economic incentive to avoid the need to provide duplicate, even if of radically different quality, entrances, toilets, and drinking facilities.[84]

White labor unions were instrumental in the declining numbers of black craftsmen at the end of the nineteenth century. In the South, in particular, there was a long-term general drive to oust blacks from the skilled positions they had occupied since emancipation. As noted earlier, by the 1890s black workers were in the process of being displaced from jobs in many areas, including shipping, construction, and the railroad. Soon it would be rare to find black electricians, plumbers, railway firemen, and machinists.[85] In addition, the low wages typical of black workers were judged below the "fair American standard" of living. It was estimated that $33 per week was needed for a family of four to meet this standard in Manhattan, New York City; however, an unskilled laborer averaged only about $20 a week. A 1927 survey by the New York Urban League found that black males in Harlem averaged $24 a week in earnings.[86] The typical black domestic's earnings of $15 per week were, therefore, indispensable if minimal standards were to be upheld.[87] The necessity for both married partners to work created an acute shortage of child care, one factor in the soaring rates of juvenile delinquency.[88] New patterns of incarceration of black males began to develop, as they represented over 15 percent of the prisoners in New York area jails within an overall population that was only 5 percent black.[89] Many of these arrests stemmed from activities associated with the illegal "numbers game" lottery. In addition, with 85 illegal drinking establishments located in Harlem—all but 4 white-owned—and heroin, cocaine, and morphine trafficking on the rise, the stage was set for a dramatic expansion of black income derived from illegal activity.[90] In Cleveland, too, during the 1920s and 1930s, there was an appreciable increase in crime and vice.[91]

The harsh employment conditions facing black males involving the limited number of occupations open to them, regardless of skill level, training, or education, made the railroad sleeping car porter one of their most coveted jobs. Yet, even after an increase in 1919, the Pullman Company paid the porters only $60 a month. When their tips were included their income still amounted to only less than two-thirds of the contemporary federal minimum family income.[92] After 15 years of seniority their pay increased to approximately only $95 per month plus tips.[93] The social interaction involved in tipping had an impact on their dignity also, since the money was a critical portion of their subsistence. By being forced by the Pullman Company to stick their hands out as if they were receiving a "handout" or charity, when, in fact, they performed usually arduous service work had a damaging impact on their dignity. To make matters worse, many of the porters were grossly underemployed, having more education than the vast majority of whites they served. They were constantly overworked, regularly working more hours than they received pay for. Family life was often difficult for the porters, due to the irregular schedule and out-of-town travel.

In 1925 A. Phillip Randolph, then a well-known activist, publisher, and intellectual in Harlem, was asked by Ashley Totten, a sleeping car porter, to speak at a meeting of porters. Randolph spoke and explained the advantages that participating in a union could bring to them. The porters were angry about the conditions they faced routinely, which stretched them emotionally, physically, and financially to the limit. Following the introduction of the sleeping car in the 1860s, the exclusively black porters were generally former household slaves. Following the fading away of this initial generation of sleeping car porters, a more educated group of men came to make up the bulk of the porters, helping to fuel the growth of militancy within their ranks. Later, Totten asked Randolph to organize the sleeping car porters into a labor union, and Randolph subsequently marshaled the collective manhood of the sleeping car porters into a force that eventually went beyond confronting the Pullman Company over the issue of wage increases and better conditions to emerge as a force for black civil rights.[94]

Phillip S. Foner concluded that by the eve of World War I, "the black wage-earner had still to claim a place in America's developing industrial society."[95] By the eve of World War II, much had changed, yet much remained the same. The all-enveloping Jim Crow atmosphere surrounding black labor remained much the same, despite three decades of migration and urbanization.

The job market was almost completely segregated, and very few high-paying jobs hired blacks of either gender. Many black workers and professionals worked in all-black establishments, and in other firms where rigid rules governed black employment: blacks could not work alongside whites; no black could supervise a white; and blacks were to do only the least sophisticated tasks. This severely restricted employment opportunities for African Americans. Jobs on the market that involved direct contact with whites were almost all ruled out. Moreover, jobs that did not involve face-to-face contact with the white public were generally unavailable to blacks since they would have to be equipped with separate toilet, eating, and drinking facilities.[96]

With the rapid urbanization and the increasing involvement of blacks in industry, a modern black working class arose in the cities. Between 1910 and 1920, the black population grew many times over in several large, industrial urban areas. Detroit's African American population grew from 6,000, to 41,000, Philadelphia's from 84,000, to 134,000, and Chicago's from 44,000, to 109,000. The first wave of the migration included a disproportionate number of single males, detached from familial responsibilities. This was followed by a wave of young single black females and, finally, by a wave of steady working men with families.[97]

Steady employment for thousands of these workers, however, remained an illusion, as after the war ended, blacks were fired, and the returning whites were hired.[98] Returning black soldiers found it tough to find employment as they competed with the fired civilians for the few employment slots available to them. By 1921, for example, black unemployment rates in Detroit were five times those of whites.[99] Even skilled or professional status did not help the African American find suitable employment.   One August 1917 survey found chronic underemployment among black graduates, engineers, carpenters, electricians, and other skilled males, who instead worked as porters, janitors, or elevator operators.[100]

While there was a rapid influx to the cities, millions remained trapped in rural poverty. Despite the FBI's pursuit of both Jack Johnson and Marcus Garvey on "white slavery" charges, the bureau almost wholly ignored the actual peonage occurring in the South. With a federal antipeonage law on the books since 1867, the Justice Department routinely neglected to enforce it.[101] The Atlanta office of the FBI investigated 115 charges of peonage during the 1921–1922 period but convicted only one person. J. Edgar Hoover concluded that this was due to the virtual inadmissibility of black testimony as evidence. The agency's most notable case of peonage occurred in 1921, when John S. Williams, a white entrepreneur who earned his income from purchasing black inmates in state and county penal institutions, murdered from 10 to 12 of them in an effort to silence them as potential witnesses. Williams was convicted of murder by the state of Georgia.

Hating to lose cases, Hoover concluded that since "the type of person usually held a peon" was "not particularly intelligent," this fouled up cases unless a white could be found to testify to it.   This led to the end of peonage investigations for the agency.[102] The criminalization of the black male via debt slavery, peonage, and contract violations was widespread until the 1940s.[103] Conviction for certain offenses carried the punishment of either a fine or a stint on chain gangs, which were overwhelmingly and often exclusively African American. The men then were virtually purchased by planters or landlords who would pay the fines, allowing unrestricted use of their labor. Others, out of favor with these white employers, would be forced to work on the chain gang. The chain gang featured a long line of men shackled with iron bands around their ankles through which a long chain was looped and padlocked at its end. They were fed food of poor quality such as fatback pork, corn bread, molasses, and a few other consumables and were housed in cages that were boiling hot in summer and freezing cold in winter. Stocks were used to "break the spirit" of the convicts in many places.[104] In one tragedy involving a chain gang, 20 black men were burned alive in a truck cage after they tried to keep warm by setting some gasoline afire.[105]

In the South, blacks continued to be hamstrung by the sharecropping and tenancy labor arrangements, which often yielded only a subsistence-level income and an overall lack of social power. With the right of political participation denied them and labor-organizing efforts fiercely repressed, there was generally little realistic hope of immediately improving conditions. Local planters in one area during the depression heard of a Garvey-like figure who had traveled from Chicago to Mississippi selling subscriptions for settlement in Africa. Local whites immediately mobilized and surrounded the house where the organizer was staying. When a black woman refused to cooperate with the men, they hit her over the head with a pistol and attempted to subdue her. As she struggled for the pistol, more blacks came to the scene. Willing to shoot the woman but prevented by other whites, the planter gang left the scene, and the woman and organizer escaped.[106]

Particularly galling to the collective and individual self-respect of African Americans in the South was the enforcement of a code of deferential behavior. The necessity for African Americans to address whites as "Mr." or "Mrs.," only to be addressed themselves by their first names, was one standard of behavior.[107] Bowing, tipping one's hat, and behaving in a generally submissive manner were others. Disagreeing with a white male could be the cause of violence, as agreement with every assertion or declaration was fully expected. The problem of how to address the local area's rare prominent black males was often resolved by using titles other than "Mr.," such as "Professor."[108] Even for more educated and prosperous blacks, interrupting a white man or taking a seat in his office was cause for grave concern.[109]

Author Richard Wright recalled learning the racial ethics of Jim Crow as a youth after taking a job at a small factory. Working hard, Wright naively saw himself as "working his way up," but the response he received after asking a white man about the nature of his specialized task enlightened him. "What yuh tryin' t' do, nigger, get smart?," he was asked with a warning not to. Persisting in his desire to learn while he was there, the situation only worsened. He was later asked, "Nigger, you think you're white, don't you?" Later, it was reported that he referred to a white man by only his last name, dropping the required "Mr." When "Mr. Pease" asked him if this was true, the white man who had told him stood nearby holding a steel bar. He was warned violently not to "lie" on him, since he "heard" him forget the title. Wright needed to think of a "neutral" reply that would not set off either man on a frenzy of violence against him.[110]

> If I had said: No. Sir, Mr. Pease, I never called you Pease. I would have been automatically calling Morrie a liar. And if I had said: Yes, sir, Mr. Pease, I called you Pease, I would have been pleading guilty to having uttered the worst insult that a Negro can utter to a southern white man.[111]

Wright failed in his effort to find a nonexistent "neutral" reply. Saying that he didn't remember calling him that, and, if he did, he didn't mean it, he was assaulted before he finished his sentence. He promised to quit, and they allowed him to leave.[112]

A white social scientist studying a depression-era Mississippi town observed an incident in which a black youth's car was sideswiped by a vehicle driven by a white man, pushing it into a white worker on the road and injuring him slightly. Sentenced to 30 days, local people believed that he had got off easy, considering he could have been killed under the existing mores of race relations. Sent to a state farm, he was beaten and abused and returned with a back scarred by the lash of repeated whippings.[113]

The conditions that African Americans had hoped were disappearing some 70 years prior remained to present problems for them in every sphere of life. For many, the 1931 trial of nine African American male youths in Scottsboro, Alabama, symbolized the continuing lack of racial justice. On 25 March 1931 the Scottsboro boys were charged with the rape of Victoria Price and Ruby Bates on a freight train. Given little opportunity to obtain a willing lawyer, they were fortunate in obtaining representation from Stephen R. Roddy. Denied a change of venue or a delay to aid in preparation of the defense, an all-white jury convicted two of the defendants after deliberating for only two hours. They were sentenced to death. Soon afterwards, six of the other defendants were sentenced to death while one trial was declared a mistrial. The contradictory stories of the alleged victims, as well as their questionable behavior during the trial, were all ignored. Alleged victim Ruby Bates, even from the outset, indicated that she was unable to identify the defendants. Prior to the alleged rape there had been a brawl on the train between some seven white youths and 17 or 18 black youths. The examination of the alleged victims failed to suggest evidence of rape. The black youths insisted that they had nothing to do with the rape and that they had even helped some of the white boys dangling between the moving cars of the train.[114] Thousands of people attended the trial, leading to the placement of machine guns around the court and the mobilization of the militia. When the initial verdicts were read, celebrations began, led by a brass band.[115] Later, as the international campaign to free the Scottsboro boys went into high gear, Ruby Bates began to speak out, admitting her complicity in the frame-up and appealing to crowds for the release of the African American youth. The impact of the Scottsboro case and its resultant publicity heightened the awareness of the lack of an impartial judicial system in the South and the region's general lack of racial and social equality. It provided an example of an organized response to consistent patterns of bias in the criminal justice system by saving the lives of the defendants and exposing the South's judicial system to the world's scrutiny.

THE BLACK MALE ON THE EVE OF WORLD WAR II

The same problems that had plagued black America since the fall of slavery persisted on the eve of the second World War II. Segregated travel continued to create serious obstacles to the free movement of blacks. Black activist Ella Baker, then an organizer for the NAACP, wrote a memo entitled "Difficulties Encountered in Securing Dining Car Service on the Seaboard Airline Railroad," in which she described her problem after she found that the "colored" section was full with white soldiers sitting in it. Despite the dining car steward's plea that she wait for a vacant "colored" table, she defiantly sat down at a "white" table.[116]

Yet, amid seeming stagnation, things were changing. By the mid-1930s African Americans represented approximately 8.5 percent of all iron and steelworkers, 17 percent of slaughter and packinghouse workers, and 9 percent of coal miners.[117] Having lost confidence that the American Federation of Labor (AFL) would ever reform by desegregating, black workers welcomed the formation of the Congress of Industrial Organizations (CIO). A. Phillip Randolph, speaking at the founding meeting of the National Negro Congress, an independent black organization representing hundreds of thousands of workers, stated that its mission was to "broaden and intensify" the effort to attract blacks to labor organizations. By 1936, when the CIO embarked upon the most massive labor-organizing campaign in American history, it had a policy of inclusion, veering sharply from the policies of the AFL. African American organizers were employed in this effort, which proved fateful for the following decades when the power of labor peaked during the twentieth century.[118]

Emerging from the long years of depression, blacks found themselves frustrated after the early years of the wartime economic boom largely bypassed them. At the outset of the mobilization for war, the prevailing segregation excluded blacks from the new civilian and military occupational opportunities.[119] Segregation continued to dominate every aspect of the lives of African Americans, north and south, even the U.S. Employment Service itself was characterized by segregated facilities and operations. The formal and informal structure of antiblack employment bias effectively doomed chances for earning a decent living for millions of black workers. Within this framework blacks could not supervise whites, work in "refined" positions, work as customer service representatives or salespersons if the customers were white, or work alongside whites. With the massive migration north, some 125,000 blacks migrated north during the 1940s, and with the burning demand for labor, new conflicts with white workers erupted.[120] In 1943, for example, almost 7,000 African Americans worked at the Alabama Dry Dock and Shipbuilding Company (ADDSCO), a firm that had grown from 1,000 employees before the war to 30,000 during the war. Prior to the issuance of the Fair Employment Practices Commission (FEPC), almost none of the black employees worked in skilled positions, and moving into compliance resulted in an outbreak of violence as blacks were assaulted with pipes and clubs, necessitating the dispatch of U.S. troops to restore order. Racial violence occurred during World War II in Detroit, Beaumont, Texas, Harlem, and other cities, and incidents, such as that in Mobile in 1942, in which a white bus driver shot and killed a black soldier as he got off the bus, resulted from the rapid changes accompanied by violence.[121]

During the World War II era, the March on Washington movement occupied the forefront of the black struggle for equal rights. Led by A. Phillip Randolph, the movement sought to end segregation within the armed forces. The movement drew on the desperation and stridency of blacks emerging from the depression and from the memory of the broken promises made during World War I. Energized by a sense of growing political power, black marchers threatened to inundate the segregated bastion of Washington as it geared up for the war overseas.

The impetus for the march emerged after a frustrating meeting between black leaders and President Franklin D. Roosevelt. Defying pleas from the president, his wife, and other powerful figures, this movement eventually wrested Executive Order 8802 from a reluctant Roosevelt only one week prior to the planned march.

Unlike in World War I, blacks did not merely "close ranks" and take a back seat in the war effort. There was an actual stepping up of the protest movement. In 1943 the Congress of Racial Equality staged sit-ins against racial discrimination in several cities.[122] The clearly observable eagerness of African Americans to support such a movement, an all-black effort, was an important factor in Roosevelt's caving in to the demand, a fact that in and of itself marked a new peak in black political power. An angry and determined sentiment left tens of thousands in black America ready to support the March on Washington at a pivotal moment of international tension. The editor of the NAACP's *Crisis*, Roy Wilkins, commented then:

> No agitators were needed to point out to him the discrepancies between what we said we were fighting for, and what we did to him. He did not need the NAACP to show him that it sounds pretty foolish to be against park benches marked "Jude" in Berlin, but to be for park benches marked "Colored" in Tallahassee, Florida.
>
> It is pretty grim . . . to have a black boy in uniform get an orientation lecture in the morning on wiping out Nazi bigotry, and that same evening be told he can buy a soft drink only in the "Colored" post exchange! [123]

The enactment of the FEPC was an important milestone for black America. While its implementation and enforcement were spotty, during its five-year life span, nearly 14,000 complaints were filed by African Americans.[124] Later, this momentum led to the signing by President Harry Truman of Executive Order 9981, desegregating the armed forces.[125]

For the most part, however, African Americans emerged from World War ll full of hope that racial barriers would fall soon. This would prove to be an important factor fueling the Civil Rights movement for years to come.

NOTES

1. Robert A. Hill and Barbara Bair (eds.), *Marcus Garvey: Life and Lessons* (Berkeley: University of California Press, 1987), 286.

2. Robert A. Hill, *The Marcus Garvey and Universal Negro Improvement Association Papers: Volume 1* (Berkeley: University of California Press, 1983), lxxix.

3. Amy Jacques Garvey, "The Early Years of Marcus Garvey," in John Henrik Clarke (ed.), *Marcus Garvey and the Vision of Africa* (New York: Vintage, 1974), 30; Tony Martin, *Marcus Garvey, Hero* (Dover, MA: Majority Press, 1983), 8; Rupert Lewis, *Marcus Garvey: Anti-Colonial Champion* (Trenton, NJ: Africa World Press, 1988), 18.

4. Martin, *Marcus Garvey*, 9.

5. Garvey, "The Early Years," 32; Martin, *Marcus Garvey*, 10.

6. Martin, *Marcus Garvey*, 14.

7. Ibid., 15.

8. Ibid., 19.

9. Ibid., 19–20.

10. Ibid., 60.

11. Ibid., 61.

12. Ibid.

13. Lewis, *Marcus Garvey*, 68.

14. Portia P. James, "Hubert H. Harrison and the New Negro Movement," *The Western Journal of Black Studies* 13 (1989): 83.

15. Martin, *Marcus Garvey*, 70, 96.

16. Ibid., 96.

17. Ibid., 83.

18. Ibid., 70.

19. James, "Hubert H. Harrison," 83.

20. Martin, *Marcus Garvey*, 43.

21. Ibid., 59.

22. Alain Locke, "The New Negro," in Abraham Chapman (ed.), *Black Voices: An Anthology of Afro-American Literature* (New York: Mentor Books, 1968), 512–13.

23. Ibid., 514.

24. William. W. Sales Jr., *From Civil Rights to Black Liberation: Malcolm X and the Organization of Afro-American Unity* (Boston: South End Press, 1994), 29.

25. Reynolds Farley, *Growth of the Black Population: A Study of Demographic Trends* (Chicago: Markham, 1971), 50.

26. Ibid., 51.

27. W. A. Domingo, "The Tropics in New York," *Survey Graphic* (March 1925), n.p.

28. Cheryl Lynn Greenberg, *"Or Does It Explode?": Black Harlem in the Great Depression* (New York: Oxford University Press, 1991), 17.

29. Farley, *Growth*, 62.

30. Martin, *Marcus Garvey*, 41.

31. Hill and Bair, *Marcus Garvey*, xxvii.

32. Ibid., 143.

33. Ibid., 144.

34. Ibid., 146.

35. Ibid., 149.

36. Ibid., 150.

37. Ibid.

38. Ibid., 151.

39. Ibid., 155.

40. Ibid.

41. Ibid., 150.

42. Ibid., 152.

43. Martin, *Marcus Garvey*, 63.

44. Kenneth O'Reilly, *"Racial Matters": The F.B.I.'s Secret File on Black America, 1960–1972* (New York: Free Press, 1989), 13.

45. Ibid., 14.

46. Hill and Bair, *Marcus Garvey*, 152.

47. Ibid., 184.

48. Ibid., 189.

49. Ibid., 185.

50. Ibid., 187.

51. Ibid., 191.

52. Ibid., 194.

53. Ibid., 199–203.

54. Ibid., 202.

55. Ibid., 203.

56. Ibid., 204.

57. Ibid., 196.

58. Ibid.

59. Ibid., 283.

60. Ibid., 286.

61. Ibid., 237.

62. Ibid., 239.

63. Beryl Satter, "Marcus Garvey, Father Divine and the Gender Politics of Race Difference and Race Neutrality," *American Quarterly* 48 (1996): 48.

64. Ibid.

65. Ibid., 50.

66. Ibid., 51.

67. Hill and Bair, *Marcus Garvey*, 211.

68. Tony Martin, *Literary Garveyism: Garvey, Black Arts and the Harlem Renaissance* (Dover, MA: Majority Press, 1983), 6.

69. Satter, "Marcus Garvey," 50.

70. Ibid., 49.

71. Clarke, *Marcus Garvey*, 180–82; Martin, *Literary Garveyism*, 7.

72. Malcolm X, *The Autobiography of Malcolm X* (New York: Grove Press, 1965), 6.

73. Ibid.

74. Ibid., 9.

75. Martin, *Marcus Garvey, Hero*, 110.

76. Ibid., 113.

77. Ibid., 114.

78. Joseph A. Hill, "The Recent Northward Migration of the Negro," *Opportunity Magazine* (April 1924): 19–32; Malaika Adero (ed.), *Up South: Stories,*

Studies, and Letters of African American Migrations (New York: New Press, 1993), 19.

79. Mary Beth Norton et al., *A People & a Nation* (Boston: Houghton Mifflin, 1990), 682.

80. Hill, "The Recent Northward Migration," 28.

81. Phillip S. Foner, *Organized Labor and the Black Worker, 1619–1981* (New York: International, 1981), 120.

82. Ibid., 121.

83. Ibid., 122.

84. Ibid., 123.

85. Ibid., 125.

86. Greenberg, "Or Does It Explode," 22.

87. Ibid., 24.

88. Ibid., 35.

89. Ibid., 37.

90. Ibid., 38.

91. Kenneth L. Kusmer, *A Ghetto Takes Shape* (Chicago: University of Illinois Press, 1976), 220.

92. Foner, *Organized Labor*, 125.

93. Sally Hanley, *A. Phillip Randolph* (New York: Chelsea House, 1989), 56.

94. Foner, *Organized Labor*, 178.

95. Ibid., 125.

96. Dorothy K. Newman et al., *Protest, Politics, and Prosperity: Black Americans and White Institutions, 1940–75* (New York: Pantheon Books, 1978), 34.

97. George E. Haynes, "Negro Migration: Its Effect on Family and Community Life in the North," in Adero, Malaika (ed.), *Up South: Stories, Studies, and Letters of African American Migrations* (New York: New Press, 1993), 77.

98. Foner, *Organized Labor*, 131.

99. Ibid., 132.

100. Ibid., 134.

101. Mary Frances Berry and John W. Blassingame, *Long Memory: The Black Experience in America* (New York: Oxford University Press, 1992), 234.

102. O'Reilly, *"Racial Matters,"* 15.

103. Berry and Blassingame, *Long Memory*, 234.

104. Arthur F. Raper, *Preface to Peasantry* (New York: Atheneum, 1968), 295.

105. Berry and Blassingame, *Long Memory*, 239.

106. John Dollard, *Caste and Class in a Southern Town* (Garden City, NY: Doubleday, 1937), 119–20.

107. Hortense Powdermaker, *After Freedom: A Cultural Study in the Deep South* (New York: Atheneum, 1969), 44.

108. Dollard, *Caste and Class*, 181.

109. Ibid., 185.

110. Richard Wright, "The Ethics of Living Jim Crow: An Autobiographical Sketch," in Abraham Chapman (ed.), *Black Voices: An Anthology of Afro-American Literature* (New York: Mentor Books, 1968) , 290–291.

111. Ibid., 292.

112. Ibid.

113. Dollard, *Caste and Class*, 288.

114. Stephen R. Roddy, "The Scottsboro Case," in Gilbert Osofsky (ed.), *The Burden of Race: A Documentary History of Negro–White Relations in America* (New York:

Harper and Row, 1967), 362; Mark Naison, *Communists in Harlem during the Depression* (New York: Grove Press, 1985), 57–58; see also Dan T. Carter, *Scottsboro: A Tragedy of the American South* (Baton Rouge: Louisiana State University Press, 1979).

115. Roddy, "The Scottsboro Case," 363.

116. Joanne Grant, *Ella Baker: Freedom Bound* (New York: John Wiley and Sons, 1998), 95.

117. Foner, *Organized Labor*, 213.

118. Ibid, 214.

119. Newman, *Protest*, 11.

120. Ibid., 33.

121. Bruce Nelson, "Organized Labor and the Struggle for Black Equality in Mobile during World War II," *The Journal of American History*, 80, no. 3, (December 1993): 959; Lerone Bennett Jr., *Before the Mayflower* (Chicago: Johnson, 1966), 307.

122. Bennett, *Before the Mayflower*, 306.

123. Herbert Garfinkel, *When Negroes March* (New York: Atheneum, 1969), 23.

124. Newman, *Protest,* 12–13.

125. Ibid., 33.

Chapter 9

The Emergence of the Urban Black Male: Increasing Black Power, 1945–1972

> We shall have our manhood. We shall have it or the earth will be leveled by our attempts to gain it.
>
> —Eldridge Cleaver, 1968[1]

Twenty-four black men and six black women marched toward the California State Assembly on 2 May 1967, their loaded guns pointed straight up. Encountering Governor Ronald Reagan greeting 200 promising young leaders amid the placid greenery of the state Capitol, they watched the future president make a hasty departure. Bobby Seale, the leader of this delegation of Black Panthers, recalled later:

One of the brothers saw Reagan turn around and start trotting away from the whole scene because here came all these hardfaced brothers. These were brothers off the block; righteous brothers off the block.[2]

Seale later wrote that one "could look at their faces and see the turmoil they've lived through."[3]

Climbing the stairs leading to the assembly, Seale stopped to read the Black Panther Party's Executive Mandate Number One, in keeping with the objective of the action to both attract media coverage for the new organization and protest a law designed to prevent armed Panther activity. Marching through the halls of the building, they finally located the assembly itself, already having achieved their first objective of publicity. Stopped by a police officer before they arrived, Seale argued that it was his constitutional right to be able to observe the

---

Excerpts from *Soul On Ice* (McGraw-Hill, 1968) by Eldridge Cleaver reproduced by permission of The McGraw-Hill Companies.

assembly in action.

It was the news-hungry reporters, not Panthers, according to Seale, who, in the crush, pushed an officer aside, allowing them to enter. Upon viewing the black legislators, the Panthers dismissed them as "Toms, bootlickers, and sellouts," Seale recalls. "They hated us being there, those bootlickers. I looked at those booklickers, those Uncle Toms, very intensely," the Panther chairman later wrote.[4] Even their demeanor irritated Seale, representative of a new brand of grassroots assertive, even aggressive black manhood. "I didn't care for them because they never represented us there. And this kind of humble-shoulderedness and looking back."[5]

Soon, however, Seale witnessed an officer holding onto young Bobby Hutton, who was "cussing out the pig," in Seale's words. Seale intervened to ask why Hutton's gun was seized and he himself was collared by the officer. During this time, Hutton, the "brother from the block," was, in the most explicit language, demanding that the white officer give him his gun back. Seale, Hutton, and the other Panthers argued that if they were not under arrest, the officers had no right to take their arms. The guns were finally returned to them as they left the building.[6] After leaving for home, their car ran hot, and they were arrested at a police station after a tense, armed confrontation with the officers.[7] While only one episode during the tumultuous "black revolutionary" days of the 1960s, this episode illustrates the style and the tone of the black masculine militancy of the era and the changes undergone since the cautious days of Booker T. Washington. For semi-impoverished African Americans to take their challenge directly to the state Capitol is also illustrative of both the heightened sense of personal power and real power of individual black males far removed from the traditional bases of social status and political power. This chapter discusses the development and essence of the aggressive black masculinity that developed as the decade of the 1960s progressed. The transformation from the assertive and determined masculinity of the southern-based Civil Rights movement, as epitomized in the life and thought of Martin Luther King, is described briefly. The Black Panther Party, the most outstanding crystallization of the black male anger and revolt of the 1960s, is analyzed with respect to the masculine gender-role ideals it promoted.

SOCIAL CHANGE IN THE POST–WORLD WAR II PERIOD

The new level of assertiveness and militancy represented by the Black Panther Party and other groups by the late 1960s did not emerge overnight. New demographic factors brought about by the massive black migration northward and westward toward a new urban working-class life; the accompanying development of an important presence in the trade union movement; the progressive development of the institutional structure of the black communities nationally; the natural protection offered by densely populated urban communities; and, at the international level, the quickened movement of colonized and subjugated peoples—all figured in the socioeconomic and political context within which the organization emerged.[8]

Nationally, black income in constant dollars increased from $5,156 in 1959, to $8,074 in 1969. Particularly important was the rise in the percentage of black workers in "high wage" sectors from 7 percent in 1940, to 24 percent in 1975.[9] Accompanying these rapid demographic changes was a spurt in the development of black institutions. For example, the black community of the city of Detroit witnessed an unparalleled institutional growth, with important implications for black male political, economic, and social power. Much of this growth and development stemmed from the rapid increase in the number of blacks in the motor vehicle and motor vehicle equipment industry from the 1930s to the 1970, which led to an increase in the black presence within the United Automobile Workers (UAW).[10]

Black communities within the southern cities were also growing rapidly from the influx of migrants from the surrounding countryside. The Montgomery bus boycott, according to sociologist Aldon Morris, "demonstrated the political potential of the black church and church-related direct-action organizations."[11] Significantly, this new breed of ministers, who were able to devote full-time to their positions, facilitated the development of the Civil Rights movement, which was launched by means of this solid institutional basis.[12] It was upon this institutional edifice that the Montgomery Improvement Association was founded, and Martin Luther King Jr. emerged as a powerful new leader.

With a favorable international climate, influential elements within the national political, business, and cultural elite came to favor a more liberal racial climate. As historian George M. Frederickson noted, "[A]s the United States attempted to guarantee its social equilibrium and embarked on efforts to influence the non-Western world in behalf of its interests and ideology, overt and virulent intellectual racism came to be recognized as a dangerous liability."[13] For change to occur, however, it would take a "push" from African Americans.

PERSISTENT RESTRICTIONS ON BLACK MALE MOBILITY

Discharged after three years of service in the South Pacific, Isaac Woodward was headed home on a bus to North Carolina from a camp in Georgia when he requested to use the rest room during a stop. Verbally abused for taking too long when he reboarded the bus, the bus driver at another rest stop in South Carolina asked police to arrest Woodward, claiming he was drunk and disorderly. Protesting that this was not the case, Woodward was brutally beaten, blinding him for life. Later, the police chief responsible for the beating was acquitted. To add insult to injury, Woodward was denied any pension from the army, which maintained that his injuries occurred after his discharge.[14]

In October 1957 H. A. Gbedemah, the finance minister of the newly independent nation of Ghana, was ejected from a Howard Johnson's restaurant in Dover, Delaware. After Gbedemah was rudely told that black people were not served, this routine incident of discrimination mushroomed into an international incident that further damaged the worldwide image of the United States in a bipolar Cold War era.[15] President Dwight Eisenhower, reportedly angered by the incident, soon invited the Ghanian official to have breakfast with him at the White House in an effort to put a positive spin on the affair.[16]

In February 1964 Colin Powell, a young black officer, an early veteran of the then relatively unknown conflict in distant Vietnam, stopped at a hamburger place in Columbus, Georgia. After ordering a hamburger, he was politely asked by the waitress if he was a student from Africa. Powell replied no. She then asked if he were a Puerto Rican; he replied no. Finally, she stated questioningly, "You're a Negro?" Powell answered, "That's right." She replied, "Well, I can't bring out a hamburger." She told him that he would have to go around to the back door, which Powell declined to do; instead he quietly left.[17]

The cases of Isaac Woodward, H. A. Gbedemah, and Colin Powell illustrate the problems interstate travel posed for African Americans, males and females, during the post-World War II period. Despite the progress that had been made in advancing African American political, social, and economic status during the preceding decades, not only were African Americans routinely terrorized by random acts of racial violence, but they remained under the yoke of Jim Crow and de facto segregation in every other public sphere of life.

The legal edifice of Jim Crow had been eroded by the victories of the NAACP in five important Supreme Court education cases. The May 1954 *Brown v. Board of Education* decision was based on these earlier decisions, gradually weakening the legal basis of segregation. The impact of the Supreme Court decision was not confined to the area of education alone but implied a thorough transformation of racial practices in all the spheres of American society. It served as a catalyst to African Americans, creating a renewed sense of momentum in the movement to destroy the structures of racism and discrimination.[18] Yet, the hard core of the institutional framework of the Jim Crow order remained intact, with its besieged defenders battling with renewed determination. Public space in American life remained riddled with segregation, including museums, schools, parks, restaurants, public transportation, and other vital institutions. To a considerable extent the legacy of slavery remained.

Bayard Rustin spent 22 days on a chain gang in March 1949 for sitting in the "white" section of a bus in North Carolina. Deposited in a filthy, vermin-invested dormitory, the African American Quaker proponent of nonviolent resistance later wrote of the conditions he found there. Inmates rose at 5:30 A.M. sharp, worked from 7 A.M. until 5:30 P.M. except for a half-hour lunch break at noon. The slavery-like camp conditions included a ban on personal possessions except for clothes, a towel, and soap. Toothbrushes, razors, stamps, writing paper, pens, and pencils were banned. Inmates were given only a pair of underwear, a pair of pants, a shirt, and a pair of socks each week, forcing them to work in dirty, encrusted, and sweat-drenched clothes for the vast majority of the time.[19] Rustin found that inmates would often be repeatedly arrested for minor crimes, including "vagrancy," staying out of the camp only for a few days before being rearrested.

A man in his mid-50s was heavily bandaged, with one eye seriously injured after his arrest and beating by the Durham, North Carolina, police. He complained of not being able to work due to his ill condition after he was initially confined to the camp. After the camp doctor pronounced him fit and able to work, he refused to. This drew the penalty of being "hung on the bars" for three days.

When a man is hung on the bars he is stood up facing his cell, with his arms chained to the vertical bars, until he is released (except for being unchained periodically to go to the toilet). After a few hours, his feet and often the glands in his groin begin to swell. If he attempts to sleep, his head falls back with a snap, or falls forward into the bars, cutting and bruising his face.[20]

The man finally was cut down after his feet swelled to alarming proportions. After he was put back on the chain gang, he simply collapsed. This time, however, the doctor generously allowed him to stay away from the work for a week. Rustin observed another incident of a sick prisoner's being struck repeatedly in the face for working too slowly.[21] Other traditional aspects of the racial oppression in the South persisted, such as tenancy and peonage, despite their gradual decline.

The racial prejudice that fueled the systematic institutional bias against African Americans continued to be strong during the 1950s and 1960s. Traditional views of black males continued to permeate white communities across the nation, making equal treatment virtually impossible. An elderly Baltimore woman was typical in her response to a survey. "You don't know what they're going to do. You're leery. They carry razors, knives, rape women. You can't trust them. Don't know what they'll do. I'm scared of them."[22] A mid-1960s national survey found that some 68 percent of whites agreed that "Negroes laugh a lot," 66 percent agreed that "Negroes tend to have less ambition," 60 percent agreed that blacks "smell different," and 55 percent agreed that blacks had "looser morals." In a similar vein, 41 percent agreed that blacks wanted handouts, 39 percent agreed that blacks had "less native intelligence," and 35 percent agreed that "Negroes are inferior to whites."[23] Despite this, a significant percentage of whites did accurately perceive black grievances and felt some degree of empathy.[24]

THE ERA OF THE LONG HOT SUMMERS
Along with the impact of the war in Vietnam and the development of the Civil Rights movement, the emergence of the overlapping Black Power and Black Nationalist movements as important political forces within the national African American community exerted considerable influence on the development of black masculinity during the mid- to late 1960s. Intertwined with these factors was another powerful motor of change in the African American political, cultural, and social consciousness—the successive summers marked by spontaneous, collective outbreaks of violence across the entire nation. Touching virtually every corner of the national black community, the riots sparked a wide-ranging and far-reaching debate on strategies to quickly gain complete equality, self-determination, and freedom. Chronologically, the years of the "long hot summers" span from 1963 to 1968, reaching their apex during the period between the summer of 1967 and the spring of 1968. During the summer of 1967, a total of 71 cities experienced riots, including the massive disorders in Newark and Detroit. The riots of the

spring of 1968 occurred in the wake of the assassination of Martin Luther King Jr. in Memphis, Tennessee. The total number of days consumed by riots grew from only 16 in 1963, to 92 in 1966, to 286 in 1968.[25]

In Detroit an early morning raid in July 1967 on an after-hours drinking spot, termed a "blind pig," led to an extensive rebellion for a weeklong period. The outbreak led to 7,200 arrests, 43 deaths, and the massive destruction of property.[26] The widespread sniping over the week-long period was a notable feature of the Detroit conflagration. Massive force was finally used to crush the rebellion. Reluctantly, President Lyndon B. Johnson called the Third Brigade of the 82d Airborne Division, based in Fort Bragg, North Carolina, with 2,500 men and the Second Brigade of the 101st Airborne Division from Fort Campbell, Kentucky, with 2,200 men into Detroit, reinforcing the 4,000-strong Detroit police force and the 8,000-strong National Guard troops.[27]

The reality and the consequences of the brutality meted out in repressing the rebellion should not be underestimated. Leon Atchison, then an administrative assistant to Congressman John Conyers, was standing near a police garage when he witnessed police brutality:

We were just standing around there, and the door from the garage flew open, and here came this cop with no shirt on, with a judo lock around the neck of this fellow, a colored man, and he was shouting, "You big black motherf--ker, you come on now, come on, get in here." He couldn't move him so he took the handcuffs and put them around his head and hit him in the forehead and just split his head open. And then a little bit later the interrogation room door flew open, and this prisoner came out all bloody and with a smashed nose.[28]

From the perspective of many, if not most, black males in the cities swept by major riots, these events were not tragedies but, rather, turning points, mass epiphanies linking politics, economics, and history. For many the outbreaks of violence meant the end of hope in what they viewed as the "American Dream" and symbolized the latent strength that would be visited upon America if things continued on the same path. In Eldridge Cleaver's *Soul on Ice*, his chapter "Four Vignettes" contains a prison yard scene that vividly depicts the pride many African American men felt after mass rebellions that shook the nation. One character describes what is occurring in the Los Angeles section of Watts:

"Baby," he said, "They walking in fours and kicking in doors; dropping Reds and busting heads; drinking wine and committing crime, shooting and looting; high-sliding and low-riding, setting fires and slashing tires; turning over cars and burning down bars; making Parker mad and making me glad; putting an end to that "go slow" crap and putting sweet Watts on the map—my black ass is in Folsom this morning but my black heart is in Watts!"

Cleaver wrote, "[T]ears of joy were rolling from his eyes."[29]

For Ali Bey Hassan, the riots were also an important personal turning point. He explained that the 1967 Newark events, termed a "riot" by the media, were a "true rebellion" of "the people," as they viewed it as a response to "intolerable ghetto conditions and police brutality and murder."[30] Witnessing a pregnant woman being gunned down by the police, Hassan was distressed that people lacked arms to defend themselves. Hassan said, "I and some other bloods tried to form a self-defense organization to protect the people in our community. But the cops found out about it before we could really begin to move on our ideas."[31]

The increasing sense of crisis on the part of blacks fed into the increased opposition nationally to the war in Vietnam. The increasing difficulties in winning clear victories against segregation and discrimination in the South contributed to the black opposition to the war, where outright victories for the United States were also increasingly rare. Painful sacrifices, disproportionately borne by the contemporary generation of black male youth, forced many to ask revealing questions about their society. Particularly important was the witnessing of unprecedented levels of violence in Vietnam at the same time African Americans were being counseled to turn away from violence as a strategy or tactic in their quest for civil rights. The Reverend Martin Luther King Jr. spoke out against sending the young black men America had "crippled" to "guarantee liberties in Southeast Asia which they had not found in Southwest Georgia and East Harlem."[32] King's antiwar convictions grew out of his experiences in northern black communities during the turbulent years of the "long, hot summers." He spoke of his exasperation at having to explain his philosophy of nonviolence to the budding black militants of the ghettos. Their pointed question, "What about Vietnam?," King said, "hit home." Was it not a fact, they queried, that "our own nation" was using "massive doses of violence to solve its problems, to bring the changes it wanted?"[33]

Certainly, being drafted into the army was viewed as an opportunity by some of those black males inducted, many having been raised in poverty. Despite this, it grated on many that these sudden "opportunities" coincided with a high risk of loss of life and limb.[34] Wallace Terry views 1969 as a decisive year in the transformation of the type of black soldier in Vietnam. Prior to that time, blacks seeking careers and better opportunities found some satisfaction from their participation in the armed forces. With the war in Vietnam taking a heavy toll among black men, who represented 23 percent of the fatalities early during the war, by 1969 black male draftees came to predominate within the service. Many of these men had participated in protests, riots, and other assertive moves toward equal rights on the part of African Americans.[35] There was a high level of awareness among black soldiers in Vietnam that they were being exposed to risks far out of proportion to their numbers. In many cases the front-line units were over 50 percent black.[36]

The physical, psychological, spiritual, and economic toll exacted on the bulk of a generation of black males by the war in Vietnam is incalculable. The damaging psychic consequences that stemmed from merely following orders could be lifelong. Private First Class Reginald "Malik" Edwards, a U.S. Marine, one of the early wave of black servicemen in the war, said that their orders were that if they received a single incoming round of artillery from a village, they were to raze it.[37] After one such incident in which three marines were wounded, Edwards deliberately missed shooting an older Vietnamese civilian, but other soldiers fired a grenade launcher at the man. Afterward he learned that the man was warning a schoolroom full of children, who were hurt by the grenade blast. Later, Edwards almost massacred a room full of women and children. He recalled that he was preparing to "wipe them off the planet," as the anxious troops had been taught to fire first through the walls before entering a village, home, or room.[38] After Edwards realized the enormity of the crime he had nearly committed, he fell to his knees and cried. "I almost killed all them people."[39]

Malik Edwards and other black veterans describe a process of brutalization of the soldier, where atrocities become acceptable amid the socialization into a new morality. Several cited the common practice of torching villages and straw houses with Zippo lighters. Edwards explained that setting "hooches" on fire with tracers "used to be a fun thing to do."[40] Colin Powell, unusual in his extraordinary rise in rank, prominence, and celebrity, had quite common experiences during the war, recalling that once his unit approached an uninhabited Montagnard village whose population had fled to avoid the Americans. Powell wrote, "[W]e burned down the thatched huts, starting the blaze with Ronson and Zippo cigarette lighters."[41]

Richard J. Ford III of Washington, D.C., had an experience in Vietnam typical of that of the black men who were sent to the front lines of the war. Recipient of two Bronze Stars and wounded three times, Ford served around Tan Son Nhut, an area of intense warfare. He described the macho of the black front-line soldier in Vietnam:

Black guys would wear sunglasses, too. We would put on sunglasses walking in the jungle. Think about it, now. It was ridiculous. But we want to show how bad we are. How we're not scared. We be saying, "The Communists haven't made a bullet that can kill me." We had this attitude that I don't give a damn. That made us more aggressive, more ruthless, more careless. And a little more luckier than the person that was scared.[42]

Ford's introduction to crime and drugs came in Vietnam. He recalled how the North Vietnamese propagandist would raise questions on why African Americans would get involved in such a conflict. He recalled her saying: "Soul brothers, go home. Whitey raping your mothers and daughters, burning down your homes. What you over here for? This is not your war."[43]

Ford eventually committed many killings in Vietnam. On one occasion he heard some rustling in the back of a hut and fired blasts from his machine gun at its rear. He heard the scream of a little girl and found that he had slain her and a man who appeared to be in his 80s. "I killed an old man and a little girl in the hut by accident," he recalled, still haunted by the memories.[44] Later, they received flame throwers to burn the entire village and destroyed everything of value that they could find, including vegetables, grain, and livestock. Chemicals were poured in wells, in order that no drinking water would be available to local inhabitants.[45]

After the black veterans left Vietnam, they returned to make up a disproportionate number of the unemployed in the black community. While many baby boomers spent the years of the Vietnam War in colleges and universities or otherwise sharpening the skills to launch meaningful and lucrative careers, the soldiers in Vietnam endured the hazards of war. The difference between years spent in investment in career activities and those spent surviving and fighting in the field was just one of the disadvantages suffered disproportionately by the black Vietnam veteran. Wounds, psychological problems, and homelessness also dogged this population long after they left the front lines. In the aftermath of the war in Vietnam, rates of addiction to drugs and of violence sharply increased. Clearly, the war in Vietnam's toll on the black male exerted a profoundly damaging impact on the black family and the black community.

THE NEW BLACK MALE: ASSERTION, SELF-DEFENSE, AND PATRIARCHY

Following 381 days of the boycott of buses launched by the Montgomery Improvement Association in 1955, a decision by the U.S. Supreme Court against the segregated transportation system of Alabama meant a victory for the Civil Rights movement. It was a victory that propelled young Reverend Martin Luther King Jr. into national prominence. King's philosophy of nonviolence subsequently became the movement's philosophy as it carried the battle against segregation to other cities and states. Embodied within this philosophy were the values of sacrifice and suffering, as well as continual resistance and nonviolent aggression. Key to its success and to its aggression is its sense of moral superiority. [46]

King explained that for the nonviolent protester, self-defense must be rethought from another angle. In aiming to eliminate a specific evil, the "demonstrator agrees that it is better for him to suffer publicly for a short time to end the crippling evil of school segregation than to have generation after generation of children suffer in ignorance."[47] King implied that the ideal black masculinity would include a very high degree of personal discipline. The ability to suffer—including enduring the blows, kicks, and curses of adversaries—was key, in his view, to the type of personality demanded by the era. The ability to adapt one's behavior to the needs of the larger collectivity would enable the individual to achieve a real moral superiority over an enemy with superior military might. King's method, to the extent that it was adhered to, was a strategic innovation that allowed masses of people to be involved in the wresting of civil rights gains. Its persistent character and assumption of moral superiority allowed it to gain important advantages. Thus, for King, it had both moral and strategic advantages. Masculine toughness, then, for King, did not involve the ability to "dish it out" and "take it"; rather it involved the latter and the ability to persist and continue to struggle. In this sense, a persistent and disciplined assertiveness coupled with mass organization was the key to victory. The confidence of the moral faultlessness of their struggle lent to this sense of moral superiority. If the struggle were reduced sheerly to a question of violence, this edge would be lost. King stressed that the nonviolent method of resistance does not seek to "humiliate" the enemy but, rather "win his friendship and understanding" with a humanistic "agape."[48]   Clearly, King's "love" could not be equated with Booker T. Washington's "meekness."

Not surprisingly, King ridiculed the notion that supermasculine African American men were unable to demonstrate nonviolently.

It is always amusing to me when a Negro man says that he can't demonstrate with us because if someone hit him he would fight back. Here is a man whose children are being plagued by rats and roaches, whose wife is robbed daily at overpriced ghetto food stores, who himself is working for about two-thirds of the pay of a white person doing a similar job and with similar skills, and in spite of all this daily suffering it takes someone spitting on him or calling him a nigger to make him want to fight.[49]

Following the launching of the southern sit-in movement in February 1960 and the formation of the Student Non-Violent Coordinating Committee (SNCC), King's basic strategic innovation, African American nonviolent direct action spread to new adherents.

The speech at the August 1963 March on Washington delivered by young John Lewis of the SNCC reflected the views of both militants of his organization and increasingly angry and impatient African Americans as a whole during the period. Dispensing with the usual introductory niceties, Lewis made clear his opposition to the Kennedy administration's civil rights bill at the very beginning of his speech. For Lewis it was "too little, and too late."[50] He also attacked the administration's attempt to control the Civil Rights movement and its promotion of a "cooling off period." "We won't stop now," Lewis declared. Not only would they not stop but he threatened that the "next time we march, we won't march on Washington, but we will march through the South, through the Heart of Dixie, the way Sherman did. We will make the action of the past few months look pretty."[51]

Early on during its southern campaigns the young activists of SNCC had hoped a federal intervention would help protect them and help break down the system of segregation there. Despite the bloody events of the early 1960s, the federal government made a determined effort not to be forced to intervene. After finding the bodies of three missing civil rights workers in an earth-fill dam on 21 June 1964 near Philadelphia, Mississippi, the debate among black activists on the role of violence and self-defense grew more intense. With the inaction on the part of the federal government, the tradition of armed self-defense was revived. Charles Sims, president of the Bogalusa chapter of Deacons for Defense and Justice in Louisiana, said that "the reason why we had to organize the Deacons in the city of Bogalusa was the Negro people and civil rights workers didn't have no adequate police protection." He said that the Deacons' patrols had stopped the activities of the "night-riders." Throughout the South, the Deacons had some 50 chapters.[52]

With his philosophy of nonviolence under increasing attack, Martin Luther King further elaborated its advantages. In one speech, "The Social Organization of Non-violence," King describes self-defensive violence as morally acceptable to all societies. "The principle of self-defense, even involving weapons and bloodshed, has never been condemned, even by Gandhi."[53] King emphasized that "nonviolent resistance is not a method of cowardice. It does resist."[54]

Following the election of Stokely Carmichael (later known as Kwame Ture) as chairman of SNCC in 1966, the organization embarked upon a more radical course. The slogan "Black Power" emerged after a speech by staff member Willie Ricks. Carmichael's use of the slogan on the Meredith march later captured the attention of the national media and thrust Carmichael into international prominence. Immediately, a hue and cry arose over the connotation and meaning of the term "Black Power." Carmichael's vague and sometimes contradictory statements further confused the issue. A raging debate engulfed the nation, especially among African Americans, over the meaning and implications of the term. Roy Wilkins of the NAACP said that "no matter how endlessly they try to explain it, the term 'black power' means anti-white power." When Bayard Rustin attempted to convince Carmichael and SNCC not to demonstrate at President Lyndon B. Johnson's daughter's wedding, Carmichael denounced him for disrespecting the "black brothers engaged in acts of rebellion in our cities."[55]

The path toward a "new," more traditionally "masculine" attitude was blazed by Carmichael, who asserted that the only "power that Negro leaders have is the power to condemn black people," referring to the media-encouraged condemnations of Black Power and of Carmichael himself. The tip-toeing around the sensitivities of those whites who were, at best, in his view, neutral and, at worst, hostile toward black civil rights was demeaning. "Negro leaders," he complained, "even before they would begin to move, . . . were apologizing" when faced with the charge that their ultimate objective was miscegenation. Carmichael's response to the charge would be to tell his accuser, "Your mother, your daughter, your sister is not the queen of the world; she's not the Virgin Mary. She can be made. Let's move on."[56] By striking directly at the anxieties of the white opponents of civil rights, Carmichael made clear his contempt for their perspective.

In the twilight of its organizational existence, SNCC had moved closer to black nationalism philosophically as it increasingly agreed with the thought of the martyred Malcolm X. As the longtime chief spokesman for the Nation of Islam, an organization that grew by leaps and bounds during the 1950s to claim an estimated membership of 250,000 a decade later, Malcolm X had gained a broad following among both Muslims and non-Muslims. Subsequent to his suspension by Elijah Muhammad for making his "chickens come home to roost" remark linking America's history of violence to the assassination of President John F. Kennedy, Malcolm X's ideology moved leftward. Increasingly, he was critical of his organization's abstinence from the mass protests, demonstrations, and other activities of the Civil Rights movement. He complained later, "It could be heard increasingly in the Negro communities: 'Those Muslims talk tough, but they never do anything, unless somebody bothers Muslims.'"[57]

Malcolm X felt that blacks had the right to use a broader range of strategies and tactics than had been previously utilized. Like SNCC, he increasingly called into question the sincerity of white liberals and blamed the federal government for the lack of enforcement of the constitutional right to vote, which effectively disfranchised blacks in the South.[58] While many maintain, with considerable justification, that Martin Luther King and Malcolm X were converging ideologically, after the 1963 events in Birmingham, King was the recipient of some of his most critical verbal blasts. Using some of the harshest terms in the repertoire of contemporary black political discourse, X termed King "the best weapon that the white man, who wants to brutalize Negroes, has ever gotten in this country" since his "foolish" philosophy ruled out self-defense.[59] On another occasion he labeled King a "twentieth-century or modern Uncle Tom or religious Uncle Tom, who is doing the same thing today to keep Negroes defenseless . . . that Uncle Tom did on the plantation."[60] X vowed that "black nationalists" would give "the civil rights struggle" "a new interpretation." The "old handkerchief-heads who have been dillydallying and pussyfooting and compromising—we don't intend to let them pussyfoot and dillydally and compromise any longer," he declared.[61] Malcolm X seemed to be in sync with the mood of the rising generation of militant youth, commenting that they "don't want to hear that 'turn-the-other cheek' stuff."[62]

Some of the more biting commentaries of X were based on contemporary standards of masculine behavior, which he knew could be used to illustrate political points. X focused on the disjuncture between African American interpersonal behavior and their behavior as a collective body:

A person can come to your home, and if he's white and wants to heap some kind of brutality on you, you're nonviolent; or he can come to take your father and put a rope around his neck and you're nonviolent. But if another Negro just stomps his foot, you'll rumble with him in a minute. Which shows you that there's an inconsistency there.[63]

Malcolm X made it clear that he stood for self-defense, particularly when the government failed to protect people.[64] Urging his audience not to "go out shooting people," he chided the men in the audience by reminding them of their masculine role as protector of the family and community. Pointing to men in the audience, he said that "some of you wearing Congressional Medals of Honor, with shoulders this wide and chests this big, muscles that big—any time you and I sit around and read where they bomb a church and murder in cold blood, not some grown-ups, but four little girls while they were praying," it represented an intolerable situation that males must address.[65]

In time, Malcolm X became an important embodiment of the new black urban man. By the time of his assassination, the notion of Malcolm as the true or ideal black "man" was fixed in the minds of his admirers. One editor of a magazine asked actor Ossie Davis, "Why did you eulogize Malcolm X?" Davis pointed to X's political independence and defiance of white power holders. In

contrast to the traditional black politicians, he explained, Malcolm X said, "Get
up off your knees and fight your own battles. That's the way to win back your
self-respect."[66] Davis said that Malcolm X also "knew"

that every Negro who did not challenge on the spot every instance of racism, overt or
covert, committed against him and his people, who chose instead to swallow his spit and
go on smiling, was an Uncle Tom and a traitor, without balls or guts, or any other
commonly accepted aspects of manhood! [67]

William Sales points to another aspect of Malcolm X's life that became a concrete
social force in the African American communities across the nation. Malcolm X's
life became "a model for the social transformation of African Americans in the
1960s," citing Abdul Alkalimat's work periodizing his life into four stages, "the
Exploited; Detroit Red: the Exploiter; Malcolm X: the Self-Emancipator; and El
Hajj Malik El Shabazz: the Social Liberator."[68] Malcolm X remains such a model,
especially important for black males, many of whom share his involvement with
the criminal justice system.

     For over three decades, *The Autobiography of Malcolm X* has been one
of the best-read books in the black community nationally. Malcolm X's profound
distrust of women and patriarchalism are clearly stated in his own words this
classic book. Much of Malcolm's socialization as an adolescent and young adult
with respect to women derived from his experiences hustling on the streets. In
Harlem, he lived in a rooming house next to several prostitutes. He recalled that
there he "learned more about women than" he did anywhere else. "It was these
working prostitutes who schooled me to things that every wife and every husband
should know. Later on, it was chiefly the women who weren't prostitutes who
taught me to be very distrustful of most women." Citing what he regarded as "a
higher code of ethics and sisterliness among those prostitutes than among
numerous ladies of the church who have more men for kicks than the prostitutes
have for pay," he stressed his distrust of the gender.

     Citing a rush of male customers of the prostitutes in the early morning
hours, X attributed this to "domineering, complaining, demanding wives who had
just about psychologically castrated their husbands." The root cause of their visits
to prostitutes was their wives' "disagreeable" personalities, which "had made their
men so tense that they were robbed of the satisfaction of being men." Fleeing this
one-sided conflict, fearing "being ridiculed by his own wife," a man went to the
comfort of a prostitute.[69]

     The prostitutes, according to Malcolm X, understood the basic nature of
men.

Most men, the prostitutes felt, were too easy to push around. . . . The prostitutes said that
most men needed to know what the pimps knew. A woman should occasionally be babied
enough to show her the man had affection, but beyond that she should be treated firmly.
These tough women said that it worked with them. All women, by their nature, are fragile
and weak; they are attracted to the male in whom they see strength.[70]

Occasionally, complaints that X was excessively hard on women would be lodged against him while he was a Nation of Islam minister.[71] When he began to consider marriage, he knew it was problematic for him. "I wouldn't have considered it possible for me to love any woman. I'd had too much experience that women were only tricky, deceitful, untrustworthy flesh." Offering a variety of potential problem areas for men with women, he related that he "had seen too many men ruined, or at least tied down, or in some other way messed up by women." Besides, Malcolm added, "[W]omen talked too much."[72]

Guided by Elijah Muhammad in his quest for a suitable mate, [73] X had only praise for his wife, Betty Shabazz, one of four women he ever trusted, explaining that "Islam is the only religion that gives both husband and wife a true understanding of what love is." [74] Following the marriage of Malcolm X to Betty Shabazz, however, it was a different story. Shabazz wrote that X was a tolerant and understanding husband and father. Rather than domination, trust and mutual consideration prevailed. Shabazz wrote that her husband favored "some sort of mutual cooperation and understanding within the family." According to his widow, Malcolm X "concluded that our marriage should be a mutual exchange. He thought that communication and understanding would give each of us an assurance that one wouldn't do anything to violate the trust of the other."[75]

THE BLACK PANTHER MODEL OF MANHOOD

The Black Panther Party was a national organization dominated by young African American males, but while at its peak of influence, it counted more females than males as members.[76] By and large, party members belonged to a political generation that was heavily influenced by the Civil Rights movement, the Black Power movement, and the black urban rebellions.

For future Black Panther Clark Squire, the summer of 1964 was an eye-opener. "One morning in 1964 I opened the paper and learned that three brothers had been murdered registering voters in Mississippi. I became angry, and that summer I went down to Parola County in the Mississippi Delta to register voters." For Abayama Katara, the summer of 1964 was quite memorable as well. The young black male suffered the loss of his mother that year, forcing a change in his way of thinking. Increasingly, he viewed the "American Dream" as an illusion veiling an actual "nightmare" for African Americans. "Housewives, young bloods, pimps, pushers, whores, bloods with so-called 'good jobs,'" Katara wrote, "were all in the streets telling the man in the only way they knew how that black people" were waking from the "American dream."[77]

For future Black Panther chairman, Bobby Seale, Malcolm X's assassination in February 1965 proved a turning point in his way of thinking. When he heard the news, he flew into a rage. He said in his anger, "We need guns, . . . Guns and underground operations to get some righteous revolution on," feeling that Malcolm X had been his "personal friend in a certain sense." When his immediate rage subsided, and he began to accept the reality of his leader's death, he vowed to "make" a "Malcolm" out of himself.[78]

Huey Percy Newton was born into a working-class setting common to millions of contemporary African Americans. Having moved to Oakland, California, Newton as a child quickly became acquainted with the hostility of the local police, in his words, "because the police were very brutal to us even at that age. There would be a policeman in the movie house, and if there was any disturbance, we would get kicked out and the police would call us niggers."[79] After Newton began working politically with Bobby Seale, they joined the Soul Students Advisory Council and quickly became embroiled in a crisis within the organization involving their unapproved spending of the organization's treasury on bail. Defending the use of the funds to bail out a black man who they felt had been unjustly arrested, Newton argued that blacks must arm themselves, suggesting that the organization sponsor an influx of armed blacks on campus.

The two men met to form an organization designed to monitor police activities and defend the rights of African American citizens. "A law book, a tape recorder, and a gun," was all Newton felt was needed. They agreed that they would accept arrests nonviolently and that they would keep their guns in plain view when they patrolled the police "so as not to break the law." They vowed to "do battle only at the point when a fool policeman drew his gun unjustly."[80] Their organization was formalized late one evening in October 1966 in the back offices of the North Oakland Neighborhood Anti-Poverty Center. By New Year's Day 1967, the Black Panther Party moved into the first of many storefront offices that it would occupy in the ensuing years. The publicity attending the key events in the Panthers' early history sparked a firestorm of growth that would increase their national membership to an estimated 2,000 in 32 chapters spread over 15 states within the next two years.[81]

With the increase in Panther popularity, new problems of recruitment emerged. Many black males began to look to Black Panther Party membership as a means of status acquisition. Seale complained that these "cats" would wear the impressive Panther uniform of black beret, black pants, blue shirt and black turtleneck but only posture and pose in front of the office "with a mean face on, their chests stuck out and their arms folded."[82] The Panther chairman complained that the "only thing they did was rap to the sisters."[83]

For the contemporary black male, the Panther look was the symbol of the new aggressive masculinity, which would no longer plead and beg for equality but, rather, engage in a protracted outward thrust to seize it. The key feature in the Panther's image was the gun. This attracted many to the organization. Cleaver describes one scene that occurred when the Panthers entered a meeting to plan the security of the widow of Malcolm X, Betty Shabazz. Cleaver stressed that the image of the Panthers was incomplete without the presence of a firearm:

I spun around in my seat and saw the most beautiful sight I had ever seen: four black men wearing black berets, powder blue shirts, black leather jackets, black trousers, shiny black shoes—and each with a gun! In front was Huey P. Newton with a riot pump shotgun in his right hand, barrel pointed to the floor. Beside him was Bobby Seale, the handle of a .45 caliber automatic showing from its holster on his right hip.[84]

Central to their goal of achieving political power was the Black Panther insistence that millions of African Americans take up arms, often quoting Black Panther founder Huey P. Newton that "an unarmed people is subject to slavery at any time." Immediately prior to the assassination of Martin Luther King Jr. in April 1968, an imprisoned Huey Newton issued "Executive Mandate No. 3," an internal Panther rule that proved key to the party's development:

We draw the line at the threshold of our doors. It is therefore mandated as a general order to all members of the Black Panther Party for Self-Defense that all members must acquire the technical equipment to defend their homes and their dependents and shall do so.[85]

The penalty for violating this mandate was expulsion.

Early in 1969 in an essay entitled the "Functional Definition of Politics," Newton described the Panthers' view of politics as "war without bloodshed" and war as "politics with bloodshed." For the masses of impoverished and struggling blacks he felt that the sole means by which they could become "political" was by engaging in armed self-defense. Newton wrote, "[B]lack people can develop self-defense power by arming themselves from house to house, block to block, community to community, throughout the nation."[86]

The Black Panther Party stressed the sacrifice of one's life for the future of the black masses. Reflecting the perpetual state of siege inflicted by the federal government's relentless attacks and their own actions and reactions, Newton tied the concept of "revolutionary suicide" to the question of organizational self-defense. Declaring that the Black Panther Party would not tolerate "the total destruction of the people" or "fascism, aggression, brutality and murder of any kind," Newton said it would be tantamount to "reactionary suicide" if they remained passive in the face of these attacks upon them. He declared "[W]e will not die the death of the Jews in Germany. We would rather die the death of the Jews in Warsaw." He continued to say that "where there is courage, where there is self-respect and dignity, there is a possibility" that they could emerge victorious. "Revolutionary suicide" would mean that they would not be repressed easily.[87]

One article in the *Black Panther*, the official news organ of the party, was authored by New York State prisoners of the Jonathan P. Jackson Commune. The imprisoned activists lauded "those qualities that make the new man–the revolutionary guerrilla fighter–love and devotion for our people, true brotherhood and solidarity with all oppressed peoples, discipline, dedication, self-reliance, willingness to sacrifice, knowledge, wisdom and understanding."[88]

Black Panther leaders were hardly bashful in displaying their assertive brand of manhood. At the Black Panther-sponsored United Front against Fascism Conference in Oakland on 18–20 July 1969, the Weathermen faction of the Students for a Democratic Society disagreed with the Panther demand for community control of the police in white areas since they felt this would "undermine the fight against white supremacy." This mild and confusing disagreement infuriated the Panthers, who denounced the group.

SDS had better get their politics straight because the Black Panther Party is drawing some very clear lines between friends and enemies. . . . We'll beat those little sissies, those little schoolboys' ass if they don't straighten up their politics. So we want to make it known to SDS and the first motherf--ker that get out of order had better stand in line for some kind of disciplinary actions from the Black Panther Party.[89]

For the Black Panthers and others steeped in their brand of masculinity, as the quote indicates, it would have been laughable that the lack of property ownership or officially recognized status in America detracted from their manhood.

On the afternoon of 29 October 1969, Black Panther Party chairman Bobby Seale, on trial in Chicago with the other "Chicago 8" defendants for a violation of the 1968 Conspiracy Act, making it a crime to cross federal lines to incite a riot, was bound, gagged, and shackled by Judge Julius J. Hoffman. At issue was the right of Seale to defend himself versus Hoffman's insistence that he already had a lawyer. Seale defiantly resisted the imposition of an attorney and repeatedly disrupted the court in protest. After Hoffman threatened Seale if he did not remain silent Seale adamantly insisted that the "law protects my right not to be discriminated against in my legal defense. Why don't you recognize that? Let me defend myself."[90]

As the back-and-forth contention continued, Hoffman instructed the marshal to take Seale into a room, and, when he returned, Seale was bound by a gag and strapped to a chair. The Black Panther leader continued to try as hard as he could to be heard, shouting through the gag. Words calling the judge and the marshals "fascist dogs" were distinctly heard despite the gag. Attorney William Kunstler complained to Hoffman, asking, "Are we going to stop this medieval torture that is going on in this courtroom? I think it is a disgrace." The photos of Seale chained to a chair, angrily denouncing the judge and the entire system, publicized widely by the media, made Seale a symbol of the contemporary black male militant.[91] The young Black Panther leader's steely defiance, his willingness to endure pain and suffering, and his adherence to principle harked back to the hard-core masculinity of his field slave ancestors.

"THE OTHER HALF": WOMEN AND THE BLACK PANTHER PARTY

Consistent with their socialist ideology, the Black Panther Party theoretically upheld the equality of women in all spheres of life. Reality, however, was clogged with examples contradicting these ostensibly good intentions. Formally, the Black Panther Party position contrasted sharply with that of their ideological opponents of other organizations, including, "the cultural nationalists," such as Ron Karenga's United Slaves (US) and Amiri Baraka's Congress of Afrikan People (CAP), which generally maintained that women were unfit for overall leadership and should be restricted to supportive and subordinate roles. The Baraka of the 1960s and early 1970s upheld a principle of male superiority, declaring at one point, "Nature had made women submissive, she must submit to man's creation in order for it to exist." Ron Karenga, for his part, tied the appeal of women to a "femininity" that is "submissive" and declared that gender "equality is false."[92]

The Black Panthers were vehement in their rejection of the more conservative nationalists' position on women. Fred Hampton, a popular Black Panther slain by police in a predawn raid in Chicago, once derisively denounced the "cultural nationalists" who "tell their women, 'Walk behind me.'" Hampton declared that the only reason that a woman should do so is "so she can put a foot knee-deep in his ass."[93]

The statements of Panther women wavered between uncompromising positions against sexism and those suggestive of a subordinate role for women. One article by a woman Panther begins by inquiring, Why are "black men so blind as not to see the beauty lying dormant in black woman; waiting to be discovered by the black man?" Historically, the article explained, the role of the black woman since slavery has been twofold: to act as a "sounding board for the black man" and as "provider and sympathizer for the black man since his castration by the white racist." The writer explained that as "long as her man is deprived of manhood," the woman herself is deprived of a "full womanhood." Appealing to him to "come to the aid of [his] black mothers, sisters and wives," the article portrays black women as collectively abandoned and alone. The role of the black woman within this situation is to "assist in the re-birth of the black man's mind," allowing him to "test this new mind" and gain confidence in it. The genuine test of his manhood will be realized when he comes to full consciousness of black feminine beauty in its entirety.[94] The article chastises the "Negro" woman, as opposed to the conscious "Black" woman, for engaging in a constant criticism of men. "Black" women, in contrast, "sing the praises of their men." She implies that the black woman's value derives directly from "what she can contribute to the black man."[95] Similarly, Linda Greene wrote that the ideal black revolutionary woman "fulfills the needs of her Black man when they are made known to her and when they are not evident, she will and does seek them out."[96] A contrasting article, demonstrating the range of views on feminist issues within the Panther organization, cites examples of women's participation in the Chinese, Cuban, and Vietnamese revolutions as support for women's equality. June Culberson's May 1969 essay, entitled "The Role of the Revolutionary Woman," stressed that Panther women don't want to be termed "Pantherettes" but rather "Panthers."[97]

Eldridge Cleaver wrote that in prison he first "encountered" the "Ogre," one of his terms for white women. Cleaver confessed she "possessed a tremendous and dreadful power" over him, whose nature he failed to comprehend.[98] While he found it easy to reject the symbols and icons of white culture and life, he could not break free of this power.[99] He soon experienced a real-life conflict over a fantasy "Ogre" that he had pinned up on his cell wall, when a prison guard ripped it down while suggesting that he pin up a "colored girl" instead.[100] In his anger and humiliation Cleaver admits to himself that he preferred white women over black and pondered the significance of this. Later, in the prison yard, he raises this question to his fellow black prisoners, who freely admitted their distaste for African American women. Cleaver's poem, "To a White Girl," is illustrative of his love-hate emotional relationship with white women. He later described how this led to his becoming a rapist, first, to "refine my technique and modus operandi," he began by "practicing on black girls in the ghetto—in the black ghetto where dark and vicious deeds appear not as aberrations or deviations from the norm, but as part of the sufficiency of the Evil of the day." Later, his technique down pat, he "crossed the tracks and sought out white prey." For him, "rape was an insurrectionary act" that gave him the satisfaction of revenge upon the "white man" and his system, citing the long history of similar actions by white men against black women.[101] He added, "There are, of course, many young blacks out there right now who are slitting white throats and raping the white girl." Later, Cleaver realized his grave crimes, confessing, "I lost my self-respect. My pride as a man dissolved and my whole fragile moral structure seemed to collapse."[102] He reemerged a new man, transformed with the supposed wisdom that "the black man's sick attitude toward the white woman is a revolutionary sickness," as it kept him out of sync with the oppressive "system." He argued that while many "whites flatter themselves" that the black "male's lust and desire for the white dream girl is purely an esthetic attraction," it was in reality "a bloody, hateful, bitter, and malignant" lust.[103]

Cleaver elaborated upon his perception of the black male's view of women in his "The Allegory of the Black Eunuchs." One of the black eunuchs, an old man named Lazarus, is asked if he ever hit a black woman. He replied, "I wish I had a nickel for every bitch whose ass I've put my foot in!"[104] Lazarus claims, "Black women take kindness for weakness. Leave them the least little opening and they will put you on the cross." Unlike white women, they can't be trusted, he says. He freely admits that he hates "a black bitch," comparing them with cobras. The white woman, in contrast, is described as a "goddess" who is both soft and submissive.

In a view echoed by George Jackson and others, Lazarus feels that there is a "war going on between the black man and the black woman, which makes her the silent ally, indirectly but effectively, of the white man." For this reason, the white man has historically "propped her up economically above you and me, to strengthen her hand against us."[105] Cleaver's allegory merely vividly captures the perceptions of thousands of black men of conscious or unconscious hostility toward black women embodied in black male folklore. The distrust implicit in this suspected betrayal instinct exerts a corrosive force on the relationships that some black males have with black women.[106] Tracey Matthews similarly points to Huey Newton's assertion of the "desirability of Black male domination and Black female acquiescence, while assuming that this pattern has been unduly interrupted," as the Panther leader refers to "recapturing our balls" and "regaining our manhood."[107]

Jean Carey Bond and Patricia Peery ask, in their important 1969 *Liberator* magazine article, "Is the Black Male Castrated?" The authors explain that one of the two versions of the black male emasculation thesis "arrives at the point that black men are weak via the route that black women have castrated them by, among other things, playing their economic ace in the hole. . . . Also linked to this thesis is the woefully misbegotten notion that black women complied with their rapists and used their bodies to rise on the socio-economic ladder, leaving black men behind."[108] They ask seriously whether black people believe that the label "emasculated" applies to black males. "Specifically applied to a male," they explain, "emasculation connotes the absence of virility and can mean, though not necessarily, effeminacy." Acknowledging African Americans' long history of hardship, they nevertheless ask: "[D]o our people truly fit the description given above? [and] [H]ave black men really been stripped of their virility?" They answer their own question contending that "as a whole people, Afro-Americans lack neither spirit nor strength nor vigor."[109]

Eldridge Cleaver's chapter "The Primeval Mitosis" further rounds out his perception of race, class, and gender relationships in America. Expressing another common black male view, Cleaver's "Omnipotent Administrator," the white man, "is markedly effeminate and delicate by reason of his explicit repudiation and abdication of the body in preference for his mind."[110] The white woman, "the Ultrafeminine," stands in stark contrast to the hard "Amazon," the black woman. He explains that the "Amazon" has been "deprived" of her womanhood as the "Supermasculine Menial" has been denied his manhood. The "Amazon" is angered by the adulation poured upon the "Ultrafeminine" by both the white and black males but envies her at the same time for her "pampered, powderpuff existence." She "finds it difficult to respect the Supermasculine Menial," viewing him as a half-man. She is attracted to the "Omnipotent Administrator," the white man, and "is lost between two worlds."[111]

For Cleaver, however, the black male dilemma centers on regaining "his mind" and ceasing to be the "embodiment of Brute Power." Cleaver writes of the "bias and reflex" of American society that discourage the development of the black male's "mind":

The products of his mind, unless they are very closely associated with his social function of Brute Power, are resented and held in contempt by society as a whole. The further away from Brute Power his mental productions stand, the more emphatically will they be rejected and scorned by society, and treated as upstart invasions of the realm of the Omnipotent Administrator. His thoughts count for nothing.[112]

In his essay "To All Black Women, From All Black Men," Cleaver declared that it was a new day for the black man, confessing that for years he was not acting like a man. Cleaver wrote: "For four hundred years you have been a woman alone, bereft of her man, a manless woman."[113] This "negated masculinity of four hundred years minus my Balls" has resulted in his feeling "a deep hurt, . . . the pain of humiliation of the vanquished warrior."[114] Cleaver indicates that black men heard the black woman's screams but in "a cowardly stupor, with a palpitating heart and quivering knees," watched the slave masters' whip tear away at the black woman's flesh, the "tender flesh of African Motherhood."[115] The lengthy black male guilt trip includes Cleaver's confession of becoming "a sniveling craven, a funky punk, a vile, groveling bootlicker," among other things.[116] Eldridge Cleaver's practical politics illustrated the formidable obstacles facing the full and equal participation of women within the Panther organization. In a speech at Stanford University, Cleaver, in remarks specifically directed to "the ladies," reminded them of the seriousness of the situation and then called for "pussy power." Apologizing to "the Victorians who have had their morals ruffled," he posits both a "revolutionary" and a "counterrevolutionary" form of sex. Advising women to tell their male mates "that they're going to have to become part of the solution or don't call you up on the telephone any more. . . . Tell them to go away, . . . You can put them under more pressure than I can with speeches. You can cut off their sugar."[117] Tracye Matthews notes how unusual it is for "an influential leader to promote this as a preferred mode of political praxis."[118]

The evidence suggests that, for the most part, the Panthers fell far short of the goal of sexual equality and a gender-neutral organization. Indeed, the Black Panther Party remained a male-dominated organization throughout its organizational heyday. However, Angela D. LeBlanc-Ernest's analysis of gender in the organization found that following the suspension of the process of inducting new members women rose to positions of leadership. With many of the male leaders imprisoned, hiding, or dead, many women such as Elaine Brown rose to lead local branches.[119]

Imprisoned Black Panther Party leader George Jackson's views on women were also noteworthy. Jackson held, discussing his mother, that "Women like to be dominated, love being strong-armed, need an overseer to supplement their weakness."[120] He regarded this as being the opposite of himself. In addition, women are not capable of understanding men like himself. Jackson explained that, because of this, "we should never allow women to express any opinions on the subject, but just to sit, listen to us, and attempt to understand. It is for them to obey and aid us, not to attempt to think."[121] A few days later in a letter to his father, Jackson wrote: "Women and children enjoy and need a strong hand poised above them."[122]

George Jackson's male chauvinism was apparently rejected by his sister Frances. He wrote that she was angry at him for cutting her off and not allowing her to speak during a visit to see him in prison. "I didn't make things any better either when she wrote two months later decrying my supposed rudeness. When I explained to her that she was not supposed to hold any opinions other than those of her menfolk, she stopped writing. Tell her that I feel no ill will toward her, but when she hears us debating method and policy, she is supposed to be silent, listen, and try to learn something. . . . I've bummed around this country three times, seen everything eight times, now what am I going to do with some advice from a twenty-three-year-old girl who has been sheltered from the real world all her life!"[123] Jackson stood reality on its head: *he* was the one limited to the confines of penal institutions for a considerable part of his life, whereas his sister was not confined by prison bars. Yet, Jackson was contemptuous of any advice whatsoever from her.

The experience of women and the extent of sexual equality within the Panther organization were quite varied and uneven. Roberta Alexander's speech at the Panther-sponsored "United Front against Fascism" conference noted the controversy over women's role in the organization. She said that the battles within the party over women's equality had run "the whole gamut" of possible problems, the issues involving whether women as well as men could use arms, whether they were confined to office work, and whether men deserve sex because of their revolutionary activity. Unequivocally, Alexander declares that African American women are "oppressed by black men and that's got to go."[124] Kathleen Cleaver felt that suggestions from women received less consideration despite their key logistical roles from the early days of the Party.[125]

Assata Shakur's most important criticism of the Black Panther Party's work, from the perspective of a former Panther, was not its sexism. She did, however, refer to "the macho cult that was an official body in the BPP [Black Panther Party]."[126] The lumpen influence in the Black Panther views of black male–black female relationships is unmistakable. One article praised the personal attributes and contributions of "pimps and whores" to the African American freedom movement and ignored the sexual exploitation of black women.[127] John Seale recalled that "a lot of guys still had that chauvinistic attitude. A guy'd pop a woman in the eye and bruise her all up. That was wrong."[128]

In 1969 FBI director J. Edgar Hoover termed the Black Panther Party "the greatest security threat to the internal security of the country." The FBI's fear was fueled by its suspicion that a quarter of African Americans were in support of the organization. After Attorney General John Mitchell designated the organization as a threat to "national security," it marked a turning point in the government's effort to destroy the Panthers. For example, the San Francisco FBI office was ordered to embark upon a "disruptive information operation" against the Panthers. Another FBI memo outlined the production of documents "ridiculing, or discrediting Panther leaders through their ineptness or personal escapades; espousing personal philosophies and promoting factionalism among Black Panther Party members; indicating electronic coverage where none exists; outlining fictitious plans for police raids or other counteractions revealing misuse or misappropriation of Panther funds."[129]

The Black Panther Party's attitude served to set an aggressive standard for black masculinity during the period of the late 1960s and early 1970s. In virtually every area where blacks were a presence during the period, black males displayed an attitude of ceaselessly striving to push forward against real and perceived obstacles of racism. On college campuses, in workplaces, on military bases, and in the athletic arenas, black males stood up to the powers, often sacrificing their individual status for the generations of the future. Like their predecessors who mobilized in similar ways during the 1850s, 1860s, and 1920s, in particular, they fought and died in search of respect, their families' security, and social justice.

The period at the cusp of the decade of the 1960s and 1970s marked a new high point in black masculine assertion. The killings at Attica prison, the raids of Black Panther offices, and the winding down of the Vietnam War marked the end of a distinctive phase of black masculine history in which strident protest, as well as ambitious projects of community and cultural development, came to a close. In the new period, more uncertainty would trouble the black male psyche as, with the forward march halted, new crises would overtake them. Soon, questions as to the actual survival of the black male would arise in many quarters of the African American community.

NOTES

1. Eldridge Cleaver, *Soul on Ice* (New York: Delta, 1968), 61.

2. Bobby Seale, *Seize the Time* (New York: Vintage Books, 1970), 155.

3. Ibid.

4. Ibid., 159.

5. Ibid., 162.

6. Ibid.

7. Ibid., 170.

8. Doug McAdam, *Political Process and the Development of Black Insurgency, 1930–70* (Chicago: University of Chicago Press, 1982), 95–96; Manning Marable, *From the Grassroots: Social and Political Essays towards Afro-American Liberation* (Boston: South End Press, 1980), 142; D. R. Deskins Jr., *Residential Mobility of Negroes in Detroit, 1837–1965, before the Ghetto: Black Detroit in the Nineteenth Century* (Urbana: University of Illinois Press, 1973).

9. Dorothy K. Newman et al., *Protest, Politics, and Prosperity: Black Americans and White Institutions, 1940–75* (New York: Pantheon Books, 1978), 269.

10. James A. Geschwender, *Class, Race, and Worker Insurgency: The League of Revolutionary Black Workers* (Cambridge: Cambridge University Press, 1977), 41.

11. Aldon Morris, "Black Southern Sit-In Movement: An Analysis of Internal Organization," *American Sociological Review* 46 (1981): 744.

12.. Ibid., 766.

13. George M. Frederickson, *The Black Image in the White Mind: The Debate on Afro-American Character and Destiny, 1817–1914* (New York: Harper and Row, 1971), 13–14.

14. Newman et al., *Protest*, 3.

15. E. F. Morrow, *Black Man in the White House* (New York: MacFadden Books, 1963), 126–27.

16. Ibid., 127.

17. D. Roth, *Sacred Honor: Colin Powell, The Inside Account of His Life and Triumphs* (New York: HarperCollins, 1993), 81.

18. Newman et al., *Protest*, 15.

19. Bayard Rustin, *Down the Line: The Collected Writings of Bayard Rustin* (Chicago: Quadrangle Books, 1971), 27–28.

20. Ibid., 31.

21. Ibid., 42.

22. Louis Harris, *The Negro Revolution in America* (New York: Simon and Schuster, 1964), 140.

23. Ibid., 140–41.

24. Ibid., 146.

25. McAdam, *Political Process*, 222.

26. National Advisory Commission on Civil Disorders, *The Kerner Report: The 1968 Report of the National Advisory Commission on Civil Disorders* (New York: Pantheon Books, 1988), 106.

27. *New York Times*, 27 July 1967, 18.

28. John Hersey, *The Algiers Motel Incident* (New York: Bantam Books, 1968), 59.

29. Cleaver, *Soul on Ice*, 27.

30. K. Balagoon et al., *Look for me in the Whirlwind: The Collective Autobiography of the New York 21* (New York: Random House, 1971), 89.

31. Ibid., 89.

32. Martin Luther King Jr., "A Time to Break Silence" in Philip S. Foner (ed.), *The Voice of Black America* (New York: Capricorn Books, 1975), 435–45. See also David Garrow, *Bearing the Cross: Martin Luther King, Jr. and the Southern Christian Leadership Conference* (New York: Morrow, 1986).

33. King, "A time to Break Silence," 438.

34. Stanley Goff and Robert Sanders, *Brothers: Black Soldiers in the Nam* (New York: Berkeley Books, 1982), x.

35. Wallace Terry, *Bloods: An Oral History of the Vietnam War by Black Veterans* (New York: Ballantine Books, 1984), xiv.

36. Goff and Sanders, *Brothers*, ix.

37. Terry, *Bloods*, 1.

38. Ibid., 3.

39. Ibid.

40. Ibid.

41. Colin L. Powell, *My American Journey* (New York: Random House, 1995), 87.

42. Terry, *Bloods*, 36.

43. Ibid., 39.

44. Ibid., 42.

45. Ibid., 43.

46. James Melvin Washington (ed.), *A Testament of Hope: The Essential Writings of Martin Luther King, Jr.* (San Francisco: Harper and Row, 1986), 5.

47. Ibid., 57.

48. Ibid., 13.

49. Ibid., 57.

50. John Lewis, "We Are in a Serious Revolution," in Foner, *The Voice of Black America*, 359.

51. Ibid., 361.

52. Joanne Grant, *Black Protest: History, Documents, and Analyses, 1619 to the Present* (New York: Fawcett, 1968), 397.

53. Washington, *A Testament of Hope*, 32–33.

54. Ibid., 12.

55. Clayborne Carson, *In Struggle: SNCC and the Black Awakening of the 1960s* (Cambridge: Harvard University Press, 1981), 220–21.

56. Ibid., 219.

57. Malcolm X, *The Autobiography of Malcolm X* (New York: Grove Press, 1965), 289.

58. Ibid., 31.

59. R. H. Brisbane, *Black Activism: Racial Revolution in the United States, 1954–70* (Valley Forge, PA: Judson Press, 1974), 70.

60. Ibid., 113.

61. Malcolm X, *Malcolm X Speaks* (New York: Grove Press, 1965), 31.

62. Ibid., 31–32.

63. Malcolm X, "To Young People," in Foner, *The Voice of Black America*, 395.

64. Malcolm X, *Malcolm X Speaks*, 43.

65. Ibid.

66. Ossie Davis, "Malcolm Was a Man," in Grant, *Black Protest*, 457.

67. Ibid., 458.

68. William W. Sales Jr., *From Civil Rights to Black Liberation: Malcolm X and the Organization Of Afro-American Unity* (Boston: South End Press, 1994), 28.

69. Malcolm X, *Autobiography of Malcolm X*, 91.

70. Ibid., 92.

71. Ibid., 92–93.

72. Ibid., 226.

73. Ibid.

74. Ibid., 229.

75. Betty Shabazz, "Malcolm X as a Husband and Father," in John Henrik Clarke (ed.), *Malcolm X: The Man and His Times* (Trenton, NJ: Africa World Press, 1990), 134.

76. Bobby Seale, *A Lonely Rage: The Autobiography of Bobby Seale* (New York: Times Books, 1978), 177; Angela D. LeBlanc-Ernest, "'The Most Qualified Person to Handle the Job'; Black Panther Party Women, 1966–1982," in Charles E. Jones (ed.), *The Black Panther Party Reconsidered* (Baltimore: Black Classic Press, 1998), 308–09.

77. Balagoon, et al., *Look for Me*, 12–13.

78. Bobby Seale, *A Lonely Rage*, 134–36.

79. Gene Marine, *The Black Panthers* (New York. Signet Books, 1969), 10.

80. Seale, *Seize the Time*, 154.

81. *The Black Panther*, 1 November 1969, 20.

82. Seale, *Seize the Time*, 367.

83. Ibid.

84. Eldridge Cleaver, *Post-Prison Writings and Speeches* (New York: Ramparts Books, 1969), 29.

85. Huey P. Newton, "Executive Mandate No. 3," *The Black Panther*, 16 March 1968.

86. Philip S. Foner (ed.), *The Black Panthers Speak* (Philadelphia: J. B. Lippincott Company, 1970), 45–47.

87. Huey P. Newton, "Let Us Hold High the Banner of Intercommunalism and the Invincible Thoughts of Huey P. Newton, Minister of Defense and Supreme Commander of the Black Panther Party," *The Black Panther* 2 January 1971, A–H.

88. "Brothers in the New York State Concentration Camp From the Jonathan P. Jackson Commune," *The Black Panther*, 9 January 1971, 8.

89. Kirkpatrick Sale, *SDS* (New York: Vintage Books, 1974), 516.

90. *The "Trial" of Bobby Seale* (New York: Priam Books, 1970), 96.

91. Ibid.

92. Paula Giddings, *When and Where I Enter: The Impact of Black Women on Race and Sex in America* (New York: William Morrow, 1984), 318; Tracye Matthews, "'No One Ever Asks, What a Man's Place in the Revolution Is': Gender and the Politics of the Black Panther Party 1966–1971" in Charles E. Jones (ed.), *The Black Panther Party Reconsidered* (Baltimore: Black Classic Press, 1998), 272.

93. "You Can Kill a Revolutionary but You Can't Kill a Revolution," *The Black Panther*, 16 January 1970, 12.

94. "Black Woman," *The Black Panther*, 14 September 1968, 6.

95. Ibid., 9.

96. Linda Greene, "The Black Revolutionary Woman," *The Black Panther*, 28 September 1968, 11.

97. June Culberson, "The Role of the Revolutionary Woman," *The Black Panther*, 4 May 1969, 8.

98. Cleaver, *Soul on Ice*, 6.

99. Ibid., 8.

100. Ibid., 14.

101. Ibid., 17.

102. Ibid., 15.

103. Ibid., 158.

104. Ibid., 162.

105. Ibid.

106. Matthews, "'No One Ever Asks,'" 279–80.

107. Ibid., 280.

108. J. C. Bond and P. Peery, "Is the Black Male Castrated?," in Toni Cade (ed.), *The Black Woman: An Anthology* (New York: Signet, 1970), 115.

109. Ibid.

110. Cleaver, *Soul on Ice*, 181.

111. Ibid., 188.

112. Ibid., 186.

113. Ibid., 205.

114. Ibid., 206.

115. Ibid., 208.

116. Ibid., 209.

117. Ibid., 395.

118. Matthews, "'No One Ever Asks,'" 281.

119. LeBlanc-Ernest, "'The Most Qualified Person,'" 310.

120. George Jackson, *Soledad Brother: The Prison Letters of George Jackson* (New York: Bantam Books, 1970), 101.

121. Ibid.

122. Ibid., 107.

123. Ibid., 117.

124. Giddings, *When and Where I Enter*, 69.

125. Ibid., 317.

126. Assata Shakur, *Assata: An Autobiography* (Westport, CT: Lawrence Hill, 1987), 223.

127. Al Carroll, "On Illegitimate Capitalist 'The Game,'" *The Black Panther*, July 1970.

128. David Hilliard, *The Autobiography of David Hilliard and the Story of the Black Panther Party* (Boston: Little, Brown, and Company, 1993), 235.

129. Winston A. Grady-Willis, "The Black Panther Party: State Repression and Political Prisoners," in *The Black Panther Party Reconsidered* (Baltimore: Black Classic Press, 1998), 363–89.

Chapter 10

African American Males in Contemporary Society, 1972–Present

> Carry this love all the way back to our cities and towns and never let
> it die, brothers, never let it die.
> —Minister Louis Farrakhan, Million Man March, 16 October 1995[1]

On 16 October 1995 a massive gathering of roughly 1 million black males was held on the Mall in Washington, DC. The Million Man March was sponsored to demonstrate to the world that African American men were "filled with the determination that we should no longer and never again be looked at as the criminals, the clowns, the buffoons, the dregs of society," in the words of the organizer of the event, Minister Louis Farrakhan. [2]

On the Mall in Washington, DC, the mood was one of seriousness guided by a general sentiment that a turning point had been reached and that it was time for the direction in which the black male has been traveling to change. A strong, pervading spirit of positive and unifying black-male-to-black-male solidarity vibrated through the crowd. The males were united, in part, from the common experience of being treated as pariahs or violent criminals merely due to their race and gender. At the same time, a collective guilt seemed to be shared concerning the devastation that has been wrought by some black males on their families, communities, and collective image. Yet, there was a broad recognition that those unfortunate acts were direct consequences of a long history of restricted opportunities and victimization of the black male.

Scores of speakers entertained the crowd while they waited for the man of the hour: Louis Farrakhan. The Nation of Islam leader began by relating the story of mythical slaveholder Willie Lynch. Lynch's strategy of maintaining blacks in slavery consisted of focusing on observable differences among black people and using them systematically to divide and weaken them.[3] Pronouncing the Willie Lynch strategy for controlling the African slave population of the United States a resounding success, Farrakhan declared that the Million Man

March had overcome those divisions and united those with vastly different socioeconomic statuses, skin color, religions, and lifestyles.[4] Fact or fiction, the Willie Lynch myth became real in the minds of tens of thousands of black males at that moment. Farrakhan's point, the dire importance of overcoming these divisions in order to slay Willie Lynch, the demon of black disunity, once and for all, carried the day. Farrakhan proclaimed triumphantly that there are "a new Black man" and "a new Black woman" in America now.

Indeed, the march attracted a broad base of support. Even those public figures, such as Colin Powell, to whom it would have been politically costly to appear at a gathering led by Louis Farrakhan, could readily embrace the conservative official goals of the march. The focus inward on the shortcomings and weaknesses of the African American male himself garnered considerable approving comments from blacks, as well as many whites, across the political spectrum. Colin Powell approvingly commented, "We have got to get ourselves together . . . we have to be better fathers," "providers," and "we have to reconcile with each other; we have to begin solving our own problems."[5]

Farrakhan could not resist commenting on the irony that the massive demonstration of black male power, designed to inaugurate a new era in African American history, was occurring in the very place where 14 decades, before slaves had been sold and where slave coffles could daily be observed moving along the District of Columbia's avenues. Farrakhan also defiantly commented that the "commands" to kill historic black prophets, including David Walker, Malcolm X, and Martin Luther King, came from the White House that Clinton now occupied. The Muslim leader charged that despite this historic persecution of black prophets, he didn't need White House approval since African Americans had "validated" him. Farrakhan, who would only months later court conservative Republican politicians, defiantly said, "I don't need to be in any mainstream."[6]

Speaking before the assembled thousands of black males, whose very real and potential power was readily apparent to themselves as well as other observers, Farrakhan struck another resonant chord within the black psyche. The notion that whites either handpick black leaders or exercise veto power over them—having experienced past weeks of intense anti-Farrakhan coverage in the media—was thus rejected en masse at this gathering.

Speaking for many African Americans out of the "mainstream," angry with what they witness daily in the media, the Muslim leader speculated about what spin the newspapers and media would put on this story. He wondered, Would they "respect the beauty of this day?"

All of these black men that the world sees as savage, maniacal, and bestial. Look at them. A sea of peace. A sea of tranquility. A sea of men ready to come back to God. Settle their differences and go back home to turn our communities into decent and safe places to live.[7]

Seeming to move far beyond his previously relatively small base of support, Farrakhan, in the spirit of black unity, called on blacks to register 8 million unregistered voters, males and females.[8] His vision of how a monthly contribution of ten dollars could fuel an economic rebirth of black America, via an entity he termed an "Exodus Economic Fund," also captured the imagination of thousands.

As his speech progressed, some of the major elements of Farrakhan's model of manhood stood out: political independence from whites; civic and political involvement; and several moral principles to use as guides to behavior. Many of these can be seen in the public pledge that Farrakhan led the crowd through, which was the high point of the long day for many participants. Leading the pledge, Farrakhan and millions of black males dedicated themselves publicly to a moral and committed posture toward life. The assembled thousands pledged to have "love" for their "brother as" they loved themselves and to "strive to improve" themselves "spirtually, morally, socially, politically and economically" to the benefit of themselves, their family and their "people." More ambiguously, thousands also pledged to endeavor to "build business, build houses, build hospitals, build factories, and to enter international trade." The assembled thousands also pledged to "never raise" their hands "with a knife or a gun to beat, cut, or shoot any member of [their] family or any human being, except in self defense."[9] The men also committed themselves to never engaging in the abuse of their wives, children, or others. In a move that elicited an almost audible collective national shout of approval by black women, Farrakhan led the crowd in another pledge designed to eliminate the word "bitch" from the vocabulary of the African American male. At the end of Farrakhan's speech he instructed the audience to "turn to your brother and hug your brother and tell your brother you love him." Farrakhan urged the Million Man marchers to "carry this love all the way back to our cities and towns and never let it die, brothers," he repeated, "Never let it die."[10]

This chapter discusses the contemporary social, political and economic problems confronting the African American male, and the general situation that culminated in a Million Man March. The continued reality of black male criminalization, in its latest permutation, is analyzed in relationship to the overall crisis of the African American male.

THE ECONOMIC AND HEALTH STATUS OF THE CONTEMP-ORARY AFRICAN AMERICAN MALE

The Million Man March was the culmination of over two decades of accumulating direct pressures on the African American male. It followed a long period of stagnation and decline in the economic, social, political, and cultural sense. This followed the upsurge in power experienced during the 1960s, peaking in the urban rebellions, militant organizations, and new culture of the late 1960s. By the early 1970s, the exhilaration experienced by black males upon joining the Black Panther Party or other activist organizations, participating in a movement event, or even vicariously experiencing the new assertiveness was a fading memory. By the late 1980s, the black male bogeyman was so salient a symbol in

American culture that Willie Horton could be profitably used by ambitious Republican strategists. The early 1990s witnessed a further intensification of this trend.

The roots of the contemporary crisis of the black male lie deep in the history of slavery and Jim Crow oppression and the economic downturn of Rust Belt industry coupled with profound changes in the global economy. For millions of black males this means a degradation of their productive capacity via damaging prejudices and impaired skill development and results in a diminished earning power. By the mid-1990s, 35 percent of black males earned less than $9,999, compared to only 19.8 percent of white males. At the higher levels, a similar disparity can be seen, as only 21.7 percent of black males compared to 40.3 percent of white males earned over $30,000. Black male median income is almost $10,000 less than that of their white male counterparts, languishing at $14,982 compared to $24,122. Despite its meagerness, the annual median income for black males remains considerably higher than that for black females, $10,544.[11] Black male poverty is associated with age; an enormous 43.3 percent of those below the age of 18 are impoverished under the official definition. During the prime working years of age 18 to 64 this rate stood at 17.4 percent, rising slightly for those older than 64. In contrast, the white male poverty rate for those under age 18 was only 12.2, considerably lower than the black male rate for any age.[12]

The disproportionate impoverishment of single black males is also reflected in the statistic that slightly over one-third (34.8 percent) of black males living as unrelated individuals were impoverished compared to only slightly less than one-fifth (18.2 percent) of white males living alone.[13] Occupationally, black males continue to lack representation within the professional and managerial fields. In 1995 only 15.0 percent of employed black males were managers or professionals, compared to 30.0 percent of white males. Strikingly, black males are more than twice as likely to be found in service occupations (18.5 percent) compared to white males (8.5 percent), a trend likely to continue for the foreseeable future. In occupations that include the skilled trades, sites of decades of exclusion of blacks, 13.5 percent of African American males compared to 18.6 percent of white males performed this type of labor.

Almost one-third of working black males were "operators, fabricators, and laborers," with 32.3 percent working in occupations of this type compared to only 18.1 percent of white males.[14] When black males are professionals or managers, they tend to earn less than comparable white males, as the status disparities across occupations are matched by disparities within occupational categories. For example, black male "executive, administrative, and managerial workers" had a median income of $34,458, and black male "professional specialty workers" had a median income of $36,080. In contrast, white males of the former occupational category enjoyed median earnings of $48,308, amounting to a black-to-white earnings ratio of 72.2. Those in the latter category, the "professional speciality workers," earned $47, 379, a 76.2 black-to-white income ratio. Other categories reflect this earnings differential as well. Black male "sales workers," for example, had median earnings amounting to $25,221 per year compared to $36,084 for white male "sales workers." The category of "handlers, equipment cleaners, helpers, and laborers," the status of a huge mass of African American male workers, had median earnings of $17,964 compared to $21,818 for white workers of this status, an 82.3 black-to-white ratio.[15]

Postwar American society has taken a heavy toll on the health of the black male whose life expectancy at birth in 1987, 65.2, was shorter than that of the white male whose stood at 72.2, white female, 75.2, or black female, 73.6.[16] Increasingly, however, African Americans are beset by the problems of AIDS, the lack of health insurance, and disappearing urban hospitals.[17] Poor health care delivery services in the black community led to lower rates of recovery in many areas. For example, white Americans almost thirteen percent more white males survived cancer for five years or more than African American males.[18]

During the 1980s, black America experienced an alarming increase in homicides involving black males. Prior to this, the period between 1970 and 1983 witnessed dramatic declines in the black male homicide rates, which at the end of the period stood at 37.4 per 100,000, a figure 6.7 times higher than that of white males.[19] The present upsurge of concern with the black male homicide rate stems from the striking rise in homicide and violence during the mid-1980s. During the 1984–1987 period the rate of homicides among black males increased by a staggering 39 percent.[20] Of the 16 cities that *Washington Post* researchers examined, 15 experienced increases in rates of homicide since the previous year. Some cities witnessed remarkable increases in violence: Boston, 45 percent; Denver 29 percent; and Chicago, Dallas, and New Orleans, in excess of 20 percent.[21] Approximately half of the black males between the ages of 18 and 35 in many cities, such as the District of Columbia in early 1997, were either incarcerated, on parole or probation, awaiting trial, or being sought for arrest.[22]

There is a consensus among criminologists, law enforcement officials, and the public at large that the root cause of this upsurge in violence, mainly involving urban black male youth, was due to the use and sale of crack cocaine. This booming illegal drug market within the depressed inner-city economies of the late 1980s has increasingly become an important source of income for the youth of these communities. Prior to crack's dramatic entry onto the stage of African American history, the homicide rate for black men had experienced a significant decline of 20.4 percent during the 1976 to 1984 period. This was accompanied by a similar decrease in homicide rates for their female counterparts of 19.4 percent during the same eight-year period.[23]

For black males the high-risk status with respect to becoming a victim of homicide is a cradle-to-grave phenomenon. In 1987 the age-adjusted black homicide rate for all ages was 53.8 per 100,000. The ages most at risk for homicide victimization for black males were between 25 and 34, whose rate was 98.9. While the peak white age group for homicide victimization was also between 25 and 34, the figure only stood at 13.2. Moreover, the age that the black male becomes at high risk for homicide victimization is much younger. Among African Americans, the homicide victimization rate for the 15-to-24 year-old age group, 85.6 was almost as high as that of that of the twenty-five to thirty-four year old group. Even among black male seniors aged 75 to 84 years, it remained high at 29.5. During the mid-1980s, for all ages of African American males it stood approximately seven times as high as that of white males.[24]

A large proportion of these black male homicides was committed by friends, acquaintances, and family members. During the period from 1976 to 1983, fully 59.8 percent of black homicide victims knew their assailant. By way of comparison, only 48.4 percent of white victims knew their assailant. Overall, black males are proportionately less victimized by homicide by family members than black females. Of black female homicide victims, 28.8 percent were killed by a relative compared to only 13.3 percent of black male homicide victims.[25]

One of the more graphic statistics measuring the impact of homicide is the measure of the number of years of potential of life lost before age 65 (YPLL). Homicide ranked as the third leading cause of death as measured by YPLL in 1983 for African Americans. More recently, for black males, especially for young black males, homicide has exacted an even more frightful toll. In Michigan homicide led to more YPLL for black males than any other cause, while among black females murder was the third leading cause of YPLL. Overall, the YPLL for black males stood at over 16 times that of white males. The fact that the average number of potential years of life lost by means of firearms was 34.9 speaks dramatically to the magnitude of the tragic loss of life among black males.[26]

The implication of this high number of potential years of life lost is both enormous and far-reaching. For the families concerned, it means the loss of a loved one, a potential pillar of emotional support. Financially, whatever the material resources invested in the individual, often involving important sacrifices by the parents and loved ones, there are only loss and no return. Family formation in the black community is further impaired by this ongoing carnage, skewing the ratio of single, female-headed families to two-parent families to an even greater imbalance. For the community or municipality, it means further erosion of its tax base, as at least one potential income-earner has been eliminated, and one or more individuals requiring social services are added to the local, state, and federal fiscal burden. Clearly, a high homicide rate terrorizes many, paralyzing them in fear, leading them to spend more time inside the home, chilling their social relationships with neighbors, and aborting the formation of new ones. Community integration and cohesion are thus impaired, and a downward spiral gains strength. Yet, it is precisely such community unity that is needed to begin to combat the very problems spawned by this social crisis.

Bell discussed the depression and mental anguish that invariably follow the sudden murder of a loved one. Often accompanied by severe financial losses, the ensuing psychological trauma can scar families and relatives for years afterward.[27] Dennis noted the existence of a "homicide trauma syndrome," characterized by acute grief, sleeplessness, headaches, chest pains, and stomach problems. Psychological trauma resulting from violence has particularly serious consequences for children, many of whom happen to witness this carnage.[28] A survey of 538 second, fourth, sixth, and eighth graders within Chicago's Community Mental Health Council's catchment area revealed that 31 percent of the children had seen someone shot, 34 percent had seen someone stabbed, and 84 percent seen someone brutally assaulted. The impact of this violence upon children has been compared to the posttraumatic stress syndrome (PTSS) suffered by Vietnam veterans.[29]

CONTEMPORARY SOURCES OF BLACK MALE VIOLENCE

Frantz Fanon wrote extensively on the phenomenon of decolonization and its social, psychological, and psychiatric consequences. He concluded that the lack of collective racial pride coupled with the absence of a sense of dignity and self-worth created a potentially volatile individual psychological disposition. The social, economic, and political context of restricted social and physical mobility formed the basic framework within which these feelings developed. This "collective autodestruction" manifested itself in the "native's muscular tension." In the situation, individual violence serves as a release for this tension and stress. Whereas great hesitancy and restraint would be displayed by the black colonized vis-à-vis the colonial establishment, Fanon observed that the "slightest hostile or aggressive glance cast on him by another native" could potentially give rise to violence. In the last resort, the oppressed black sought to defend "his personality vis-à-vis his brother."[30] This represented, at the same time, an avoidance of the actual barriers to social, economic, and political upward mobility and forced the internalization of aggressive drives creating a tension that manifested itself in soaring murder rates, riots, gang violence, fratricide, and interpersonal conflict.[31]

This internalized self-devaluation of their worth and that of the African Americans with whom they interact on a daily basis, coupled with the high frequency and intensity of stressful situations, creates a volatile social context. Psychologist Na'im Akbar noted that a "by-product of racism is a tremendous sense of frustration, anger, and helplessness." The resulting "free-floating anger" manifests itself in a "displaced aggression," leading to many black homicides. Akbar described black homicide not as a "rational process" but, rather as "a situational process."[32] Amos Wilson similarly stresses the factor of the "internalization of White racist projections" within the black psyche, citing a "conscious and/or unconscious tendency to disavow membership" in the particular African ethnic group they are a part of. This has a corrosive effect on unity and community, as it tends to be accompanied by a lack of concern or contempt for the traditional morality of the group. Wilson termed these problems "sociopathoid" and stressed that they are amenable to change since they "are stimulus-specific responses to circumscribed conditions, usually . . . learned as a consequence of faulty past experiences."[33]

Both James Comer and Frantz Fanon stressed the displacement of black anger toward whites and the social system onto fellow blacks as a source of violence.[34] Fanon contended that the problem would be at least partially resolved with the onset of the anticolonial struggle during which blacks would cease displacing the hostility onto their fellow blacks and, instead, vent them on the actual source of their frustration, the colonizer. Noel Cazenave stressed the importance of the black male's "quest for manhood" as a precipitant of homicides among the group.[35] Violence becomes a means of demonstrating that one is not impotent and has the means to control his destiny. Viewed in a typical, contemporary, daily social context within the black low-income community, this assertive thrust for masculine identity is often combined with alcohol and drug use, an illegal means of earning income, and an atmosphere of competition among individuals attempting to obtain a "reputation."

Harvey also points to the mass media as an important causal factor in the overall high rates of black homicide, noting the disproportionate amount of time lower-income blacks spend watching television programs infused with a heavy dose of violence. Harvey's fear is that the impact of this encourages similar violence in the viewers' personal lives, citing the ingredient of the "contempt and disrespect" meted out by businesses, social service agencies, stores, and courts, and practically the whole of civil society treating the lower-income black male youth with "contempt and disrespect."[36]

In a like manner, Harvey views the high rate of unemployment among African American male youth as a shortage of legitimate outlets for youth's transition into adulthood. He writes that contemporary society "has failed to provide constructive means for the simultaneous affirmation of their manhood" and "the release" of their "pent-up energy." Harvey wrote that from the "dawning of their manhood," the American social system operated in ways that deny young black men the opportunity to realize masculinity in the most basic, socially sanctioned sense—the ability to be a "worker and provider." He warns against underestimating the significance of the lack of meaningful work on the youthful psyches of black males. The lack of meaningful labor results in a sense of inner rage, leading to the development of mass individual "toughness."[37]

While there are distinct differences between the "primary" interpersonal violence between friends and relatives and the "secondary" violence surrounding the illegal drug trades, there are common elements to both. The intensity of the violence of the drug trade may surpass that "necessary" for the settling of disputes, for example. The same type of "lack of impulse control" that ignites family and friend disputes within the confines of the informal social network can manifest itself on the streets in the display of "trigger-happy" characteristics of criminals during robberies. In other instances, the pent-up anger within the individual is released in a frenzy of violence with little or no provocation.

Clearly, the state of frustration characterized by hypersensitivity to perceived slights and offenses heightens the probability of homicidal violence within conflict situations of both primary and secondary social interaction. The inability to control and rechannel anger or defuse potentially dangerous interpersonal encounters is an important causal factor in both situations. In this specific historical conjuncture, new drugs, new social relationships, new, more powerful weapons, and a new economy, characterized by more widespread unemployment and low-paying service employment, combine to make for a volatile environment.

The significance of the high proportion of crimes of passion featuring a marked lack of impulse control lies in the high percentage of unintended homicides resulting from spiraling cycles of disputes or spontaneous violent conflicts. Without a doubt, the increased availability of guns heightens the risk that a minor dispute will escalate into a tragedy. During the years from 1976 to 1983, fully 66.4 percent of murders of blacks were committed with guns; 51 percent, with handguns.[38] The African American teen population, in particular, has suffered from the increased presence of handguns. In 1987 the rate of homicide from firearms among black male teenagers was 49.2 per 100,000 compared to 5.1 per 100,000 for white male teenagers.[39]

BLACK MALE CRIMINALIZATION AND THE "PRISON-INDUSTRIAL COMPLEX"

While the 1990 report by the Sentencing Project received a tremendous amount of publicity due to its finding that one in four black males was under some form of criminal justice system supervision, the 1995 follow-up report was perhaps even more shocking. By 1995 fully 32.2 percent of African American males in their 20s, up from 30.2 percent in 1994, suffered under this status.[40] This shocking increase in incarceration has led some analysts to label it the "prison-industrial complex."[41]

The "prison-industrial complex" refers to the tripartite relationship binding private enterprise, government officials, and political leaders in a mutually beneficial relationship that has fueled the construction of prisons and jails at a record pace. Financiers such as Goldman Sach and Co. and Smith Barney Shearson have profited, as have Westinghouse Electric and other defense corporations, from the mass criminalization of black males.[42] Yet, the intimate connection between the growth of the illegal drug trade and the black male frustration with the dearth of opportunities in the legitimate economy has been well documented. A 1990 study by Peter Reuter of Rand Institute found that financial need was the key motivating force compelling thousands of young black males to risk life, limb, and imprisonment to sell illegal drugs. The study revealed that the vast majority of those arrested for drug dealing had jobs and used the drug profits to supplement their income. The median earnings were estimated at $2,000 per month for daily sellers.[43]

Criminal justice has become increasingly a matter of dollars and cents. The total cost of incarcerating and supervising the 827,440 African American males amounts to some $6 billion annually. The reality that most of these males were involved in crimes that are highly related to their impoverished surroundings and lack of legitimate opportunities is highly significant. The en masse character of these crimes, suggestive of the Prohibition era, calls into question traditional reasoning with respect to criminal behavior. Within one brief decade the number of drug offenders imprisoned increased sixfold. At the same time, between 1980 and 1989, the proportion of blacks in all drug arrests increased from 24 percent to 39 percent in 1993.[44] The annual survey of the National Institute on Drug Abuse (NIDA) found that blacks, while constituting only 13 percent of monthly drug users, represented 39 percent of the drug arrests.[45] This upsurge in drug-related arrests was much more dramatic for the most impoverished sectors of the black community, as one study found a sixfold increase in arrests among black "underclass" residents.[46] The racial focus of the drug war is apparent by the finding that not a single white conviction occurred for crack cocaine in the Los Angeles metropolitan area since 1986, while surveys indicate that whites constitute the majority of crack cocaine users.[47]

In early 1996 President Bill Clinton rejected the recommendations of the U.S. Sentencing Commission to reform the drug laws to correct this clear racial disparity in sentencing practices. The Sentencing Commission found that blacks were 84.5 percent of those convicted of crack cocaine possession in 1993 while making up only 38 percent of those using the drug in the prior year. On the average a person possessing five grams of cocaine would tend to receive the same sentence as one charged with the sale of 500 grams of powder cocaine.[48]

A tendency that poses a distinct obstacle to the passage of legislation that would ameliorate the growing problem of black male criminalization is the incentive politicians have to demonize the black male. Crafty and unprincipled politicians, desperate to secure election, are able, at little cost, to enhance their chances of electoral victory by appealing to the "get tough" sentiments of voters. By calling for tough measures against crime and building more prisons, they also gain campaign contributions. They can make use of a pervasive perception that crime is out of control, despite the actual decline of many types of serious crime—since 1973 robbery has fallen 12 percent, burglary has fallen 47 percent, and murder has not appreciably increased. While homicide by juveniles has significantly increased, the public view that crime has soared is fueled largely by the media, political campaigns, and, increasingly, private firms that earn profits in direct proportion to the number that society incarcerates. The growth of the California Correctional Peace Officers Association, for example, has been phenomenal, from 4,000 to 23,000 in only a decade. The average salary of a correctional officer in the state, $55,000 per year, now exceeds that of a public school teacher, who averages $43,000 annually. Not surprisingly, this association has an interest in increased incarceration and was the second largest donor to statewide political campaigns. It heavily supported the "Three Strikes and You're Out" ballot initiative.[49]

Alabama became the first state to revive chain gangs in 1995, signaling the continuing legacy of Jim Crow criminalization and the plummeting of black male status in America. Once again coerced black males can be seen toiling along the roads of southern states. Howling dogs and snarling guards aiming shotguns at the predominantly black prisoners, hobbled by the three-pound chains, bring thoughts of their slave ancestors to the men. The pain of enslavement is revisited by the men, some of whom were driven by economic desperation to crime. One of them termed it "degrading"; another, "a zoo." Even in public the guards call them "boy."[50]

Ron Jones, Alabama's correction's chief, was pleased by the response he received from other prison agencies eager to replicate a program whose guards openly refer to the black men as "boys." Jones, saying that he didn't want to see the prisoners shot, explained, "[I]t's not that I'm a softy. It's expensive. You shoot someone and you send him to the hospital and it costs $100,000 to patch him up."[51]

More commonly, the black male is languishing in wretched, filthy, unhealthy, and dangerous prisons. In city after city across the country, local, state, and federal prisons are overcrowded, bulging with black men. Many of these prisons are grossly substandard and fail to meet international human rights standards. In May 1996 the Maryland Division of Corrections, for example, was threatened by the U.S. Department of Justice with a lawsuit if it did not correct alleged violations of the civil rights of inmates housed in its "Supermax" unit. In the "pink room" of the Baltimore prison, inmates are chained in an isolation unit, semiclad in underwear. This room, with cold concrete and with no heat, had only a hole in the floor for a toilet. The cell, completely littered with human waste, removed from fresh air, dark, and hellish, was judged as "grossly deficient" by the Justice Department. The cell is designed to house the most violent and incorrigible of inmates, allowing them only one hour a day outside the cell. Investigators found that inmates would be taken out only once every two or three days, were never exposed to fresh air, were not allowed any recreation, and were allegedly violently abused. Inmates were held indefinitely, even when they abided by the rules, and medical care was judged as unsatisfactory. With chains attached to their waists, the prisoners in the "pink room" had no choice but to soil themselves with their own urine and feces.[52] In February 1996, following the stabbing of three guards, approximately 50 inmates were subjected to tortuous treatment in a similar unit known as "South-One," a high-security unit. One adolescent improperly jailed with adult prisoners told investigators that he was forced to stay in a cell with feces on the wall, with underwear as his only clothes and deprived of any opportunity to shower or obtain more clothing. Another inmate was strapped to his bed naked for 12 hours despite his suicidal tendencies. Other cells were infested with rats, roaches, and other vermin, while the prisoners were denied blankets or eating utensils. They were forced to wear their dirty clothing and were denied showers. Many were in need of medical attention.[53]

"Get tough" initiatives such as "three strikes, you're out" promise to further increase the black male prison population. The California law, the model for many other states, requires people having a record of a serious felony conviction to receive a sentence twice as long upon their second conviction. Upon their third conviction, they are to receive a mandatory 25 years to life sentence. The first man convicted under these provisions was Jerry Dewayne Williams, a 27-year-old convicted of taking pizza from a group of children at Redondo Beach. Normally, this offense is a misdemeanor; however, under the "three strike" provisions, it was determined to be a felony. This tough law will cost taxpayers in excess of $500,000 for this case alone, it is estimated.[54] "Truth in sentencing" laws are keeping greater numbers imprisoned for longer periods of time, straining the fiscal capacities of many states. At the same time, prisons are grossly overcrowded and substandard, while politicians campaign to make them even more harsh. In April 1994 the Pryce-Stupak amendment proposed "a simple, commonsense step toward reducing violence in America" by banning weight training in prisons. Congresswoman Pryce complained that "we have unwittingly been mass producing a super breed of criminals."[55] Yet, contrary to popular opinion, most of the imprisoned black males are not violent offenders at the time of imprisonment. The prison experience, however, often matures and socializes individuals into "hardened" criminals.[56]

The respect generated by certain illegal occupations within the African American communities, for at least the past 60 years, arises from a recognition that many legitimate avenues for enterprise were blocked. The turn to "crime" is not taken in revolt against middle-class values, but rather to "stretch" or "adapt" these to their lives, according to Earl Ofari Hutchinson. "Poor young black males have become especially adept at this," he writes.

Even though by all economic indicators black women are at the bottom of the economic barrel, poor young black males are the ones weighted down with the burden of proving their "manhood." They are trapped by society's definition of the successful male as breadwinner and family protector.[57]

By the mid-1990s the significance to social status of having ready cash on hand had grown to unheard-of dimensions, as the spread of consumerism, the decline of family and community, and the dearth of both education and social mobility greatly enhanced the lure of materialistic values. With the attraction of consumer goods for the sheer status attached to the labels steadily increasing, it is reasonable to expect black males to pour their energies into whatever "industry" or sector, legal or illegal, yields the necessary income to obtain a minimum of these precious commodities. The intractable nature of the immediate crisis of the black male, involving high levels of criminalization and violence, flows from this basic gap between the aspirations engendered by a consumer society and the ability of black males to obtain them by legitimate means.

"HORTONIZING" THE BLACK MALE

Jesse Jackson's successive efforts to capture the American presidency represent the high-water marks for the black male image during the post–civil rights era. While Jackson was repeatedly disrespected by commentators, and his significant achievements during the campaigns were grossly minimized, his solid campaign performance and clear dominance in face-to-face debates among the candidates was a shot in the arm for the collective African American male image. At the opposite end of the spectrum, the emergence of a fictionalized "Willie Horton" was one of the low points that served to dramatize the extent to which the black male had been linked to crime in the American mind. "Willie" Horton was used by former president George Bush as a symbol of African Americans and African American interests. Not only violent crime by black males but high wages, social programs, and inflation were all subtly captured by the general focus on Horton. By placing the spotlight on Horton's real crimes, the campaign of Vice

President George Bush make clear to their overwhelmingly white constituency their opposition to liberalism and the perceived interests of black Americans. That the target was an African American male rapist added to the appeal of this tactic. As Horton himself says, "Willie Horton" was a media creation that emerged from the actual William Horton, a convicted murderer who in April 1987 raped a white woman after tying up her husband. Bush tied this heinous act to the Massachusetts furlough program that Horton escaped from. In speech after speech, Bush and Republican campaigners hammered away at this theme tying Democratic nominee Michael Dukakis to both Horton and black crime. This connection to other African Americans and "liberal" and black issues and interests was unmistakable. Liberal policies, programs, sympathies, and taxes that blacks took advantage of were making life miserable for decent white Americans. The Republican support group "Americans for Bush" paid for the Horton ads and a national tour for Horton's victims, the Barnes.[58]

This strategy was the brainchild of Lee Atwater, a southern-born Republican strategist who had no qualms about appealing to the rawest racial prejudices of white Americans. Atwater licked his lips in anticipation of confronting Dukakis with the constant image of Horton, especially before southern white audiences, viewed as the key factor in a Republican victory. To the extent that Dukakis was forced to give respect to the figure of Jesse Jackson, Atwater sought to exploit this fact and win votes for George Bush.[59] On his deathbed, Atwater later apologized to William Horton Jr. for vilifying him.[60]

COLIN POWELL, O. J. SIMPSON, AND THE BLACK MALE IMAGE

Aside from President George Bush's nomination of Clarence Thomas for the Supreme Court, the appointment of General Colin Powell as chairman of the Joint Chiefs of Staff was his most important African American appointment. Powell's appointment represented the individual achievement of perhaps the most powerful official position an African American has ever occupied in the history of the United States, and, despite its irrelevance in terms of black political power, it represents a new stage in relationships between black appointees and chief executives. The inclusion of Powell in heretofore closed corners of American policy making marks a new level of inclusion for blacks within the American political elite.

By 1995 Colin Powell, retired, was touted by the media as a viable potential candidate for president. Polls showed widespread support for a Powell candidacy, and speculation abounded as to whether he would run. Powell, like Michael Jackson before him, was applauded as achieving a "raceless" status—a neutral status enjoying more prestige than that of an African American. Others saw his widespread popularity as the ultimate proof of the inherent fairness and justness of American society. Black conservative Orlando Patterson expresses the view that his prominence is genuine, writing that it "would be ridiculous to dismiss these developments as mere tokens." In a world-class overstatement the social commentator wrote that Powell's rise demonstrates "beyond a doubt" that "being black is no longer a significant obstacle to participation in the public life of the nation."[61]

Yet, Powell's own unusual career route illustrates the improbability of his rise being duplicated by many. Indeed, many of the advantages and good fortune that aided his rise will not be extended to many in this generation of tight budgets, conservatism, and racial stereotypes. Powell benefitted from the timing of the decision of the American elite to liberalize the racial structure of the nation. Born 5 April 1937, Powell came of age at an ideal time, as his academic career in both high school and college was undistinguished. Graduating from high school in February 1954, he enrolled in City College of New York, where he benefitted from the ten dollar per semester tuition. Choosing a career in engineering, Powell had difficulty and soon switched to geology but found out that the Reserve Officers Training Corps was more suited to his interests. Before long he had decided upon a long-term career in the military.[62] Yet, on his graduation day, Powell's mother was forced to send friends to his regular drinking spot, across the street from the ceremonies, "to ask" him if he would "be kind enough to join the graduation ceremonies."[63] Graduating with a C average, Powell's demonstration of excellence was some years away. It was in Vietnam during the early 1960s that Powell distinguished himself as an officer and began his rapid ascent up the ranks.[64] By mid-1966 Powell had been promoted to major and was clearly a rising star of the military. It was a military that was beginning to address the disproportionate lack of African Americans in its upper ranks. By the late 1980s Colin Powell had risen to become the chairman of the Joint Chiefs of Staff, the most powerful official position ever held by a black in the nation's bureaucracy, civilian or military. Overseeing the U.S. forces in the Persian Gulf War, Powell came to be regarded as a possible presidential candidate, although not often by African Americans.

Yet, if Colin Powell ever becomes president, it will not be as a black man but as a raceless savior who somehow transcended the thorny issues of race, class, and politics. Clearly, much of the white support for Powell in the mid-1990s would evaporate in the heat of a presidential campaign. The recent Republican victories have utilized the terrifying specter of black male crime as a means of mobilizing and attracting white voters; this strategy will be difficult if a black man is the party's nominee. In the long run, the negative image of the black male would eventually catch up to General Powell. Nor could he, unless he devoted himself to making a direct appeal, garner the majority of blacks as supporters. Their support would damage his support among whites, many of whom would think twice about voting in a bloc along with blacks for a candidate whose skin is black. While, in the abstract, there are many reasons that whites would profess support for Colin Powell, to appear fair on race at little cost to them, holding onto their support would be quite difficult for him.

Following the murder of Nicole Brown Simpson on 12 July 1994, the O. J. Simpson trial became the media event of the century. The elements of sex, race, and violence of the case within the post–Cold War financial jungle made its eventual transformation into a superprofitable commodity all but inevitable. The idea of the physically powerful black male having sexual and romantic relationships with a blond white woman and then slaying her viciously somehow tantalized the American psyche. The unprecedented quantity of publicity and the transformation of the case into a temporary industry were the most remarkable aspects of the entire ordeal.

While many aspects of the case and its outcome can be disputed, it is certain that the black male image suffered during the trial. For many, it appeared that no black male was immune from the pathology of violence. O. J. Simpson, such a familiar face on network television that millions of people, of all races and ethnicities, felt that they personally knew him, was now seen as a wanton murderer. Despite the countervailing images of an intelligent, clever, slick, if unscrupulous, Simpson attorney, Johnny Cochran, black males took another powerful hit to their image by the long trial. Even prior to his acquittal, the fact that O. J. was not condemned and made a pariah in the black community was seen as complicity in his crimes or, at least, as a sign of black moral fragility.

Several aspects of the trial will leave a lasting impact on the image of the African American male. First, the image of the black male inordinately obsessed with gaining the attentions of white women was reinforced by the long trial. This aspect was drummed in by the focus on Simpson's individual obsession with his former wife. Second, the uncontrollable nature of the violence of black males, even those you believe you know, was strongly suggested. Third, the immorality of blacks, especially after the verdict of acquittal, and their innate criminality were suggested since, if a millionaire superstar, with time, money, and fame on his hands, could commit a heinous crime, it suggests that lesser-known black males could do likewise. Although the long-term impact of the trial on the black male image will hardly equal the impact of the daily stereotyped portrayal of the black male in movies, television programs, and videos as violence-prone, volatile, and irresponsible, it served to reinforce these stereotyped traits in the American mind.

The cumulative impact of the whole history of the black male in American society has made him today, in many respects, a pariah. Throughout every stage of American history, black male mobility has been severely curtailed as a measure to halt or minimize what was officially defined as crime. During slavery, Reconstruction, and Jim Crow, there existed only a blurred line separating the criminal justice system from the economic sphere for the black male. Today, black male freedom in public space continues to be severely circumscribed. As has been shown by several revelations during the 1990s, including those of Mark Fuhrman during the trial of O. J. Simpson, police across the nation remain attuned to the presence of any black male beyond implicit community and neighborhood boundaries. An automatic search is mandated in many communities by police when a black male is spotted driving or walking through. For the individual black male, knowledge that this is likely to happen in vast stretches of territory across the nation has a chilling impact on his free movement. At a milder level, when arrests, detentions, and searches are not practiced upon mere sight of the black male, the constant perception of him in white areas as a violence-prone criminal discourages his presence. Historian Robin D. G. Kelley's amusing personal anecdote about rushing into an Ann Arbor theater, to be met by a young white woman who said, "I don't have anything in the cash register" to the puzzled

African American intellectual is an all-too-common occurrence in contemporary America.[65] These de facto geographical restrictions severely limit the job prospects of black males, as does the practice of firms' locating far from the black communities of the nation.

As during the heyday of the lynch mob, the current racial climate has encouraged the scapegoating of black males. Claiming that a black man jumped in her car, threw her out, and sped off with her two kids in it, Susan Smith told the media: "I can't even describe what I'm going through. It just aches so bad. I can't sleep. I can't eat. I can't do anything but think about them."[66] The Union, South Carolina, mother described a detailed tale of horror that the local, national, and international press accepted with little resistance. Inconsistencies within her story were ignored as a massive air, sea, and land search was launched, guided by an artist's depiction of a shady-looking black man. Frustrated in their search, suspicion finally turned to Smith. Following a search of her house and intense interrogation, she broke down and confessed. Soon, divers were pulling her car from a lake with her two young boys in it.

Many African Americans in Union, South Carolina, had participated in the search for the children. They were especially irate at the false attribution of the crime to a black man. McElroy Hughes, local NAACP president, said that the affair "with her labeling a black man as the criminal sends a message of the black male as savage and barbarian."[67] Lee A. Daniels in *Emerge* observed: "There was that image again—the one that had proven so valuable to three generations of white Southern politicians during the era of Grand Apartheid" and to presidential candidate, George Bush, in 1988.[68]

The image of the black male as a predatory beast was also utilized by Charles Stuart, who murdered his pregnant wife in 1989. Seeking to collect on a life insurance policy on her, Stuart fabricated a tale that his wife was slain by a black man while he was shot and wounded. This led to the detaining of hundreds of black men and the arrest of one for the crime itself. He remained incarcerated until Stuart committed suicide months later.[69]

THE MILLION MAN MARCH, THE PROBLEM OF BLACK PATRIARCHY, AND THE FUTURE

In mid-December 1994 Minister Louis Farrakhan of the Nation of Islam outlined the objectives of the planned event that they formally termed the "One Million Man March." Citing the 440-year-old oppression of the African American male, Minister Farrakhan called on "all able-bodied black men" to devote 16 October 1995 to the march in order to declare to the world that they "are ready" to assume family and community leadership as well as "shoulder the responsibility of being the maintainers of our women and children and the builders of our communities."[70]

Citing the Honorable Elijah Muhammad's vow to someday sponsor a march on Washington, Farrakhan asserted that this march would "now show the world our resolve; for it is we, black men, who cleared the underbrush, laid the tracks for the railroad, built the homes in the south for the slave masters. It is we who plowed their fields, helped build their roads. It is we who fought in all of America's wars for a freedom that we have yet to enjoy." The Nation of Islam leader also cited the "inertia" afflicting the contemporary African American male while attacks against the black community are occurring as a motivating factor in launching the march. Citing the rise of the Republican Party and its commitment to imprisoning greater numbers and the "three-strikes law," he said that "prisons are now private enterprise" that makes it profitable to "incarcerate the black, the weak, the poor and the ignorant," warning that this "new wave of anticrime legislation is to legitimize a return to slavery in the name of crime-reduction."[71]

The most controversial aspect of the Million Man March was its all-black male character. In an article "To Our Women and Girls," Farrakhan requested that they stay home in order to allow the black man to "stand up" for them and their families. No work was to be performed that day, nor were any purchases to be made. Prayer, instead, was to take place.[72] Many black women took offense at this request and the logic it reflected. "How dare anyone ask us to show unity by silence," said Jewell Jackson McCabe. "What price for our own dignity and what price for our community's dignity?"[73]

The Nation of Islam's views on marriage, the family, and male–female relationships represent a radical departure from the historic forms of flexibility, complementarity, and the relatively egalitarian, if patriarchal, black family. A two-part article entitled, "Allah (God) Hates Divorce" by Farrakhan firmly establishes the importance Muslims place on marriage and the family. The "sacredness of marriage" carries with it a "duty" on each mate to prevent the intrusion of "anything that is destructive of this institution, even to thoughts, imagery, or fantasy of another individual other than the husband or wife." Marriage is based on the "demand" of Allah and the Holy Qur'an that "teaches that the man has rights over the woman, but the woman also has rights over the man," according to Farrakhan. The "nature of the female demands from the male that she be made secure. . . . To be made secure is to be made safe from fear, harm, or danger." This includes being safe not only from physical harm but also from mental harm or anxiety. She must also be made spiritually and morally secure as well by the man. Men, in turn, were "created" by Allah to "struggle" and have "a duty to multiply and replenish the earth and subdue it." "Power," "dominion," and "knowledge" are the male's as he builds society and "maintains" his woman. Upon performing and accomplishing tasks in pursuit of this goal, a man "has a natural demand on the nature of a woman," who is obligated, in turn, to "give to him peace and contentment of mind."[74]

Farrakhan summarized his views on the general role of women:

The Holy Qur'an teaches that the woman is the consoler of the man. What is consolation? It is to ease the man from the pain and burden of the labor that Allah (God) has imposed upon the man. Allah has given man a female whose duty by nature is to ease the burden on man, to console, to give peace, and quiet of mind.[75]

For the Nation of Islam, "Man is the maintainer of woman and she is the consoler of man." According to Elijah Muhammad, the founder of the Nation of Islam, "the woman is man's heaven."[76] In another article Farrakhan asserted that while independence in women is positive, in some respects, it gives rise to problems in the black community. According to the Muslim minister, "Allah says in the Qur'an that men are a degree above women," while the Nation of Islam leader acknowledged that "in our condition now" "we're several degrees below you." Nevertheless, his message to his male audience was that "in the nature in which God created you, brother, he created you a degree above the woman. Otherwise the woman would not be able to look up to you." He warns that "anytime you have a woman that does not look up to you, brother, you're in trouble."[77]

The prime political motivation of the black male should be to protect black women. Farrakhan said that a "man should die before he lets a stranger contaminate his woman. A man should kill. We ought to be the number one killers on the earth to keep any man away from our woman." More specifically, he declared, "[W]hen the White man comes into our society, he goes to war with that society so that he may have free access to the woman. He has conquered us as men, and therefore we cannot be to our women what God commanded us to be until we are made free of the mind and the power of our enemies."[78]

Politically, he contends that manhood means not having to ask for freedom, as it is a God-given right, and men must seize their freedom. Yet, the theme of atonement adopted by the march at the behest of Farrakhan reflected a view of black history that seemed to dovetail with other varieties of blame-the-victim theories. Farrakhan declared: "We, as men, must atone for the abuse of our women and girls, and our failure to be the leaders of and builders of our community."[79]

These beliefs indicate the depth of the unmitigated patriarchalism of the Nation of Islam and suggest that black male–female conflict will rise dramatically if their views become more popular. For this reason it is not surprising that many respected figures within the black community questioned the morality and aims of the event. Angela Davis said, "No march, movement or agenda that defines manhood in the narrowest terms and seeks to make women lesser partners. . . . can be considered a positive step." Black feminists, such as Michelle Wallace, spoke out against the march, while political scientist Linda Williams declared in a similar vein that the exclusion of "half of the race" served to undermine the moral authority of the event.[80] This failed to faze the Nation of Islam author, who asserted that "black women have cried and prayed for this day since we were on the slave plantations" and that 99 percent of black women supported the Million Man March. The 1 percent who dissented "need our prayers" and were charged with "merely parroting the White, feminist party line."[81]

Robert Allen wrote in *The Black Scholar* approvingly of the image of black men projected by the massive gathering on the Mall. He commented that the march was "one of the few times in recent memory when black men were on the front pages of newspapers and featured on national television, and the news wasn't about murders, drugs, riots or sports."[82] Expressing the optimistic view that "more black men are coming to realize this cannot be achieved by men reclaiming their 'rightful' place as head of the family," Allen wrote that "many supporters and organizers of the march understood that we cannot go back to a patriarchal system that never really worked in the black community. The call for male responsibility and respect for women at the march was not necessarily a demand for patriarchal privilege" but rather an admission of past wrongs and a signal of a new determination to rebuild the black family. Allen, calling for both greater tolerance and the elimination of sexist patriarchy in order to attain African American unity, also cautioned that this "will require a new notion of masculinity, not the old idea of a manhood based on domination and submission, but one based on mutual respect and mutual responsibility."[83]

An automatic assumption of male dominance is a recipe for prolonged intrafamilial, intracommunity, and intraracial conflict for African Americans. When one party to a relationship, on its own, announces that it will be the ultimate arbiter of disputes, conflict can be expected. The development and fostering of a greater capacity to arrive at an equal, fair, and just working relationship between the genders is essential for black progress. All areas of life should be open to both males and females and mutual respect should be fostered by African American institutions. Not only is this principled behavior, but it is the most efficient way to work for, and achieve, African American progress. It is completely consistent with a heritage containing powerful elements of egalitarianism extending from the antebellum era through Reconstruction to the present. While black political, cultural, and social life has been, for the most part, dominated by males and supported by dominant patriarchal views, the reality is that black women have often been the principal forces underlying the strength of institutions, movements, and organizations. Strengthening sexual equality within African American civil society will serve the cause of progress and offer immediate benefits to the national community as a whole.

The ever-increasing ethnic, philosophical, ideological, cultural, gender, and economic diversity of the national black community makes it imperative that old forms of divisiveness be overcome, lest the black community be fractured into tiny segments.[84] African American history illustrates that during periods of progress, trends toward gender equality are strongest. During periods of stagnation, tendencies favoring gender inequality have grown. In the new millennium, it is clear that any movement that seeks to foist a postmodern patriarchalism on black America is doomed to failure. Not only would this clash with the trends of contemporary history, but it would go against the grain of African American history and culture. Black males will march in equality with their female counterparts, or there will be no forward march.

NOTES

1. "Minister Farrakhan Challenges Black Men," *CNN*, 17 October 1995.
2. "To Our Women and Girls," *The Final Call*, 14 December 1994.
3. "Minister Farrakhan Challenges Black Men."

4. Ibid.

5. J. Mendens, "The Million Man March." (http://www.newslink.net/ojtrial.html, 1995).

6. "Minister Farrakhan Challenges Black Men."

7. Ibid.

8. Ibid.

9. Ibid.

10. Ibid.

11. U.S. Bureau of the Census,. Table 11, "Total Money Earnings in 1994 of Persons 15 Years Old and Over, by Sex, Region, and Race," May 1996.

12. U.S. Bureau of the Census, Table 15, "Selected Characteristics of the Population below the Poverty Level in 1994, by Region and Race," May 1996.

13. Ibid.

14. U.S. Bureau of the Census,. Table 13, "Occupation of Longest Job in 1994 of Year- Round, Full-Time Workers 25 Years Old and Over, by Total Money Median Earnings, Educational Attainment, Sex, and Race," May 1996.

15. Ibid..

16. U.S. Department of Health and Human Services, *Health Status of Minorities and Low-Income Groups, 3d ed.* (Washington, DC: Public Health Service, 1991), Table 18, "Life Expectancy at Birth by Race and Sex: United States, 1940, 1950, 1960, and 1970–87," 32.

17. Ibid., Table 6, "Acquired Immunodeficiency Syndrome (AIDS) Deaths, by Age, Sex, and Race/Ethnicity: United States, 1982–1988," 208.

18. Ibid., Table 8. "Five-year Relative Cancer Survival Rates by Sex and Race, and Excess of White Rates over Black for Selected Cancer Sites: United States, 1980–85,." 146.

19. Centers for Disease Control, *Homicide Surveillance: High-Risk Racial and Ethnic Groups—Blacks and Hispanics, 1970 to 1983* (Atlanta: Centers for Disease Control, 1986).

20. L. A. Fingerhut, and J. C. Kleinman, "International and Interstate Comparisons of Homicide among Young Males," *Journal of the American Medical Association* 263 (1990): 3292–95.

21. "Violence in the 90s, Drugs' Deadly Residue," *Washington Post*, 14 October 1990, A1.

22. "Young Blacks Entangled in Legal System," *Washington Post*, 26 August 1997, B1. See also Eric Lotke, "Hobbling a Generation," *African American Male Research*, 2, no. 2, (January/February 1998), (http://www.pressroom.com/~afrimale/hobb.htm)

23. P. W. O'Carroll and J. A. Mercy, "Patterns and Recent Trends in Black Homicide," in Darnell Hawkins (ed.), *Homicide among Black Americans* (London: University Press of America, 1986), 29–42.

24. National Center for Health Statistics, "Male Death Rates for Homicide and Legal Intervention, according to Race and Age, 1987," *Health, United States, 1989* (Hyattsville, MD: Public Health Service, 1990), 139.

25. Centers for Disease Control, *Homicide Surveillance.*

26. D. G. Sienko, J. Thrush, and K. R. Wilcox, "Impact of Homicide on Years of Potential Life Lost in Michigan's Black Population," *Journal of the American Medical Association* 261 (1989): 686–687.

27. C. C. Bell, "Preventive Strategies for Dealing with Violence among Blacks," *Community Mental Health Journal* 23 (1987): 217–28.

28. R. E. Dennis, "Social Costs of Black Male Homicide to Families And

Communities," in Summary Proceedings of Symposium on Homicide among Black Males (Washington, DC: Howard University, 1980), 21–24.

29. Bell, "Preventive Strategies," 217–18.

30. Frantz Fanon, *The Wretched of the Earth* (New York: Grove Press, 1963), 54.

31. Ibid.,

32. Na'im Akbar, "Causal Factors," *Public Health Reports* 95 (1980): 554–55.

33. A. N. Wilson, *Understanding Black Adolescent Male Violence: Its Remediation and Prevention* (New York: Afrikan World Infosystems, 1992), 29.

34. James D. Comer, "The Dynamics of Black and White Violence," in H. Graham and Ted Gurr (eds.), *Violence in America: The Complete Official Report to the National Commission on Causes and Prevention of Violence* (New York: Signet, 1969), 434

35. Noel A. Cazenave, "Black Men in America: The Quest for 'Manhood,'" in H. P. McAdoo (ed.), *Black Families* (Beverly Hills, CA: Sage, 1981), 176–84.

36. Harvey, William "Pride and Purpose as Antidotes to Black Homicidal Violence," *Journal of the National Medical Association*. 79, no. 2, (1986) 159.

37. Ibid., 161.

38. Centers for Disease Control, *Homicide Surveillance*.

39. National Center for Health Statistics, "Male Death Rates," 139.

40. Marc Mauer and T. Huling, *Young Black Americans and the Criminal Justice System: Five Years Later* (Washington, DC: Sentencing Project, 1995), 1.

41. S. Donziger, "The Prison-Industrial Complex,"*Washington Post*, 17 March 1996, C3; see also Clarence Lusane, *Pipe Dream Blues: Racism and the War on Drugs* (Boston: South End Press, 1991).

42. Donziger, "The Prison-Industrial Complex," C3.

43. Mauer and Huling, *Young Black Americans*, 15.

44. Ibid., 1.

45. J. P. Lynch and W. Sabol "The Use of Coercive Social Control and Changes in the Race and Class Composition of U.S. Prison Populations," paper presented at the American Society of Criminology, November 1994.

46. Mauer and Huling, *Young Black Americans*, 11.

47. Ibid., 10.

48. Donziger, "The Prison-Industrial Complex," C3.

49. Ibid., C3.

50. "The Return of the Chain Gang," *Washington Post*," 4 May 1995, A1, A14.

51. Ibid., A14.

52. K. Shatzkin, "State May Face Prison Lawsuit," *Baltimore Sun*, 8 May 1996, 1A, 6A.

53. T. Locy, "'Deplorable' Unit Alleged at D.C. Jail," *Washington Post*, 28 March 1996, A1, A15.

54. "Return of Chain Gang," A1.

55. "Support the Pryce-Stupak Amendment to the Crime Bill," *Congressional Record*, 20 April 1994, H2512.

56. John Allen, *Assault with a Deadly Weapon: The Autobiography of a Street Criminal* (New York: Pantheon Books, 1977), 19.

57. Earl Ofari Hutchinson, *The Mugging of Black America* (Chicago: African American Images, 1990), 19.

58. J. M. Elliot, "The 'Willie' Horton Nobody Knows," *The Nation* (August

1993): 201–05.

    59. Thomas B. Edsall, *Chain Reaction* (New York: W. W. Norton, 1991), 223–24.

    60. Elliot, "The 'Willie' Horton Nobody Knows," 203–04.

    61. Orlando Patterson, "Why Whites and Blacks Seem So Divided. The Paradox of Integration," *The New Republic* (6 November1995), n.p.

    62. D. Roth, *Sacred Honor: Colin Powell, The Inside Account of His Life and Triumphs* (New York: HarperCollins, 1993), 35.

    63. Ibid.

    64. Ibid., 67.

    65. Robin D. G. Kelley, "Confessions of a Nice Negro, or Why I Shaved My Head," in Don Belton (ed.), *Speak My Name: Black Men on Masculinity and the American Dream.* (Boston: Beacon Press, 1995), 12.

    66. "Mother Murders Her Sons," *Time* 14 November 1994, n.p.

    67. Ibid.

    68. L. A. Daniels, "The American Way: Blame a Black Man," *Emerge* (February 1995), 60–62, 64.

    69. Ibid., 60.

    70. Louis Farrakhan, "Minister Louis Farrakhan Calls for One Million Man March," *The Final Call* (14 December 1994), 1.

    71. Ibid.

    72. "To Our Women and Girls." *The Final Call* (14 December 1994), 6.

    73. "Behind Million Men, Black Women—'No Girls Allowed' Request Leaves Community Divided," *CNN,* 16 October 1995.

    74. Louis Farrakhan, "Allah (God) Hates Divorce-Part Two." *The Final Call* (14 April 1995), 7–8.

    75. Ibid.

    76. Ibid.

    77. Louis Farrakhan, "Minister Louis Farrakhan Speaks on Domestic Violence," *The Final Call* (21 June 1995), 1–3.

    78. Ibid.

    79. Ibid.

    80. D. Jackson, "Farrakhan Getting Much of the Attention of Million Man March," *Dallas Morning News*, (12 October 1995).

    81. A. A. Muhammad, "Black Woman, This March Is for You," *The Final Call* (14 April 1995), 11.

    82. Allen, *Assault with a Deadly Weapon*, 24.

    83. Robert Allen, "Racism, Sexism and a Million Men," *The Black Scholar* 25 (1995), 24–26.

    84. Ibid., 25.

Bibliography

Abrahams, Roger D. *Singing the Master: The Emergence of African American Culture in the Plantation South*. New York: Pantheon Books, 1992.

Adero, Malaika (ed.). *Up South: Stories, Studies, and Letters of African American Migrations*. New York: New Press, 1993.

Akbar, Na'im. "Causal Factors." *Public Health Reports* 95 (1980): 554–55.

Allen, James E. *The Negro in New York*. New York: Exposition Press, 1964.

Allen, John. *Assault with a Deadly Weapon: The Autobiography of a Street Criminal*. New York: Pantheon Books, 1977.

Allen, Richard. *Constitution of the American Society of Free Persons of Colour, for Improving Their Condition in the United States; for Purchasing Lands; and for the Establishment of a Settlement in Upper Canada, Also the Proceedings of the Convention, with Their Address to the Free Persons of Colour in the United States*. Philadelphia: W. Allen, 1831. (http://www.nuinfo.edu/ speech.htm).

Allen, Robert. "Racism, Sexism and a Million Men." *The Black Scholar* 25 (1995): 24–26.

Allen, Theodore W. *The Invention of the White Race. Vol. 2: The Origin of Racial Oppression in Anglo-America*. London: Verso, 1997.

American Moral Reform Society, *The Minutes and Proceedings of the First Annual Meeting of the American Moral Reform Society*. (Washington, DC: Library of Congress, 1837). (Http://memory.loc.gov).

American Society for Colonizing the Free People of Color of the United States. *The First Annual Report of the American Society for Colonizing the Free People of Color of the United States: And the Proceedings of the Society At their Annual Meeting in the City of Washington, on the First Day of January, 1818*. Washington, DC: Library of Congress, 1818. (Http://www.memory.loc.gov).

Andrews, William, L. "The Black Male in American Literature." In Richard G. Majors and Jacob U. Gordon (eds.), *The American Black Male: His Present Status and His Future* Chicago: Nelson-Hall, 1994.

Aptheker, Herbert. *American Negro Slave Revolts*. New York: International Publishers, 1978.

Ayers, Edward L. *Vengeance and Justice: Crime and Punishment in the 19th Century*

American South (New York: Oxford University Press, 1984).

Bailey, Anne J. "A Texas Cavalry Raid: Reaction to Black Soldiers and Contrabands." *Civil War History*, 35, no. 2 (June 1989): 138–52.

Balagoon, K., et al. *Look for Me in the Whirlwind: The Collective Autobiography of the New York 21*. New York: Random House, 1971.

Bauer, Raymond A. and Bauer, Alice H. "Day to Day Resistance to Slavery." *Journal of Negro History* 27, no. 4 (October 1942): 388–419.

Bayliss, John F. *Black Slave Narratives*. New York: Macmillan, 1970.

Beckford, George L. *Persistent Poverty: Underdevelopment in Plantation Economies of the Third World*. NewYork: Oxford University Press, 1972.

"Behind Million Men, Black Women—'No Girls allowed' Request Leaves Community Divided." *CNN*, 16 October 1995.

Bell, C. C. "Preventive Strategies for Dealing with Violence among Blacks." *Community Mental Health Journal* 23 (1987): 217–28.

Belton, Don (ed.). *Speak My Name: Black Men on Masculinity and the American Dream*. Boston: Beacon Press, 1995.

Bennett, B. Kevin. "The Jacksonville Mutiny." *Civil War History* 38, no. 1 (March 1992): 40–50.

Bennett, Lerone, Jr. *Before the Mayflower: A History of the Negro in America, 1619–1964*. Baltimore: Penguin Books, 1966.

Berlin, Ira *Slaves without Masters: The Free Negro in the Antebellum South*. New York: New Press, 1974.

Berlin, Ira, Fields, Barbara J., Glymph, Thavolia, Reidy, Joseph P., and Rowland, Leslie S. (eds.) *Freedom: A Documentary History of Emancipation, 1861–1867*. Cambridge: Cambridge University Press, 1985.

Bernstein, Iver. *The New York City Draft Riots: Their Significance for American Society and Politics in the Age of the Civil War*. New York: Oxford University Press, 1990.

Berry, Mary Frances. *Black Resistance, White Law: A History of Constitutional Racism in America*. New York: Allen Lane Penguin Press, 1994.

Berry, Mary Frances and Blassingame, John W. *Long Memory: The Black Experience in America*. New York: Oxford University Press, 1992.

"Black Woman." *The Black Panther* 14 September 1968: 6.

"Black Women College Graduates Closing Income Gap with Whites." *Baltimore Sun*, 27 June 1997, 3A.

Blassingame, John W. *Black New Orleans, 1860–1880*. Chicago: University of Chicago Press, 1973.

Blassingame, John W. *The Slave Community: Plantation Life in the Antebellum South*. New York: Oxford University Press, 1972.

Blassingame, John W. *Slave Testimony: Two Centuries of Letters, Speeches, Interviews, and Autobiographies*. Baton Rouge: Louisiana State University Press, 1977.

"The Blessings of Slavery." *Plaindealer* (New York), 25 February 1837 (http: //www. nuinfo.nwu.edu/ speech.) .

Block, J. H. "Conceptions of Sex Role: Some Cross-Cultural and Longitudinal Perspectives." *American Psychologist* 28 (1973): 512.

Bond, J. C. and Peery, P. "Is the Black Man Castrated?" Toni Cade (ed.) in *The Black Woman: An Anthology*, New York: Signet, 1970, 113–18.

Boskin, Joseph. *Sambo: The Rise & Demise of an American Jester*. New York: Oxford University Press, 1986.

Boyd, Herb and Allen, Robert L. *Brotherman: The Odyssey of Black Men in America*. New York: Ballantine Books, 1995.

Brink, William and Harris, Louis. *The Negro Revolution in America*. New York: Simon and Schuster, 1964.

Brisbane, R. H. *Black Activism: Racial Revolution in the United States, 1954–70*. Valley Forge, PA: Judson Press, 1974.

"Brothers in the New York State Concentration Camp Form the Jonathan P. Jackson Commune." *The Black Panther*, 9 (January 1971), 8.

Brown, William Wells. *The Negro in the American Rebellion: His Heroism and His Fidelity*. New York: Citadel Press, 1971a.

Brown, William Wells. "A Pioneer Black Historian and Nat Turner." In Eric Foner (ed.), *Nat Turner*. Englewood Cliffs, NJ: Prentice-Hall, 1971b, 141–45.

Bruce, John Edward. *The Blood Red Record: Review of the Horrible Lynchings and Burning of Negroes by Civilized White Men in the United States: As Taken from the Records: With Comments by John Edward Bruce*. Albany, NY: Argus, 1901.

Brundage, W. Fitzhugh. *Lynching in the New South: Georgia and Virginia, 1880–1930*. Urbana: University of Illinois Press, 1993.

Bryne, William A. "Slave Crime in Savannah, Georgia," *Journal of Negro History* 79, no. 4, (Fall 1994): 353.

Butler, Price M. "What Became of the Slaves on a Georgia Plantation?: Great Auction Sale of Slaves, at Savannah, Georgia, March 2d & 3d, 1859. A sequel to Mrs. Kemble's Journal." Murray's African-American Pamphlets, Washington, DC: Library of Congress, 1859), 5.(http:// ww.loc.gov/ammcm/aap/aaphome.html).

Calhoun, John C. "Slavery a Positive Good," 6 February 1837. In Andrew C. McLaughlin's *Readings in the History of the American Nation*. New York: D. Appleton, 1914.

Cameron, James. *A Time of Terror: A Survivor's Story*. Baltimore: Black Classic Press, 1994.

Carroll, Al. "On Illegitimate Capitalist 'The Game.'" *The Black Panther*, July 1970.

Carson, Clayborne. *In Struggle: SNCC and the Black Awakening of the 1960s*. Cambridge: Harvard University Press, 1981.

Carter, Dan T. *Scottsboro: A Tragedy of the American South*. Baton Rouge: Louisiana State University Press, 1979.

Cashin, Herschel V., et al. *Under Fire with the Tenth U.S. Cavalry*. New York: Arno Press and the New York Times, 1969.

Castel, Albert. *The Presidency of Andrew Johnson*. Lawrence: Regents Press of Kansas, 1979.

Catton, Bruce. *This Hallowed Ground: The Story of the Union Side of the Civil War*. New York: Pocket Books, 1961.

Cazenave, Noel A. "Black Men in America: The Quest for Manhood." In Harriette P. McAdoo, (ed.), *Black Families*. Beverly Hills, CA: Sage, 1981, 176–86.

Centers for Disease Control. *Homicide Surveillance: High-Risk Racial and Ethnic Groups—Blacks and Hispanics, 1970 to 1983*. Atlanta: Centers for Disease Control, 1986.

Chesnut, Mary Boykin. *A Diary from Dixie, as Written by Mary Boykin Chesnut, Wife of James Chesnut, Jr., United States Senator from South Carolina, 1859–1861, and Afterward an Aide to Jefferson Davis and a Brigadier-General in the Confederate Army*. Gloucester, MA: Peter Smith, 1961.

Christopher, Maurine. *America's Black Congressmen*. New York: Thomas W. Crowell,

1971.

Clarke, John Henrik (ed.). *Marcus Garvey and the Vision of Africa*. New York: Vintage Books, 1974.

Clatterbaugh, Kenneth. *Contemporary Perspectives on Masculinity*. Boulder, CO: Westview Press, 1990.

Cleaver, Eldridge. *Post-Prison Writings and Speeches*. New York: Ramparts Books, 1969.

Cleaver, Eldridge. *Soul on Ice*. New York: McGraw-Hill, 1968.

Clegg, Claude Andrew. *An Original Man: The Life and Times of Elijah Muhammad*. New York: St. Martin's Press, 1997.

Clements, Kendrick A. *Woodrow Wilson: World Statesman*. Boston: Twayne, 1987.

Coffin, Levi. *Reminiscences of Levi Coffin*. New York: Arno Press, 1968.

Cohen, William. *At Freedom's Edge: Black Mobility and the Southern White Quest for Racial Control, 1861–1915*. Baton Rouge: Louisiana State University Press, 1991.

Coleman, Willi. "Architects of a Vision: Black Women and Their Antebellum Quest for Political and Social Equality." In Ann D. Gordon (ed.), *African American Women and the Vote, 1837–1965* (Amherst: University of Massachusetts Press, 1997).

Colored People of Massachusetts. "Open Letter to President McKinley by Colored People of Massachusetts." *Anniversary of Emancipation in the District of Columbia*. Murray's African American Pamphlets. Washington, DC: Library of Congress, 1996.

Comer, James D. "The Dynamics of Black and White Violence." In H. Graham and Ted Gurr (eds.),*Violence in America: The Complete Official Report to the National Commission on Causes and Prevention of Violence*. New York: Signet, 1969.

Cooper, Anna Julia. *A Voice from the South*. New York: Oxford University Press, 1988.

Cripps, Thomas. *Slow Fade to Black: The Negro in American Film, 1900–1942*. New York: Oxford University Press, 1977.

Crummell, Alexander. *The Black Woman of the South: Her Neglects and Her Needs*. Murray's African American Pamphlets. Washington, DC: Library of Congress, n.d.

Culberson, June. "The Role of the Revolutionary Woman." *The Black Panther*, 4 May 1969, 8.

Da Costa, Mariam. *The Memphis Diary of Ida B. Wells*. Boston: Beacon Press, 1995.

Daniels, L. A. "The American Way: Blame a Black Man." *Emerge* (February 1995): 60–62, 64.

Davis, Angela Y. *Blues Legacies and Black Feminism: Gertrude "Ma" Rainey, Bessie Smith, and Billie Holiday*. New York: Pantheon Books, 1998.

Davis, Angela Y. *Women, Race and Class*. New York: Vintage Books, 1983.

Davis, Benjamin O. *Benjamin O. Davis, Jr., American: An Autobiography*. Washington, DC: Smithsonian Institution Press, 1991.

Davis, David Brion. *The Problem of Slavery in Western Culture*. New York: Oxford University Press, 1966.

Davis, Ossie. "Malcolm Was a Man." In Joanne Grant (ed.), *Black Protest: History, Documents, and Analyses, 1619 to the Present*. New York: Fawcett, 1968.

De Fontaine, F. G. *History of American Abolitionism: Its Four Great Epochs, Embracing Narratives of the Ordinance of 1787, Compromise of 1820, Annexation of Texas, Mexican War, Wilmot Proviso, Negro Insurrections, Abolition Riots, Slave*

Rescues, Compromise of 1850, Kansas Bill of 1854, John Brown Insurrection, 1859, Valuable Statistics, Together With a History of The Southern Confederacy. New York Herald, 1863.(http://www.loc.gov/ammem), 15.

Dennis, R. E. "Social Costs of Black Male Homicide to Families and Communities." In *Summary Proceedings of Symposium on Homicide Among Black Males* (pp. 21–24). Washington, DC: Howard University, 1980.

Deskins, D. R., Jr. *Residential Mobility of Negroes in Detroit, 1837–1965, before the Ghetto: Black Detroit in the Nineteenth Century.* Urbana: University of Illinois Press, 1973.

Dew, Charles B. "Sam Williams, Forgeman: The Life of an Industrial Slave in the Old South." In J. Morgan Kousser and James M. McPherson (eds.), *Region, Race, and Reconstruction* (pp. 199–240). New York: Oxford University Press, 1982.

Division of Violence Prevention, Centers for Disease Control and Prevention. "Suicide Facts." 1997 dvpinfo@cdc.gov.

Documentary Sources Database. "Copy of a Letter from Benjamin Banneker." In *Documenting the African American Experience* (pp. n.p.). Charlottesville: University of Virginia Library Electronic Text Center, 1996.

Dollard, John. *Caste and Class in a Southern Town.* Garden City, NY: Doubleday, 1937.

Domingo, W. A. "The Tropics in New York." *Survey Graphic* (March 1925), n.p..

Donaldson, Gary. *The History of African-Americans in the Military, Double V.* Malabar, FL: Krieger, 1991.

Donziger, S. "The Prison-Industrial Complex." *Washington Post,.* 17 March 1996, C3.

Douglass, Frederick. *Address by Hon. Frederick Douglass, Delivered in the Congregational Church, Washington, D.C., April 16, 1883: On the Twenty-first Anniversary of Emancipation in the District of Columbia.* Murray's African American Pamphlets. Washington, DC: Library of Congress. (http://memory.loc.gov).

Dubbert, Joe I. *A Man's Place: Masculinity in Transition.* Englewood Cliffs, NJ: Prentice-Hall, 1979.

Du Bois, W.E.B. "Back to Africa." In John Henrik Clarke (ed.), *Marcus Garvey and the Vision of Africa* (pp. 115–31). New York: Vintage Books, 1974.

Du Bois, W.E.B. *Black Reconstruction in America: An Essay toward a History of the Part Which Black Folk Played in the Attempt to Reconstruct Democracy in America: 1860–1880.* New York: Atheneum, 1983.

Du Bois, W.E.B. "The Evolution of Negro Leadership." *The Dial* (July 1901):53.

Du Bois, W.E.B. "An History toward a History of the Black Man in the Great War." In J. Lester (ed.), *The Seventh Son: The Thought and Writings of W.E.B. Du Bois,* vol. 2. New York: Random House, 1971.

Du Bois, W.E.B. "Of Mr. Booker T. Washington and Others." In *The Souls of Black Folk* (pp. 42–54). New York: Fawcett, 1961.

Du Bois, W.E.B. "Of the Training of Black Men." *Atlantic Monthly* 90 (1902): 289–97.

Du Bois, W.E.B. *The Philadelphia Negro.* Milwood, NY: Kraus-Thomson.

Du Bois, W.E.B. *The Souls of Black Folk.* New York: Fawcett Publications, 1961.

Du Bois, W.E.B. "The Study of the Negro Problem." *Annals of the American Academy of Political and Social Science* 11 (1898): 1–23.

Duster, Alfreda (ed.). *Crusade for Justice: The Autobiography of Ida B. Wells.* Chicago: University of Chicago Press, 1970.

Edelstein, Tilden G. "Othello in America: The Drama of Racial Intermarriage." In J. Morgan Kousser and James. M. McPherson (eds.), *Region, Race, and*

Reconstruction. New York: Oxford University Press, 1982.

"Edgar Dinsmore Letters." *Journal of Negro History* 25, no. 3, (July 1940): 363–71.

Edsall, Thomas B. *Chain Reaction: The Impact of Race, Rights, and Taxes on American Politics*. New York: W. W. Norton, 1991.

Egerton, Douglas R. *Gabriel's Rebellion: The Virginia Slave Conspiracies of 1800 and 1802*. Chapel Hill: University of North Carolina Press, 1993.

Eisen, George and Wiggins, David K. *Ethnicity and Sport in North American History and Culture*. Westport, CT: Greenwood, 1994.

Elkins, Stanley M. *Slavery: A Problem in American Institutional and Intellectual Life*. Chicago: University of Chicago Press, 1959, 82.

Elliot, J. M. "The 'Willie' Horton Nobody Knows." *The Nation* (August 1993): 201–5.

Equiano, Olaudah. *The Interesting Narrative of the Life of Olaudah Equiano or Gustavus Vassa the African*. London, 1789.

Fanon, Franz. *The Wretched of the Earth*. New York: Grove Press, 1963.

Farley, Reynolds. *Growth of the Black Population: A Study of Demographic Trends*. Chicago: Markham, 1970.

Farrakhan, Louis. "Allah (God) Hates Divorce—Part Two." *The Final Call*, (14 April 1995), 7–8

Farrakhan, Louis. "Minister Louis Farrakhan Calls for One Million Man March." *The Final Call* (14 December 1994, 1.

Farrakhan, Louis. "Minister Louis Farrakhan Speaks on Domestic Violence." *The Final Call* (21 June 1995): 1–3.

Farrell, Warren. *The Liberated Man*. New York: Random House, 1975.

Felder, Cain Hope. *Stony the Road We Trod: African American Biblical Interpretation*. Minneapolis: Augsburg Fortress, 1991.

Fields, Barbara J. "Ideology and Race in American History." In J. Morgan Kousser and James M. McPherson (eds.), *Region, Race, and Reconstruction* (pp. 143–78) New York: Oxford University Press, 1982.

Filene, Peter G. *Him/Her/Self: Sex Roles in Modern America*. Baltimore: Johns Hopkins University Press, 1974.

Fingerhut, L. A. and Kleinman, J. C. "International and Interstate Comparisons of Homicide among Young Males." *Journal of the American Medical Association* 263 (1990): 3292–95.

Flexner, James Thomas. *George Washington, Anguish and Farewell (1793–1799)*. Boston: Little, Brown, 1972.

Fogel, Robert William and Engerman, Stanley L. *Time on the Cross Vol. 1: The Economics of American Negro Slavery*. Boston: Little, Brown, 1974.

Foner, Eric E. *Reconstruction: America's Unfinished Revolution, 1863–1877*. New York: Harper and Row, 1988.

Foner, Eric E. (ed.). *Nat Turner*. Englewood Cliffs, NJ: Prentice-Hall, 1971.

Foner, Philip S. *The Black Panthers Speak*. Philadelphia: J.B. Lippincott Company, 1970.

Foner, Philip S. *The Life and Writings of Frederick Douglass*. New York: International Publishers, 1952.

Foner, Philip S. *Organized Labor and the Black Worker, 1619–1981*. New York: International Publishers, 1981.

Foner, Philip S. and Walker, George E. (eds). *Proceedings of the Black National and State Conventions, 1865–1900*. Philadelphia: Temple University Press, 1986.

Forten, Charlotte L. *The Journal of Charlotte Forten*. New York: Dryden Press, 1953.

Fox, Stephen R. *The Guardian of Boston: William Monroe Trotter*. New York:

Atheneum, 1970.

Fox-Genovese, Elizabeth. *Within the Plantation Household: Black and White Women of the Old South*. Chapel Hill: University of North Carolina Press, 1988.

Franklin, Clyde W. *The Changing Definition of Masculinity*. New York: Plenum Press, 1984.

Franklin, John Hope. *Race and History: Selected Essays, 1938–1988*. Baton Rouge: Louisiana State University Press, 1989.

Frazier, E. Franklin. *The Free Negro Family*. New York: Arno Press and the New York Times, 1968.

Frazier, E. Franklin. *The Negro Family in the United States*. Chicago: University of Chicago Press, 1939.

Fredrickson, George, M. *The Black Image in the White Mind: The Debate on Afro-American Character and Destiny, 1817–1914*. New York: Harper and Row, 1971.

Freehling, William W. *The Road to Disunion (vol. 1): Secessionists at Bay, 1776–1854*. New York: Oxford University Press, 1990.

Friends of Eldridge Cleaver. *The FBI, OPD and Eldridge Cleaver*. Oakland, CA: Friends of Eldridge Cleaver, 1970.

Fry, Gladys-Marie. *Night Riders in Black Folk History*. Knoxville: University of Tennessee. Press, 1975.

Gaines, Kevin K. *Uplifting the Race: Black Leadership, Politics, and Culture in the Twentieth Century*. Chapel Hill: University of North Carolina Press, 1996.

Garfinkel, H. *When Negroes March: The March on Washington Movement in the Organizational Politics for FEPC*. New York: Atheneum, 1969.

Garvey, Amy Jacques. "The Early Years of Marcus Garvey." In. John Henrik Clarke (ed.), *Marcus Garvey and the Vision of Africa*. New York: Vintage, 1974.

Gary, Lawrence E., Booker, Christopher B., and Fekade, Abeba. *African American Males: An Analysis of Contemporary Values, Attitudes and Perceptions of Manhood*. Washington, DC: Howard University School of Social Work, 1993.

Gatewood, Willard B., Jr. "Booker T. Washington and the Ulrich Affair." *The Journal of Negro History* 55 (January 1970): 29–44.

Gatewood, Willard B., Jr. *"Smoked Yankees" and the Struggle for Empire: Letters from Negro Soldiers, 1898–1902*. Fayetteville: University of Arkansas Press, 1987.

Gatewood, Willard B., Jr. *Theodore Roosevelt and the Art of Controversy*. Baton Rouge: Louisiana State University Press, 1970.

Gatewood, Willard B., Jr. (ed.). *Free Man of Color: The Autobiography of Willis Augustus Hodges*. Knoxville: University of Tennessee Press, 1982.

Genovese, Eugene. *From Rebellion to Freedom: Afro-American Slave Revolts in the Making of the Modern World*. Baton Rouge: Louisiana State University Press, 1979.

Genovese, Eugene D. *Roll, Jordan, Roll: The World The Slaves Made*. New York: Pantheon Books, 1974.

Gerber, David A. *Black Ohio and the Color Line, 1860–1915*. Chicago: University of Illinois Press, 1976.

Geschwender, James A. *Class, Race, and Worker Insurgency: The League of Revolutionary Black Workers*. Cambridge: Cambridge University Press, 1977.

Gibbs, Jewell Taylor. *Young, Black, and Male in America: An Endangered Species*. Dover, MA: Auburn House, 1988.

Gibbs, Mifflin W. *Shadow and Light: An Autobiography*. New York: Arno Press and the

New York Times, 1968.

Giddings, Paula. *When and Where I Enter: The Impact of Black Women on Race and Sex in America*. New York: William Morrow, 1984.

Gilmore, David D. *Manhood in the Making: Cultural Concepts of Masculinity*. New Haven, CT: Yale University Press, 1990.

Gilmore, Glenda Elizabeth. *Gender and Jim Crow: Women and the Politics of White Supremacy in North Carolina, 1896–1920*. Chapel Hill: University of North Carolina Press, 1996.

Ginzburg, Ralph. *100 Years of Lynchings*. Baltimore: Black Classic Press, 1988.

Goff, Stanley and Sanders, Robert. *Brothers: Black Soldiers in the Nam*. New York: Berkeley Books, 1982.

Goldfield, Michael. *The Color of Politics: Race and the Mainsprings of American Politics*. New York: New Press, 1997.

Gordon, Ann D. (ed). *African American Women and the Vote, 1837–1965*. Amherst: University of Massachusetts Press, 1997.

Gould, L. L. *The Presidency of William McKinley*. Lawrence: Regents Press of Kansas, 1980.

Grant, Donald L. (ed.). *The Way It Was in the South: The Black Experience in Georgia*. New York: Birch Lane Press, 1993.

Grant, Jacquelyn. "Black Theology and the Black Woman." In Beverly Guy-Sheftall, *Words of Fire: An Anthology of African-American Feminist Thought*. New York: New Press, 1995.

Grant, Joanne. *Black Protest: History, Documents, and Analyses, 1619 to the Present*. New York: Fawcett, 1968.

Grant, Joanne. *Ella Baker: Freedom Bound*. New York: John Wiley and Sons, 1998.

Green, Constance McLaughlin. *The Secret City: A History of Race Relations in the Nation's Capital*. Princeton: Princeton University Press, 1967.

Greenberg, Cheryl Lynn. *"Or Does It Explode?": Black Harlem in the Great Depression*. New York: Oxford University Press, 1991.

Grover, Kathryn. *Make a Way Somehow: African-American Life in a Northern Community, 1790–1965*. Syracuse, NY: Syracuse University Press, 1994.

Gutman, Herbert G. *The Black Family in Slavery and Freedom, 1750–1925*. New York: Vintage Books, 1976.

Hair, William Ivy. *Carnival of Fury: Robert Charles and the New Orleans Race Riot of 1900*. Baton Rouge: Louisiana State University Press, 1976.

Hall, Gwendolyn Midlo. *Africans in Colonial Louisiana: The Development of Afro-Creole Culture in the Eighteenth Century*. Baton Rouge: Louisiana State University Press, 1992.

Hallowell, Norwood P. *The Negro as a Soldier in the War of the Rebellion. Read before the Military Historical Society of Massachusetts, 5 January 1892*. Boston: Little, Brown, 1897.

Hammon, Jupiter. "An Address to the Negroes in the State of New York, by Jupiter Hammon, Servant of John Lloyd, Jun. Esq; of the Manor of Queen's Village, Long-Island." In Documentary Sources Database. American Multicultural Series, Unit One, Documenting the American Experience, (http://www.lib.virginia.edu/etext/ readex/readex.html).

Hanley, Sally. *A. Phillip Randolph*. New York: Chelsea House, 1989.

Harlan, Louis R. *Booker T. Washington: The Wizard of Tuskegee, 1901–1915*. New York: Oxford University Press, 1983.

Harris, Joel Chandler. *The Complete Tales of Uncle Remus*. Boston: Houghton Mifflin, 1955.

Harrison, Hubert H. *When Africa Awakes: The Inside Story of the Stirrings and Strivings of the New Negro*. New York: Poro Press, 1920.

Haynes, Robert V. *A Night of Violence: The Houston Riot of 1917*. Baton Rouge: Louisiana State University Press, 1976.

Haywood, Harry. *Black Bolshevik: Autobiography of an Afro-American Communist*. Chicago: Liberator Press, 1978.

Henry, Patrick. "Patrick Henry to Robert Pleasants, Jan. 18, 1773." In Roger Bruns (ed.), *Am I Not a Man and a Brother: The Antislavery Crusade of Revolutionary America, 1688–1788*. New York: Chelsea House, 1977.

Hersey, John. *The Algiers Motel Incident*. New York: Bantam Books, 1968.

Hill, Robert A. *Marcus Garvey and the Universal Negro Improvement Association Papers. Vol.1*. Berkeley: University of California Press, 1983.

Hill, Robert A. and Bair, Barbara (eds.). *Marcus Garvey: Life and Lessons*. Berkeley: University of California Press, 1987.

Hilliard, David. *The Autobiography of David Hilliard and the Story of the Black Panther Party*. Boston: Little, Brown, 1993.

Holt, Thomas. *Black over White: Negro Political Leadership in South Carolina during Reconstruction*. Urbana: University of Illinois Press, 1977.

Horton, James Oliver (ed.). *Free People of Color: Inside the African American Community*. Washington, DC: Smithsonian Institution Press, 1993.

Horton, James Oliver and Horton, Lois E. *In Hope of Liberty: Culture, Community, and Protest among Northern Free Blacks, 1700–1860*. New York: Oxford University Press, 1997.

Horton, James Oliver and Horton, Lois E. "Violence, Protest, and Identity: Black Manhood in Antebellum America." In James Oliver Horton (ed.), *Free People of Color: Inside the African American Community*. Washington: Smithsonian Institution Press, 1993.

Huggins, Nathan Irvin. *Black Odyssey: The African American Ordeal in Slavery*. New York: Random House, 1977.

Hutchinson, Earl Ofari. *The Mugging of Black America*. Chicago: African American Images, 1990.

"In District's War on Drugs, Bennett Seems to Favor Short-Term Answers." *Washington Post*, 16 April 1989, A25.

Jackson, D. "Farrakhan Getting Much of the Attention of Million Man March." *Dallas Morning News*, 12 October 1995.

Jackson, George. *Soledad Brother: The Prison Letters of George Jackson*. New York: Bantam Books, 1970.

Jakoubek, R. *Jack Johnson*. New York: Chelsea House, 1990.

James, Joy. *Transcending the Talented Tenth: Black Leaders and American Intellectuals*. New York: Routledge, 1997.

James, Portia P. "Hubert H. Harrison and the New Negro Movement." *The Western Journal of Black Studies* 13 (1989).

Jaynes, Gerald D. *Branches without Roots: Genesis of the Black Working-Class in the American South, 1862–1882*. New York: Oxford University Press, 1986.

Jefferson, Thomas. "Notes on Virginia." In *The Writings of Thomas Jefferson*, vol. 2. Washington, D.C.: Thomas Jefferson Memorial Association, 1903.

Jefferson, Thomas. *Thomas Jefferson on Slavery*. Dep. Alfa: Informatica University of

Groningen, 1996.

Jeffords, Susan. *The Remasculinization of America: Gender and the Vietnam War*. Bloomington: University of Indiana Press, 1989.

Johnson, Andrew. "The Civil Rights Bill of 1866 Should Not Be Enacted." In Brenda Stalcup (ed.), *Reconstruction: Opposing Viewpoints*. San Diego: Greenhaven Press, 1995.

Johnson, Charles S. *Shadow of the Plantation*. Chicago: University of Chicago Press, 1939.

Johnson, Jack. *Jack Johnson—In the Ring—and Out*. New York: Carol, 1992.

Johnson, James Weldon. *Along This Way: The Autobiography of James Weldon Johnson*. New York: Penguin Books, 1993.

Johnson, Michael P. and Roark, James L. *Black Masters: A Free Family of Color in the Old South*. New York: W. W. Norton, 1984.

Jones, Charles E. (ed.). *The Black Panther Party Reconsidered*. Baltimore: Black Classic Press, 1998.

Jones, Jacqueline. *Labor of Love, Labor of Sorrow: Black Women, Work, and the Family from Slavery to the Present*. New York: Basic Books, 1985.

Jordan, Winthrop D. *Tumult and Silence at Second Creek: An Inquiry Into a Civil War Slave Conspiracy*. Baton Rouge: Louisiana State University Press, 1993.

Jordan, Winthrop D. *White over Black: American Attitudes toward the Negro, 1550–1812*. Baltimore: Penguin Books, 1969.

Kaplan, Sidney. *The Black Presence in the Era of the American Revolution 1770–1800*. Washington, DC: National Portrait Gallery, Smithsonian Institution, 1973.

Kelley, Robin D. G. "Confessions of a Nice Negro, or Why I Shaved My Head." In Don Belton (ed.), *Speak My Name: Black Men on Masculinity and the American Dream*. Boston: Beacon Press, 1995.

Kemble, Frances. *Journal of a Residence on a Georgia Plantation in 1838–1839*. Athens, GA: University of Georgia Press, 1984.

Kennedy, Randall. "The Justice System and Black America: After the Cheers." *The New Republic*, 23 October 1995.

Kennedy, Randall. *Race, Crime, and the Law*. New York: Pantheon Books, 1997.

Kimmel, Michael. *Manhood in America: A Cultural History*. New York: Free Press, 1996.

King, Wilma. *Stolen Childhood: Slave Youth in Nineteenth-Century America*. Bloomington: Indiana University Press, 1995.

King, Martin Luther, Jr. "A Time to Break Silence." In Philip S. Foner (ed.), *The Voice of Black America. Vol. 2*. New York: Capricorn Books, 1975.

Kolchin, Peter. *First Freedom: The Responses of Alabama's Blacks to Emancipation and Reconstruction*. Westport, CT: Greenwood Press, 1972.

Kusmer, Kenneth L. *A Ghetto Takes Shape: Black Cleveland, 1870–1930*. Chicago: University of Illinois Press, 1976.

Lamon, Lester C. *Blacks in Tennessee 1791–1970*. Knoxville: University of Tennessee Press, 1981.

Lane, A. J. *The Brownsville Affair: National Crisis and Black Reaction*. Port Washington, NY: Kennikat Press, 1971.

Lane, Roger. *Roots of Violence in Black Philadelphia, 1860–1900*. Cambridge: Harvard University Press, 1986.

Lang, Robert (ed.) *The Birth of a Nation*. New Brunswick, NJ: Rutgers University Press, 1994.

Langston, John Mercer. *From the Virginia Plantation to the National Capital or the First and Only Negro Representative in Congress from the Old Dominion*. Hartford, CT: American, 1894.

Lanning, Michael Lee. *The African American Soldier: From Crispus Attucks to Colin Powell*. Secaucus, NJ: Carol, 1997.

Levine, Lawrence W. *Black Culture and Black Consciousness: Afro-American Folk Thought from Slavery to Freedom*. New York: Oxford University Press, 1977.

Lewis, David Levering. *W.E.B. Du Bois: Biography of a Race, 1868–1919*. New York: Henry Holt, 1993.

Lewis, John. "We are in a Serious Revolution." In Philip S. Foner (ed.), *The Voice of Black America: Major Speeches by Negroes in the United States, 1797–1973*. Vol. 2: 1900–1973. New York: Capricorn Books, 1975.

Lewis, R. *Marcus Garvey: Anti-Colonial Champion*. Trenton, NJ: Africa World Press, 1988.

Lincoln, Abraham. *Second Inaugural Address*. Saturday, 4 March 1865. The Avalon Project at the Yale Law School (http://www.yale.edu/lawweb/avalon/presiden/inaug/ lincoln2.htm).

Litwack, Leon F. *Been in the Storm So Long: The Aftermath of Slavery*. New York: Vintage Books, 1979.

Litwack, Leon F. *North of Slavery: The Negro in the Free States, 1790–1860*. Chicago: University of Chicago Press, 1961.

Locke, Alain. "The New Negro." In Abraham Chapman (ed.), *Black Voices: An Anthology of Afro-American Literature*. New York: Mentor Books, 1968.

Locy, T. "'Deplorable' Unit Alleged at D.C. Jail." *Washington Post*, 28 March 1996, A1, A15.

Logan, Rayford W. *The Betrayal of the Negro: From Rutherford B. Hayes and Woodrow Wilson*. New York: Collier, 1954.

Loguen, Jermain Wesley. "Jermain Wesley Loguen to Frederick Douglass, [March 1855]." In Peter Ripley et al.(eds.), *The Black Abolitionist Papers*. New York: Microfilm Corporation of America, 1981.

Lotke, Eric. "Hobbling a Generation." *African American Male Research* 2, no. 2, (January/February 1998), (*http://www.pressroom.com/~afrimale/hobb.htm*).

Lott, Eric. *Love and Theft: Blackface Minstrelsy and the American Working Class*. New York: Oxford University Press, 1993.

Louis, Joe. *Joe Louis: My Life* New York: Harcourt Brace Jovanovich, 1978.

"Louisiana Planters to the Commander of the Department of the Gulf Terrebonne Parish, Louisiana, January 14, 1862." *The Black Military Experiment*. (http:// www.coax. net/people/ lwf/default.htm).

Lunardini, C. "Standing Firm: William Monroe Trotter's Meetings with Woodrow Wilson, 1913–1914." *Journal of Negro History* 64 (1979): 255–62.

Lusane, Clarence. *Pipe Dream Blues: Racism and the War on Drugs*. Boston: South End Press, 1991.

Lyman, Stanford M. *The Black American in Sociological Thought*. New York: Capricorn Books, 1972.

Lynch, J. P. and Sabol, W. "The Use of Coercive Social Control and Changes in the Race and Class Composition of U.S. Prison Populations." Paper presented at the American Society of Criminology, November 1994.

Mabee, Carleton. *Sojourner Truth: Slave, Prophet, Legend*. New York: New York University Press, 1993.

Majors, Richard and Billson, Janet. *Coolpose: The Dilemmas of Black Manhood in America*. New York: Lexington Books, 1992.

Marable, Manning. *From the Grassroots: Social and Political Essays toward Afro-American Liberation*. Boston: South End Press, 1980.

Marine, Gene. *The Black Panthers*. New York: Signet Books, 1969.

Martin, Tony. *Literary Garveyism: Garvey, Black Arts and the Harlem Renaissance*. Dover, MA: Majority Press, 1983.

Martin, Tony. *Marcus Garvey, Hero: A First Biography*. Dover, MA: Majority Press, 1983.

Mauer, Marc and Huling, T. *Young Black Americans and the Criminal Justice System: Five Years Later*. Washington DC: Sentencing Project, 1995.

McAdam, Doug. *Political Process and the Development of Black Insurgency, 1930–70*. Chicago: University of Chicago Press, 1982.

McFeely, William S. *Frederick Douglass*. New York: W. W. Norton, 1991.

McKaye, James. *The Mastership and Its Fruits: The Emancipated Slave Face to Face with His Old Master. A Supplemental Report to Hon. Edwin M. Stanton, Secretary of War by James McKaye, Special Commissioner*. New York: Loyal Publication Society, 1864.

McManus, Edgar J. *Black Bondage in the North*. Syracuse, NY: Syracuse University Press, 1973.

McPherson, James M. *The Negro's Civil War: How American Blacks Felt and Acted during the War for the Union*. New York: Ballantine Books, 1991.

Meier, August and Rudwick, Elliott. "A Strange Chapter in the Career of Jim Crow." In August Meier and Elliot Rudwick (eds.), *The Making of Black America: Essays in Negro Life & History, vol. 2: The Black Community in Modern America*. New York: Atheneum, 1973.

Mellon, James (ed.). *Bullwhip Days: The Slaves Remember, an Oral History*. New York: Avon Books, 1988.

Miller, Edward A., Jr. *Gullah Statesman: Robert Smalls from Slavery to Congress, 1839–1915*. Columbia: University of South Carolina Press, 1995.

Miller, John Chester. *The Wolf by the Ears: Thomas Jefferson and Slavery*. New York: Free Press, 1977.

Miller, Kelly. *Radicals and Conservatives and Other Essays on the Negro in America*. New York: Schocken Books, 1968.

Miller, Nathan. *Theodore Roosevelt: A Life*. New York: William Morrow, 1992.

"Minister Farrakhan Challenges Black Men." *CNN*, 17 October 1995. Transcript from Minister Louis Farrakhan's remarks at the Million Man March.

Mintz, Sidney W. and Price, Richard. *The Birth of African-American Culture*. Boston: Beacon Press, 1972.

Moore, George H. *Historical Notes on the Employment of Negroes in the American Army of the Revolution*. Washington, DC: Library of Congress, 1863, 3–4.

Morison, Elting E. *The Letters of Theodore Roosevelt*. Cambridge: Harvard University Press, 1951.

Morris, Aldon. "Black Southern Sit-In Movement: An Analysis of Internal Organization." *American Sociological Review* 46 (1981): 744–766.

Morris, Lorenzo (ed.). "The Range and Limits of Campaign Politics." In *The Social and Political Implications of the 1984 Jesse Jackson Presidential Campaign*. New York: Praeger, 1990.

Morrow, E. F. *Black Man in the White House*. New York: MacFadden Books, 1963.

Moses, William J. *Alexander Crummell: A Study of Civilization and Discontent.* New York: Oxford University Press, 1989.

Moses, William J. *The Golden Age of Black Nationalism, 1850–1925.* New York: Oxford University Press, 1978.

"Mother Murders Her Sons." *Time* (14 November 1994), http://www.time.com/time, n.p..

Muhammad, A. A. "Black Woman, This March Is for You." *The Final Call* 14 April 1995, 11.

Mullin, Gerald W. *Flight and Rebellion: Slave Resistance in Eighteenth-Century Virginia.* New York: Oxford University Press, 1974.

Naison, Mark. *Communists in Harlem during the Depression.* New York: Grove Press, 1985.

Nash, Gary B. *Forging Freedom: The Formation of Philadelphia's Black Community, 1720–1840.* Cambridge: Harvard University Press, 1988.

Nash, Gary B. *Race and Revolution.* Madison: Madison House, 1990.

National Advisory Commission on Civil Disorders. *The Kerner Report: The 1968 Report of the National Advisory Commission on Civil Disorders.* New York: Pantheon Books, 1988.

National Centers for Health Statistics. *Health, United States, 1989.* Hyattsville, MD: Public Health Service, 1990.

Nelson, Bruce. "Organized Labor and the Struggle for Black Equality in Mobile during World War II." *The Journal of American History* 80, no. 3 (December 1993): 959.

Newman, Dorothy K., et al. *Protest, Politics, and Prosperity: Black Americans and White Institutions, 1940–75.* New York: Pantheon Books, 1978.

Newton, Huey P. "Executive Mandate No. 3." *The Black Panther,* 16 March 1968.

Newton, Huey P. "Let Us Hold High the Banner of Intercommunalism and The Invincible Thoughts of Huey P. Newton, Minister of Defense and Supreme Commander of the Black Panther Party." *The Black Panther,* 2 January 1971, A–H.

Nichols, Roy Franklin. *Franklin Pierce: Young Hickory of Granite Hills.* Norwalk, CT: Easton Press, 1969.

Norton, Mary Beth, et al. *A People and a Nation: A History of the United States.* Boston: Houghton Mifflin, 1990.

Norton, Mary Beth, Gutman, Herbert G., and Berlin, Ira. "The Afro-American Family in the Age of Revolution." In Ira Berlin and Ronald Hoffman (eds.), *Slavery and Freedom in the Age of the American Revolution.* Charlottesville: University of Virginia Press, 1983.

Oakes, James. *The Ruling Race: A History of American Slaveholders.* New York: Alfred A. Knopf, 1982.

Oakes, S. B. *The Fires of Jubilee: Nat Turner's Fierce Rebellion.* New York: Harper and Row, 1975.

Oakes, S. B. *With Malice toward None: The Life of Abraham Lincoln.* New York: Harper and Row, 1977.

O' Carroll, P. W. and Mercy, J. A. "Patterns and Recent Trends in Black Homicide." In Darnell Hawkins (ed.), *Homicide among Black Americans.* London: University Press of America, 1986.

Oliver, W. "Black Males and Social Problems: Prevention through Afrocentric Socialization." *Journal of Black Studies* 20 (1989): 15-39.

O' Reilly, Kenneth. *Nixon's Piano: Presidents and Racial Politics from Washington to Clinton.* New York: Free Press, 1995.

O' Reilly, Kenneth. "Racial Matters": *The F.B.I.'s Secret File on Black America, 1960–1972*. New York: Free Press, 1989.

Osofsky, Gilbert (ed.). "A View of the Negro as a Beast." In *The Burden of Race: A Documentary History of Negro–White Relations in America*. New York: Harper Torchbooks, 1967.

Ottley, Roi and Weatherby, William J. (eds.). *The Negro in New York: An Informal Social History*. New York: New York Public Library, 1967.

Owens, Leslie Howard. *This Species of Property: Slave and Culture in the Old South*. New York: Oxford University Press, 1976.

Painter, Irvin Nell. *Sojourner Truth: A Life, a Symbol*. New York: W. W. Norton, 1996.

Painter, Irvin Nell. *Standing at Armageddon: The United States 1877–1919*. New York: W. W. Norton, 1987.

Patterson, Orlando. "Why Whites and Blacks Seem So Divided. The Paradox of Integration." *The New Republic Online* (6 November 1995), n.p..

Perkins, Linda. "Black Women and Racial 'Uplift' Prior to Emancipation." In Filomina Chioma Steady (ed.), *The Black Woman Cross-Culturally*. Rochester, VT: Schenkman Books, 1981.

Pollard, Edward A. *Black Diamonds Gathered in the Darkey Homes of the South*. New York: Pudney and Russel, 1859.

Poole, Jason. "On Borrowed Ground: Free African-American Life in Charleston, South Carolina, 1810–61." *Essays in History* 36 (1994): 4. (http://www.lib. virginia.edu/ journals).

Powdermaker, Hortense. *After Freedom: A Cultural Study in the Deep South*. New York: Atheneum, 1969.

Powell, Colin L. *My American Journey*. New York: Random House, 1995.

Powers, Bernard E., Jr. *Black Charlestonians: A Social History, 1822–1885*. Fayetteville: University of Arkansas Press, 1994.

Quarles, Benjamin. *The Negro in the Civil War*. Boston: Little, Brown, 1969.

Quarles, Benjamin. *The Negro in the Making of America*. New York: Collier Books, 1964.

Raboteau, Albert J. *Slave Religion: The "Invisible" Institution in the Antebellum South*. New York: Oxford University Press, 1978.

Raper, Arthur F. *Preface to Peasantry: A Tale of Two Black Belt Counties*. New York: Atheneum, 1968.

Raper, Arthur F. *The Tragedy of Lynching*. New York: Dover, 1933.

Rapier, James T. "Segregation Should Be Abolished." In Brenda Stalcup (ed.), *Reconstruction: Opposing Viewpoints*. San Diego: Greenhaven Press, 1995.

Rawick, George P. *The American Slave: A Composite Autobiography*. Vol. 2: Texas Narratives, Part 1. Westport, CT: Greenwood Press, 1979.

Rawick, George P. *The American Slave: A Composite Autobiography*. Vol. 2: South Carolina Narratives, Parts 1 and 2. Westport, CT: Greenwood, 1972.

Redkey, Edwin S. (ed.). *A Grand Army of Black Men: Letters from African American Soldiers in the Union Army, 1861–1865*. Cambridge: Cambridge University Press, 1992.

"The Return of the Chain Gang." *Washington Post*, 4 May 1995,: A1, A14.

Rice, C. Duncan. *The Rise and Fall of Black Slavery*. Baton Rouge: Louisiana State University Press, 1975

Rice, Spotswood. Letter to "My Children," 3 September 1864. Enclosed in F. W. Diggs to Genl. Rosecrans, 10 September 1864, D-296 1864, Letters Received, ser. 2593, Department of the MO, U.S. Army Continental Commands, Record Group

393 Pt. 1, National Archives.

Rice, Spotswood. Letter to "Kittey Diggs," 3 September 1864. Enclosed in F. W. Diggs to Genl. Rosecrans, 10 September 1864, D-296 1864, Letters Received, ser. 2593, Department of the MO, U.S. Army Continental Commands, Record Group 393 Pt. 1, National Archives.

Ripley, Peter, et al. (eds.). *The Black Abolitionist Papers*. New York: Microfilm Corporation of America, 1981.

Roark, James L. *Masters without Slaves: Southern Planters in the Civil War and Reconstruction*. New York: W. W. Norton, 1977.

Roberts, Randy. *Papa Jack: Jack Johnson and the Era of White Hopes*. New York: The Free Press, 1983.

Roddy, Stephen R. "The Scottsboro Case." In Gilbert Osofsky (ed.), *The Burden of Race: A Documentary History of Negro–White Relations in America*. New York: Harper and Row, 1967.

Roediger, David R. *The Wages of Whiteness: Race and the Making of the American Working Class*. London: Verso, 1991.

Rogin, Michael. "'The Sword Became a Flashing Vision.'" In Robert Lang (ed.), *The Birth of a Nation*. New Brunswick, NJ: Rutgers University Press, 1994.

Roosevelt, Theodore. "Letter to Dr. Lyman Abbott." 29 October 1903. In E. E. Morison (ed.), *The Letters of Theodore Roosevelt*. Cambridge: Harvard University Press, 1951.

Roosevelt, Theodore. "Letter to Governor Winfield T. Durbin." 6 August 1903. In E.E. Morison, (ed.), *The Letters of Theodore Roosevelt*. Cambridge: Harvard University Press, 1951.

Roosevelt, Theodore. *The Strenuous Life: Essays and Addresses*. New York: Century, 1904.

Rose, Willie Lee. *Rehearsal for Reconstruction: The Port Royal Experiment*. New York: Oxford University Press, 1962.

Roth, D. *Sacred Honor: Colin Powell, The Inside Account of His Life and Triumphs*. New York: HarperCollins, 1993.

Rudwick, Elliott. *Race Riot at East St. Louis, July 2, 1917*. Urbana: University of Illinois Press, 1982.

Rustin, Bayard. *Down the Line: The Collected Writings of Bayard Rustin*. Chicago: Quadrangle Books, 1971.

Sale, Kirkpatrick. *SDS*. New York: Vintage Books, 1974.

Sales, William W., Jr. *From Civil Rights to Black Liberation: Malcolm X and the Organization of Afro-American Unity*. Boston: South End Press, 1994.

Salvatore, Nick. *We All Got History: The Memory Books of Amos Webber*. New York: Random House, 1996.

Satter, Beryl. "Marcus Garvey, Father Divine and the Gender Politics of Race Difference and Race Neutrality." *American Quarterly* 48 (1996): 48–52.

Seale, Bobby. *A Lonely Rage: The Autobiography of Bobby Seale*. New York: New York Times Books, 1978.

Seale, Bobby. *Seize the Time*. New York: Vintage Books, 1970.

"Secret Information Concerning Black American Troops," in Bernard C. Nalty and Morris J. MacGregor (eds.), *Blacks in the Military: Essential Documents* (Wilmington, DE: Scholarly Resources, 1981)

Shabazz, Betty. "Malcolm X as a Husband and Father." In John Henrik Clarke (ed.), *Malcolm X: The Man and His Times*. Trenton, NJ: Africa World Press, 1990.

Shakur, Assata. *Assata: An Autobiography*. Westport, CT: Lawrence Hill, 1987.

Shatzkin, K. "State May Face Prison Lawsuit." *Baltimore Sun*, 8 May 1996, 1A, 6A.

Sienko, D. G., Thrush, J., and Wilcox, K. R. "Impact of Homicide on Years of Potential Life Lost in Michigan's Black Population." *Journal of the American Medical Association* 261 (1989): 686–687.

Slaughter, Thomas P. *Bloody Dawn: The Christiana Riot and Racial Violence in the Antebellum North*. New York: Oxford University Press, 1991.

Spear, Allan H. *Black Chicago: The Making of a Negro Ghetto, 1890–1920*. Chicago: The University of Chicago Press, 1967.

Stampp, Kenneth M. *The Era of Reconstruction, 1865–1877*. New York: Alfred A. Knopf, 1965.

Stampp, Kenneth M. *The Peculiar Institution: Slavery in the Antebellum South*. New York: Vintage Books, 1989.

Staples, Robert. *Black Masculinity: The Black Males' Role in American Society*. San Francisco: Black Scholar Press, 1982.

Starling, M. W. *The Slave Narrative: Its Place in American History*. Washington, DC: Howard University Press, 1981.

Sterling, Dorothy. *The Making of an Afro-American: Martin Robison Delany, 1812–1885*. Garden City, NY: Doubleday, 1971.

Sterling, Dorothy (ed.). *The Trouble They Seen: The Story of Reconstruction in the Words of African Americans*. New York: Da Capo Press, 1994.

Sterling, Dorothy (ed.). *We Are Your Sisters: Black Women in the Nineteenth Century*. New York: W. W. Norton, 1984.

Steward, Austin. *Twenty-two Years a Slave, and Forty Years a Freeman. Rochester, New York, 1861*.(http://memory.loc.gov). Murray's African American Pamphlets. Washington, DC: Library of Congress, 1996.

Stroyer, Jacob. *My Life in the South*. Salem, MA: 1988.1861. Murray's African American Pamphlets. Washington, DC: Library of Congress, 1996. (http://memory.loc.gov).

"Support the Pryce-Stupak Amendment to the Crime Bill." *Congressional Record*. 20 April 1994, H2512.

Takaki, Ronald. *Iron Cages: Race and Culture in 19th-Century America*. New York: Oxford University Press, 1990.

Terrell, Mary Church. *The Progress of Colored Women: An Address Delivered before the National American Women's Suffrage Association at the Columbia Theater, Washington, D.C., February 18, 1898, on the Occasion of Its Fiftieth Anniversary*. Washington, DC Smith Brothers, 1898.   Murray's African American Pamphlets.   Washington, DC: Library of Congress, 1996. 1861.(http://memory.loc.gov).

Terry, Wallace. *Bloods: An Oral History of the Vietnam War by Black Veterans*. New York: Ballantine Books, 1984.

Testi, Arnaldo. "The Gender of Reform Politics: Theodore Roosevelt and the Culture of Masculinity." *The Journal of American History*, 81, no. 4 (March 1995): 1509–1533.

Thomas, Lamont D. *Rise to Be a People: A Biography of Paul Cuffe*. Urbana: University of Illinois Press, 1986.

Thomas, Samuel. *Samuel Thomas, Assistant Commissioner, Bureau of Refugees, Freedmen and Abandoned Lands*. WPA Archives Web site, 1995.

Tise, Larry E. *Proslavery: A History of the Defense of Slavery in America, 1701–1840*.

Athens: University of Georgia Press, 1987.

"To Our Women and Girls." *The Final Call* (14 December 1994).

Toll, Robert C. *Blacking Up: The Minstrel Show in Nineteenth-Century America.* New York: Oxford University Press, 1974.

The "Trial" of Bobby Seale. New York: Priam Books, 1970.

Trudeau, Noah Andre. *Like Men of War: Black Troops in the Civil War, 1862–1865.* New York: Little, Brown, 1998.

Turner, Patricia A. *Ceramic Uncles & Celluloid Mammies: Black Images and Their Influence on Culture.* New York: Anchor Books, 1994.

Tuttle, William M. *Race Riot: Chicago in the Red Summer of 1919.* Chicago: University of Chicago Press, 1996.

U.S. Bureau of the Census. *Statistical Abstract of the United States: 1994.* "No. 723. Money Incomes of Persons-Percent Distribution, by Income Level, in Constant (1992) Dollars: 1970 to 1992." Washington, DC: U.S. Government Printing Office, 1994.

U.S. Department of Commerce. *The Social and Economic Status of the Black Population of the United States: An Historical View, 1790–1978.* Washington, DC: U.S. Government Printing Office, 1980.

U.S. Department of Health and Human Services. *Health Status of Minorities and Low-Income Groups.* 3d ed. Washington, DC: Public Health Service, 1991.

Van Deburg, William L. *The Slave Drivers: Black Agricultural Labor Supervisors in the Antebellum South.* New York: Oxford University Press, 1979.

Vincent, Theodore G. *Black Power and the Garvey Movement.* Berkeley, CA: The Ramparts Press, n.d.

"Violence in the 90s, Drugs' Deadly Residue." *The Washington Post*, 1990 October 14, 1990, A1.

Walling, William English. "A Description of Racial Violence in the North." In Gilbert Osofsky (ed.), *The Burden of Race: A Documentary History of Negro–White Relations in America.* New York: Harper, 1967.

Walters, Ronald W. "The Issue Politics of the Jesse Jackson Campaign for President in 1984." In *The Social and Political Implications of the 1984 Jesse Jackson Presidential Campaign.* New York: Praeger, 1990.

Washington, Booker T. *"Address of Booker T. Washington, Principal of the Tuskegee Normal and Industrial Institute, Tuskegee, Alabama, Delivered at the Opening of the Cotton States and International Exposition, at Atlanta, Ga, September 18, 1895: With a Letter of Congratulation from the President of the United States."* Murray's African American Pamphlets. Washington, DC: Library of Congress, 1996.(http://memory.loc.gov).

Washington, Booker T. *The Story of the Negro: The Rise of the Race from Slavery.* New York: Negro Universities Press, 1969.

Washington, James Melvin (ed.). *A Testament of Hope: The Essential Writings of Martin Luther King, Jr.* San Francisco: Harper and Row. 1986.

Watkins, F. and Clemente, F. *Keep Hope Alive: Jesse Jackson's 1988 Presidential Campaign.* Boston: Keep Hope Alive PAC and South End Press, 1989.

Watkins, William J. "Editorial by William J. Watkins," 7 April 1854. In *The Black Abolitionist Papers.* New York: Microfilm Corporation of America, 1981.

Weaver, John D. *The Brownsville Raid.* New York: W. W. Norton, 1970.

Wells- Barnett, Ida M. "Booker T. Washington and His Critics." In Mildred I. Thompson (ed.), *Ida B. Wells-Barnett: An Exploratory Study of an American Black*

Woman, 1893–1930. Brooklyn, NY: Carlson, 1990.

Wells-Barnett, Ida M. "Lynch Law in America." In Mildred I. Thompson (ed.), *Ida B. Wells-Barnett: An Exploratory Study of an American Black Woman, 1893–1930.* Brooklyn, NY: Carlson, 1990.

Wells-Barnett, Ida M. "Lynching Our National Crime." In Philip S. Foner (ed.), *The Voice of Black America: Major Speeches by Blacks in the United States, 1797–1973.* New York: Capricorn Books, 1975.

Wharton, Vernon Lane. *The Negro in Mississippi, 1865–1890.* New York: Harper and Row, 1965.

Whipper, William. Letter to Frederick Douglass, October 1854. In Peter Ripley (ed.), *The Black Abolitionist Papers.* New York: Microfilm Corporation of America, 1981.

White, Deborah Gray. *Ar'n't I a Woman?: Female Slaves in the Plantation South.* New York: W. W. Norton, 1985.

White, George. *"Additional Regiments of Artillery: Speech of the Hon. George H. White, of North Carolina, in the House of Representatives, Monday, March 7, 1898."* Murray's African American Pamphlets. Washington, DC: Library of Congress. (http://memory.loc.gov)

White, George C. *Racial Violence in Kentucky, 1865–1940: Lynchings, Mob Rule and "Legal Lynchings."* Baton Rouge: Louisiana State University Press, 1990.

White, Shane. *Somewhat More Independent: The End of Slavery in New York City, 1770–1810.* Athens: University of Georgia Press, 1991.

White, Walter. *Rope and Faggot.* New York: Arno Press and the New York Times, 1969.

Williamson, Joel. *After Slavery: The Negro in South Carolina during Reconstruction, 1861–1877.* Hanover, NH: University Press of New England, 1965.

Williamson, Joel. *The Crucible of Race: Black–White Relations in the American South since Emancipation.* New York: Oxford University Press, 1984.

Wilson, A. N. *Understanding Black Adolescent Male Violence: Its Remediation and Prevention.* New York: Afrikan World Infosystems, 1992.

Wilson, Joseph T. *The Black Phalanx.* Hartford, CT: American, 1892.

Wilson, Sondra Kathryn (ed.). *The Selected Writings of James Weldon Johnson. Vol.1: The New York Age Editorials (1914–1923).* New York: Oxford University Press, 1995.

Winch, Julie. *Philadelphia's Black Elite: Activism, Accommodation, and the Struggle for Autonomy, 1787–1848.* Philadelphia: Temple University Press, 1988.

Windley, Lathan A. (ed.). *Runaway Slave Advertisements: A Documentary History from the 1730s to 1790s.* Westport, CT: Greenwood, 1983.

Wood, J. Taylor. "The Capture of a Slaver." *Atlantic Monthly* (1900): 451–463.

Wood, Peter H. *Black Majority: Negroes in Colonial South Carolina from 1670 through the Stono Rebellion.* New York: W. W. Norton, 1974.

Woodward, C. Vann. *The Strange Career of Jim Crow.* New York: Oxford University Press, 1974.

Wooten, James. *Dasher: The Roots and the Rising of Jimmy Carter.* New York: Summit Books, 1978.

Wright, Richard. "The Ethics of Living Jim Crow: An Autobiographical Sketch." In Abraham Chapman (ed.), *Black Voices: An Anthology of Afro-American Literature.* New York: Mentor Books, 1968.

Wyatt-Brown, Bertram. "The Mask of Obedience: Male Slave Psychology in the Old South." *American Historical Review* 98 (1988): 1228–52.

Wyatt-Brown, Bertram. "Modernizing Southern Slavery: The Proslavery Argument

Reinterpreted." In J. Morgan Kousser and James M. McPherson (eds.), *Region, Race, and Reconstruction*. New York: Oxford University Press, 1982.

Wyatt-Brown, Bertram. *Southern Honor: Ethics and Behavior in the Old South*. New York: Oxford University Press, 1982.

X, Malcolm. *The Autobiography of Malcolm X*. New York: Grove Press, 1965.

X, Malcolm. *Malcolm X Speaks*. New York: Grove Press, 1965.

X, Malcolm. "To Young People." Speech at New York's Hotel Theresa on 31 December 1964. In Philip S. Foner (ed.), *The Voice of Black America*. New York: Capricorn Books, 1975.

"You Can Kill a Revolutionary but You Can't Kill a Revolution." *Black Panther*, 16 (January 1970): 6.

"Young Blacks Entangled in Legal System." *Washington Post*, 26 August 1997, B1.

Index

About the Author

CHRISTOPHER B. BOOKER is a part-time Research Associate in the School of Social Work at Howard University. He is also the editor of African American Male Research, a social research and advocacy website dedicated to the interests of African American males. He has contributed newspaper and journal articles to various publications.